W9-AEP-162

MICROECONOMIC THEORY

Economics Handbook Series
SEYMOUR E. HARRIS, *Editor*

ADVISORY COMMITTEE: Edward H. Chamberlain, Gottfried Haberler, Alvin H. Hansen, Edward S. Mason, and John H. Williams. *All of Harvard University.*

Burns · SOCIAL SECURITY AND PUBLIC POLICY

Duesenberry · BUSINESS CYCLES AND ECONOMIC GROWTH

Hansen · THE AMERICAN ECONOMY

Hansen · A GUIDE TO KEYNES

Hansen · MONETARY THEORY AND FISCAL POLICY

Harris · INTERNATIONAL AND INTERREGIONAL ECONOMICS

Henderson and Quandt · MICROECONOMIC THEORY

Hoover · THE LOCATION OF ECONOMIC ACTIVITY

Kindleberger · ECONOMIC DEVELOPMENT

Lerner · ECONOMICS OF EMPLOYMENT

Mikesell · UNITED STATES ECONOMIC POLICY
   AND INTERNATIONAL RELATIONS

Schelling · NATIONAL INCOME BEHAVIOR

Wright · CAPITALISM

Microeconomic Theory

A MATHEMATICAL APPROACH

JAMES M. HENDERSON
Assistant Professor of Economics
Harvard University

RICHARD E. QUANDT
Assistant Professor of Economics
Princeton University

McGraw-Hill Book Company, Inc.
New York   Toronto   London
1958

HB
171
H52

MICROECONOMIC THEORY

Copyright © 1958 by the McGraw-Hill Book Company, Inc. Printed in the United States of America. All rights reserved. This book, or parts thereof, may not be reproduced in any form without permission of the publishers. *Library of Congress Catalog Card Number:* 58-8844

THE MAPLE PRESS COMPANY, YORK, PA.

CANISIUS COLLEGE LIBRARY
BUFFALO, N. Y.

EDITOR'S INTRODUCTION

For years many teachers of economics, as well as other professional economists, have felt the need for a series of books on economic subjects—a need which is not filled by the usual textbook or by the highly technical treatise.

This series, published under the general title *Economics Handbook Series*, was planned with these needs in mind. Designed first of all for students, the volumes are useful in the ever-growing field of adult education and also are of interest to the informed general reader.

The volumes are not long—they give the essentials of the subject matter within the limits of a few hundred pages; they present a distillate of accepted theory and practice without the detailed approach of the technical treatise. Each volume is a unit, standing on its own.

In the classroom the books included in the *Economics Handbook Series* will, it is hoped, serve as brief surveys in one-semester courses and as supplementary reading in introductory courses, as well as in other courses in which the subject is pertinent.

In the current volume of the *Economics Handbook Series*, Professors Henderson and Quandt discuss microeconomics with the help of mathematics. The amount of mathematics required for understanding the text is not great, and an appendix helps the reader refresh his memory on the indispensable mathematical techniques. With economists increasingly in command of the mathematics essential for professional work in their field, this book should contribute greatly to an understanding of microeconomics. This volume suggests the many clarifications and advances made possible by the use of mathematics.

It is our hope that undergraduates at the better colleges, graduate students, and professional economists will find this well-organized, clearly and logically presented work helpful. From the case of a single consumer and a single producer, the authors move on to that of exchange among producers and consumers in a single market and then to the general case in which all markets are shown in their interrelations with one another. The book deals with competitive markets, as well as imperfect markets, and also with problems of welfare.

One author took the primary responsibility for four chapters, and the other for three chapters and the Appendix. But each author also contributed to the final preparation of his coauthor's chapters. In this sense the book is a joint product.

From San Diego State College, James M. Henderson moved on to Harvard, where he received his Ph.D. and won the Wells Prize for *The Efficiency of the Coal Industry*, which is slated for publication in 1958. At present, Professor Henderson is on the Harvard teaching staff and is a member of the senior research staff of the Harvard University Economic Research Project.

After an early education in Europe, Richard Quandt migrated to this country and received his A.B. at Princeton, *summa cum laude*. He obtained his Ph.D. at Harvard and, while on the teaching staff there, began the collaboration which produced the current volume. Quandt, now an assistant professor at Princeton, has written articles for several scientific journals.

The editor welcomes this volume to the series. Its quality indicates that many other important contributions are to be expected from these first-class economists.

Seymour E. Harris

PREFACE

The last two decades have witnessed an increasing application of mathematical methods to nearly every branch of economics. The theories of individual optimizing units and market equilibrium which are included within the microeconomics branch are no exception. Traditional theory has been formulated in mathematical terms, and the classical results proved or disproved. The use of mathematics has also allowed the derivation of many new results. Mathematical methods are particularly useful in this field since the underlying premises of utility and profit maximization are basically mathematical in character.

In the early stages of this development economists were rather sharply divided into two groups: the mathematical economists and the literary, or nonmathematical, economists. Fortunately, this sharp division is breaking down with the passage of time. More and more economists and students of economics are becoming acquainted with at least elementary mathematics and are learning to appreciate the advantages of its use in economics. On the other side, many mathematically inclined economists are becoming more aware of the limitations of mathematics. It seems a safe prediction that before too many more years have passed the question of the use of mathematics in microeconomic theory will be only a matter of degree.

As the number of economists and students of economics with mathematical training increases, the basic problem shifts from that of teaching mathematics to economists to that of teaching them economics in mathematical terms. The present volume is intended for economists and students of economics who have some mathematical training but do not possess a high degree of mathematical sophistication. It is not intended as a textbook on mathematics for economists. The basic concepts of microeconomic theory are developed with the aid of intermediate mathematics. The selection of topics and the order of presentation are indicated by economic, rather than mathematical, content.

This volume is intended for readers who possess some knowledge, though not necessarily a great deal, of both economics and mathematics. The audience at which it is aimed includes advanced undergraduate and graduate students in economics and professional economists who desire to see how intermediate mathematics contributes to the understanding of some familiar concepts.   Advanced knowledge in one of these fields can partially compensate for a lack of training in the other.   The reader with a weak background in microeconomics will not fully appreciate its problems or the limitations of the mathematical methods unless he consults some of the purely literary works in this area.   A limited number of these are contained in the lists of selected references at the end of each chapter.

A one-year college course in calculus, or its equivalent, is sufficient mathematical preparation for the present volume.[1]   A review of the mathematical concepts employed in the text is contained in the Appendix. The Appendix is not adequate for a reader who has never been exposed to calculus, but it should serve the dual purpose of refreshing the reader's memory on topics with which he has some familiarity and of introducing him to the few concepts that are employed in the text but are not usually covered in a first course in calculus—specifically, Cramer's rule, Lagrange multipliers, and simple difference equations.   The reader interested in extending his knowledge of specific mathematical concepts will find a list of references at the end of the Appendix.

In order to simplify the reader's introduction to the use of mathematical methods in microeconomic theory, two- and three-variable cases are emphasized in Chapters 2 and 3.   The more general cases are emphasized in the later chapters.   The analysis is frequently accompanied by diagrams, in order to provide a geometric interpretation of the formal results. The formal analysis is also illustrated with specific numerical examples. The reader may test his comprehension by working through the examples and working out the proofs and extensions of the analysis that are occasionally left as exercises.

The authors have both served as senior partners in the preparation of this volume, with each contributing approximately one-half of the material.   Henderson is primarily responsible for Chapters 3, 5, 6, and 8, and Quandt is primarily responsible for Chapters 2, 4, 7, and the Appendix. However, the manuscript was prepared in very close collaboration, and each author helped plan, review, and revise the work of the other. Therefore, all errors and defects are the responsibility of both.

The authors are indebted to many of their teachers, colleagues, and students for direct and indirect aid in the production of this volume. Their greatest debt is to their former teacher, Wassily W. Leontief.   His general outlook is in evidence throughout the volume, and he is responsible for much of the authors' affection for microeconomic theory.   The authors gratefully acknowledge the advice and criticism of William J.

[1] The reader without this background is referred to the first fifteen chapters of R. G. D. Allen, *Mathematical Analysis for Economists* (London: Macmillan, 1938).

Baumol, who read the entire manuscript in an intermediate stage and offered numerous suggestions for its improvement.   Others who deserve specific mention are Robert Dorfman, W. Eric Gustafson, Franklin M. Fisher, Carl Kaysen, and Seymour E. Harris.   The marginal productivities of the inputs of the authors' above-mentioned friends are strictly positive in all cases.

The authors also owe a very significant debt to the economists who pioneered the application of mathematical methods to microeconomic theory.   Their written works provide the framework for this book.   The outstanding pioneers are J. R. Hicks and Paul A. Samuelson, but there are many others.   The names and works of many of the pioneers can be found in the lists of selected references at the end of each chapter.

James M. Henderson
Richard E. Quandt

CONTENTS

CHAPTER 1

INTRODUCTION

Economics is not a clearly defined discipline. Its frontiers are constantly changing, and their definition is frequently a subject of controversy. A commonly used definition characterizes economics as the study of the use of limited resources for the achievement of alternative ends. This definition is adequate if interpreted broadly enough to include the study of unemployed resources and to cover situations in which the ends are selected by economists themselves. More specifically, economics may be defined as a social science which covers the actions of individuals and groups of individuals in the processes of producing, exchanging, and consuming goods and services.

1-1. The Role of Theory

Explanation and prediction are the goals of economics as well as most other sciences. Both theoretical analyses and empirical investigations are necessary for the achievement of these goals. The two are usually inextricably intertwined in concrete examples of research; yet there is a real distinction between them. Theories employ abstract deductive reasoning whereby conclusions are drawn from sets of initial assumptions. Purely empirical studies are inductive in nature. The two approaches are complementary, since theories provide guides for empirical studies and empirical studies provide tests of the assumptions and conclusions of theories.

Basically, a theory contains three sets of elements: (1) data which play the role of parameters and are assumed to be given from outside the analytical framework; (2) variables, the magnitudes of which are determined within the theory; and (3) behavior assumptions or postulates which define the set of operations by which the values of the variables are determined. The conclusions of a theoretical argument are always of a *what would happen if* nature. They state what the results of economic processes would be if the initial assumptions were satisfied, i.e., if the data were in fact given and the behavior assumptions justified.

Empirical investigations allow comparisons of the assumptions and conclusions of theories with observed facts.   However, the requirement of a strict conformity between theory and fact would defeat the very purpose of theory.   Theories represent simplifications and generalizations of reality and therefore do not completely describe particular situations. The data-variable distinctions and behavior assumptions of the theories presented in subsequent chapters are satisfied by few, if any, actual market situations.   A stricter conformity to facts would require a separate, highly detailed theory for each individual market situation, since each possesses its own distinctive characteristics.   Applied theories of this nature, however valuable for specific research projects, are of little general value.   The more general theories are fruitful because they contain statements which abstract from particulars and find elements which many situations have in common.   Increased understanding is realized at the cost of the sacrificed detail.   It is then possible to go from the general to the specific.   The cases described by pure theories provide insight into economic processes and serve as a background and starting point for applied theories and specific empirical studies.

1-2. Microeconomics

Like most other disciplines, economics is divided into branches and sub-branches.   In recent years two major branches have been distinguished: *microeconomics*, which is the study of the economic actions of individuals and well-defined groups of individuals, and *macroeconomics*, which is the study of broad aggregates such as total employment and national income. This dichotomy is in a sense artificial, since aggregates are merely sums of individual figures.   However, it is justified by the basic differences in the objectives and methods of the two branches.

The microscopic versus the macroscopic view of the economy is the fundamental, but not the only, difference between these two branches of economics.   Before the micro-macro distinction came into vogue, the fundamental distinction was between price and income analyses.   This distinction can be carried over into the micro and macro branches. Prices play a major role in microeconomic theories, and their goal is generally the analysis of price determination and the allocation of specific resources to particular uses.   On the other hand, the goals of macroeconomic theories generally are the determination of the levels of national income and aggregate resource employment.

One cannot say that income concepts are ignored in micro theories or that prices are nonexistent in macro theories.   However, in micro theories the determination of the incomes of individuals is encompassed within the general pricing process: individuals earn their incomes by selling factors of production, the prices of which are determined in the same manner as all other prices. On the other hand, prices are relevant in macro theories, but macro theorists usually abstract from the problems of determining individual prices and their relations to one another and deal with aggregate price indices as determined by the level of aggregate spending.

Since the problems of individual price determination are assumed away in macro theory, the relationship between individual units and the aggregates is not clear. If it were, the analysis would be classified as micro theory. The simplifications introduced by aggregation are not without reward, since they make it possible to describe the position and progress of the economy as a whole in terms of a few simple aggregates. This would be impossible if the micro emphasis on individual behavior and relative prices were maintained.

Following this established separation of subject matter, the present volume is limited to a systematic exposition of traditional microeconomic theory. The theories of individual behavior and price determination for a perfectly competitive economy are developed in three stages of increasing generality in Chapters 2 through 5. The behavior of individual consumers (Chapter 2) and producers (Chapter 3) is the focal point of the first stage. Each individual is assumed to consider the prices of the goods that he buys and sells as given parameters, the magnitudes of which he is unable to influence. The quantities of his purchases and sales are the variables determined in these theories. The market for a single commodity is the focal point of the second stage (Chapter 4). The prices of all other commodities are assumed to be given parameters, and the price of the commodity in question, as well as the volume of its purchases and sales, is shown to be determined by the independent actions of all its buyers and sellers. Finally, in the third stage (Chapter 5) the interrelations between the various markets in the system are explicitly taken into account, and all prices are determined simultaneously.

Microeconomic theories are sufficiently flexible to permit many variations in their underlying assumptions. For example, the assumption that no single individual is able to influence prices or the actions of other individuals is modified in Chapter 6. Despite the variation of this basic premise, the family resemblance between the analyses of Chapter 6 and those of earlier chapters is quite evident. The assumption of a static world in which consumers and producers do not plan for the future is relaxed in Chapter 8. Again the logical connection with the earlier chapters is easily discernible. The possibility of relaxing these and other assumptions increases the flexibility and generality of the basic theories.

Another important use of theory is to serve as a guide to *what ought to be*. The subbranch of microeconomics which covers these problems is known as welfare economics and is the subject of Chapter 7. The degree of conformity between theory and fact is of great importance in welfare economics. If one were interested in pure description, a divergence between theory and fact would suggest that the theory is faulty for that particular purpose. When the theory becomes a welfare ideal, such a divergence leads to the conclusion that the actual situation is faulty and should be remedied.

1-3. The Role of Mathematics

The theories of the present volume are cast in mathematical terms. The mathematics is not an end in itself, but rather a set of tools which facilitates the derivation and exposition of the economic theories. Mathematics is useful for translating verbal arguments into concise and consistent forms. However, it does more than this. Mathematics provides the economist with a set of tools often more powerful than ordinary speech in that it possesses concepts and allows operations for which no manageable verbal equivalents exist. The use of mathematics enlarges the economist's tool kit and widens the range of possible inferences from initial assumptions.

Purely verbal analysis was the first stage in the historical development of economic theory. However, as quantitative relationships were formulated in increasing numbers and as theories became increasingly complex, purely verbal analyses became more tedious and more difficult to formulate consistently. Mathematical functions underlay most of these early theories, though they were seldom made explicit. The recognition that more rigorous formulations were often necessary led to the acceptance of geometry as an important tool of analysis. Geometry was and is highly useful, but possesses many limitations. One of the most serious of these is the limitation of theoretical arguments to two, or at most three, variables. The increasing use of mathematics in recent years reflects the belief that geometry is not adequate for rigorous economic reasoning in many cases.

When an economic theory is put into mathematical terms, one must make some assumptions about the mathematical properties of the phenomena under investigation. These assumptions, like the strictly economic assumptions, represent simplifications of reality. However, it is fruitful to abstract from reality if increased understanding results from the sacrifice of some detail.

The use of mathematics in the present volume does not mean that the authors believe that all verbal and geometric analyses should be discarded. All three approaches are of value. Verbal analyses serve to fill in many details, and geometry is adequate, even preferable, for many problems. In order to highlight the similarities between the geometric and mathematical approaches, the two are used side by side in the development of many propositions in the present volume.

The mathematical concepts used in the text are reviewed in the Appendix. All except mathematically sophisticated readers should read, or at least skim, the Appendix *before* beginning Chapter 2.

CHAPTER 2

THE THEORY OF CONSUMER BEHAVIOR

The postulate of rationality is the customary point of departure in the theory of the consumer's behavior. The consumer is assumed to choose among the alternatives available to him in such a manner that the satisfaction derived from consuming commodities (in the broadest sense) is as large as possible. This implies that he is aware of the alternatives facing him and is capable of evaluating them. All information pertaining to the satisfaction that the consumer derives from various quantities of commodities is contained in his *utility function*.

The concepts of utility and its maximization are void of any sensuous connotation. The assertion that a consumer derives more satisfaction or utility from an automobile than from a suit of clothes means that if he were presented with the alternatives of receiving as a gift either an automobile or a suit of clothes, he would choose the former. Things that are necessary for survival—such as vaccine when a smallpox epidemic threatens—may give the consumer the most utility, although the act of consuming such a commodity has no pleasurable sensations connected with it.

The nineteenth-century economists W. Stanley Jevons, Léon Walras, and Alfred Marshall considered utility measurable, just as the weight of objects is measurable. The consumer was assumed to possess a *cardinal* measure of utility, i.e., he was assumed to be capable of assigning to every commodity or combination of commodities a number representing the amount or degree of utility associated with it. The numbers representing amounts of utility could be manipulated in the same fashion as weights. Assume, for example, that the utility of A is 15 units and the utility of B 45 units. The consumer would "like" B three times as strongly as A. The differences between utility numbers could be compared, and the comparison could lead to a statement such as "A is preferred to B twice as much as C is preferred to D." It was also assumed by the nineteenth-century economists that the additions to a consumer's total utility resulting from consuming additional units of a commodity decrease as he consumes more of it. The consumer's behavior can be deduced from the above assumptions. Imagine that a certain price, say 2 dollars, is charged for coconuts. The consumer, confronted with coconuts, will not buy any if the amount of utility he surrenders by paying the price of a coconut (i.e., by parting with purchasing power) is greater than the utility he gains by consuming it. Assume that the utility of a dollar is 5 utils and remains approximately constant for small variations in income and that the consumer derives the following increments of utility by consuming an additional coconut:

Unit	Additional utility
Coconut 1	20
Coconut 2	9
Coconut 3	7

He will buy at least one coconut, because he surrenders 10 utils in exchange for 20 utils and thus increases his total utility.[1] He will not buy a second coconut, because the utility loss exceeds the gain. In general, the consumer will not add to his consumption of a commodity if an additional unit involves a net utility loss. He will increase his consumption only if he realizes a net gain of utility from it. For example, assume that the price of coconuts falls to 1.6 dollars. Two coconuts will now be bought. A fall in the price has increased the quantity bought. This is the sense in which the theory predicts the consumer's behavior.

The assumptions on which the theory of cardinal utility is built are very restrictive. Equivalent conclusions can be deduced from much weaker assumptions. Therefore it will *not* be assumed in the remainder of this chapter that the consumer possesses a cardinal measure of utility or that the additional utility derived from increasing his consumption of a commodity diminishes.

If the consumer derives more utility from alternative A than from alternative B, he is said to prefer A to B.† The postulate of rationality is equivalent to the following statements: (1) for all possible pairs of alternatives A and B the consumer knows whether he prefers A to B or B to A, or whether he is indifferent between them; (2) only one of the three possibilities is true for any pair of alternatives; (3) if the consumer prefers A to B and B to C, he will prefer A to C. The last statement ensures that the consumer's preferences are consistent or *transitive:* if he prefers an automobile to a suit of clothes and a suit of clothes to a bowl of soup, he must prefer an automobile to a bowl of soup.

The postulate of rationality, as stated above, merely requires that the

---

[1] The price is 2 dollars; the consumer loses 5 utils per dollar surrendered. Therefore the gross loss is 10 utils, and the gross gain is 20 utils.

† A chain of definitions must eventually come to an end. The word "prefer" could be defined to mean "would rather have than," but then this expression must be left undefined. The term "prefer" is also void of any connotation of sensuous pleasure.

consumer be able to rank commodities in order of preference.   The consumer possesses an *ordinal* utility measure, i.e., he need not be able to assign numbers that represent (in arbitrary units) the degree or amount of utility that he derives from commodities.   His ranking of commodities is expressed mathematically by his utility function.   It associates certain numbers with various quantities of commodities consumed, but these numbers provide only a ranking or ordering of preferences.   If the utility of alternative A is 15 and the utility of B is 45 (i.e., if the utility function associates the number 15 with alternative or commodity A and the number 45 with alternative B), one can only say that B is preferred to A, but it is meaningless to say that B is liked three times as strongly as A. This reformulation of the postulates of the theory of consumer behavior was effected only around the turn of the last century.   It is remarkable that the consumer's behavior can be explained just as well in terms of an ordinal utility function as in terms of a cardinal one.   Intuitively one can see that the consumer's choices are completely determinate if he possesses a ranking (and only a ranking) of commodities according to his preferences.   One could visualize the consumer as possessing a list of commodities in decreasing order of desirability; when the consumer receives his income he starts purchasing commodities from the top of the list and descends as far as his income allows.[1]   Therefore it is not necessary to assume that he possesses a cardinal measure of utility. The much weaker assumption that he possesses a consistent ranking of preferences is sufficient.

The basic tools of analysis and the nature of the utility function are discussed in Sec. 2-1.   Two alternative but equivalent methods are employed for the determination of the individual consumer's optimum consumption level in Sec. 2-2.   It is shown in Sec. 2-3 that the solution of the consumer's maximum problem is invariant with respect to monotonic transformations of his utility function.   Demand curves are derived in Sec. 2-4, and the analysis is extended to the problem of choice between income and leisure in Sec. 2-5.   The effect of price and income variations on consumption levels is examined in Sec. 2-6.   The theory is generalized to an arbitrary number of commodities in Sec. 2-7 and is reformulated in terms of an alternative approach, the theory of revealed preference, in Sec. 2-8.   Finally, the problem of choice is analyzed with respect to situations with uncertain outcomes in Sec. 2-9.

2-1. Basic Concepts

The Nature of the Utility Function.   Consider the simple case in which the consumer's purchases are limited to two commodities.   His ordinal

---

[1] How much a particular item on the list is liked is irrelevant; an item which is higher up on the list will always be chosen before one which comes later.

utility function is

$$U = f(q_1, q_2) \tag{2-1}$$

where q_1 and q_2 are the quantities of the two commodities Q_1 and Q_2 which he consumes. It is assumed that $f(q_1, q_2)$ is continuous and has continuous first- and second-order partial derivatives. The consumer's utility function is not unique (see Sec. 2-3). In general, any single-valued increasing function of q_1 and q_2 can serve as a utility function. The utility number U^0 assigned to any particular commodity combination indicates that it is preferable or superior to all combinations with lower numbers and inferior to those with higher numbers.

The utility function is defined with reference to consumption during a specified period of time. ⌈The level of satisfaction that the consumer derives from a particular commodity combination depends upon the length of the period during which he consumes it.⌋ Different levels of satisfaction are derived from consuming ten portions of ice cream within one hour and within one month. There is no unique time period for which the utility function *should* be defined. However, there are restrictions upon the possible length of the period. The consumer usually derives utility from variety in his diet and diversification among the commodities he consumes. Therefore, the utility function must not be defined for a period so short that the desire for variety cannot be satisfied. On the other hand, tastes (the shape of the function) may change if it is defined for too long a period. Any intermediate period is satisfactory for the static theory of consumer behavior.[1] The present theory is static in the sense that the utility function is defined with reference to a single time period, and the consumer's optimal expenditure pattern is analyzed only with respect to this period. No account is taken of the possibility of transferring consumption expenditures from one period to another.[2]

Indifference Curves. A particular level of utility or satisfaction can be derived from many different combinations of Q_1 and Q_2.† For a

---

[1] The theory would break down if it were impossible to define a period that is neither too short from the first point of view nor too long from the second.

[2] The present analysis is static in that it does not consider what happens after the current income period. The consumer makes his calculations for only one such period at a time. At the end of the period he repeats his calculations for the next one. If he were capable of borrowing, one would consider his total liquid resources available in any time period instead of his income proper. Conversely, he may save, i.e., not spend all his income on consumption goods. Provision can be made for both possibilities without changing the essential points of the analysis (see Sec. 8-2).

† By definition, a commodity is an item of which the consumer would rather have more than less. Otherwise he is dealing with a discommodity. In reality a commodity may become a discommodity if its quantity is sufficiently large. For example, if the consumer partakes of too many portions of ice cream, it may become a discommodity for him. It is assumed in the remainder of the chapter that such a point of saturation has not been reached.

given level of utility U^0 Eq. (2-1) becomes

$$U^0 = f(q_1, q_2) \tag{2-2}$$

where U^0 is a constant.   Since the utility function is continuous, (2-2) is satisfied by an infinite number of combinations of Q_1 and Q_2.   Imagine that the consumer derives a given level of satisfaction U^0 from 5 units of Q_1 and 3 units of Q_2.   If his consumption of Q_1 were decreased from 5 to 4 without an increase in his consumption of Q_2, his satisfaction would certainly decrease.   In general, it is possible to compensate him for the loss of 1 unit of Q_1 by allowing an increase in his consumption of Q_2.

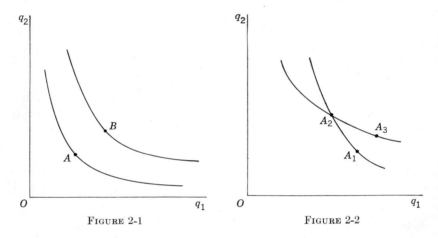

FIGURE 2-1   FIGURE 2-2

Imagine that an increase of 3 units in his consumption of Q_2 makes him indifferent between the two alternative combinations.   Other commodity combinations which yield the consumer the same level of satisfaction can be discovered in a similar manner.   The locus of all commodity combinations from which the consumer derives the same level of satisfaction forms an *indifference curve*.   An *indifference map* is a collection of indifference curves corresponding to different levels of satisfaction. The quantities q_1 and q_2 are measured along the axes of Fig. 2-1.   One indifference curve passes through every point in the positive quadrant of the $q_1 q_2$ plane.   Indifference curves correspond to higher and higher levels of satisfaction as one moves in a northeasterly direction in Fig. 2-1. A movement from point A to point B would increase the consumption of both Q_1 and Q_2.   Therefore B must correspond to a higher level of satisfaction than A.†

Indifference curves cannot intersect as shown in Fig. 2-2.   Consider

† The term "level of satisfaction" should not mislead the reader to think in terms of a cardinal measure of utility.   The term is relevant only in that a particular level of satisfaction is *higher* or *lower* than some other level.   Only the ordinal properties of levels of satisfaction are relevant.

the points A_1, A_2, and A_3. Let the consumer derive the satisfaction U_1 from the batch of commodities represented by A_1 and similarly U_2 and U_3 from A_2 and A_3. The consumer has more of both commodities at A_3 than at A_1, and therefore $U_3 > U_1$. Since A_1 and A_2 are on the same indifference curve, $U_1 = U_2$. The points A_2 and A_3 are also on the same indifference curve, and therefore $U_2 = U_3$. This implies $U_1 = U_3$. Therefore, A_1 and A_3 are on the same indifference curve contrary to assumption.

The Rate of Commodity Substitution. The total differential of the utility function is

$$dU = f_1 \, dq_1 + f_2 \, dq_2 \qquad (2\text{-}3)$$

where f_1 and f_2 are the partial derivatives of U with respect to q_1 and q_2. The total change in utility (compared to an initial situation) caused by variations in q_1 and q_2 is approximately the change in q_1 multiplied by the change in utility resulting from a unit change of q_1 plus the change in q_2 multiplied by the change in utility resulting from a unit change in q_2. Let the consumer move along one of his indifference curves by giving up some Q_1 in exchange for Q_2. If his consumption of Q_1 decreases by dq_1 (therefore, $dq_1 < 0$), the resulting loss of utility is approximately $f_1 \, dq_1$. The gain of utility caused by acquiring some Q_2 is approximately $f_2 \, dq_2$ for similar reasons. Taking arbitrarily small increments, the sum of these two terms must equal zero in the limit, since the total change in utility along an indifference curve is zero by definition.[1] Since the analysis runs in terms of ordinal utility functions, the magnitudes of $f_1 \, dq_1$ and $f_2 \, dq_2$ are not known. However, it must still be true that the sum of these two terms is zero. Setting $dU = 0$,

$$f_1 \, dq_1 + f_2 \, dq_2 = 0$$

yields

$$-\frac{dq_2}{dq_1} = \frac{f_1}{f_2} \qquad (2\text{-}4)$$

The slope of an indifference curve, dq_2/dq_1, is the rate at which a consumer would be willing to substitute Q_1 for Q_2 or Q_2 for Q_1 in order to maintain a given level of utility. The negative of the slope, $-dq_2/dq_1$, is the rate of commodity substitution (RCS) of Q_1 for Q_2 or Q_2 for Q_1, and it equals the ratio of the partial derivatives of the utility function.[2]

---

[1] Imagine the utility function as a surface in three-dimensional space. Then the total differential (2-3) is the equation of the tangent plane to this surface at some point. This justifies the use of the word approximate in the above argument (see Sec. A-3).

[2] The rate of commodity substitution is frequently referred to in the literature of economics as the *marginal* rate of substitution, although the term marginal is redundant. Cf. J. R. Hicks, *Value and Capital* (2d ed.; Oxford: Clarendon Press, 1946), part I.

The RCS at a point on an indifference curve is the same for movements in either direction. It is immaterial whether the verbal definition is in terms of substituting Q_1 for Q_2 or vice versa.

In a cardinal analysis the partial derivatives f_1 and f_2 are defined as the *marginal utilities* of the commodities Q_1 and Q_2.† This definition is retained in the present ordinal analysis. However, the partial derivative of an ordinal utility function cannot be given a cardinal interpretation. Therefore, the numerical magnitudes of individual marginal utilities are without meaning. The consumer is not assumed to be aware of the existence of marginal utilities, and only the economist need know that the consumer's RCS equals the ratio of marginal utilities. The signs as well as the ratios of marginal utilities are meaningful in an ordinal analysis. A positive value for f_1 signifies that an increase in q_1 will increase the consumer's satisfaction level and move him to a higher indifference curve.

2-2. The Maximization of Utility

The rational consumer desires to purchase that combination of Q_1 and Q_2 from which he derives the highest level of satisfaction. His problem is one of maximization. However, his income is limited, and he is not able to purchase unlimited amounts of the commodities. The consumer's budget constraint can be written as

$$y^0 = p_1 q_1 + p_2 q_2 \qquad (2\text{-}5)$$

where y^0 is his (fixed) income and p_1 and p_2 are the prices of Q_1 and Q_2 respectively. The amount he spends on the first commodity ($p_1 q_1$) plus the amount he spends on the second ($p_2 q_2$) equals his income (y^0).

Method 1. In order to maximize the utility function subject to the budget constraint the consumer must find a combination of commodities that satisfies (2-5) and also maximizes the utility function (2-1). Transposing $p_1 q_1$ to the left in (2-5) and dividing through by p_2, the budget constraint becomes

$$\frac{y^0 - p_1 q_1}{p_2} = q_2$$

Substituting this value of q_2 into (2-1), the utility function becomes a function of q_1 alone:

$$U = f\left(q_1, \frac{y^0 - p_1 q_1}{p_2}\right) \qquad (2\text{-}6)$$

---

† The marginal utility of a commodity is often loosely defined as the increase in utility resulting from a unit increase in its consumption.

Because of the fixed relationship between q_1 and q_2 via the budget constraint, it is sufficient to maximize (2-6) with respect to q_1. Sufficient conditions are satisfied if $dU/dq_1 = 0$ (first-order condition) and $d^2U/dq_1^2 < 0$ (second-order condition).

Setting the first derivative of (2-6) equal to zero,†

$$\frac{dU}{dq_1} = f_1 + f_2\left(-\frac{p_1}{p_2}\right) = 0 \qquad (2\text{-}7)$$

Transposing the second term of (2-7) to the right and dividing by f_2 yields

$$\frac{f_1}{f_2} = \frac{p_1}{p_2} \qquad (2\text{-}8)$$

The ratio of the marginal utilities must equal the ratio of prices for a maximum. Since f_1/f_2 is the RCS, the first-order condition for a maximum is expressed by the equality of the RCS and the price ratio. Equation (2-8) can be rewritten as

$$\frac{f_1}{p_1} = \frac{f_2}{p_2} \qquad (2\text{-}9)$$

Marginal utility divided by price must be the same for all commodities. This ratio gives the rate at which satisfaction would increase if an additional dollar were spent on a particular commodity. If more satisfaction could be gained by spending an additional dollar on Q_1 rather than Q_2, the consumer would not be maximizing utility. He could increase his satisfaction by shifting some of his expenditure from Q_2 to Q_1. Equation (2-9) is necessary for a maximum, but it does not ensure that a maximum is actually reached.

Denoting the second direct partial derivatives of (2-1) by f_{11} and f_{22} and the second cross partial derivatives by f_{12} and f_{21}, the second-order condition for a maximum requires that

$$\frac{d^2U}{dq_1^2} = f_{11} + 2f_{12}\left(-\frac{p_1}{p_2}\right) + f_{22}\left(-\frac{p_1}{p_2}\right)^2 < 0$$

Multiplying by p_2^2 (a positive number),

$$f_{11}p_2^2 - 2f_{12}p_1p_2 + f_{22}p_1^2 < 0 \qquad (2\text{-}10)$$

A maximum is obtained if (2-10) holds in addition to (2-8) and (2-9).

By further differentiation of (2-4) the rate of change of the slope of

† The composite-function rule and the function of a function rule have been used (see Secs. A-2 and A-3).

the indifference curve is†

$$\frac{d^2q_2}{dq_1{}^2} = -\frac{1}{f_2{}^3}(f_{11}f_2{}^2 - 2f_{12}f_1f_2 + f_{22}f_1{}^2) \qquad (2\text{-}11)$$

Substituting $f_1 = p_1f_2/p_2$ from (2-8) into (2-11),

$$\frac{d^2q_2}{dq_1{}^2} = -\frac{1}{f_2p_2{}^2}(f_{11}p_2{}^2 - 2f_{12}p_1p_2 + f_{22}p_1{}^2) \qquad (2\text{-}12)$$

Inequality (2-10) ensures that the bracketed term on the right-hand side of (2-12) is negative. Hence $d^2q_2/dq_1{}^2$ is positive, and the indifference curves are convex from below. Equations (2-4) and (2-8) together imply that indifference curves are negatively sloped, since prices are positive. If maxima exist, indifference curves are of the general shape presented in Fig. 2-1.

Assume that the utility function is $U = q_1q_2$, that $p_1 = 2$ dollars, $p_2 = 5$ dollars, and that the consumer's income for the period is 100 dollars. The budget constraint is

$$100 - 2q_1 - 5q_2 = 0$$

Expressing q_2 as a function of q_1 from the budget constraint,

$$q_2 = 20 - \frac{2q_1}{5}$$

Substituting into the utility function,

$$U = 20q_1 - \frac{2q_1{}^2}{5}$$

Therefore $\dfrac{dU}{dq_1} = 20 - \dfrac{4q_1}{5}$

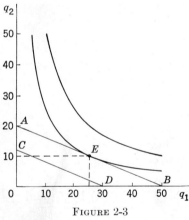

FIGURE 2-3

Setting dU/dq_1 equal to zero and solving for q_1 gives $q_1 = 25$. Substituting this into the budget constraint gives $q_2 = 10$. The second derivative of the utility function is negative for these values of q_1 and q_2, as the reader may verify by performing the necessary differentiation. The consumer maximizes utility by consuming this combination.

Figure 2-3 contains a graphic presentation of this example. The price line AB is the geometric counterpart of the budget constraint and shows all possible combinations of Q_1 and Q_2 that the consumer *can* purchase. Its equation is $100 - 2q_1 - 5q_2 = 0$. The consumer can purchase 50 units of Q_1 if he buys no Q_2, 20 units of Q_2 if he buys no Q_1, etc. A

† Note that (2-11) is obtained by taking the total derivative of the slope of the indifference curve instead of the partial derivative.

different price line corresponds to each possible level of income; if the consumer's income were 60 dollars, the relevant price line would be CD. The indifference curves in this example are a family of rectangular hyperbolas.[1] The consumer desires to reach the highest indifference curve that has at least one point in common with AB. His equilibrium is at point E, at which AB is tangent to an indifference curve. Movements in either direction from point E result in a diminished level of utility. The constant slope of the price line, $-p_1/p_2$ or $-\frac{2}{5}$ in the present example, must equal the slope of the indifference curve. Forming the ratio of the

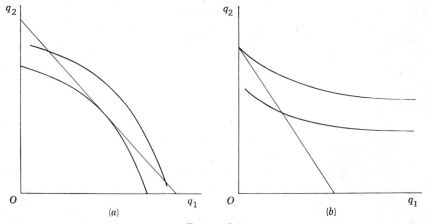

FIGURE 2-4

partial derivatives of the utility function, the slope of the indifference curves in the present example is $-q_2/q_1$, and hence the RCS equals $q_2/q_1 = \frac{10}{25}$, which equals the ratio of prices $\frac{2}{5}$ as required. The indifference curves are convex from below because $d^2q_2/dq_1^2 = 2q_2/q_1^2 > 0$.

The first-order condition (2-8) or (2-9) is not necessary for a maximum in two special cases: (1) if the indifference curves are concave from below, and (2) if the indifference curves are convex from below but are everywhere steeper (or less steep) than the price line. The consumer's optimum position is given by a corner solution in both cases. In case (1) the first-order condition for a maximum is satisfied at the point of tangency between the price line and an indifference curve, but the second-order condition is not (see Fig. 2-4a). Therefore this point represents a situation of minimum utility, and the consumer can increase his utility by moving from the point of tangency toward either axis. He consumes only one commodity at the optimum. If he spends all his income on one commodity, he can buy y^0/p_1 units of Q_1 or y^0/p_2 units of Q_2. Therefore he will buy only Q_1 or only Q_2, depending upon whether $f(y^0/p_1, 0) \gtrless$

[1] Hyperbolas the asymptotes of which coincide with the coordinate axes.

$f(0, y^0/p_2)$.   In case (2) tangency cannot be achieved (the first-order condition cannot be fulfilled) although the second-order condition could be satisfied (see Fig. 2-4b).   The methods of calculus cannot be applied because of the restrictions $q_1 \geqq 0$, $q_2 \geqq 0$.   As before, the consumer purchases only one commodity at the optimum.

Method 2.   The same conclusions can be obtained by using the technique of Lagrange multipliers.   From the utility function (2-1) and the budget constraint (2-5) form the function

$$V = f(q_1, q_2) + \lambda(y^0 - p_1 q_1 - p_2 q_2) \tag{2-13}$$

where λ is the as yet undetermined Lagrange multiplier (see Sec. A-3). V is a function of q_1, q_2, and λ.   Moreover, V is identically equal to U for those values of q_1 and q_2 which satisfy the budget constraint, since then $y^0 - p_1 q_1 - p_2 q_2 = 0$.   To maximize V, calculate the partial derivatives of V with respect to the three variables and set them equal to zero:

$$\frac{\partial V}{\partial q_1} = f_1 - \lambda p_1 = 0$$

$$\frac{\partial V}{\partial q_2} = f_2 - \lambda p_2 = 0 \tag{2-14}$$

$$\frac{\partial V}{\partial \lambda} = y^0 - p_1 q_1 - p_2 q_2 = 0$$

The first-order condition (2-8) is immediately obtained from (2-14) by transposing the second terms in the first two equations of (2-14) to the right-hand side and dividing the first equation by the second.   The second-order condition for a constrained maximum is that the relevant bordered Hessian determinant be positive:

$$\begin{vmatrix} f_{11} & f_{12} & -p_1 \\ f_{21} & f_{22} & -p_2 \\ -p_1 & -p_2 & 0 \end{vmatrix} > 0 \tag{2-15}$$

Expanding (2-15),

$$2f_{12}p_1 p_2 - f_{22}p_1{}^2 - f_{11}p_2{}^2 > 0$$

which is the same as (2-10).†

2-3. The Choice of a Utility Index

The numbers which the utility function assigns to the alternative commodity combinations need not have cardinal significance; they need only serve as an *index* of the consumer's satisfaction.   Imagine that one wishes to compare the satisfaction a consumer derives from one hat and

† See Sec. A-1 on expanding a determinant and Sec. A-3 on constrained maxima.

two shirts and from two hats and five shirts. The consumer is known to prefer the latter to the former combination. The numbers that are assigned to these combinations for the purpose of showing the strength of his preferences are arbitrary in the sense that the difference between them has no meaning. Since the second batch is preferred to the first batch, the number 3 could be assigned to the first, and the number 4 to the second. However, any other set of numbers would serve as well, as long as the number assigned to the second batch exceeded that assigned to the first. Thus 3 for the first batch and 400 for the second would provide an equally satisfactory utility index. If a particular set of numbers associated with various combinations of Q_1 and Q_2 is a utility index, any monotonic transformation of it is also a utility index.[1] Assume that the original utility function is $U = f(q_1, q_2)$. Now form a new utility index $W = F(U) = F[f(q_1, q_2)]$ by applying a monotonic transformation to the original utility index. The function $F(U)$ is then a monotonic (increasing) function of U.† It can be demonstrated that maximizing W subject to the budget constraint is equivalent to maximizing U subject to the budget constraint. Form the function

$$Z = F[f(q_1, q_2)] + \lambda(y^0 - p_1 q_1 - p_2 q_2)$$

and set the partial derivatives with respect to q_1, q_2, and λ equal to zero:

$$\frac{\partial Z}{\partial q_1} = F'f_1 - \lambda p_1 = 0$$

$$\frac{\partial Z}{\partial q_2} = F'f_2 - \lambda p_2 = 0 \qquad (2\text{-}16)$$

$$\frac{\partial Z}{\partial \lambda} = y^0 - p_1 q_1 - p_2 q_2 = 0$$

where F' is the derivative of F with respect to its argument.[2] Transposing the second terms of the first two equations of (2-16) and dividing the first equation by the second,

$$\frac{f_1}{f_2} = \frac{p_1}{p_2} \qquad (2\text{-}17)$$

This proves that the first-order conditions are invariant with respect to the particular choice of the utility index.[3] The ratio of the marginal utilities must equal the ratio of the corresponding prices, irrespective of

---

[1] A function $F(U)$ is a monotonic transformation of U if $F(U_1) > F(U_0)$ whenever $U_1 > U_0$.

† Examples are provided by the transformations $W = aU + b$, provided that a is positive, and by $W = U^2$, provided that all utility numbers are nonnegative.

[2] The arguments of a function are the variables of which it is a function. Note that the function of a function rule is applied (see Sec. A-2).

[3] The assumption that F is a monotonic transformation guarantees that $F' \neq 0$.

the choice of a utility index. The marginal utilities for different indices may be quite different, but they are not important for the maximization of utility; the ratio of the marginal utilities is the same, irrespective of the utility index.

The second-order partial derivatives of Z are

$$\frac{\partial^2 Z}{\partial q_1{}^2} = F''f_1{}^2 + F'f_{11}$$

$$\frac{\partial^2 Z}{\partial q_2{}^2} = F''f_2{}^2 + F'f_{22}$$

$$\frac{\partial^2 Z}{\partial \lambda^2} = 0$$

$$\frac{\partial^2 Z}{\partial q_1 \partial q_2} = F''f_1 f_2 + F'f_{12}$$

$$\frac{\partial^2 Z}{\partial q_2 \partial q_1} = F''f_1 f_2 + F'f_{21}$$

$$\frac{\partial^2 Z}{\partial q_1 \partial \lambda} = -p_1$$

$$\frac{\partial^2 Z}{\partial q_2 \partial \lambda} = -p_2$$

The second-order condition for a maximum states that

$$\mathbf{A} = \begin{vmatrix} F''f_1{}^2 + F'f_{11} & F''f_1 f_2 + F'f_{12} & -p_1 \\ F''f_1 f_2 + F'f_{21} & F''f_2{}^2 + F'f_{22} & -p_2 \\ -p_1 & -p_2 & 0 \end{vmatrix} > 0 \qquad (2\text{-}18)$$

This determinant can be shown to be the same as (2-15). The value of a determinant does not change if a multiple of one row is added to some other row or if a multiple of a column is added to some other column. Multiplying a row or a column of the array by a given number is equivalent to multiplying the value of the determinant by that number (see Sec. A-1). From the first two equations of (2-16)

$$p_1 = \frac{F'f_1}{\lambda}$$

$$p_2 = \frac{F'f_2}{\lambda}$$

Substituting these values of p_1 and p_2 into (2-18),

$$\mathbf{A} = \begin{vmatrix} F''f_1{}^2 + F'f_{11} & F''f_1 f_2 + F'f_{12} & -F'f_1/\lambda \\ F''f_1 f_2 + F'f_{21} & F''f_2{}^2 + F'f_{22} & -F'f_2/\lambda \\ -F'f_1/\lambda & -F'f_2/\lambda & 0 \end{vmatrix} > 0 \qquad (2\text{-}19)$$

Multiplying the last row and the last column of (2-19) by λ/F',

$$\mathbf{A} = \left(\frac{F'}{\lambda}\right)^2 \begin{vmatrix} F''f_1{}^2 + F'f_{11} & F''f_1 f_2 + F'f_{12} & -f_1 \\ F''f_1 f_2 + F'f_{21} & F''f_2{}^2 + F'f_{22} & -f_2 \\ -f_1 & -f_2 & 0 \end{vmatrix} > 0$$

Now add $F''f_1$ times the last row to the first row and $F''f_2$ times the last row to the second row. This leaves $\mathbf{A}$ unchanged:

$$\mathbf{A} = \left(\frac{F'}{\lambda}\right)^2 \begin{vmatrix} F'f_{11} & F'f_{12} & -f_1 \\ F'f_{21} & F'f_{22} & -f_2 \\ -f_1 & -f_2 & 0 \end{vmatrix} > 0$$

Substitute $-\lambda p_1/F'$ for $-f_1$ and $-\lambda p_2/F'$ for $-f_2$ from the first two equations of (2-16) and then multiply the last row and the last column by F'/λ:

$$\mathbf{A} = \begin{vmatrix} F'f_{11} & F'f_{12} & -p_1 \\ F'f_{21} & F'f_{22} & -p_2 \\ -p_1 & -p_2 & 0 \end{vmatrix} > 0$$

Now multiply the last column by F' and divide the first two rows by F':

$$\mathbf{A} = \begin{vmatrix} f_{11} & f_{12} & -p_1 \\ f_{21} & f_{22} & -p_2 \\ -p_1 & -p_2 & 0 \end{vmatrix} (F') > 0 \qquad (2\text{-}20)$$

F is a monotonic transformation by hypothesis; hence F' is positive, and the sign of $\mathbf{A}$ is the same as the sign of the determinant on the right-hand side of (2-20). However, the determinant on the right-hand side of (2-20) is identical with that given by (2-15). This proves that the second-order condition is invariant with respect to the choice of the utility index. It follows from the invariance of the first- and second-order conditions that if the utility index U is maximized, so will be the utility index W. It can be concluded that if the consumer maximizes his utility subject to the budget constraint for one given utility index, he will behave in identical fashion irrespective of the utility index chosen, as long as the index selected is a monotonic transformation of the original one. If a utility function is maximized by a particular batch of commodities, the same batch will maximize all other utility functions that are monotonic transformations of it. The consumer's utility function is unique except for a monotonic transformation.[1]

Choose the utility index $U^* = q_1{}^2 q_2{}^2$, which is a monotonic transfor-

---

[1] This proposition can be proved intuitively as follows. Any single-valued function U can serve as a utility function if it is *order-preserving*, i.e., $U(A) > U(B)$ if and only if A is preferred to B. If $F(U)$ is a monotonic transformation, $F[U(A)] > F[U(B)]$, and the function $F(U)$ is itself order-preserving.

mation of $U = q_1 q_2$.† Form the function

$$V^* = q_1^2 q_2^2 + \lambda(y^0 - 2q_1 - 5q_2)$$

and set its partial derivatives equal to zero:

$$\frac{\partial V^*}{\partial q_1} = 2q_1 q_2^2 - 2\lambda = 0$$

$$\frac{\partial V^*}{\partial q_2} = 2q_1^2 q_2 - 5\lambda = 0$$

$$\frac{\partial V^*}{\partial \lambda} = y^0 - 2q_1 - 5q_2 = 0$$

Substituting $y^0 = 100$ and solving for q_1 and q_2, the same values are obtained as before: $q_1 = 25$ and $q_2 = 10$.

2-4. Demand Curves

The consumer's demand curve for a commodity gives the quantity he will buy as a function of its price. Demand curves can be derived from the analysis of utility maximization. The first-order conditions for maximization (2-14) consist of three equations in the three unknowns: q_1, q_2, and λ.‡ The demand curves are obtained by solving this system for the unknowns. The solutions for q_1 and q_2 are in terms of the parameters p_1, p_2, and y^0. The quantity of Q_1 (or Q_2) that the consumer purchases in the general case depends upon the prices of all commodities and his income.

As above, assume that the utility function is $U = q_1 q_2$ and the budget constraint $y^0 - p_1 q_1 - p_2 q_2 = 0$. Form the expression

$$V = q_1 q_2 + \lambda(y^0 - p_1 q_1 - p_2 q_2)$$

and set its partial derivatives equal to zero:

$$\frac{\partial V}{\partial q_1} = q_2 - p_1 \lambda = 0$$

$$\frac{\partial V}{\partial q_2} = q_1 - p_2 \lambda = 0$$

$$\frac{\partial V}{\partial \lambda} = y^0 - p_1 q_1 - p_2 q_2 = 0$$

† The new utility function is obtained by squaring the original one. Squaring is not a monotonic transformation if negative numbers are admissible. However, squaring is proper for the present purposes, since the possibility of negative purchases by the consumer is not admitted.

‡ Assume that the second-order conditions are fulfilled.

Solving for q_1 and q_2 gives the demand functions:[1]

$$q_1 = \frac{y^0}{2p_1} \qquad q_2 = \frac{y^0}{2p_2}$$

The demand functions derived in this fashion are contingent on continued optimizing behavior by the consumer. Given the consumer's income and prices of commodities, the quantities demanded by him can be determined from his demand functions. Of course, these quantities are the same as those obtained directly from the utility function. Substituting $y = 100$, $p_1 = 2$, $p_2 = 5$ in the demand functions gives $q_1 = 25$ and $q_2 = 10$, as in Sec. 2-2.

Two important properties of demand functions can be deduced: (1) the demand for any commodity is a single-valued function of prices and income, and (2) demand functions are homogeneous of zeroth degree in prices and income; i.e., if all prices and income change in the same proportion, the quantity demanded remains unchanged.

The first property follows from the convexity of the indifference curves: a single maximum, and therefore a single commodity combination, corresponds to a given set of prices and income. To prove the second property assume that all prices and income change in the same proportion. The budget constraint becomes

$$ky^0 - kp_1q_1 - kp_2q_2 = 0$$

where k is the factor of proportionality. Expression (2-13) becomes

$$V = f(q_1, q_2) + \lambda(ky^0 - kp_1q_1 - kp_2q_2)$$

and the first-order conditions are

$$\begin{aligned} f_1 - \lambda k p_1 &= 0 \\ f_2 - \lambda k p_2 &= 0 \\ ky^0 - kp_1q_1 - kp_2q_2 &= 0 \end{aligned} \qquad (2\text{-}21)$$

The last equation of (2-21) is the partial derivative of V with respect to the Lagrange multiplier and can be written as

$$k(y^0 - p_1q_1 - p_2q_2) = 0$$

Since $k \neq 0$,

$$y^0 - p_1q_1 - p_2q_2 = 0$$

Eliminating k from the first two equations of (2-21) by moving the second terms to the right-hand side and dividing the first equation by the second,

$$\frac{f_1}{f_2} = \frac{p_1}{p_2}$$

[1] Notice that these demand curves are a special case in which the demand for each commodity depends only upon its own price and income.

The last two equations are the same as (2-5) and (2-8). Therefore the demand curve for the price-income set (kp_1, kp_2, ky^0) is derived from the same equations as for the price-income set (p_1, p_2, y^0). It is equally easy to demonstrate that the second-order conditions are unaffected. This proves that the demand functions are homogeneous of degree zero in prices and income. If all prices and the consumer's income are increased in the same proportion, the quantities demanded by the consumer do not change. This implies a relevant and empirically testable restriction upon the consumer's behavior; it means that he will not behave as if he were richer (or poorer) in terms of real income if his income and prices rise in the same proportion. A rise in money income is desirable for the consumer, *ceteris paribus*, but its benefits are illusory if prices change proportionately. If such proportionate changes leave his behavior unaltered, there is an absence of "money illusion."[1]

In general, the consumer's demand curve for commodity Q_1 is written as

$$q_1 = \phi(p_1, p_2, y^0) \tag{2-22}$$

or, assuming that p_2 and y are given parameters,[†]

$$q_1 = D(p_1) \tag{2-23}$$

The shape of the demand function depends upon the properties of the consumer's utility function. It is generally assumed that demand curves are negatively sloped: the lower the price, the greater the quantity demanded. In exceptional cases the opposite relationship may hold. An example is provided by ostentatious consumption: if the consumer derives utility from a high price, the demand function may have a positive slope. The nature of price-induced changes in the quantity demanded is analyzed in detail in Sec. 2-6. Elsewhere in this volume it is assumed that the demand function is negatively sloped.

---

[1] If the consumer possesses a hoard of cash, he may feel richer in spite of a proportional fall in commodity prices and income, since the purchasing power of his hoard increases. He may consequently increase his demand for commodities. This is the Pigou effect.

[†] In general, the demand curve can also be written as $p_1 = \psi(q_1)$. If the price is p_1^0, and the consumer purchases q_1^0 units, his total expenditure on the commodity is $p_1^0 q_1^0$ dollars. It has been argued that the area under the demand curve up to the point $q_1 = q_1^0$ represents the sum of money that the consumer would be willing to pay for q_1^0 units rather than not have the commodity at all. The difference between what he would be willing to pay and what he actually pays, $\int_0^{q_1^0} \psi(q_1)\, dq_1 - p_1^0 q_1^0$, is the "consumer surplus," i.e., a measure of the net benefit he derives from buying Q_1. There are several alternative definitions of consumer surplus, and the concept has been refined considerably, but it has failed to result in notable advances, since it depends upon the assumption of cardinality.

2-5. Income and Leisure

If the consumer's income is payment for work performed by him, the optimum amount of work that he performs can be derived from the analysis of utility maximization.   One can also derive the consumer's demand curve for income from this analysis.   Assume that the consumer's satisfaction depends on income and leisure.   His utility function is

$$U = g(L,y) \qquad (2\text{-}24)$$

where L denotes leisure.   Both income and leisure are desirable.   In the preceding sections it is assumed that the consumer derives utility from the commodities he purchases with his income.   In the construction of (2-24) it is assumed that he buys the various commodities in fixed proportions at constant prices, and income is thereby treated as generalized purchasing power.

The rate of substitution of income for leisure is

$$-\frac{dy}{dL} = \frac{g_1}{g_2}$$

Denote the amount of work performed by the consumer by W and the wage rate by r.   By definition,

$$L = T - W \qquad (2\text{-}25)$$

where T is the total amount of available time.[1]   The budget constraint is

$$y = rW \qquad (2\text{-}26)$$

Substituting (2-25) and (2-26) into (2-24),

$$U = g(T - W, rW) \qquad (2\text{-}27)$$

To maximize utility set the derivative of (2-27) with respect to W equal to zero:[2]

$$\frac{dU}{dW} = -g_1 + g_2 r = 0$$

and therefore

$$-\frac{dy}{dL} = \frac{g_1}{g_2} = r \qquad (2\text{-}28)$$

which states that the rate of substitution of income for leisure equals the wage rate.   The second-order condition states

$$\frac{d^2U}{dW^2} = g_{11} - 2g_{12}r + g_{22}r^2 < 0$$

[1] For example, if the period for which the utility function is defined is one day, $T = 24$ hours.

[2] The composite-function rule is employed.

Equation (2-28) is a relation in terms of W and r and is based on the individual consumer's optimizing behavior. [It is therefore the consumer's offer curve for work and states how much he will work at various wage rates. Since the offer of work is equivalent to the demand for income, (2-28) indirectly provides the consumer's demand curve for income.]

Assume that the utility function is of the same form as in previous sections: $U = Ly$. Then

$$U = (T - W)Wr$$

and setting the derivative equal to zero,

$$\frac{dU}{dW} = Tr - 2Wr = 0$$

Therefore

$$W = \frac{T}{2}$$

and substituting this in (2-26),

$$y = \frac{rT}{2}$$

One can infer that the consumer will work 12 hours per day irrespective of the wage level. The second-order condition is fulfilled:

$$\frac{d^2U}{dW^2} = -2r < 0$$

An alternative example is provided by the utility function

$$U = Ly - 0.1L^2 - 0.1y^2 = (T - W)Wr - 0.1(T - W)^2 - 0.1W^2r^2$$

Then

$$\frac{dU}{dW} = -Wr + (T - W)r + 0.2(T - W) - 0.2Wr^2 = 0$$

and

$$W = \frac{T(r + 0.2)}{2(0.1 + r + 0.1r^2)}$$

The amount of work performed now depends upon the wage rate. If $r = 1$ dollar, the individual will work 12 hours per day. The second-order condition is fulfilled:

$$\frac{d^2U}{dW^2} = -2(0.1 + r + 0.1r^2) < 0$$

2-6. Substitution and Income Effects

The Slutsky Equation. The quantities purchased by a rational consumer will always satisfy Eqs. (2-14). Changes in prices and income will normally alter his expenditure pattern, but the new quantities (and prices and income) will still satisfy (2-14). In order to find the magnitude of the effect of price and income changes on the consumer's purchases, allow all variables to vary simultaneously. This is accomplished by total differentiation of Eqs. (2-14):

$$\begin{aligned} f_{11}\,dq_1 + f_{12}\,dq_2 - p_1\,d\lambda &= \lambda\,dp_1 \\ f_{21}\,dq_1 + f_{22}\,dq_2 - p_2\,d\lambda &= \lambda\,dp_2 \\ -p_1\,dq_1 - p_2\,dq_2 \qquad\qquad &= -dy + q_1\,dp_1 + q_2\,dp_2 \end{aligned} \qquad (2\text{-}29)$$

In order to solve this system of three equations for the three unknowns, dq_1, dq_2, and $d\lambda$, the terms on the right must be regarded as constants. The array of coefficients formed by (2-29) contains the same elements as the bordered Hessian determinant (2-15). Denoting this determinant by $\mathbf{D}$ and the cofactor of the element in the first row and the first column by $\mathbf{D}_{11}$, the cofactor of the element in the first row and second column by $\mathbf{D}_{12}$, etc., the solution of (2-29) by Cramer's rule (see Sec. A-1) is

$$dq_1 = \frac{\lambda\mathbf{D}_{11}\,dp_1 + \lambda\mathbf{D}_{21}\,dp_2 + \mathbf{D}_{31}(-dy + q_1\,dp_1 + q_2\,dp_2)}{\mathbf{D}} \qquad (2\text{-}30)$$

$$dq_2 = \frac{\lambda\mathbf{D}_{12}\,dp_1 + \lambda\mathbf{D}_{22}\,dp_2 + \mathbf{D}_{32}(-dy + q_1\,dp_1 + q_2\,dp_2)}{\mathbf{D}} \qquad (2\text{-}31)$$

Dividing both sides of (2-30) by dp_1 and assuming that p_2 and y do not change ($dp_2 = dy = 0$),

$$\frac{\partial q_1}{\partial p_1} = \frac{\mathbf{D}_{11}\lambda}{\mathbf{D}} + q_1\frac{\mathbf{D}_{31}}{\mathbf{D}} \qquad (2\text{-}32)$$

The partial derivative on the left-hand side of (2-32) is the rate of change of the consumer's purchases of Q_1 with respect to changes in p_1, all other things being equal. *Ceteris paribus*, the rate of change with respect to income is

$$\frac{\partial q_1}{\partial y} = -\frac{\mathbf{D}_{31}}{\mathbf{D}} \qquad (2\text{-}33)$$

Changes in commodity prices change the consumer's level of satisfaction, since a new equilibrium is established which lies on a different indifference curve. Imagine now that a price change is accompanied by an income change that compensates for the effect of the price change such that the consumer remains neither better off nor worse off. He is thereby forced to stay on the same indifference curve. A decrease in the price of a commodity is accompanied by a corresponding decrease in his income such that $dU = 0$ and $f_1\,dq_1 + f_2\,dq_2 = 0$ by (2-3). Since $f_1/f_2 = p_1/p_2$, it is also true that $p_1\,dq_1 + p_2\,dq_2 = 0$. Hence, from the last equation of (2-29), $-dy + q_1\,dp_1 + q_2\,dp_2 = 0$, and

$$\left(\frac{\partial q_1}{\partial p_1}\right)_{U=\text{const}} = \frac{\mathbf{D}_{11}\lambda}{\mathbf{D}} \qquad (2\text{-}34)$$

Equation (2-32) can now be rewritten as

$$\frac{\partial q_1}{\partial p_1} = \left(\frac{\partial q_1}{\partial p_1}\right)_{U=\text{const}} - q_1 \left(\frac{\partial q_1}{\partial y}\right)_{\text{prices}=\text{const}} \tag{2-35}$$

Equation (2-35) is known as the *Slutsky equation*.

Substitution and Income Effects. The first term on the right-hand side of (2-35) is the *substitution effect*, or the rate at which the consumer substitutes Q_1 for other commodities when the price of Q_1 changes and he moves along a given indifference curve.[1] The second term on the

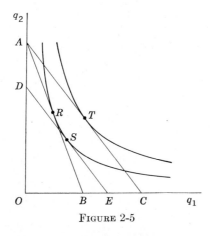

right is the *income effect*, which states the consumer's reaction with respect to purchases of Q_1 to changes in his income, prices remaining constant. The sum of the two terms gives the total effect on the consumer's purchases of Q_1 as p_1 changes. Imagine that the price of Q_1 falls. The consumer may wish to substitute Q_1 for Q_2 because (1) Q_1 has become cheaper and (2) the fall in the price of Q_1 is equivalent to an increase in the consumer's income. The substitution effect describes the realloca-

FIGURE 2-5

tion that will take place among the consumer's purchases if a price change is compensated by a simultaneous income change which forces him to remain on the same indifference curve. The discrepancy between this point and the final point of equilibrium is accounted for by the income effect. These concepts are illustrated in Fig. 2-5. The original price line is AB, and the corresponding point of equilibrium is at R. After the change in p_1 the price line is represented by AC, and the final equilibrium is at T. The movement from R to T can be decomposed into the steps from R to S and from S to T. The point S is the tangency point between the original indifference curve and a price line DE which has the same slope (and therefore represents the same price ratio) as AC. The movement from R to S is accounted for by the substitution and the movement from S to T by the income effect.[2]

[1] Slutsky called this the *residual variability* of the commodity in question.

[2] Figure 2-5 is not an exact representation of the foregoing mathematical discussion. The Slutsky equation involves rates of change which cannot be represented directly in an indifference-curve diagram. In Fig. 2-5 the sum of two discrete changes (rather than of two rates) is the total discrete change (rather than the total rate of change). These two discrete changes *correspond to* (rather than *are*) the substitution effect and the income effect.

The extra utility gained by consuming an additional unit of any commodity divided by its price equals λ. The utility gained from the last dollar spent is the marginal utility of income. Alternatively, the marginal utility of income can be determined from (2-13). Since $\partial V/\partial y = \lambda$, the Lagrange multiplier λ is the marginal utility of income which is positive. The direction of the substitution effect is then easily ascertained. By (2-34) the substitution effect is $\mathbf{D}_{11}\lambda/\mathbf{D}$. Expanding the determinant $\mathbf{D}$,

$$\mathbf{D} = 2f_{12}p_1p_2 - p_1{}^2f_{11} - p_2{}^2f_{22}$$

which is known to be positive by (2-10). Expanding $\mathbf{D}_{11}$,

$$\mathbf{D}_{11} = -p_2{}^2$$

which is clearly negative. This proves that the sign of the substitution effect is always negative. If the price of Q_1 rises and the consumer's income is so adjusted that his final equilibrium point is on the same indifference curve, his purchases of Q_1 will decrease.

A change in real income may cause a reallocation of the consumer's resources even if prices do not change or if they change in the same proportion. The income effect is $-q_1(\partial q_1/\partial y)_{\text{prices=const}}$ and may be of either sign. The final effect of a price change on the purchases of the commodity is thus unknown. However, an important conclusion can still be derived: the smaller the quantity of Q_1, the less significant is the income effect. If the income effect is positive and its absolute value is large enough to make $\partial q_1/\partial p_1$ positive, Q_1 is said to be an inferior good.[1] This means that as the price of Q_1 falls, the consumer's purchases of Q_1 will also fall. This may occur if a consumer is sufficiently poor so that a considerable portion of his income is spent on a commodity such as potatoes which he needs for his subsistence. Assume now that the price of potatoes falls. The consumer who is not very fond of potatoes may suddenly discover that his real income has increased as a result of the price fall. He will then buy fewer potatoes and purchase a more palatable diet with the remainder of his income.

The Slutsky equation can be derived for the specific utility function assumed in the previous examples. State the budget constraint in the general form $y - p_1q_1 - p_2q_2 = 0$, and form the function

$$V = q_1q_2 + \lambda(y - p_1q_1 - p_2q_2)$$

---

[1] An alternative definition of inferior goods may be given by the following statement: a commodity Q_1 is an inferior good if $\partial q_1/\partial y$ is negative, i.e., if the consumer's purchases of Q_1 decrease when his income rises. This is a weaker definition in the sense that it does not imply the definition given in the text above, whereas the definition in the text does imply this one.

Setting the partial derivatives equal to zero,

$$q_2 - \lambda p_1 = 0$$
$$q_1 - \lambda p_2 = 0$$
$$y - p_1 q_1 - p_2 q_2 = 0$$

The total differentials of these equations are

$$dq_2 - p_1 \, d\lambda = \lambda \, dp_1$$
$$dq_1 - p_2 \, d\lambda = \lambda \, dp_2$$
$$-p_1 \, dq_1 - p_2 \, dq_2 = -dy + q_1 \, dp_1 + q_2 \, dp_2$$

Denote the determinant of the coefficients of these equations by $\mathbf{D}$ and the cofactor of the element in the ith row and jth column by $\mathbf{D}_{ij}$. Simple calculations show that

$$\mathbf{D} = 2p_1 p_2$$
$$\mathbf{D}_{11} = -p_2{}^2$$
$$\mathbf{D}_{21} = p_1 p_2$$
$$\mathbf{D}_{31} = -p_2$$

Solving for dq_1 by Cramer's rule gives

$$dq_1 = \frac{-p_2{}^2 \lambda \, dp_1 + p_1 p_2 \lambda \, dp_2 - p_2(-dy + q_1 \, dp_1 + q_2 \, dp_2)}{2p_1 p_2}$$

Assuming that only the price of the first commodity varies,

$$\frac{\partial q_1}{\partial p_1} = -\frac{p_2 \lambda}{2p_1} - \frac{q_1}{2p_1}$$

The value of λ can be obtained by substituting the values of q_1 and q_2 from the first two equations of (2-14) into the third one and solving for λ in terms of the parameters p_1, p_2, and y. Thus $\lambda = y/2p_1 p_2$. Substituting this value into the above equation and then introducing into it the values of the parameters ($y = 100$, $p_1 = 2$, $p_2 = 5$) and also the equilibrium value of q_1 (25), a numerical answer is obtained:

$$\frac{\partial q_1}{\partial p_1} = -12.5$$

The meaning of this answer is the following: if, starting from the initial equilibrium situation, p_1 were to change, *ceteris paribus*, the consumer's purchases would change at the rate of 12.5 units of Q_1 per dollar of change in the price of Q_1; furthermore the direction of the change in the consumer's purchases is opposite to the direction of the price change. The expression $-p_2 \lambda / 2p_1$ is the substitution effect, and its value in the present example is $-2\frac{5}{4}$. The expression $-q_1/2p_1$ is the income effect, also with a value of $-2\frac{5}{4}$.

Cross Effects. The analysis can be extended to account for the change in the demand for one commodity resulting from a change in the price of some other commodity. From Eqs. (2-30) and (2-31)

$$\frac{\partial q_1}{\partial p_2} = \frac{D_{21}\lambda}{D} + q_2 \frac{D_{31}}{D} \qquad (2\text{-}36)$$

and

$$\frac{\partial q_2}{\partial p_1} = \frac{D_{12}\lambda}{D} + q_1 \frac{D_{32}}{D} \qquad (2\text{-}37)$$

Since D is a symmetric determinant,[†] $D_{12} = D_{21}$. The first terms on the right-hand sides of (2-36) and (2-37) are the substitution effects for each commodity with respect to a change in the price of the other. The sign of the substitution effect is unknown in the present case. Denote the substitution effect when the quantity of the ith commodity is adjusted as a result of a variation in the jth price by S_{ij}. It follows from the symmetry of D that the substitution effect on the ith commodity resulting from a change in the jth price is the same as the substitution effect on the jth commodity resulting from a change in the ith price: $S_{ij} = S_{ji}$.

This is a remarkable conclusion. Imagine that the consumer's demand for tea increases at the rate of 2 cups of tea per 1-cent increase in the price of coffee. One can infer from this that his purchases of coffee would increase at the rate of 2 cups of coffee per 1-cent increase in the price of tea.

Substitutes and Complements. Two commodities are substitutes if both can satisfy the same need of the consumer; they are complements if they are consumed jointly in order to satisfy some particular need. These are loose definitions, but everyday experience may suggest some plausible examples. Coffee and tea are most likely substitutes, whereas coffee and sugar are complements. A more rigorous definition of substitutability and complementarity is provided by the substitution term of the Slutsky equations (2-36) and (2-37). Accordingly, Q_1 and Q_2 are substitutes if the substitution effect $D_{21}\lambda/D$ is positive; they are complements if it is negative. If Q_1 and Q_2 are substitutes (in the everyday sense) and if compensating variations in income keep the consumer on the same indifference curve, an increase in the price of Q_1 will induce the consumer to substitute Q_2 for Q_1. Then $\left(\dfrac{\partial q_2}{\partial p_1}\right)_{U=\text{const}} > 0$. For analogous reasons, $\left(\dfrac{\partial q_2}{\partial p_1}\right)_{U=\text{const}} < 0$ in the case of complements.[1]

[†] A determinant is symmetric if its array is symmetric around the principal diagonal.

[1] This provides a rationale for the definitions. When $\left(\dfrac{\partial q_2}{\partial p_1}\right)_{U=\text{const}} = 0$, Q_1 and Q_2 are independent.

All commodities cannot be complements for each other. Hence only substitutability can occur in the present two-variable case. This theorem is easily proved. Multiply (2-32) by p_1, (2-33) by y, and (2-36) by p_2 and add:

$$\frac{\mathbf{D}_{11}\lambda}{\mathbf{D}} p_1 + q_1 \frac{\mathbf{D}_{31}}{\mathbf{D}} p_1 + \frac{\mathbf{D}_{21}\lambda}{\mathbf{D}} p_2 + q_2 \frac{\mathbf{D}_{31}}{\mathbf{D}} p_2 - \frac{\mathbf{D}_{31}}{\mathbf{D}} y$$

$$= \frac{1}{\mathbf{D}} [\mathbf{D}_{11}\lambda\, p_1 + \mathbf{D}_{21}\lambda\, p_2 - \mathbf{D}_{31}(y - p_1q_1 - p_2q_2)]$$

$$= \frac{1}{\mathbf{D}} [\mathbf{D}_{11}\lambda\, p_1 + \mathbf{D}_{21}\lambda\, p_2 - \mathbf{D}_{31}(0)] = 0 \quad (2\text{-}38)$$

The expression (2-38) equals zero since it is an expansion of the determinant of (2-31) in terms of alien cofactors; i.e., the cofactors of the elements in the first column are multiplied by the elements in the last column. Substituting $\mathbf{D}_{12} = \mathbf{D}_{21}$ and $S_{ij} = \mathbf{D}_{ij}\lambda/\mathbf{D}$,

$$S_{11}p_1 + S_{12}p_2 = 0 \quad (2\text{-}39)$$

Equation (2-39) can be verified for the utility function used in the previous examples. Substituting the values of $\mathbf{D}$, $\mathbf{D}_{11}$, and $\mathbf{D}_{21}$ obtained by assuming the utility function $U = q_1q_2$,

$$- \frac{p_1p_2{}^2\lambda}{2p_1p_2} + \frac{p_1p_2{}^2\lambda}{2p_1p_2} = 0 \quad (2\text{-}40)$$

Since the left-hand side of (2-40) equals zero, Eq. (2-39) has been verified. But S_{11}, the substitution effect for Q_1 resulting from changes in p_1, is known to be negative. Hence (2-39) implies that S_{12} must be positive, and in terms of the definitions of substitutability and complementarity this means that Q_1 and Q_2 are necessarily substitutes.

2-7. Generalization to n Variables

The foregoing analysis of the consumer is now generalized to the case of n commodities. The generalization is not carried out in detail, but the first few steps are indicated. If there are n commodities, the utility function is

$$U = f(q_1, q_2, \ldots, q_n) \quad (2\text{-}41)$$

and the budget constraint is given by

$$y - \sum_{i=1}^{n} p_iq_i = 0 \quad (2\text{-}42)$$

Forming the function as above,

$$V = f(q_1, q_2, \ldots, q_n) + \lambda \left(y - \sum_{i=1}^{n} p_i q_i \right) \qquad (2\text{-}43)$$

Setting the partial derivatives equal to zero,

$$\frac{\partial V}{\partial q_i} = f_i - \lambda p_i = 0 \qquad (i = 1, \ldots, n) \qquad (2\text{-}44)$$

Conditions (2-44) can be modified to state the equality for all commodities of marginal utility divided by price. The partial derivative of V with respect to λ is again the budget constraint. There are a total of $(n + 1)$ equations in $(n + 1)$ variables (n qs and λ). The demand curves for the n commodities can be obtained by solving for the qs. Conditions (2-44) can be stated alternatively as

$$-\frac{\partial q_i}{\partial q_j} = \frac{p_j}{p_i} \qquad (2\text{-}45)$$

for all i and j; i.e., the rate of commodity substitution of commodity i for commodity j must equal the price ratio p_j/p_i. Second-order conditions must be fulfilled in order to ensure that a batch of commodities that satisfies (2-44) is optimal. The bordered Hessian determinants must alternate in sign:

$$\begin{vmatrix} f_{11} & f_{12} & -p_1 \\ f_{21} & f_{22} & -p_2 \\ -p_1 & -p_2 & 0 \end{vmatrix} > 0, \qquad \begin{vmatrix} f_{11} & f_{12} & f_{13} & -p_1 \\ f_{21} & f_{22} & f_{23} & -p_2 \\ f_{31} & f_{32} & f_{33} & -p_3 \\ -p_1 & -p_2 & -p_3 & 0 \end{vmatrix} < 0,$$

$$\ldots, \quad (-1)^n \begin{vmatrix} f_{11} & f_{12} & \cdots & f_{1n} & -p_1 \\ f_{21} & f_{22} & \cdots & f_{2n} & -p_2 \\ \cdots & \cdots & \cdots & \cdots & \cdots \\ f_{n1} & f_{n2} & \cdots & f_{nn} & -p_n \\ -p_1 & -p_2 & \cdots & -p_n & 0 \end{vmatrix} > 0$$

Other theorems can also be generalized in straightforward fashion. For example, the Slutsky equation becomes

$$\frac{\partial q_i}{\partial p_j} = \left(\frac{\partial q_i}{\partial p_j} \right)_{U=\text{const}} - q_j \left(\frac{\partial q_i}{\partial y} \right)_{\text{prices}=\text{const}} \qquad (2\text{-}46)$$

The generalization of (2-39) is

$$\sum_{j=1}^{n} S_{ij} p_j = 0 \qquad (2\text{-}47)$$

It still follows that all commodities cannot be complements for each other.

2-8. The Theory of Revealed Preference

It was assumed in the previous sections that the consumer possesses a utility function. If his behavior conforms to certain simple axioms, the existence and nature of his indifference map can be inferred from his actions.

Assume that there are n commodities. A particular set of prices p_1^0, p_2^0, . . . , p_n^0 is denoted by $[p^0]$, and the corresponding quantities bought by the consumer by $[q^0]$. The consumer's total expenditures are given by $\Sigma p^0 q^0$.

Consider an alternative batch of commodities $[q^1]$ that could have been purchased by the consumer but was not. The total cost of the batch $[q^1]$, at prices $[p^0]$, must be no greater than the total cost of $[q^0]$:

$$\Sigma p^0 q^1 \leqq \Sigma p^0 q^0 \qquad (2\text{-}48)$$

Since $[q^0]$ is at least as expensive a combination of commodities as $[q^1]$, and since the consumer refused to choose combination $[q^1]$, $[q^0]$ is "revealed" to be preferred to $[q^1]$.

Axiom 1. If $[q^0]$ is revealed to be preferred to $[q^1]$, the latter must never be revealed to be preferred to $[q^0]$.

The only way in which $[q^1]$ can be revealed to be preferred to $[q^0]$ is to have the consumer purchase the combination $[q^1]$ in some price situation in which he could also afford to buy $[q^0]$. In other words, $[q^1]$ is revealed to be preferred if

$$\Sigma p^1 q^0 \leqq \Sigma p^1 q^1 \qquad (2\text{-}49)$$

The axiom states that (2-49) can never hold if (2-48) does. Consequently (2-48) implies the opposite of (2-49) or

$$\Sigma p^0 q^1 \leqq \Sigma p^0 q^0 \quad \text{implies} \quad \Sigma p^1 q^0 > \Sigma p^1 q^1 \qquad (2\text{-}50)$$

Axiom 2. If $[q^0]$ is revealed to be preferred to $[q^1]$, which is revealed to be preferred to $[q^2]$, . . . , which is revealed to be preferred to $[q^n]$, $[q^n]$ must never be revealed to be preferred to $[q^0]$.† This axiom ensures the transitivity of revealed preferences, but is stronger than the usual transitivity condition.

At the beginning of this chapter the cardinal approach to utility theory was rejected on the grounds that there is no reason to assume that the consumer possesses a cardinal measure of utility. By the same token one could question whether he even possesses an indifference map. It

---

† The two axioms can be collapsed into a single one, but have been kept separate for the sake of clarity.

can fortunately be proved that a consumer who always conforms to the above axioms must possess an indifference map. His indifference map could be reconstructed with a high degree of accuracy (the "true" indifference map could be approximated as closely as is desired) by confronting him with various appropriately chosen price sets and observing his purchases.[1] If the consumer does not conform to the axioms, he is irrational by the definition of the earlier sections. If he is irrational and acts inconsistently, he does not possess an indifference map, and the shape of his utility function cannot be determined by observing his behavior.

The Substitution Effect. It can be proved from revealed-preference theory that the substitution effect is negative.[2] Assume that the consumer is forced to move along a given indifference curve. When prices are given by $[p^0]$, he purchases the batch $[q^0]$ rather than the batch $[q^1]$ which lies on the same indifference hypersurface. Since he is indifferent between $[q^0]$ and $[q^1]$ and yet purchases $[q^0]$, the latter combination must not be more expensive than the former:

$$\Sigma p^0 q^0 \leqq \Sigma p^0 q^1 \tag{2-51}$$

The combination $[q^1]$ is purchased at prices $[p^1]$. This implies that the combination $[q^0]$ must not be cheaper at the $[p^1]$ prices than $[q^1]$:

$$\Sigma p^1 q^1 \leqq \Sigma p^1 q^0 \tag{2-52}$$

Moving the right-hand terms in (2-51) and (2-52) to the left,

$$\Sigma p^0 q^0 - \Sigma p^0 q^1 = \Sigma p^0 (q^0 - q^1) = \Sigma(-p^0)(q^1 - q^0) \leqq 0 \tag{2-53}$$
$$\Sigma p^1 q^1 - \Sigma p^1 q^0 = \Sigma p^1 (q^1 - q^0) \leqq 0 \tag{2-54}$$

Adding together (2-53) and (2-54),

$$\Sigma(-p^0)(q^1 - q^0) + \Sigma p^1(q^1 - q^0) = \Sigma(p^1 - p^0)(q^1 - q^0) \leqq 0 \tag{2-55}$$

This inequality asserts that the sum of all quantity changes multiplied by the corresponding price changes is nonpositive if the consumer moves along a given indifference curve. Assume now that only the price of the first commodity changes, all other prices remaining constant. Then (2-55) reduces to

$$(p_1{}^1 - p_1^0)(q_1{}^1 - q_1^0) < 0 \tag{2-56}$$

[1] The proof of this theorem is somewhat difficult and is not reproduced here. See H. S. Houthakker, "Revealed Preference and the Utility Function," *Economica*, n.s., vol. 17 (May, 1950), pp. 159–174.

[2] This is only one of several theorems that can be deduced from the theory. Others are (1) the homogeneity of the demand functions of zeroth degree in prices and incomes (Sec. 2-4), and (2) the equality of the cross-substitution effects (Sec. 2-6). See P. A. Samuelson, *Foundations of Economic Analysis* (Cambridge, Mass.: Harvard University Press, 1948), pp. 111–112; and J. R. Hicks, *A Revision of Demand Theory* (Oxford: Clarendon Press, 1956), p. 127.

The strict inequality must hold in (2-56) by the assumption that the price change is nonzero and that $q_1{}^1$ and q_1^0 are distinct, i.e., that demand is a single-valued function of price. If the price increases, the quantity bought must decrease and vice versa. This again proves that the substitution effect is negative.

2-9. The Problem of Choice in Situations Involving Risk

The traditional theory of consumer behavior does not include an analysis of uncertain situations. Von Neumann and Morgenstern showed that under certain circumstances it is possible to construct a set of numbers for a particular consumer that can be used to predict his choices in uncertain situations. Great controversy has centered around the question of whether the resulting utility index is ordinal or cardinal. It will be shown that von Neumann–Morgenstern utilities possess at least some cardinal properties.

The previous analysis is unrealistic in the sense that it assumes that particular actions on the part of the consumer are followed by particular, determinate consequences which are knowable in advance. All automobiles of the same model and produced in the same factory do not always have the same performance characteristics. As a result of random accidents in the production process some substandard automobiles are occasionally produced and sold. The consumer has no way of knowing ahead of time whether the particular automobile which he purchases is of standard quality or not. Let A represent the situation in which the consumer possesses a satisfactory automobile, B a situation in which he possesses no automobile, and C one in which he possesses a substandard automobile. Assume that the consumer prefers A to B and B to C.† Present him with a choice between two alternatives: (1) He can maintain the *status quo* and have no car at all. This is a choice with certain outcome, i.e., the probability of the outcome equals unity. (2) He can obtain a lottery ticket with a chance of winning either a satisfactory automobile (alternative A) or an unsatisfactory one (alternative C). The consumer may prefer to retain his income (or money) with certainty, or he may prefer the lottery ticket with dubious outcome, or he may be indifferent between them. His decision will depend upon the chances of winning or losing in this particular lottery. If the probability of a loss is very high, he might prefer to retain his money with certainty; if the probability of a win is very high, he might prefer the lottery ticket.

The Axioms. It is possible to make an ordinal utility index which can also be used to predict choice in uncertain situations if the consumer conforms to five axioms:

† Not having a car is assumed preferable to owning a substandard one because of the nuisance and expense involved in its upkeep.

Complete-ordering axiom. For the two alternatives A and B one of the following must be true: the consumer prefers A to B, he prefers B to A, or he is indifferent between them. The consumer's evaluation of alternatives is transitive: if he prefers A to B and B to C, he prefers A to C.

Continuity axiom. Assume that A is preferred to B and B to C. The axiom asserts that there exists some probability P, $0 < P < 1$, such that the consumer is indifferent between outcome B with certainty and a lottery ticket offering the outcomes A and C with probabilities P and $1 - P$ respectively.

Independence axiom. Assume that the consumer is indifferent between A and B and that C is any outcome whatever. If one lottery ticket offers outcomes A and C with probabilities P and $1 - P$ respectively and another the outcomes B and C with the same probabilities P and $1 - P$, the consumer is indifferent between the two lottery tickets.

Unequal-probability axiom. Assume that the consumer prefers A to B. If two lottery tickets, L_1 and L_2, both offer the same outcomes, A and B, the consumer prefers the lottery ticket L_2 if and only if the probability of winning A is greater for L_2 than for L_1.

Axiom of complexity. Assume that a person engages in the following game of chance: he throws a die, and if a one or two comes up, his opponent pays him 9 dollars. He pays his opponent 3 dollars in every other case. The probability of a win is $\frac{1}{3}$, and the probability of a loss $\frac{2}{3}$. The player can expect to win, on the average,

$$(\tfrac{1}{3})(9) + (\tfrac{2}{3})(-3) = 1 \text{ dollar per game}$$

If A and B are the money values of two outcomes with probabilities P and $1 - P$, the mathematical expectation of the game, or the expected win, is $PA + (1 - P)B$. Assume now that the consumer is offered a choice between two lottery tickets. The first one, L_1, offers the outcomes A and B with given probabilities. The other, L_2, is a complex one in the sense that the prizes themselves are lottery tickets: if the consumer chooses L_2 and wins, he gets a lottery ticket L_3 (offering A and B with some given probabilities); if he loses he is given another lottery ticket L_4 (also offering A and B with some given probabilities). Assume finally that the probabilities of winning on each ticket happen to be such that the consumer's expectation of winning (as defined above) is the same whether he chooses L_1 or L_2. The axiom asserts that the consumer is then indifferent between L_1 and L_2.

These axioms are very general, and it may be difficult to object to them on the grounds that they place unreasonable restrictions upon the consumer's behavior. However, they rule out some types of plausible behavior. Consider a person who derives satisfaction from the sheer act of gambling. It is conceivable that there exists no P other than $P = 1$

or $P = 0$ for such a person, so that he is indifferent between outcome B with certainty and the uncertain prospect consisting of A and C: he will always prefer the gamble.   If he has a fear of gambling, he may always prefer the "sure thing" to the dubious prospect.   This type of behavior is ruled out by the continuity axiom and the axiom of complexity.

Construction of the Utility Numbers.   Imagine that the consumer derives the satisfaction U_A from outcome A and U_C from outcome C. Given that these outcomes have the probabilities P and $1 - P$, the consumer's expected utility is $PU_A - (1 - P)U_C$.   It can be proved that a consumer who conforms to the axioms will maximize expected utility. If he faces a set of uncertain prospects (i.e., he has to decide which lottery ticket to select), he will choose the one with the highest expected utility. The consumer's prospects can be arranged in order of decreasing expected utility or desirability.   In the special case in which a prospect has a certain (rather than uncertain or dubious) outcome, the expected utility of the prospect equals the utility number associated with the (single) outcome.   Thus the utility numbers associated with various outcomes are an ordinal utility index and provide a correct ranking.

Consider the earlier example in which the outcomes A, B, and C represented the possession of a satisfactory automobile, no automobile, or a substandard one.   The consumer prefers A to B and B to C.   In order to derive a utility index, an origin and a unit have to be chosen.   This can be accomplished by assigning numbers to represent the utilities of any two outcomes.   These numbers are completely arbitrary, except for the fact that a higher number must be assigned to the preferred outcome. The utility index $U_A = 100$ and $U_C = 10$ can be used, since A is preferred to C.   The continuity axiom ensures that there exists some probability P for which the consumer is indifferent between B and a chance between A and C.   Since the consumer is an expected-utility maximizer, the utility of B with certainty must equal, for some value of P, the expected utility of the prospect (or lottery ticket) involving A and C, or

$$U_B = PU_A + (1 - P)U_C \tag{2-57}$$

He could be asked to reveal the value of P for which he is indifferent between B with certainty and a chance between A and C.   Assume that this value is $P = 0.1$.   Then

$$U_B = (0.1)(100) + (0.9)(10) = 19 \tag{2-58}$$

Proceeding in this fashion one can find utility numbers U_A, U_B, U_C, U_D, . . . , etc., for all possible quantities and combinations of all commodities; hence a complete utility index can be derived by taking two arbitrary starting points and successively confronting the consumer with various choice situations involving probabilities or risk.   For example, if the consumer is indifferent between a satisfactory automobile with certainty and a 0.8 chance of winning a yacht (outcome D) or a 0.2 chance of winning a substandard car, the application of the previous technique gives 122.5 as the utility of a yacht. The consumer's choice between more complicated alternatives can be predicted on the basis of these utility numbers. The rational consumer would prefer a 40:60 chance of D and B to a 50:50 chance of A and C, since

$$(0.5)(100) + (0.5)(10) < (0.4)(122.5) + (0.6)(19)$$

The Uniqueness of the Utility Index. Imagine that a set of utility numbers satisfying the above axioms has been found for a particular consumer. Ordinal utility functions have been demonstrated to be unique except for a monotonic transformation. The results obtained from the present (cardinal) utility index might change under some monotonic transformations. This can be illustrated with reference to the example used above. As before,

$$U_A = 100 \qquad U_B = 19$$
$$U_C = 10 \qquad U_D = 122.5$$

The consumer prefers a 40:60 chance of D and B to a 50:50 chance of A and C. Perform a monotonic transformation on these numbers such that they become[1]

$$U_A = 120 \qquad U_B = 20$$
$$U_C = 18 \qquad U_D = 125 \,.$$

The consumer will now prefer the 50:50 chance of A and C. It is no longer true that any monotonic transformation of a utility index in the present sense can also serve as a utility index. However, monotonic linear transformations of utility functions are also utility functions.[2] $U_B = PU_A + (1 - P)U_C$ for some P. Transform the utility function so that $U^* = aU + b, a > 0$. Then $U = (U^* - b)/a$ or $U = cU^* + d$ (where $c = 1/a$ and $d = -b/a$), and

$$cU_B^* + d = P(cU_A^* + d) + (1 - P)(cU_C^* + d)$$
$$= PcU_A^* + (1 - P)cU_C^* + d$$

Hence $\qquad\qquad cU_B^* = PcU_A^* + c(1 - P)U_C^*$

and therefore $\qquad\qquad U_B^* = PU_A^* + (1 - P)U_C^*$

This proves that a monotonic linear transformation of the original utility function is itself a utility function giving the same results.

---

[1] The exact form of the transformation is not indicated. The reader may check that the transformation is monotonic.

[2] Y is a monotonic linear transformation of X if $Y = aX + b$ and $a > 0$.

The utilities in the von Neumann–Morgenstern analysis are cardinal in a restricted sense. They are derived from the consumer's risk behavior and are valid for predicting his choices as long as he maximizes expected utility. They are derived by presenting him with mutually exclusive choices; therefore, it is meaningless to attempt to infer from the utility of event A and the utility of event B the utility of the joint event A and B. Von Neumann–Morgenstern utilities possess some, but not all, the properties of cardinal measures. Let the utilities of three alternatives be $U_A = 10$, $U_B = 30$, and $U_C = 70$. It is not meaningful to assert that the consumer prefers C "seven times as much" as A, since the choice of the origin is arbitrary: the same preferences are described by $U_A = 1$, $U_B = 21$, and $U_C = 61$. Utility numbers differ from measures of weight, distance, or volume. It can be meaningfully asserted that one object weighs seven times as much as another. However, differences between utility numbers are meaningful. This follows from the fact that the relative magnitudes of differences between utility numbers are invariant with respect to linear transformations. In the above example

$$U_C - U_B > U_B - U_A$$

Choose a linear transformation $U = cU^* + d$, $c > 0$, and substitute in the above inequality:

$$cU_C^* + d - cU_B^* - d > cU_B^* + d - cU_A^* - d$$

and
$$U_C^* - U_B^* > U_B^* - U_A^*$$

In contrast to the traditional theory of the consumer, the sign of the rate of change of marginal utility (the second derivative of the utility function) is relevant, since it is invariant with respect to linear transformations. Such comparisons do not imply, however, that the consumer would prefer to have C over B to B over A, since the chosen alternative must have the highest utility number.

Interpersonal comparisons of utility are still impossible. However, the construction of von Neumann–Morgenstern utilities does permit (1) the complete ranking of alternatives in situations characterized by certainty, (2) the comparison of utility differences by virtue of the above cardinal property, and (3) the calculation of expected utilities, thus making it possible to deal with the consumer's behavior under conditions of uncertainty.

2-10. Summary

Nineteenth-century economic theorists explained the consumer's behavior on the assumption that utility is measurable. This restrictive assumption was abandoned around the turn of the last century, and the consumer was assumed to be capable only of ranking commodity combinations consistently in order of preference. This ranking is described mathematically by the consumer's ordinal utility function, which always assigns a higher number to a more desirable combination of commodities. The basic postulate of the theory of consumer behavior is that the consumer maximizes utility. Since his income is limited, he maximizes the utility function subject to the budget constraint, which expresses the income limitation in mathematical form. The ratio of the marginal utilities must equal the price ratio for a maximum. In diagrammatic terms, the optimum commodity combination is given by the point at which the price line is tangent to an indifference curve. The second-order condition for a maximum requires the indifference curves to be convex from below.

The consumer's utility function is not unique. If a particular function describes appropriately the consumer's preferences, so does any other which is a monotonic transformation of the first. Other kinds of transformations do not preserve the correct ranking, and the utility function is unique up to a monotonic transformation.

The consumer's demand curve for a commodity can be derived from his first-order conditions for utility maximization. A demand curve states the quantity demanded as a function of all prices and the consumer's income. Demand curves are single-valued and homogeneous of degree zero in prices and income: a proportionate change in all prices and the consumer's income leaves the quantity demanded unchanged.

In general, the amount of labor performed by a consumer affects his level of utility. The amount of labor performed by the consumer can be determined on the basis of the rational-decision criterion of utility maximization. The equilibrium conditions are similar to those which hold for the selection of an optimal commodity combination.

The consumer's reaction to price and income changes can be analyzed in terms of substitution and income effects. The effect of a given price change can be analytically decomposed into a substitution effect, which measures the rate at which he would substitute commodities for each other by moving along the same indifference curve, and an income effect as a residual category. If the price of a commodity changes, the quantity demanded changes in the opposite direction if the consumer is forced to move along the same indifference curve: the substitution effect is negative. If the income effect is positive and exceeds the substitution effect in absolute value, the commodity is an inferior good. Substitutes and complements are defined in terms of the sign of the substitution effect for one commodity when the price of another changes: a positive cross-substitution effect means substitutability, and a negative one, complementarity.

The theory can be generalized to an arbitrary number of commodities.

It can also be restated in terms of the theory of revealed preference, which makes no use of differential calculus and arrives at essentially the same conclusions as the preceding analysis. The results are obtained by presenting the consumer with hypothetical price-income situations and observing his choices. His indifference curves can be derived, and future choices can be predicted on the basis of past choices if his behavior satisfies the fundamental axioms of revealed preference.

The approach of von Neumann and Morgenstern is concerned with the consumer's behavior in situations characterized by uncertainty. If the consumer's behavior satisfies certain crucial axioms, his utility function can be derived by presenting him with a series of choices between a certain outcome on the one hand and a probabilistic combination of two uncertain outcomes on the other. The utility function thus derived is unique up to a linear transformation and provides a ranking of alternatives in situations that do not involve risk. Consumers maximize expected utility, and von Neumann–Morgenstern utilities are cardinal in the sense that they can be combined to calculate expected utilities and can be used to compare differences in utilities. The expected utility calculation can be used to determine the consumer's choices in situations involving risk.

SELECTED REFERENCES

Alchian, A. A., "The Meaning of Utility Measurement," *American Economic Review*, vol. 43 (March, 1953), pp. 26–50. A nonmathematical discussion of the von Neumann–Morgenstern utility index.

Ellsberg, D., "Classic and Current Notions of 'Measurable Utility,'" *Economic Journal*, vol. 64 (September, 1954), pp. 528–556. A comparison of the nineteenth-century concept of measurable utility with the von Neumann–Morgenstern index. Nonmathematical.

Friedman, M., and L. J. Savage, "The Utility Analysis of Choices Involving Risk," *Journal of Political Economy*, vol. 56 (August, 1948), pp. 279–304. Also reprinted in American Economic Association, *Readings in Price Theory* (Homewood, Ill.: Irwin, 1952), pp. 57–96. An analysis of situations with uncertain outcomes leading to a hypothesis concerning utility as a function of income. Simple mathematics.

Georgescu-Roegen, N., "The Pure Theory of Consumer Behavior," *Quarterly Journal of Economics*, vol. 50 (August, 1936), pp. 545–593. A mathematical analysis of ordinal utility theory.

Hicks, J. R., *A Revision of Demand Theory* (Oxford: Clarendon Press, 1956). A discussion of consumer theory relying on the theory of revealed preference and employing little mathematics.

———, *Value and Capital* (2d ed.; Oxford: Clarendon Press, 1946). Chapters I–III contain an exposition of ordinal utility theory. The mathematical analysis is in an appendix.

Houthakker, H. S., "Revealed Preference and the Utility Function," *Economica*, n. s. vol. 17 (May, 1950), pp. 159–174. Contains a proof of the existence of indifference curves for consumers who satisfy the axioms of revealed-preference theory.

Marschak, J., "Rational Behavior, Uncertain Prospects and Measurable Utility," *Econometrica*, vol. 18 (April, 1950), pp. 111–141. A further development of the von Neumann–Morgenstern approach. Moderately difficult mathematics.

Marshall, Alfred, *Principles of Economics* (8th ed., London: Macmillan, 1920). Chapters I–IV, Book III, contain a nonmathematical discussion of wants, utility, marginal utility, and demand from the cardinalist viewpoint.

Neumann, J. von, and O. Morgenstern, *Theory of Games and Economic Behavior* (2d ed.; Princeton, N.J.: Princeton University Press, 1947). Chapter 1 and an appendix contain the original statement of the von Neumann–Morgenstern approach.

Samuelson, Paul A., "Consumption Theory in Terms of Revealed Preference," *Economica*, n.s. vol. 15 (November, 1948), pp. 243–253. Presents a proof that the revealed-preference approach can lead to the determination of indifference curves.

———, *Foundations of Economic Analysis* (Cambridge, Mass.: Harvard University Press, 1948). Chapters V and VII contain a comprehensive analysis of utility theory using fairly advanced mathematics.

Slutsky, E. E., "On the Theory of the Budget of the Consumer," *Giornale degli Economisti*, vol. 51 (July, 1915), pp. 1–26. Also reprinted in American Economic Association, *Readings in Price Theory* (Homewood, Ill.: Irwin, 1952), pp. 27–56. The article upon which the modern mathematical theory of consumer behavior is based. Fairly difficult mathematics.

CHAPTER 3

THE THEORY OF THE FIRM

A firm is a technical unit in which commodities are produced. Its entrepreneur (owner and manager) decides how much of and how one or more commodities will be produced, and gains the profit or bears the loss which results from his decision. An entrepreneur transforms inputs into outputs, subject to the technical rules specified by his production function. The difference between his revenue from the sale of outputs and the cost of his inputs is his profit, if positive, or his loss, if negative.

The entrepreneur's production function gives mathematical expression to the relationship between the quantities of inputs he employs and the quantity of output he produces. The concept is perfectly general. A specific production function may be given by a single point, a single continuous or discontinuous function, or a system of equations. The first six sections of this chapter are limited to production functions given by a single continuous function with continuous first- and second-order partial derivatives. The analysis is first developed for the relatively simple case in which two inputs are combined for the production of a single output, and then extended to more general cases. The seventh section is devoted to the case in which the production function is given by a system of linear equations.

An input is any good or service which contributes to the production of an output. An entrepreneur will usually use many different inputs for the production of a single output. Generally, some of his inputs are the outputs of other firms. For example, steel is an input for an automobile producer and an output for a steel producer. Other inputs— such as labor, land, and mineral resources—are not produced. For a given period of production, inputs are classified as either fixed or variable. A fixed input is necessary for production, but its quantity is invariant with respect to the quantity of output produced. Its costs are incurred by the entrepreneur regardless of his *short-run* maximizing decisions. The necessary quantity of a variable input depends upon the quantity of output produced. The distinction between fixed and variable inputs is temporal. Inputs which are fixed for one period of time are variable for a longer period. The entrepreneur of a machine shop may require a period of three months in order to buy new machinery or dispose of existing machinery. He will consider machinery as a fixed input in planning production for a one-month period, and as a variable input in planning production for a one-year period. All inputs are variable, given a sufficiently long period of time.

The formal analysis of the firm is similar to the formal analysis of the consumer in a number of respects. The consumer purchases commodities with which he "produces" satisfaction; the entrepreneur purchases inputs with which he produces commodities. The consumer possesses a utility function; the firm, a production function. The consumer's budget equation is a linear function of the amounts of commodities he purchases; the competitive firm's cost equation is a linear function of the amounts of inputs it purchases. The postulate of rational maximizing behavior also has a counterpart in the theory of the firm. The rational consumer desires to maximize the utility he obtains from the consumption of commodities; the rational entrepreneur desires to maximize the profit he obtains from the production and sale of commodities.

The differences between the analyses of the consumer and firm are not quite as obvious as the similarities. A utility function is subjective, and utility does not possess an unambiguous cardinal measure; a production function is objective, and the output of a firm is easily measured. A single firm may produce more than one output. The maximization process of the entrepreneur usually goes one step beyond that of the consumer. The rational consumer maximizes utility for a given income. The analogous action for the entrepreneur is to maximize the quantity of his output for a given cost level, but generally his cost is variable, and he desires to maximize his profit.

The problems of an entrepreneur who uses two inputs for the production of a single output are discussed in the first two sections of this chapter. The first covers the nature of his production function and the derivation of productivity curves and isoquants, and the second covers alternative modes of optimizing behavior. In Sec. 3-3 cost functions are derived from the production relations. Returns to scale and the special case of homogeneous production functions are considered in Sec. 3-4. The problems of an entrepreneur who uses one input for the production of two outputs are covered in Sec. 3-5, and the analysis is generalized for arbitrary numbers of inputs and outputs in Sec. 3-6. The entrepreneur's optimization problem is considered within the linear-programming framework in Sec. 3-7.

3-1. Basic Concepts

The Production Function. Consider a simple production process in which an entrepreneur utilizes two variable inputs (X_1 and X_2) and one or more fixed inputs in order to produce a single output (Q). His production function states the quantity of his output (q) as a function of the quantities of his variable inputs (x_1 and x_2):

$$q = f(x_1, x_2) \tag{3-1}$$

where (3-1) is assumed to be a single-valued continuous function with continuous first- and second-order partial derivatives. The production function is defined only for nonnegative values of the input and output levels. Negative values are meaningless within the present context. The production function is constructed with the assumption that the quantities of the fixed inputs are at predetermined levels which the entrepreneur is unable to alter during the time period under consideration.

The entrepreneur is able to use many different combinations of X_1 and X_2 for the production of a given level of output. In fact, since (3-1) is continuous, the number of possible combinations is infinite. The entrepreneur's technology is all the technical information about the combination of inputs necessary for the production of his output. It includes all physical possibilities. The technology may state that a single combination of X_1 and X_2 can be utilized in a number of different ways and therefore can yield a number of different output levels. The production function differs from the technology in that it presupposes technical efficiency and states the *maximum* output obtainable from every possible input combination. The best utilization of any particular input combination is a technical, not an economic, problem. The selection of the best input combination for the production of a particular output level depends upon input and output prices and is the subject of economic analysis.

Input and output levels are rates of flow per unit of time. The period of time for which these flows, and hence the short-run production function, are defined is subject to three general restrictions: it must be (1) sufficiently short so that the entrepreneur is unable to alter the levels of his fixed inputs, (2) sufficiently short so that the shape of the production function is not altered through technological improvements, and (3) sufficiently long to allow the completion of the necessary technical processes. The selection of a particular time period within the specified limits is arbitrary. The analysis can be shifted to a long-run basis by relaxing condition (1) and defining the production function for a period long enough to allow variation of the heretofore fixed inputs. The major difference between a short-run and long-run analysis is the number of variable inputs. Nearly all the results for a short-run period will follow in a slightly altered form for a long-run period.

Productivity Curves. The total productivity of X_1 in the production of Q is defined as the quantity of Q that can be secured from the input of X_1 if X_2 is assigned the fixed value x_2^0:

$$q = f(x_1, x_2^0) \tag{3-2}$$

The input level x_2^0 is treated as a parameter, and q becomes a function of x_1 alone. The relation between q and x_1 may be altered by changing x_2^0. A representative family of total productivity curves is presented in Fig. 3-1. Each curve gives the relationship between q and x_1 for a different value of x_2^0. Normally, an increase of x_2^0 will result in a reduction of the quantity of X_1 necessary to produce each output level within the feasible

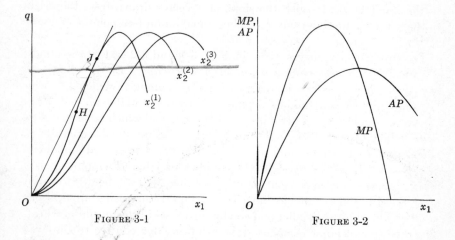

FIGURE 3-1   FIGURE 3-2

range. If one total productivity curve lies to the left of another, it corresponds to a higher value for x_2^0: $x_2^{(1)} > x_2^{(2)} > x_2^{(3)}$.

Average and marginal productivities for X_1 are defined in an analogous manner for particular values of x_2^0. The *average productivity* (AP) of X_1 is its total productivity divided by its quantity:

$$AP = \frac{q}{x_1} = \frac{f(x_1, x_2^0)}{x_1} \tag{3-3}$$

The *marginal productivity* (MP) of X_1 is the rate of change of its total productivity with respect to variations of its quantity, i.e., the partial derivative of (3-1) with respect to x_1:

$$MP = \frac{\partial q}{\partial x_1} = f_1(x_1, x_2^0) \tag{3-4}$$

Families of AP and MP curves can be constructed by assigning different values to x_2^0.

The AP and MP curves corresponding to one of the total productivity curves in Fig. 3-1 are presented in Fig. 3-2. Both AP and MP increase and then decline as the application of X_1 is expanded. The MP curve reaches a maximum at a lower input level than the AP curve and intersects the AP curve at its maximum point.[1] [The input level at which MP equals zero is the same as the input level at which the corresponding total productivity curve is at a maximum, i.e., the point at which the slope of its tangent equals zero.] The input level at which MP reaches a maximum is the same as the input level at the point of inflection on the corresponding total productivity curve, i.e., the point at which the slope of its tangent is at a maximum (see point H on curve $x_2^{(1)}$ in Fig. 3-1). The input level at which the AP curve reaches a maximum is the same as the input level at which the slope of a vector drawn from the origin to the total productivity curve reaches a maximum (see point J on curve $x_2^{(1)}$ in Fig. 3-1).

The productivity curves given in Figs. 3-1 and 3-2 satisfy the almost universal *law of diminishing marginal productivity*: The MP of X_1 will eventually decline as x_1 is increased with x_2^0 remaining unchanged.[2]   This law does not rule out the initial phase of increasing MP exhibited in the present example.   Consider a production process in which labor and land are combined for the production of wheat and compute the quantity of wheat produced as more and more labor is applied to a fixed amount of land.   Initially an increase in the number of laborers employed may allow specialization and result in an increasing MP of labor.   However, after these initial economies have been realized, increasing applications of labor will result in smaller and smaller increases in the output of wheat. The quantity of labor becomes greater and greater relative to the fixed quantity of land.   The law of diminishing marginal productivity concerns the relative quantities of the inputs and is not applicable if both inputs are increased.   The entire productivity analysis may be applied to variations of x_2 with x_1 as the parameter.

For a specific example, consider the production function given by the sixth-degree equation

$$q = Ax_1^2x_2^2 - Bx_1^3x_2^3 \qquad (3\text{-}5)$$

---

[1] To determine the maximum value of AP, set its partial derivative with respect to x_1 equal to zero:

$$\frac{\partial AP}{\partial x_1} = \frac{x_1 f_1(x_1,x_2^0) - f(x_1 x_2^0)}{x_1^2} = 0$$

If a fraction equals zero, its numerator must equal zero:

$$x_1 f_1(x_1,x_2^0) - f(x_1,x_2^0) = 0$$

Moving the second term to the right, and dividing through by x_1,

$$f_1(x_1,x_2^0) = \frac{f(x_1,x_2^0)}{x_1}$$

MP and AP are equal at the point of maximum AP if such a point exists.

[2] This law has been stated in a number of alternative forms.   See K. Menger, "The Laws of Return," O. Morgenstern (ed.), *Economic Activity Analysis* (New York: Wiley, 1954), pp. 419–482.

where $A, B > 0$. The corresponding productivity curves are depicted in Figs. 3-1 and 3-2.[†] Letting $Ax_2{}^2 = k_1$ and $Bx_2{}^3 = k_2$, the family of total productivity curves for X_1 is given by the cubic equation

$$q = k_1 x_1{}^2 - k_2 x_1{}^3$$

where k_1 and k_2 depend upon the fixed value assigned to x_2. The AP and MP curves are given by the quadratic equations

$$\text{AP} = k_1 x_1 - k_2 x_1{}^2 \qquad \text{MP} = 2k_1 x_1 - 3k_2 x_1{}^2$$

AP reaches a maximum at $x_1 = k_1/2k_2$, and MP reaches a maximum at $x_1 = k_1/3k_2$. Since x_1, k_1, $k_2 > 0$, MP reaches its maximum at a smaller input of X_1 than AP. The reader may verify that AP = MP at $x_1 = k_1/2k_2$.

Isoquants. An isoquant is the firm's counterpart of the consumer's indifference curve. It is the locus of all combinations of x_1 and x_2 which yield a specified output level. For a given output level, (3-1) becomes

$$q^0 = f(x_1, x_2) \qquad (3\text{-}6)$$

where q^0 is a parameter. The locus of all the combinations of x_1 and x_2 which satisfy (3-6) forms an isoquant. Since the production function is continuous, an infinite number of input combinations lie on each isoquant. Three curves from a family of isoquants are shown in Fig. 3-3. All the input combinations which lie on an isoquant will result in the output indicated for that curve. Within

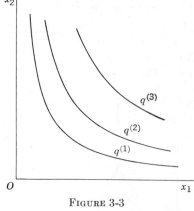

FIGURE 3-3

the relevant range of operation an increase of both inputs will result in an increased output. The further an isoquant lies from the origin, the greater the output level which it represents: $q^{(3)} > q^{(2)} > q^{(1)}$.

The slope of the tangent to a point on an isoquant is the rate at which X_1 must be substituted for X_2 (or X_2 for X_1) in order to maintain the corresponding output level. The negative of the slope is defined as the *rate of technical substitution* (RTS):

$$\text{RTS} = -\frac{dx_2}{dx_1} \qquad (3\text{-}7)$$

The RTS for the firm is analogous to the RCS for the consumer. The RTS at any point is the same for movements in either direction.

[†] The values $A = 0.09$ and $B = 0.0001$ were used for the construction of the curves in Figs. 3-1 and 3-2.

The total differential of the production function is

$$dq = f_1 \, dx_1 + f_2 \, dx_2 \qquad (3\text{-}8)$$

where f_1 and f_2 are the partial derivatives of q with respect to x_1 and x_2 (the MPs of X_1 and X_2). Since $dq = 0$ for movements along an isoquant,

$$0 = f_1 \, dx_1 + f_2 \, dx_2$$

and
$$\text{RTS} = -\frac{dx_2}{dx_1} = \frac{f_1}{f_2} \qquad (3\text{-}9)$$

The RTS at a point equals the ratio of the MP of X_1 to the MP of X_2 at that point.

Isoquants of the shape presented in Fig. 3-3 (rectangular hyperbolas which are negatively sloped throughout) can be derived for the production function given by (3-5). Let $z = x_1 x_2$, and rewrite (3-5) as

$$q^0 = Az^2 - Bz^3$$

Form the cubic equation

$$Bz^3 - Az^2 + q^0 = 0$$

which can be solved for z. Treat the smallest positive real root as the solution for z. The value of z depends upon the parameter q^0:

$$z = \psi(q^0) \qquad \text{or} \qquad x_1 x_2 = \psi(q^0) \qquad .$$

which defines the isoquants as a family of rectangular hyperbolas, since $\psi(q^0)$ is constant for any fixed value of q^0.

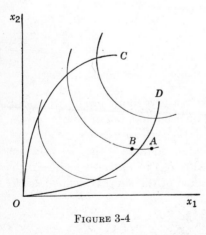

FIGURE 3-4

The MP of X_1 may become negative if the application of X_1 is sufficiently large. One can imagine a situation in which the quantity of labor employed relative to the quantities of the other inputs is so large that an increase of labor would result in congestion and inefficiency. The definition of the production function as giving the maximum output for every possible input combination does not rule out this possibility. If the MP of X_1 is negative and the MP of X_2 positive,[1] the RTS is negative, as at point A in Fig. 3-4. A movement along the isoquant from A to B would result in a reduc-

[1] This situation will never arise for the production function given by (3-5). If the MP of one of its inputs is negative, the MP of the other must also be negative.

tion of both x_1 and x_2. Clearly, point B is preferable to A if the entrepreneur must pay positive prices for the inputs. A rational entrepreneur will never operate on a positively sloped section of an isoquant; i.e., he will never use a factor combination which results in a negative MP for one of the inputs. The *ridge lines* OC and OD enclose the area of rational operation.

3-2. Optimizing Behavior

The present analysis is limited to the case in which the entrepreneur purchases X_1 and X_2 in perfectly competitive markets at constant unit prices. His total cost of production (C) is given by the linear equation

$$C = r_1 x_1 + r_2 x_2 + b \tag{3-10}$$

where r_1 and r_2 are the respective prices of X_1 and X_2, and b is the cost of the fixed inputs. An isocost line is defined as the locus of input combinations that may be purchased for a specified total cost:

$$C^0 = r_1 x_1 + r_2 x_2 + b \tag{3-11}$$

where C^0 is a parameter.

Solving (3-11) for x_1,

$$x_1 = \frac{C^0 - b}{r_1} - \frac{r_2}{r_1} x_2$$

The slopes of the isocost lines equal the negative of the input price ratio. The intercept of an isocost line on the x_1 axis $[(C^0 - b)/r_1]$ is the amount of X_1 that could be purchased if the entire outlay, exclusive of the cost of the fixed inputs, were expended upon X_1, and the intercept on the x_2 axis $[(C^0 - b)/r_2]$ is the amount of X_2 that could be purchased if this amount were expended upon X_2. Three of a family of isocost lines are given in Fig. 3-5. The greater the total outlay to which an isocost line corresponds, the greater the intercepts on the x_1 and x_2 axes, and therefore the further

FIGURE 3-5

it lies from the origin: $C^{(3)} > C^{(2)} > C^{(1)}$. The family of isocost lines completely fills the positive quadrant of the $x_1 x_2$ plane.

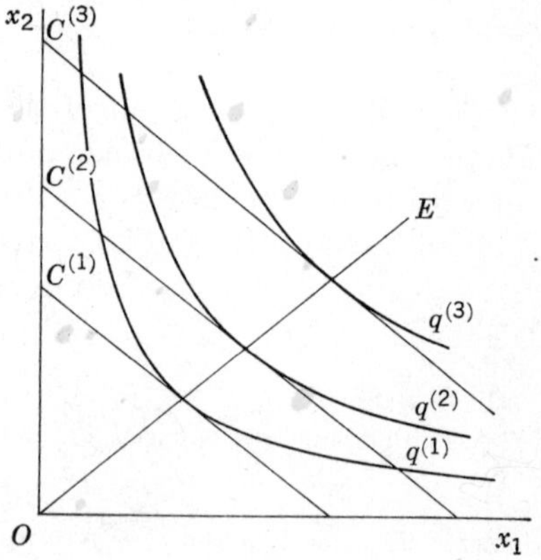

Constrained Output Maximization. The consumer maximizes utility subject to his budget constraint. The analogous problem for the firm is the maximization of output (3-1) subject to a cost constraint (3-11). The entrepreneur would desire to obtain the greatest possible output for a given cost outlay. Form the function

$$V = f(x_1, x_2) + \mu(C^0 - r_1 x_1 - r_2 x_2 - b) \tag{3-12}$$

where $\mu \neq 0$ is an undetermined Lagrange multiplier, and set the partial derivatives of V with respect to x_1, x_2, and μ equal to zero:

$$\frac{\partial V}{\partial x_1} = f_1 - \mu r_1 = 0$$

$$\frac{\partial V}{\partial x_2} = f_2 - \mu r_2 = 0$$

$$\frac{\partial V}{\partial \mu} = C^0 - r_1 x_1 - r_2 x_2 - b = 0$$

Moving the price terms to the right of the first two equations and dividing the first by the second,

$$\frac{f_1}{f_2} = \frac{r_1}{r_2} \tag{3-13}$$

First-order conditions state that the ratio of the MPs of X_1 and X_2 must be equated with the ratio of their prices.

The first-order conditions may be stated in a number of equivalent forms. Solving the first two equations for μ,

$$\mu = \frac{f_1}{r_1} = \frac{f_2}{r_2} \tag{3-14}$$

The contribution to output of the last dollar expended upon each input must equal μ. The Lagrange multiplier μ is the total derivative of output with respect to cost.[1]

Finally, substituting RTS $= f_1/f_2$ from (3-9) into (3-13),

$$\text{RTS} = \frac{r_1}{r_2} \tag{3-15}$$

---

[1] Assuming that cost is variable, the total differential of the cost equation (3-10) is

$$dC = r_1 \, dx_1 + r_2 \, dx_2$$

Substituting $r_1 = f_1/\mu$ and $r_2 = f_2/\mu$ from the first-order conditions,

$$dC = \frac{1}{\mu} (f_1 \, dx_1 + f_2 \, dx_2)$$

Dividing this expression into the total differential of the production function (3-8), the total derivative of output with respect to cost is

$$\frac{dq}{dC} = \mu \frac{f_1 \, dx_1 + f_2 \, dx_2}{f_1 \, dx_1 + f_2 \, dx_2} = \mu$$

The first-order conditions may also be expressed as the equality of the RTS and the input price ratio. The three formulations of the first-order conditions given by (3-13), (3-14), and (3-15) are equivalent alternatives. If one is satisfied, all three are satisfied.

The formulation given by (3-15) has a clear geometric interpretation. The optimum input combination is given by the point of tangency between an isoquant and the relevant isocost line. If $C^{(3)}$ (see Fig. 3-5) is the predetermined level of cost, the maximum output is $q^{(3)}$. The outputs corresponding to all other isoquants which have points in common with the given isocost line, such as $q^{(1)}$ and $q^{(2)}$, are less than $q^{(3)}$.

Second-order conditions require that the relevant bordered Hessian determinant be positive:

$$\begin{vmatrix} f_{11} & f_{12} & -r_1 \\ f_{21} & f_{22} & -r_2 \\ -r_1 & -r_2 & 0 \end{vmatrix} > 0 \qquad (3\text{-}16)$$

The second-order conditions may be utilized to demonstrate that the rate of change of the slope of the tangent to an isoquant must be positive $(d^2x_2/dx_1^2 > 0)$ at the point of tangency with an isocost line.[1] This means that the isoquants must be convex from below as shown in Fig. 3-5.

Constrained Cost Minimization. The entrepreneur may desire to minimize the cost of producing a prescribed level of output. In this case (3-10) is minimized subject to (3-2). Form the function

$$Z = r_1 x_1 + r_2 x_2 + b + \lambda[q^0 - f(x_1, x_2)] \qquad (3\text{-}17)$$

and set the partial derivatives of Z with respect to x_1, x_2, and λ equal to zero:

$$\frac{\partial Z}{\partial x_1} = r_1 - \lambda f_1 = 0$$

$$\frac{\partial Z}{\partial x_2} = r_2 - \lambda f_2 = 0$$

$$\frac{\partial Z}{\partial \lambda} = q^0 - f(x_1, x_2) = 0$$

Since r_1 and f_1 are both positive, λ is also positive. Moving the price terms of the first two equations to the right, and dividing the first by the second,

$$\frac{f_1}{f_2} = \frac{r_1}{r_2} \quad \text{or} \quad \frac{1}{\lambda} = \frac{f_1}{r_1} = \frac{f_2}{r_2} \quad \text{or} \quad \text{RTS} = \frac{r_1}{r_2}$$

---

[1] The formal derivation is identical with that used to demonstrate that the rate of change of the slope of the indifference curve must be positive at the point of maximum utility (see Sec. 2-2).

CANISIUS COLLEGE LIBRARY
BUFFALO, N. Y.

The first-order conditions for the minimization of cost subject to an output constraint are similar to those for the maximization of output subject to a cost constraint. The multiplier λ is the reciprocal of the multiplier μ, or the total derivative of cost with respect to output (defined as marginal cost in Sec. 3-3). In the present case, the entrepreneur finds the lowest isocost line which has at least one point in common with a selected isoquant. He could produce $q^{(1)}$ (see Fig. 3-5) at a cost of $C^{(3)}$ or $C^{(2)}$, but $C^{(1)}$ is lower than either of these. His minimum cost is given by the isocost line which is tangent to the selected isoquant.

Second-order conditions require that the relevant bordered Hessian determinant be negative:

$$\begin{vmatrix} -\lambda f_{11} & -\lambda f_{12} & -f_1 \\ -\lambda f_{21} & -\lambda f_{22} & -f_2 \\ -f_1 & -f_2 & 0 \end{vmatrix} < 0$$

Substituting $-f_1 = -r_1/\lambda$ and $-f_2 = -r_2/\lambda$, multiplying the first two columns of the array by $-1/\lambda$, and then multiplying the third row by $-\lambda^2$ and the third column by λ,†

$$\begin{vmatrix} -\lambda f_{11} & -\lambda f_{12} & -\dfrac{r_1}{\lambda} \\ -\lambda f_{21} & -\lambda f_{22} & -\dfrac{r_2}{\lambda} \\ -\dfrac{r_1}{\lambda} & -\dfrac{r_2}{\lambda} & 0 \end{vmatrix} = \lambda^2 \begin{vmatrix} f_{11} & f_{12} & -\dfrac{r_1}{\lambda} \\ f_{21} & f_{22} & -\dfrac{r_2}{\lambda} \\ \dfrac{r_1}{\lambda^2} & \dfrac{r_2}{\lambda^2} & 0 \end{vmatrix}$$

$$= -\frac{1}{\lambda} \begin{vmatrix} f_{11} & f_{12} & -r_1 \\ f_{21} & f_{22} & -r_2 \\ -r_1 & -r_2 & 0 \end{vmatrix} < 0$$

Since $\lambda > 0$,

$$\begin{vmatrix} f_{11} & f_{12} & -r_1 \\ f_{21} & f_{22} & -r_2 \\ -r_1 & -r_2 & 0 \end{vmatrix} > 0$$

The second-order conditions are the same as those given by (3-16).

If the second-order conditions are satisfied, every point of tangency between an isoquant and an isocost line is the solution of both a constrained-maximum and a constrained-minimum problem. If $q^{(1)}$ (see Fig. 3-5) is the maximum output which can be obtained from an outlay of $C^{(1)}$ dollars, $C^{(1)}$ dollars is the minimum cost for which the output $q^{(1)}$

† The multiplication of the first column by $-1/\lambda$ increases the value of the determinant by the same multiple. The multiplication of both the first and second columns by $-1/\lambda$ increases the value of determinant by $1/\lambda^2$. Its value is left unchanged if the entire array is now multiplied by λ^2 (see Sec. A-1).

can be produced. The locus of tangency points (OE in Fig. 3-5) gives the *expansion path* of the firm. The rational entrepreneur will select only input combinations which lie on his expansion path. Formally, the expansion path is an implicit function of x_1 and x_2:

$$g(x_1,x_2) = 0 \qquad (3\text{-}18)$$

for which the first- and second-order conditions for constrained maxima and minima are fulfilled.

If the isoquants are convex from below, the second-order conditions will always be satisfied, and the expansion path can be derived from the first-order conditions. Consider the production function given by (3-5) as an example. Compute the ratio of the MPs of X_1 and X_2:

$$\frac{f_1}{f_2} = \frac{2Ax_1x_2^2 - 3Bx_1^2x_2^3}{2Ax_1^2x_2 - 3Bx_1^3x_2^2} = \frac{x_2(2Ax_1x_2 - 3Bx_1^2x_2^2)}{x_1(2Ax_1x_2 - 3Bx_1^2x_2^2)} = \frac{x_2}{x_1}$$

and set it equal to the ratio of the input prices

$$\frac{x_2}{x_1} = \frac{r_1}{r_2}$$

Putting this first-order condition in the form of an implicit function, the expansion path is given by the linear equation

$$r_1x_1 - r_2x_2 = 0$$

This corresponds to the expansion path OE in Fig. 3-5.

Profit Maximization. The entrepreneur is usually free to vary the levels of both cost and output, and his ultimate aim is the maximization of profit rather than the solution of constrained maximum and minimum problems. The total revenue of an entrepreneur who sells his output in a perfectly competitive market is given by the number of units he sells multiplied by the fixed unit price (p) he receives. His profit (π) is the difference between his total revenue and his total cost:

$$\pi = pq - C$$

or substituting $q = f(x_1,x_2)$ from (3-1) and $C = r_1x_1 + r_2x_2 + b$ from (3-10),

$$\pi = pf(x_1,x_2) - r_1x_1 - r_2x_2 - b \qquad (3\text{-}19)$$

Profit is a function of x_1 and x_2 and is maximized with respect to these variables.

Setting the partial derivatives of (3-19) with respect to x_1 and x_2 equal to zero,

$$\frac{\partial \pi}{\partial x_1} = pf_1 - r_1 = 0 \qquad \frac{\partial \pi}{\partial x_2} = pf_2 - r_2 = 0 \qquad (3\text{-}20)$$

Moving the input-price terms to the right,

$$pf_1 = r_1 \qquad pf_2 = r_2 \tag{3-21}$$

The partial derivatives of the production function with respect to the inputs are the MPs of the inputs. The value of the MP of X_1 (pf_1) is the rate at which the entrepreneur's revenue would increase with further application of X_1. The first-order conditions for profit maximization (3-21) require that each input be utilized up to a point at which the value of its MP equals its price. The entrepreneur can increase his profit as long as the addition to his revenue from the employment of an additional unit of X_1 exceeds its cost. The maximum profit-input combination lies on the expansion path, since (3-21) is a special case of (3-13).

Second-order conditions require that the principal minors of the relevant Hessian determinant alternate in sign:

$$\frac{\partial^2 \pi}{\partial x_1{}^2} < 0; \quad \begin{vmatrix} \dfrac{\partial^2 \pi}{\partial x_1{}^2} & \dfrac{\partial^2 \pi}{\partial x_1 \, \partial x_2} \\[2ex] \dfrac{\partial^2 \pi}{\partial x_2 \, \partial x_1} & \dfrac{\partial^2 \pi}{\partial x_2{}^2} \end{vmatrix} > 0 \tag{3-22}$$

Expanding the second determinant of (3-22),

$$\left(\frac{\partial^2 \pi}{\partial x_1{}^2} \frac{\partial^2 \pi}{\partial x_2{}^2} \right) - \left(\frac{\partial^2 \pi}{\partial x_1 \, \partial x_2} \right)^2 > 0 \tag{3-23}$$

since $\partial^2 \pi / \partial x_1 \, \partial x_2 = \partial^2 \pi / \partial x_2 \, \partial x_1$. Since $\partial^2 \pi / \partial x_1{}^2 < 0$ and $(\partial^2 \pi / \partial x_1 \, \partial x_2)^2 > 0$,

$$\frac{\partial^2 \pi}{\partial x_2{}^2} < 0 \tag{3-24}$$

and the numbering of the inputs is immaterial. Profit must be decreasing with respect to further applications of *either* X_1 or X_2. Condition (3-23) ensures that profit is decreasing with respect to further applications of *both* X_1 and X_2.

The second-order conditions require that the MPs of both inputs be decreasing. Using the second-order partial derivatives of (3-20) to evaluate (3-22) and (3-24),

$$\frac{\partial^2 \pi}{\partial x_1{}^2} = pf_{11} < 0 \qquad \frac{\partial^2 \pi}{\partial x_2{}^2} = pf_{22} < 0$$

Since $p > 0$,

$$f_{11} < 0 \qquad f_{22} < 0 \tag{3-25}$$

If the MP of one of the inputs were increasing, a small movement from the point at which the first-order conditions are satisfied would result in an increase in the value of its MP. Since its price is constant, the entrepreneur could increase his profit by increasing its quantity.

3-3. Cost Functions

The economist frequently assumes that the problem of optimum input combinations has been solved and conducts his analysis of the firm in terms of its revenues and costs expressed as functions of output. The problem of the entrepreneur is then to select that output at which his profits are maximized.

Short-run Cost Functions. Cost functions can be derived from the information contained in Secs. 3-1 and 3-2.† Consider the system of equations consisting of the production function (3-1), the cost equation (3-10), and the expansion path function (3-18):

$$q = f(x_1, x_2)$$
$$C = r_1 x_1 + r_2 x_2 + b$$
$$0 = g(x_1, x_2)$$

This system of three equations in four variables can be reduced to a single equation in which cost is stated as an explicit function of the level of output plus the cost of the fixed inputs:

$$C = \phi(q) + b \tag{3-26}$$

The cost of the fixed inputs, *the fixed cost*, must be paid regardless of how much the firm produces, or whether it produces at all. The cost function gives the minimum cost of producing each output and is derived on the assumption that the entrepreneur acts rationally. A cost-output combination for (3-26) can be obtained as follows: (1) select a point on the expansion path, (2) substitute the corresponding values of the input levels into the production function to obtain the corresponding output level, (3) multiply the input levels by the fixed input prices to obtain the total variable cost for this output level, and (4) add the fixed cost.

A number of special cost relations which are also functions of the level of output can be derived from (3-26). Average total (ATC), average variable (AVC), and average fixed (AFC) costs are defined as the respective total, variable, and fixed costs divided by the level of output:

$$\text{ATC} = \frac{\phi(q) + b}{q}$$

$$\text{AVC} = \frac{\phi(q)}{q}$$

$$\text{AFC} = \frac{b}{q}$$

ATC is the sum of AVC and AFC. Marginal cost (MC) is the deriva-

---

† The term *cost function* is used to denote cost expressed as a function of output. The term *cost equation* is used to denote cost expressed in terms of input levels and input prices.

tive of total cost with respect to output:

$$\text{MC} = \frac{dC}{dq} = \phi'(q)$$

The derivatives of total and total variable cost are identical since the fixed-cost term vanishes upon differentiation.

Specific cost functions may assume many different shapes. One possibility which exhibits the properties usually assumed by economists is depicted in Figs. 3-6 and 3-7. Total cost is a cubic function of output.

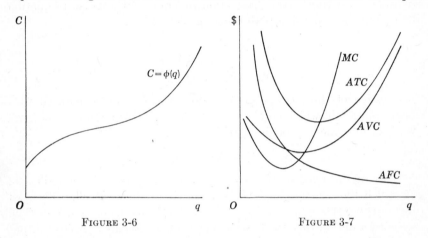

FIGURE 3-6   FIGURE 3-7

ATC, AVC, and MC are all second-degree curves which first decline and then increase as output is expanded. MC reaches its minimum before ATC and AVC, and AVC reaches its minimum before ATC. The reader may verify that the MC curve passes through the minimum points of both the AVC and ATC curves.[1] The AFC curve is a rectangular hyperbola regardless of the shapes of the other cost curves; the fixed cost is spread over a larger number of units as output is expanded, and therefore declines monotonically. The vertical distance between the ATC and AVC curves equals AFC, and hence decreases as output is increased.

The revenue of an entrepreneur who sells his output at a fixed price is also a function of the level of his output. Therefore, his profit is a function of the level of his output:

$$\pi = pq - \phi(q) - b \qquad (3\text{-}27)$$

To maximize profit, set the derivative of (3-27) with respect to q equal to zero:

$$\frac{d\pi}{dq} = p - \phi'(q) = 0$$

[1] Set the derivative of ATC (or AVC) equal to zero, and put the equation in a form which states the equality between ATC (or AVC) and MC (see Sec. A-2).

Moving the MC to the right,

$$p = \phi'(q) \tag{3-28}$$

The entrepreneur must equate his MC with the constant selling price of his output. He can increase his profit by expanding his output if the addition to his revenue (p) of selling another unit exceeds the addition to his cost (MC).

The second-order condition for profit maximization requires that

$$\frac{d^2\pi}{dq^2} = -\frac{d^2C}{dq^2} < 0$$

or multiplying by -1 and reversing the inequality,

$$\frac{d^2C}{dq^2} > 0$$

MC must be increasing at the profit-maximizing output. If MC were decreasing, the equality of price and MC would give a point of minimum profit.

The level of the entrepreneur's fixed cost (b) generally has no effect upon his optimizing decisions during a short-run period. It must be paid regardless of the level of his output and merely adds a constant term to his profit equation. The fixed-cost term vanishes upon differentiation, and MC is independent of its level. Since the first- and second-order conditions for profit maximization are expressed in terms of MC, the equilibrium output level is unaffected by the level of fixed cost. The mathematical analyses of optimization in the present section and in Sec. 3-2 can generally be carried out on the basis of variable cost alone.

The level of fixed cost has significance for the analysis of short-run profit maximization in one special case. The entrepreneur has an option not recognized by the calculus. He can discontinue production and accept a loss equal to his fixed cost. This option is optimal if his maximum profit from the production of a positive output level is a negative amount (a loss) with a greater absolute value than the level of his fixed cost. The entrepreneur need never lose more than the amount of his fixed cost. He will produce at a loss in the short run if his loss is less than the amount of his fixed cost, i.e., if revenue exceeds total variable cost, and he is able to recover a portion of his outlay on the fixed inputs.

A geometric description of profit maximization is contained in Fig. 3-8. The optimum output (q^0) is given by the intersection of a horizontal line drawn at the level of the going price (p^0) and the rising portion of the MC curve. The entrepreneur's revenue is given by the area of the rectangle Op^0Bq^0, total cost by $OADq^0$, and profit by Ap^0BD.

As an example consider the cubic total-cost function

$$C = 0.04q^3 - 0.9q^2 + 10q + 5 \tag{3-29}$$

Assume that the price of q is 4 dollars per unit.   Equating MC and price,

$$0.12q^2 - 1.8q + 10 = 4$$

which yields the quadratic equation

$$q^2 - 15q + 50 = 0$$

the roots of which are $q = 5$ and $q = 10$.   Two different outputs satisfy the first-order condition for profit maximization, and the rate of change of MC must be calculated for both. The rate of change of MC:

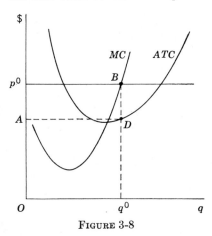

FIGURE 3-8

$$\frac{d^2C}{dq^2} = 0.24q - 1.8$$

is negative for $q = 5$ and positive for $q = 10$.   An output of 10 units yields a maximum profit, and an output of 5 a minimum.   Profit at 10 units, however, is negative:

$$\pi = 4q - (0.04q^3 - 0.9q^2 + 10q + 5)$$
$$= 40 - 55 = -15$$

The entrepreneur's ATC curve lies above the price line for every output, and his maximum profit is a loss of 15 dollars.   He should discontinue production, since his fixed cost (5 dollars) is less than the smallest loss which he can incur from a positive output level.

Long-run Cost Functions.   Let the levels of the entrepreneur's fixed inputs be represented by a parameter k, which gives the "size of his plant"—the greater the value of k, the greater the size of his plant.   The entrepreneur's short-run problems concern the optimal utilization of a plant of given size.   In the long run he is free to vary k and select a plant of optimum size.   The shapes of the entrepreneur's production and cost functions depend upon his plant size.   These are uniquely determined in the short run.   In the long run he can choose between cost and production functions with different shapes.   The number of his alternatives equals the number of different values which k may assume.   Once he has selected the shapes of these functions, i.e., selected a value for k, he is faced with the conventional short-run optimization problems.

As an illustration, consider the case of an entrepreneur operating a grocery store.   The "size of his plant" is given by the number of square feet of selling space which he possesses.   Assume that the only possible alternatives are 5,000, 10,000, and 20,000 square feet and that he currently possesses 10,000.   His present plant size is the result of a long-run decision made in the past. When the time comes for the replacement of his store, he will be able to select his plant size anew. If conditions have not changed since his last decision, he will again select 10,000 square feet. If the store has been crowded and he anticipates a long-run increase in sales, he will build 20,000 square feet. Under other conditions he may build a store with 5,000 square feet. Once he has built a new store, his problems concern the optimal utilization of a selling area of given size.

Assume that k is continuously variable and introduce it explicitly into the production function, cost equation, and expansion path function:

$$q = f(x_1, x_2, k)$$
$$C = r_1 x_1 + r_2 x_2 + \psi(k)$$
$$0 = g(x_1, x_2, k)$$

Fixed cost is an increasing function of plant size: $\psi'(k) > 0$. The shapes of the families of isoquants and iso-cost lines and the shape of the expansion path depend upon the value assigned to the parameter k. Generally, two of the above relations may be utilized to eliminate x_1 and x_2, and total cost may be expressed as a function of output level and plant size:

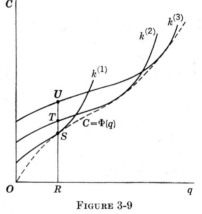

FIGURE 3-9

$$C = \phi(q, k) + \psi(k) \qquad (3\text{-}30)$$

which describes a family of total cost curves generated by assigning different values to the parameter k. As soon as plant size is assigned a particular value $k = k^0$, (3-30) is equivalent to the particular total cost function given by (3-26), and the short-run analysis is applicable.

The entrepreneur's long-run total cost function gives the minimum cost of producing each output level if he is free to vary the size of his plant. For a given output level he computes the total cost for each possible plant size and selects the plant size for which total cost is a minimum. Figure 3-9 contains the total cost curves corresponding to three different plant sizes. The entrepreneur can produce the output OR in any of the plants. His total cost would be RS for plant size $k^{(1)}$, RT for $k^{(2)}$, and RU for $k^{(3)}$. The plant size $k^{(1)}$ gives the minimum production cost for the output OR. Therefore, the point S lies on the long-run total cost curve. This process is repeated for every output level, and the long-run total cost curve is defined as the locus of the minimum-cost points.

The long-run cost curve is the envelope of the short-run curves; it touches each and intersects none. Write the equation for the family of short-run cost functions (3-30) in implicit form:

$$C - \phi(q,k) - \psi(k) = G(C,q,k) = 0 \qquad (3\text{-}31)$$

and set the partial derivative of (3-31) with respect to k equal to zero:

$$G_k(C,q,k) = 0 \qquad (3\text{-}32)$$

The equation of the envelope curve (the long-run cost curve) is obtained by eliminating k from (3-31) and (3-32) and solving for C as a function of q (see Sec. A-3):

$$C = \Phi(q) \qquad (3\text{-}33)$$

Long-run total cost is a function of output level, given the condition that each output level is produced in a plant of optimum size. The long-run cost curve is not something apart from the short-run cost curves. It is constructed from points on the short-run curves. Since k is assumed continuously variable, the long-run cost curve (see Fig. 3-9) has one and only one point in common with each of the infinite number of short-run cost curves.

Since AC equals total cost divided by output level, the minimum AC of producing a particular output level is attained at the same plant size as the minimum total cost of producing that output level. The long-run AC curve can be derived by dividing long-run total cost by output level, or by constructing the envelope of the short-run AC curves. The two constructions are equivalent.

The long-run MC curve can be constructed by plotting the derivative of long-run total cost with respect to output level, or can be derived from the short-run MC curves. However, the long-run MC curve is not the envelope of the short-run MC curves. Short-run MC equals the rate of change of short-run variable cost with respect to output level; long-run MC is the rate of change of total cost assuming that all costs are variable. Therefore, portions of short-run MC curves may lie below the long-run MC curve. The long-run MC curve may be defined as the locus of those points on the short-run MC curves which correspond to the optimum plant size for each output.[1] The equivalence of the two methods of deriving the long-run MC curve is obvious in Fig. 3-9. The long-run total cost curve is tangent to each short-run curve at the output for which

---

[1] It *is not correct* to construct the long-run MC curve by selecting the points on the short-run MC curves which correspond to the optimum output (i.e., point of minimum AC) for each plant size.

the short-run curve in question represents optimum plant size. Since the MCs are defined as the slopes of the tangents of these curves, the long-run and short-run MCs are equal at such points.

Assume that the entrepreneur desires to construct a plant for use during a number of short-run periods and that he expects to receive the same price for his product during each of the short-run periods. Since conditions remain unchanged from one period to the next, he will produce the same level of output in each period. His profit during one of the periods is the difference between his revenue and cost with plant size variable:

$$\pi = pq - \Phi(q) \tag{3-34}$$

Set the derivative of π equal to zero:

$$\frac{d\pi}{dq} = p - \Phi'(q) = 0$$

or
$$p = \Phi'(q) \tag{3-35}$$

Profits are maximized by equating long-run MC to price, if long-run MC is increasing (second-order condition). Once the optimum output is determined, the optimum value for k can be determined from (3-31) and (3-32).

Consider the family of short-run cost curves generated by

$$C = 0.04q^3 - 0.9q^2 + (11 - k)q + 5k^2 \tag{3-36}$$

For the plant size $k = 1$, the short-run cost curve is the one given by (3-29). Setting the partial derivative of the implicit form of (3-36) with respect to k equal to zero,

$$G_k(C,q,k) = -q + 10k = 0$$

which has the solution $k = 0.1q$. Substituting into (3-36) gives the long-run cost function:

$$C = 0.04q^3 - 0.9q^2 + (11 - 0.1q)q + 5(0.1q)^2$$
$$= 0.04q^3 - 0.95q^2 + 11q$$

Long-run fixed cost equals zero.

Let the price of the entrepreneur's product be 4 dollars, as in the example for a short-run cost function. Setting price equal to long-run MC,

$$4 = 0.12q^2 - 1.9q + 11$$

which yields the quadratic equation

$$0.12q^2 - 1.9q + 7 = 0$$

with the roots $q = 5.83$ and $q = 10$. Profit is maximized at an output of 10 units. Utilizing the relation $k = 0.1q$, the optimum-size plant is given by $k = 1$.   The entrepreneur's profit per short-run period is

$$\pi = pq - (0.04q^3 - 0.95q^2 + 11q) = 40 - 55 = -15$$

As in the last example, the maximum operating profit is a loss of 15 dollars.   In the long run the entrepreneur is unable to earn a positive profit and will not construct a plant of any size.

The situation is quite different if price is increased to 6 dollars.   Setting long-run MC equal to price yields the quadratic equation

$$0.12q^2 - 1.9q + 5 = 0$$

with the roots $q = 3.3$ and $q = 12.5$.   Profit is maximized at an output of 12.5 units.   Profit is positive for this plant size:

$$\pi = 75 - 67.1875 = 7.8125$$

and the entrepreneur will construct a plant of the optimum size ($k = 1.25$).

3-4. Homogeneous Production Functions

"Returns to scale" describes the output response to a proportionate increase of all inputs.   If output increases by the same proportion, returns to scale are constant for the range of input combinations under consideration.   They are increasing if output increases by a greater proportion and decreasing if it increases by a smaller proportion.   A single production function may exhibit all three types of returns.   Some economists assume that production functions exhibit increasing returns for small amounts of the inputs, then pass through a stage of constant returns, and finally exhibit decreasing returns to scale as the quantities of the inputs become greater and greater.

Properties.   Returns to scale are easily defined for homogeneous production functions.   A production function is homogeneous of degree k if

$$f(tx_1, tx_2) = t^k f(x_1, x_2) \tag{3-37}$$

where k is a constant and t is any positive real number.   If both inputs are increased by the factor t, output is increased by the factor t^k.   Returns to scale are increasing if $k > 1$, constant if $k = 1$, and decreasing if $k < 1$.   Degrees of homogeneity other than one are seldom assumed for production functions.[1]

The partial derivatives of a function homogeneous of degree k are homogeneous of degree $(k - 1)$.   Differentiate (3-37) partially with respect to x_1 using the function of a function rule (see Sec. A-2) on the left:

---

[1] A function which is homogeneous of degree one is said to be linearly homogeneous. This, of course, does not imply that the production function is linear.

$$tf_1(tx_1,tx_2) = t^k f_1(x_1,x_2)$$

Dividing through by t,

$$f_1(tx_1,tx_2) = t^{k-1} f_1(x_1,x_2)$$

which is the definition of homogeneity of degree $k - 1$. If a production function is homogeneous of degree one, the marginal productivities of X_1 and X_2 are homogeneous of degree zero, i.e., they remain unchanged for proportionate changes of both inputs:

$$f_1(x_1,x_2) = f_1(tx_1,tx_2)$$
$$f_2(x_1,x_2) = f_2(tx_1,tx_2) \tag{3-38}$$

The MPs depend only upon the proportion in which X_1 and X_2 are used.

A straight line from the origin in the isoquant plane is defined by $(0,0)$ and any arbitrary point (x_1^0, x_2^0). Such a line is the locus of all points (tx_1^0, tx_2^0) for $t \geq 0$. The RTS at any arbitrarily selected point on the line equals the ratio of the marginal productivities for the input combination corresponding to that point:

$$\frac{f_1(tx_1^0,tx_2^0)}{f_2(tx_1^0,tx_2^0)} = \frac{t^{k-1}f_1(x_1^0,x_2^0)}{t^{k-1}f_2(x_1^0,x_2^0)} = \frac{f_1(x_1^0,x_2^0)}{f_2(x_1^0,x_2^0)}$$

The RTS at (tx_1^0, tx_2^0) equals the RTS at (x_1^0, x_2^0). The expansion path which is the locus of points with RTS equal to the fixed-input-price ratio is a straight line if the production function is homogeneous of any degree. A straight-line expansion path, however, does not necessarily imply a homogeneous production function. The production function given by (3-5) possesses a straight-line expansion path, but it is not homogeneous.

One of the most widely used homogeneous production functions is the Cobb-Douglas function for the economy as a whole:

$$q = A x_1^\alpha x_2^{1-\alpha} \tag{3-39}$$

where q is an index of aggregate output, x_1 and x_2 are the aggregate inputs of labor and capital respectively, and $0 < \alpha < 1$. Increasing the levels of both labor and capital by the factor t,

$$f(tx_1,tx_2) = A(tx_1)^\alpha (tx_2)^{1-\alpha} = tA x_1^\alpha x_2^{1-\alpha}$$

The Cobb-Douglas function is homogeneous of degree one. The MPs of labor and capital are homogeneous of degree zero:

$$f_1(x_1,x_2) = \alpha(A x_1^{\alpha-1} x_2^{1-\alpha})$$
$$f_2(x_1,x_2) = (1 - \alpha)(A x_1^\alpha x_2^{-\alpha})$$
$$f_1(tx_1,tx_2) = \alpha(A t^{\alpha-1} x_1^{\alpha-1} t^{1-\alpha} x_2^{1-\alpha}) = \alpha(A x_1^{\alpha-1} x_2^{1-\alpha})$$
$$f_2(tx_1,tx_2) = (1 - \alpha)(A t^\alpha x_1^\alpha t^{-\alpha} x_2^{-\alpha}) = (1 - \alpha)(A x_1^\alpha x_2^{-\alpha})$$

The expansion path generated by the Cobb-Douglas function is linear.

The first-order conditions for a constrained optimum require that

$$\frac{r_1}{r_2} = \frac{f_1}{f_2} = \frac{\alpha(A x_1{}^{\alpha-1} x_2{}^{1-\alpha})}{(1-\alpha)(A x_1{}^{\alpha} x_2{}^{-\alpha})} = \frac{\alpha x_2}{(1-\alpha)x_1}$$

Therefore, the expansion path is given by the implicit function

$$(1-\alpha)r_1 x_1 - \alpha r_2 x_2 = 0$$

which describes a straight line emanating from the origin in the isoquant plane.

Euler's Theorem and Distribution. Euler's theorem states that the following condition is satisfied by a homogeneous function:[1]

$$x_1 f_1 + x_2 f_2 = k f(x_1, x_2) \tag{3-40}$$

Assuming that the production function is homogeneous of degree one, and substituting $q = f(x_1, x_2)$,

$$x_1 f_1 + x_2 f_2 = q \tag{3-41}$$

Total output equals the MP of X_1 multiplied by its quantity plus the MP of X_2 multiplied by its quantity. If the firm were to pay the suppliers of an input its marginal physical product, total output would be just exhausted. Total output would exceed payments if the degree of homogeneity were greater than one and would be less than payments if it were less than one.

Euler's theorem played a major role in the development of the marginal-productivity theory of distribution. The basic postulates of this theory are: (1) each input is paid the value of its marginal product, and (2) total output is just exhausted. Since these conditions are satisfied by production functions homogeneous of degree one, it was generally assumed that all production functions are of this type.

The Cobb-Douglas function was utilized to attempt an empirical verification of the marginal-productivity theory of distribution. It satisfies Euler's theorem:

$$\begin{aligned} q &= x_1(\alpha A x_1{}^{\alpha-1} x_2{}^{1-\alpha}) + x_2[(1-\alpha) A x_1{}^{\alpha} x_2{}^{-\alpha}] \\ &= \alpha A x_1{}^{\alpha} x_2{}^{1-\alpha} + (1-\alpha) A x_1{}^{\alpha} x_2{}^{1-\alpha} \end{aligned}$$

Substituting from (3-39),

$$q = \alpha q + (1-\alpha)q$$

If each factor is paid its marginal product, total output is distributed

[1] Differentiating (3-37) partially with respect to t using the composite-function rule on the left,

$$x_1 f_1(tx_1, tx_2) + x_2 f_2(tx_1, tx_2) = k t^{k-1} f(x_1, x_2)$$

Equation (3-40) is obtained by substituting $t = 1$.

between labor and capital in the respective proportions α and $(1 - \alpha)$. Paul Douglas estimated α from aggregate time-series data and compared his estimates with labor's share of total output.[1]

The condition of product exhaustion is equivalent to the condition that maximum long-run profit equal zero. Multiplying (3-41) through by the price of the product

$$x_1(pf_1) + x_2(pf_2) = pq$$

Substituting $r_1 = pf_1$ and $r_2 = pf_2$ from the first-order conditions for profit maximization,

$$r_1 x_1 + r_2 x_2 = pq \tag{3-42}$$

Long-run total outlay equals long-run total revenue. Following the assumptions of the marginal-productivity theory, Eq. (3-42) leads to the startling conclusion that long-run profit equals zero regardless of the level of the product price.

The analysis of the marginal-productivity theory of distribution is misleading, if not erroneous. The conventional analysis of profit maximization breaks down if the entrepreneur sells his output at a constant price and possesses a production function which is homogeneous of degree one. The reader can verify that in this case his profit function is also homogeneous of degree one:

$$t\pi = pf(tx_1, tx_2) - r_1 t x_1 - r_2 t x_2$$

Three outcomes are possible. If the prices are such that some factor combination yields a positive profit, profit can be increased to any level by selecting a sufficiently large value for t. In this case the profit function has no finite maximum. If the prices are such that every factor combination yields a negative profit, the entrepreneur will go out of business.

The third possibility, to which the marginal-productivity theorists generally limited their analysis, is the most interesting. In this case there is no factor combination which will yield a positive profit, but the combination (x_1^0, x_2^0) yields a zero profit. From the homogeneity of the profit function it follows that the factor combination (tx_1^0, tx_2^0) will also yield a zero profit. Maximum long-run profit equals zero, but the size of the firm is indeterminate. If the entrepreneur can earn a zero profit for a particular factor combination, his profit remains unchanged if he doubles or halves his scale of operations. If an arbitrary scale of operations is imposed upon the entrepreneur, Euler's theorem holds, and his product is just exhausted.

The assumption of a homogeneous production function is not necessary for the fulfillment of the postulates of the marginal-productivity theory.

[1] See the references listed at the end of this chapter.

The postulates are fulfilled if (1) the production function is not homogeneous, (2) the first- and second-order conditions for profit maximization are fulfilled, and (3) the entrepreneur's maximum profit equals zero. Conditions (1) and (2) have been assumed throughout the development of the theory of the firm in Secs. 3-1 and 3-2. In Chapter 4 it will be demonstrated that the free entry and exit of competing firms will result in the satisfaction of condition (3).   Condition (3) requires that

$$\pi = pq - r_1 x_1 - r_2 x_2 = 0$$

Substituting $r_1 = pf_1$ and $r_2 = pf_2$ (the first-order conditions), and solving for q,

$$q = x_1 f_1 + x_2 f_2$$

Here the result of (3-41) is attained without the use of Euler's theorem. Furthermore, since the production function is not homogeneous, the entrepreneur's optimum factor combination is generally determinate.

Long-run Cost Functions.   A production function homogeneous of degree one generates a linear long-run total cost function.   Let (x_1^0, x_2^0) be the optimum input combination for the production of 1 unit of Q.   The corresponding production cost is $r_1 x_1^0 + r_2 x_2^0$.   Since the production function is homogeneous and the expansion path linear, (qx_1^0, qx_2^0) is the optimum input combination for the production of q units of Q.   The corresponding production cost is

$$C = aq$$

where $a = r_1 x_1^0 + r_2 x_2^0$.   Marginal and average cost are both equal to the constant a.

The total cost function for the Cobb-Douglas production function can be derived more easily in the conventional manner.   Writing out the production function, cost equation, and expansion path function,

$$q = A x_1^\alpha x_2^{1-\alpha}$$
$$C = r_1 x_1 + r_2 x_2$$
$$(1 - \alpha) r_1 x_1 - \alpha r_2 x_2 = 0$$

Solving the second and third equations for x_1 and x_2,

$$x_1 = \frac{\alpha C}{r_1} \qquad x_2 = \frac{(1 - \alpha) C}{r_2}$$

and substituting these values into the production function,

$$q = A \left(\frac{\alpha C}{r_1}\right)^\alpha \left[\frac{(1 - \alpha) C}{r_2}\right]^{1-\alpha}$$

Solving for C in terms of q and the parameters, the total cost function is

$$C = aq$$

where

$$a = \frac{r_1{}^\alpha r_2{}^{1-\alpha}}{A\alpha^\alpha(1-\alpha)^{(1-\alpha)}}$$

The breakdown of the profit-maximization analysis for homogeneous production functions can be illustrated with the aid of cost and revenue functions. Expressing profit as a function of output

$$\pi = pq - aq$$

and setting its derivative equal to zero

$$p - a = 0$$

The first-order condition requires that the entrepreneur equate two constants. This is an impossible task unless price and marginal cost happen to be equal by chance. He is unable to affect either price or marginal cost through variations of his output. If price exceeds marginal cost, the entrepreneur will expand his output without limit; if $p = a$, the level of his output is indeterminate; and if $p < a$, he will go out of business.

3-5. Joint Products

Some production processes will yield more than one output. Sheep raising is the classic example of such a process. Two outputs, wool and mutton, can be produced in varying proportions by a single production process.[1] The case of joint products is distinguished on technical rather than organizational grounds and exists whenever the quantities of two or more outputs are technically interdependent. Cases in which a single firm produces two or more technically independent products are excluded by this definition.

Basic Concepts.   Consider the simplest case in which an entrepreneur uses a single input (X) for the production of two outputs (Q_1 and Q_2). In implicit form his production function is

$$H(q_1,q_2,x) = 0 \tag{3-43}$$

where q_1, q_2, and x are the respective quantities of Q_1, Q_2, and X.   Assume

[1] The production of joint products does not require an extended analysis unless they can be produced in varying proportions.   If two products are always produced in a fixed proportion: $q_1/q_2 = k$ where k is a constant, the analysis for a single output can be applied.   Define a compound unit of output as k units of Q_1 and 1 unit of Q_2 with a price of $(kp_1 + p_2)$ and treat it as a single output.

that (3-43) can be solved explicitly for x:

$$x = h(q_1, q_2) \qquad (3\text{-}44)$$

The cost of production *in terms of* X is a function of the quantities of the two outputs.

A *product transformation curve* is defined as the locus of output combinations that can be secured from a given input of X:

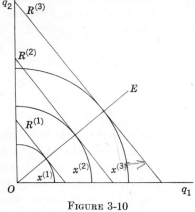

FIGURE 3-10

$$x^0 = h(q_1, q_2) \qquad (3\text{-}45)$$

Three of a family of product transformation curves are presented in Fig. 3-10. The further a curve lies from the origin, the greater the input of X to which it corresponds:

$$x^{(3)} > x^{(2)} > x^{(1)}$$

The slope of the tangent to a point on a product transformation curve is the rate at which Q_2 must be sacrificed to obtain more Q_1 (or Q_1 sacrificed to obtain more Q_2) without varying the input of X. The negative of the slope is defined as the *rate of product transformation* (RPT):

$$\text{RPT} = -\frac{dq_2}{dq_1} \qquad (3\text{-}46)$$

Taking the total differential of (3-44),

$$dx = h_1 \, dq_1 + h_2 \, dq_2$$

Since $dx = 0$ for movements along a product transformation curve,

$$\text{RPT} = -\frac{dq_2}{dq_1} = \frac{h_1}{h_2} \qquad (3\text{-}47)$$

The RPT at a point on a product transformation curve equals the ratio of the marginal cost of Q_1 *in terms of* X to the marginal cost of Q_2 *in terms of* X at that point.

Alternatively, the RPT can be expressed in terms of the MPs. The inverse-function rule applies:

$$\frac{\partial q_1}{\partial x} = \frac{1}{h_1} \qquad \frac{\partial q_2}{\partial x} = \frac{1}{h_2} \qquad (3\text{-}48)$$

Substituting (3-48) into (3-47),

$$\text{RPT} = -\frac{dq_2}{dq_1} = \frac{\partial q_2/\partial x}{\partial q_1/\partial x} \qquad (3\text{-}49)$$

The RPT equals the ratio of the MP of X in the production of Q_2 to the MP of X in the production of Q_1. If both MPs are positive, as rational operation requires, the slopes of the product transformation curves are negative, and the RPT positive.

The system of product transformation curves in Fig. 3-10 is generated by the implicit production function

$$q_1{}^2 + q_2{}^2 - x = 0$$

The product transformation curves are concentric circles:

$$x^0 = q_1{}^2 + q_2{}^2$$

with $\text{RPT} = q_1/q_2$. Since $q_1, q_2 > 0$, the slopes of the product transformation curves are negative, and the RPT positive throughout.

Constrained Revenue Maximization. If the entrepreneur sells his outputs at fixed prices, his revenue is given by the linear equation

$$R = p_1q_1 + p_2q_2 \qquad (3\text{-}50)$$

where p_1 and p_2 are the prices of Q_1 and Q_2 respectively. An isorevenue line is the revenue counterpart of an isocost line and is defined as the locus of output combinations that will earn a specified revenue. Three of a system of isorevenue lines are presented in Fig. 3-10. They are parallel straight lines with slopes equal to the negative of the ratio of the output prices $(-p_1/p_2)$.

To solve the constrained-maximization problem of an entrepreneur who desires to maximize revenue for a specified input of X, form the function

$$W = p_1q_1 + p_2q_2 + \mu[x^0 - h(q_1,q_2)] \qquad (3\text{-}51)$$

where μ is an undetermined Lagrange multiplier, and set its partial derivatives equal to zero:

$$\frac{\partial W}{\partial q_1} = p_1 - \mu h_1 = 0$$

$$\frac{\partial W}{\partial q_2} = p_2 - \mu h_2 = 0$$

$$\frac{\partial W}{\partial \mu} = x^0 - h(q_1,q_2) = 0$$

Moving the second terms of the first two equations to the right and dividing the first by the second,

$$\frac{p_1}{p_2} = \frac{h_1}{h_2} = \text{RPT} \qquad (3\text{-}52)$$

or substituting from (3-48),

$$\frac{p_1}{p_2} = \frac{\partial q_2/\partial x}{\partial q_1/\partial x} = \text{RPT} \qquad (3\text{-}53)$$

The RPT must be equated with the fixed price ratio. In geometric terms, the specified product transformation curve must be tangent to an isorevenue line.

The first-order conditions may also be stated as

$$\mu = \frac{p_1}{h_1} = \frac{p_2}{h_2}$$

or substituting from (3-48),

$$\mu = p_1 \frac{\partial q_1}{\partial x} = p_2 \frac{\partial q_2}{\partial x}$$

The value of the MP of X in the production of each output must equal μ, the total derivative of R with respect to x.†

The second-order condition requires that the relevant bordered Hessian determinant be positive:

$$\begin{vmatrix} -\mu h_{11} & -\mu h_{12} & -h_1 \\ -\mu h_{21} & -\mu h_{22} & -h_2 \\ -h_1 & -h_2 & 0 \end{vmatrix} > 0$$

Expanding,

$$\mu(h_{11}h_2{}^2 - 2h_{12}h_1 h_2 + h_{22}h_1{}^2) > 0$$

Since $\mu > 0$,

$$(h_{11}h_2{}^2 - 2h_{12}h_1 h_2 + h_{22}h_1{}^2) > 0 \qquad (3\text{-}54)$$

† The total differential of (3-50) is

$$dR = p_1\, dq_1 + p_2\, dq_2$$

or substituting $p_1 = \mu h_1$ and $p_2 = \mu h_2$,

$$dR = \mu(h_1\, dq_1 + h_2\, dq_2)$$

Dividing this by the total differential of (3-44), the total derivative of R with respect to x is

$$\frac{dR}{dx} = \frac{\mu(h_1\, dq_1 + h_2\, dq_2)}{h_1\, dq_1 + h_2\, dq_2} = \mu$$

and is called the marginal-revenue productivity of X.

Taking the total derivative of the negative of (3-47), the rate of change of the slope of a product transformation curve is

$$\frac{d^2q_2}{dq_1^2} = -\frac{1}{h_1^3}(h_{11}h_2^2 - 2h_{12}h_1h_2 + h_{22}h_1^2) \qquad (3\text{-}55)$$

If condition (3-54) is satisfied, the bracketed term of (3-55) is positive. Since $h_1 > 0$, the rate of change of the slope of the product transformation curve (3-55) must be negative. If constrained maxima exist, the product transformation curves are concave from below as shown in Fig. 3-10.

An entrepreneur might desire to minimize the amount of X necessary to obtain a specified revenue. In this case he would minimize (3-44) subject to a revenue constraint. Geometrically, he desires to reach the lowest product transformation curve that has a common point with a specified isorevenue line. For a constrained revenue maximization he desires to reach the highest isorevenue line possessing a common point with a specified product transformation curve. If the product transformation curves are concave from below, every point of tangency between an isorevenue line and a product transformation curve represents the solution of both a constrained-revenue-maximization and a constrained-input-minimization problem. The locus of all points of tangency (see OE in Fig. 3-10) is an *output expansion path* similar in interpretation to the input expansion path of the single-product firm.

Profit Maximization. Express profit as a function of q_1 and q_2:

$$\pi = p_1q_1 + p_2q_2 - rh(q_1,q_2) \qquad (3\text{-}56)$$

and set its partial derivatives equal to zero:

$$\frac{\partial \pi}{\partial q_1} = p_1 - rh_1 = 0$$

$$\frac{\partial \pi}{\partial q_2} = p_2 - rh_2 = 0$$

Moving the price terms to the right and dividing by the marginal costs in terms of X,

$$r = \frac{p_1}{h_1} = \frac{p_2}{h_2} \qquad (3\text{-}57)$$

or substituting from (3-48),

$$r = p_1\frac{\partial q_1}{\partial x} = p_2\frac{\partial q_2}{\partial x} \qquad (3\text{-}58)$$

The value of the MP of X for the production of each output must be equated to the price of X.† The entrepreneur could increase his profit by increasing his employment of X if its return in the production of either product exceeded its cost.

Second-order conditions require that

$$-rh_{11} < 0 \qquad \begin{vmatrix} -rh_{11} & -rh_{12} \\ -rh_{21} & -rh_{22} \end{vmatrix} > 0$$

Expanding the second determinant,

$$r^2[h_{11}h_{22} - (h_{12})^2] > 0$$

Since $r > 0$, the second-order conditions can be stated as

$$h_{11} > 0 \qquad h_{11}h_{22} - (h_{12})^2 > 0 \tag{3-59}$$

Both together imply that $h_{22} > 0$. The marginal cost of each output in terms of X must be increasing.

Consider profit maximization by an entrepreneur whose product transformation curves are given by a system of concentric circles. His profit is

$$\pi = p_1 q_1 + p_2 q_2 - r(q_1{}^2 + q_2{}^2)$$

Setting the partial derivatives equal to zero

$$\frac{\partial \pi}{\partial q_1} = p_1 - 2rq_1 = 0 \qquad \frac{\partial \pi}{\partial q_2} = p_2 - 2rq_2 = 0$$

The first-order conditions can be stated as

$$r = \frac{p_1}{2q_1} = \frac{p_2}{2q_2}$$

Second-order conditions (3-59) are satisfied:

$$2 > 0 \qquad 4 - 0 = 4 > 0$$

3-6. Generalization to m Variables

The analysis of the firm is easily generalized to cover a production process with n inputs and s outputs. The production function is stated in implicit form as

$$H(q_1, \ldots, q_s, x_1, \ldots, x_n) = 0 \tag{3-60a}$$

where (3-60a) is assumed to possess continuous first- and second-order partial derivatives which are different from zero for all its solutions. To

† Following the derivations of (3-53) and note 1, p. 50, it is not surprising to learn that profit maximization requires that $r = dR/dx$. The rate at which the application of an additional unit of X would increase the entrepreneur's revenue must equal its price.

simplify notation, let $q_{s+j} = -x_j$ $(j = 1, \ldots, n)$, and rewrite (3-60a) as

$$F(q_1, \ldots, q_m) = 0 \qquad (3\text{-}60b)$$

where $m = (n + s)$. Input and output levels are distinguished by sign. Input levels are negative, and output levels positive.

Profit Maximization. Profit is the difference between the total revenue from the sale of all outputs and the expenditure upon all inputs:

$$\pi = \sum_{i=1}^{m} p_i q_i \qquad (3\text{-}61)$$

where $p_{s+j} = r_j$ $(j = 1, \ldots, n)$, outputs contribute positive terms to (3-61), and inputs contribute negative terms. The entrepreneur desires to maximize profit subject to the technical rules given by his production function. Form the function

$$J = \sum_{i=1}^{m} p_i q_i + \lambda F(q_1, \ldots, q_m) \qquad (3\text{-}62)$$

and set each of its $(m + 1)$ partial derivatives equal to zero:

$$\frac{\partial J}{\partial q_i} = p_i + \lambda F_i = 0 \qquad (i = 1, \ldots, m)$$
$$\frac{\partial J}{\partial \lambda} = F(q_1, \ldots, q_m) = 0 \qquad\qquad (3\text{-}63)$$

where F_i is the partial derivative of (3-60b) with respect to q_i.

Select any two of the first m equations of (3-63), move the second terms to the right, and divide one by the other:[1]

$$\frac{p_j}{p_k} = \frac{F_j}{F_k} = -\frac{\partial q_k}{\partial q_j} \qquad (j, k = 1, \ldots, m) \qquad (3\text{-}64)$$

If both variables are outputs, (3-64) states the RPT for every pair of outputs—holding the levels of all other outputs and all inputs constant—must equal the ratio of their prices. Assume that the jth variable is an input and the kth an output. Substituting $p_j = r_{j-s}$ and $dq_j/dx_{j-s} = -1$ into (3-64),

$$\frac{r_{j-s}}{p_k} = \frac{\partial q_k}{\partial x_{j-s}} \quad \text{or} \quad r_{j-s} = p_k \frac{\partial q_k}{\partial x_{j-s}} \qquad \begin{array}{l} (k = 1, \ldots, s) \\ (j = s + 1, \ldots, m) \end{array}$$

The values of the marginal productivities of an input with respect to every output must be equated to its price. Finally, assume that both

---

[1] The implicit-function rule $F_i/F_j = -\partial q_j/\partial q_i$ is utilized in (3-64) (see Sec. A-3).

variables are inputs.   The first-order conditions become

$$\frac{r_{j-s}}{r_{k-s}} = -\frac{\partial x_{k-s}}{\partial x_{j-s}} \qquad (j, k = s + 1, \ldots , m)$$

The RTS for every pair of inputs—holding the levels of all outputs and all other inputs constant—must equal the ratio of their prices.

The second-order conditions for the maximization of profit require that the relevant bordered Hessian determinants alternate in sign:

$$\begin{vmatrix} \lambda F_{11} & \lambda F_{12} & F_1 \\ \lambda F_{21} & \lambda F_{22} & F_2 \\ F_1 & F_2 & 0 \end{vmatrix} > 0; \ldots ; (-1)^m \begin{vmatrix} \lambda F_{11} & \cdots & \lambda F_{1m} & F_1 \\ \cdots & \cdots & \cdots & \cdots \\ \lambda F_{m1} & \cdots & \lambda F_{mm} & F_m \\ F_1 & \cdots & F_m & 0 \end{vmatrix} > 0$$

$$(3\text{-}65)$$

Multiplying the first two columns of the first array and the first m of the last by $1/\lambda$, and multiplying the last row of both arrays by λ,

$$\lambda \begin{vmatrix} F_{11} & F_{12} & F_1 \\ F_{21} & F_{22} & F_2 \\ F_1 & F_2 & 0 \end{vmatrix} > 0; \ldots ; (-1)^m \lambda^{m-1} \begin{vmatrix} F_{11} & \cdots & F_{1m} & F_1 \\ \cdots & \cdots & \cdots & \cdots \\ F_{m1} & \cdots & F_{mm} & F_m \\ F_1 & \cdots & F_m & 0 \end{vmatrix} > 0$$

Since $\lambda < 0$ from (3-63), the second-order conditions require that

$$\begin{vmatrix} F_{11} & F_{12} & F_1 \\ F_{21} & F_{22} & F_2 \\ F_1 & F_2 & 0 \end{vmatrix} < 0; \ldots ; \begin{vmatrix} F_{11} & \cdots & F_{1m} & F_1 \\ \cdots & \cdots & \cdots & \cdots \\ F_{m1} & \cdots & F_{mm} & F_m \\ F_1 & \cdots & F_m & 0 \end{vmatrix} < 0 \quad (3\text{-}66)$$

Substitution Effects.   The profit-maximizing entrepreneur will respond to changes in his input and output prices by varying his input and output levels in order to continue to satisfy the first-order conditions (3-63). By total differentation of (3-63)

$$\lambda F_{11} \, dq_1 + \cdots + \lambda F_{1m} \, dq_m + F_1 \, d\lambda = -dp_1$$
$$\cdots \cdots \cdots \cdots \cdots \cdots \cdots \cdots \cdots \cdots \cdots$$
$$\lambda F_{m1} \, dq_1 + \cdots + \lambda F_{mm} \, dq_m + F_m \, d\lambda = -dp_m$$
$$F_1 \, dq_1 + \cdots + F_m \, dq_m + 0 = 0$$

$$(3\text{-}67)$$

Assume that the price changes are given and treat (3-67) as a system of $(m + 1)$ equations in $(m + 1)$ variables: dq_j $(j = 1, \ldots , m)$ and $d\lambda$. Using Cramer's rule (see Sec. A-1) to solve (3-67) for dq_j,

$$dq_j = -\frac{D_{1j} \, dp_1 + D_{2j} \, dp_2 + \cdots + D_{mj} \, dp_m}{D} \qquad (j = 1, \ldots , m)$$

$$(3\text{-}68)$$

where $\mathbf{D}$ is the determinant of the coefficients of (3-67) and $\mathbf{D}_{ij}$ is the cofactor of the element in the ith row and jth column of the array. The determinant $\mathbf{D}$ is the same as the highest-order determinant of (3-65).

The rate of change of q_j with respect to p_k is determined by dividing both sides of (3-68) by dp_k and letting $dp_i = 0$ for $i \neq k$:

$$\frac{\partial q_j}{\partial p_k} = - \frac{\mathbf{D}_{kj}}{\mathbf{D}} \qquad (j, k = 1, \ldots, m) \qquad (3\text{-}69)$$

Since $\mathbf{D}$ is a symmetric determinant, the partial derivatives (3-69) are also symmetric:

$$\frac{\partial q_j}{\partial p_k} = \frac{\partial q_k}{\partial p_j} \qquad (j, k = 1, \ldots, m)$$

There is no counterpart of the consumer's nonsymmetric income effect in the theory of the firm. The total effect for the firm is a symmetric substitution effect.

3-7. Linear Programming

Linear programming, as well as the calculus, is applicable to problems that require the determination of maxima and minima. The calculus encompasses problems in which the quantity to be maximized (or minimized) is stated as a continuous function of the independent variables with continuous first- and second-order partial derivatives. Linear programming encompasses problems in which the quantity to be maximized (or minimized) is stated as a linear function of the independent variables and is subject to a system of linear inequalities stated in terms of these variables. Both sets of mathematical tools have found wide applicability for the problems of the firm. A complete description of linear programming would require mathematics beyond the limits of the present volume. The present description merely outlines the general nature of linear programming with respect to applications for the firm.

Applications for the Firm. Linear programming replaces the continuous production function with a collection of n independent linear activities. In the present context an activity can be regarded as a particular way of combining inputs for the production of an output. The jth activity level (q_j), then, is the quantity of output that is produced using the jth activity. Activities are linear in the sense that the quantity of the ith input required to support the jth activity (x_{ij}) is a linear function of the level of the jth activity:

$$x_{ij} = a_{ij}q_j \qquad \begin{array}{l} (i = 1, \ldots, m) \\ (j = 1, \ldots, n) \end{array} \qquad (3\text{-}70)$$

The coefficient a_{ij} is the quantity of X_i required to produce 1 unit of Q_j. The jth activity is completely described by its coefficients for the m inputs: $(a_{1j}, a_{2j}, \ldots, a_{mj})$. The definition of an activity may vary from one problem to another. The various activities may represent different methods for the production of a single commodity, the production of distinct commodities, or some combination of the two. The assumption of distinct commodities is used here. The alternative definitions follow easily from this assumption.

The concept of the marginal productivity of an input is meaningless within the linear-programming framework. It is not possible to increase an activity level by increasing the quantity of a single input. All inputs must be increased proportionately.

Consider the problem of an entrepreneur who possesses fixed quantities of the m inputs which he desires to allocate among the n activities in such a way as to maximize his revenue. An example might be provided by a farmer who possesses fixed quantities of land, managerial labor, and tractor hours and desires to determine optimal plantings of a number of alternative crops. The entrepreneur's revenue (R) is a linear function of his activity (output) levels:

$$R = p_1 q_1 + p_2 q_2 + \cdots + p_n q_n \qquad (3\text{-}71)$$

where p_j is the fixed price that he receives for a unit of Q_j.† The entrepreneur will select particular activity levels such that R is as large as possible. He is not entirely free in his selection of activity levels. The sum of the amounts of the ith input that he uses to support the n activities cannot exceed his fixed endowment (x_i^0):

$$
\begin{aligned}
a_{11} q_1 + a_{12} q_2 + \cdots + a_{1n} q_n &\leqq x_1^0 \\
a_{21} q_1 + a_{22} q_2 + \cdots + a_{2n} q_n &\leqq x_2^0 \\
&\cdots\cdots\cdots\cdots\cdots \\
a_{m1} q_1 + a_{m2} q_2 + \cdots + a_{mn} q_n &\leqq x_m^0
\end{aligned}
\qquad (3\text{-}72)
$$

The constraints are expressed as weak inequalities, since the entrepreneur is free to use less than his endowments. Furthermore, the activity levels must be nonnegative:

$$q_j \geqq 0 \qquad (j = 1, \ldots, m) \qquad (3\text{-}73)$$

† The analysis is easily extended to the case in which the entrepreneur uses $(s - m)$ variable inputs which he purchases in the open market. Define the net revenue from the production of a unit of Q_j as

$$z_j = p_j - \sum_{i=m+1}^{s} a_{ij} r_i$$

where r_i is the market price of the ith variable input. Now redefine R as the net revenue attributable to the fixed inputs and replace p_j with z_j in (3-71).

Some, or all, may be zero. A negative activity level is mathematically possible, but meaningless in the economic context. The entrepreneur's linear-programming problem is to maximize (3-71) subject to the constraints given by (3-72) and (3-73).

A Method of Solution. Define m new variables u_i $(i = 1, \ldots, m)$ which give the quantities of the m inputs not used for productive activities. The definition of these variables allows the transformation of (3-72) to a system of m equations in $(n + m)$ variables:

$$\begin{aligned}
a_{11}q_1 + a_{12}q_2 + \cdots + a_{1n}q_n + u_1 \qquad\qquad &= x_1^0 \\
a_{21}q_1 + a_{22}q_2 + \cdots + a_{2n}q_n \qquad + u_2 \quad &= x_2^0 \\
\cdots\cdots\cdots\cdots\cdots\cdots\cdots\cdots\cdots\cdots\cdots\cdots\cdots\cdots\cdots\cdots& \\
a_{m1}q_1 + a_{m2}q_2 + \cdots + a_{mn}q_n \qquad\qquad + u_m &= x_m^0
\end{aligned} \qquad (3\text{-}74)$$

The nonuse of an input is interpreted as an activity. Its coefficients are $+1$ for the relevant input and zero for all others. The levels of these activities are also restricted to nonnegative values. If $u_i = 0$, the equality of the ith relation of (3-72) holds. If $u_i > 0$, the inequality holds. The act of not using an input is assumed costless. Therefore, (3-71) is unaffected.

A set of nonnegative values for the activity levels that satisfies (3-74) is a *feasible solution* for the programming problem. There are an infinite number of feasible solutions for this system of m equations in $(m + n)$ variables. The system can be reduced to m equations in m variables by setting n of the activity levels equal to zero. The reduced system can generally be solved and forms a *basic feasible solution* for the programming problem if the values of all its variables are nonnegative. Formally, a basic feasible solution for (3-74) is a feasible solution with not more than m positive activity levels. Less than m may be positive since the solution value for one or more of the m included variables may equal zero. A basic theorem of linear programming states that for every feasible solution there exists a basic feasible solution that yields at least as great a value for R. The programming problem can be solved by finding a basic feasible solution for (3-74) that maximizes R. The importance of this theorem is indicated by the fact that the number of basic feasible solutions is finite.

One method of solving the programming problem is to find all the basic feasible solutions and select the one (it may not be unique) that yields the highest value for R. However, a much easier method is available. Begin by selecting any basic feasible solution. It is not difficult to find one. One possibility is to let $q_j = 0$ $(j = 1, \ldots, n)$ and $u_i = x_i^0$ $(i = 1, \ldots, m)$. Renumber the activity levels v_j $(i = 1, \ldots, m + n)$ where the subscripts $(1, \ldots, m)$ denote the activities included in the initial basic feasible solution and the subscripts $(m + 1, \ldots,$

$m + n$) denote the activities excluded from the solution with levels set equal to zero. Renumber the j indices of the a_{ij} coefficients in the same manner. Using Cramer's rule (see Sec. A-1), the solution values for the included variables can be expressed as linear functions of the m input endowments:

$$v_j = \sum_{i=1}^{m} \frac{\mathbf{D}_{ij}}{\mathbf{D}} x_i^0 \qquad (j = 1, \ldots, m) \qquad (3\text{-}75)$$

where $\mathbf{D}$ is the determinant of the array of the coefficients of the included activities and $\mathbf{D}_{ij}$ is the cofactor of a_{ij}. Total revenue can be written as

$$R = \sum_{j=1}^{m} p_j v_j \qquad (3\text{-}76)$$

where the prices have been renumbered in the same manner as the other variables, and $p_j = 0$ if v_j is the level of a nonuse activity.

The next step is to determine the changes in the levels of the included activities and the corresponding change of total revenue that would result from the diversion of inputs to one of the excluded activities. Let $v_{m+1} = 1$ and deduct the necessary input requirements from the fixed factor endowments. The altered levels of the included activities are given by

$$v_j^* = \sum_{i=1}^{m} \frac{\mathbf{D}_{ij}}{\mathbf{D}} (x_i^0 - a_{i,m+1}) \qquad (j = 1, \ldots, m)$$

Some activity levels will be reduced. Others may be increased. The value of total revenue for the altered solution is

$$R^* = \sum_{j=1}^{m} p_j v_j^* + p_{m+1}$$

The change of total revenue with respect to the introduction of the $(m + 1)$th activity at the unit level is

$$\Delta R_{m+1} = R^* - R = \sum_{j=1}^{m} p_j(v_j^* - v_j) + p_{m+1}$$

The change of total revenue with respect to the introduction of each of the other excluded activities is computed in a similar manner.

If $\Delta R_k \leq 0$ for all of the excluded activities, the programming problem is solved. If $\Delta R_k > 0$ for at least one, the value of total revenue can be increased. Select one of the excluded activities for which $\Delta R_k > 0$. The increase of total revenue from the introduction of the kth excluded activity is $\Delta R_k v_k$. The maximum increase is obtained by making v_k as large as possible. The value of v_k is restricted by the requirement that all activity levels be nonnegative. The levels of the included activities for which $(v_j^* - v_j) < 0$ are reduced with the introduction of the kth excluded activity. For each of these compute the value of v_k at which v_j becomes zero:

$$v_k = -\frac{v_j}{(v_j^* - v_j)}$$

The smallest of these is the maximum permissible value for v_k. The level of one of the included activities is reduced to zero, and the levels of the others remain positive.

A new basic feasible solution is formed by including the kth activity and excluding the one that becomes zero as a result of its introduction. The values of the activity levels for this solution can be expressed in the form of (3-75), and revenue changes computed for the introduction of each of the variables excluded from it. If $\Delta R_k > 0$ for at least one of the excluded activities, a third basic feasible solution is formed by the introduction of an excluded activity. The computational process is repeated until a basic feasible solution is reached with $\Delta R_k \leq 0$ for all of the excluded activities. The optimum solution will be reached with a finite number of iterations.

As an example, consider the problem of an entrepreneur who can use two inputs for the production of three distinct commodities. He desires to maximize

$$R = 2q_1 + 3q_2 + 5q_3$$

subject to

$$1q_1 + 2q_2 + 4q_3 + 1u_1 + 0u_2 = 22$$
$$4q_1 + 2q_2 + 2q_3 + 0u_1 + 1u_2 = 16$$

and $q_1, q_2, q_3, u_1, u_2 \geq 0$. Let q_2, q_3 and u_2 equal zero, and begin with a basic feasible solution containing q_1 and u_1. The relevant determinant is

$$\mathbf{D} = \begin{vmatrix} 1 & 1 \\ 4 & 0 \end{vmatrix} = -4$$

and

$$q_1 = 0(22) + 0.25(16) = 4$$
$$u_1 = 1(22) - 0.25(16) = 18$$
$$R = 2(4) + 3(0) + 5(0) = 8$$

Now let $q_2 = 1$:

$$q_1^* = 0(22 - 2) + 0.25(16 - 2) = 3.5$$
$$u_1^* = 1(22 - 2) - 0.25(16 - 2) = 16.5$$
$$R^* = 2(3.5) + 3(1) + 5(0) = 10$$

The introduction of a unit of Q_2 will increase total revenue by 2 dollars. The introduction of a unit of Q_2 reduces q_1 by 0.5, and u_1 by 1.5 units. The activity level q_1 becomes zero at $q_2 = 8$ (4/0.5), and u_1 becomes zero at $q_2 = 12$ (18/1.5). The maximum permissible value for q_2 is 8 units, and q_1 is dropped from the basic feasible solution.

The second basic feasible solution contains q_2 and u_1. The relevant determinant is

$$D = \begin{vmatrix} 2 & 1 \\ 2 & 0 \end{vmatrix} = -2$$

and
$$q_2 = 0(22) + 0.5(16) = 8$$
$$u_2 = 1(22) - 1(16) = 6$$
$$R = 2(0) + 3(8) + 5(0) = 24$$

Now let $q_3 = 1$:
$$q_2^* = 0(22 - 4) + 0.5(16 - 2) = 7$$
$$u_2^* = 1(22 - 4) - 1(16 - 2) = 4$$
$$R^* = 2(0) + 3(7) + 5(1) = 26$$

The introduction of a unit of Q_3 increases total revenue by 2 dollars. The activity level q_2 becomes zero at $q_3 = 8$ (8/1), and u_2 becomes zero at $q_3 = 3$ (6/2). The maximum permissible value for q_3 is 3 units, and u_2 is dropped from the basic feasible solution.

The third basic feasible solution contains q_2 and q_3. The relevant determinant is

$$D = \begin{vmatrix} 2 & 4 \\ 2 & 2 \end{vmatrix} = -4$$

and
$$q_2 = -0.5(22) + 1(16) = 5$$
$$q_3 = 0.5(22) - 0.5(16) = 3$$
$$R = 2(0) + 3(5) + 5(3) = 30$$

Total revenue would be reduced by 1 if q_1 or u_1 were set equal to 1, and by 0.5 if u_2 were set equal to 1. The third basic feasible solution is the optimal solution. The entrepreneur will produce 5 units of Q_2 and 3 units of Q_3 and will earn a maximum total revenue of 30 dollars.

The Dual Problem. Linear-programming problems always come in pairs. The original problem is to find a nonnegative set of values for q_j $(j = 1, \ldots, n)$ that maximizes

$$R = p_1 q_1 + p_2 q_2 + \cdots + p_n q_n$$

subject to

$$
\begin{aligned}
a_{11}q_1 + a_{12}q_2 + \cdots + a_{1n}q_n &\leq x_1^0 \\
a_{21}q_1 + a_{22}q_2 + \cdots + a_{2n}q_n &\leq x_2^0 \\
&\cdots \cdots \\
a_{m1}q_1 + a_{m2}q_2 + \cdots + a_{mn}q_n &\leq x_m^0
\end{aligned}
\tag{3-77}
$$

The associated, or dual, problem is to find a nonnegative set of values for r_i $(i = 1, \ldots , m)$ that minimizes

$$Z = r_1 x_1^0 + r_2 x_2^0 + \cdots + r_m x_m^0$$

subject to

$$
\begin{aligned}
a_{11}r_1 + a_{21}r_2 + \cdots + a_{m1}r_m &\geq p_1 \\
a_{12}r_1 + a_{22}r_2 + \cdots + a_{m2}r_m &\geq p_2 \\
\cdots \cdots \cdots \cdots \cdots \cdots \cdots \cdots \\
a_{1n}r_1 + a_{2n}r_2 + \cdots + a_{mn}r_m &\geq p_n
\end{aligned}
$$

(3-78)

The original problem contains n variables and m relations; the dual problem contains m variables and n relations. Both systems of relations contain the same coefficients, though the columns and rows are interchanged in the dual problem.

A basic duality theorem states that if a finite maximum exists for R, a finite minimum exists for Z, and

$$\max R = \min Z$$

If the original problem is meaningful, the dual problem always exists, but its interpretation varies from one application to another. In the present example the variables of the dual problem are interpreted as the imputed prices of the m inputs. The value Z is the imputed value of the entrepreneur's input endowment, and the relations of the dual system state that the input costs of producing each output cannot be less than its price. The dual problem does not have an independently meaningful interpretation for the present example. The optimum values of its variables, however, are of interest.

The optimum solution for the dual problem follows easily from the optimum solution of the original problem. Each relation of the dual problem is associated with a variable of the original problem. A basic duality theorem states that the equality holds for the jth relation of the dual system if the jth variable of the original system is included in the maximum solution, and the inequality holds if it is excluded. The maximum basic feasible solution of the original system contains $(m - s)$ production activities and s nonuse activities. Assume that the relations of the dual system are numbered so that the first $(m - s)$ correspond to the productive activities included in the maximum basic feasible solution and are therefore equations:

$$
\begin{aligned}
a_{11}r_1 + a_{21}r_2 + \cdots + a_{m1}r_m &= p_1 \\
a_{12}r_1 + a_{22}r_2 + \cdots + a_{m2}r_m &= p_2 \\
\cdots \cdots \cdots \cdots \cdots \cdots \cdots \cdots \\
a_{1,m-s}r_1 + a_{2,m-s}r_2 + \cdots + a_{m,m-s}r_m &= p_{m-s}
\end{aligned}
$$

(3-79)

This is a system of $(m - s)$ equations in m variables. The number of variables can be reduced with the use of another duality theorem, which states that the ith variable in the dual problem vanishes if the inequality holds for the ith relation in the original system. Since the maximum basic feasible solution includes s nonuse activities, the inequality holds for s of the relations of (3-77). Therefore, s of the variables of (3-79) equal zero. The system of $(m - s)$ equations can be solved for the remaining $(m - s)$ variables.

The relevant equations for the example are

$$2r_1 + 2r_2 = 3$$
$$2r_1 + 4r_2 = 5$$

with the solution $r_1 = 1$ and $r_2 = 0.5$. The minimum value of Z:

$$Z = 1(22) + 0.5(16) = 30$$

equals the maximum value of R.

3-8. Summary

The production function for the one-output–two-variable-inputs case gives the maximum output level that can be secured from each possible input combination. Productivity curves are obtained by treating the quantity of one of the variable inputs as a parameter and expressing output as a function of the quantity of the other. An isoquant is the locus of all input combinations that yield a specified output level.

The entrepreneur may desire to maximize his output level for a given cost, or he may desire to minimize the cost of producing a given output level. The first-order conditions for both problems require that the rate of technical substitution between the inputs be equated to their price ratio. In diagrammatic terms, both require tangency between an isoquant and an isocost line. The locus of such tangency points is the expansion path of the firm. The entrepreneur may allow both output level and cost to vary and maximize his profit. First-order conditions require that the value of the marginal physical productivity of each input be equated to its price. Second-order conditions require that the marginal productivities of both inputs be decreasing.

Given the entrepreneur's production function, cost equation, and expansion path function, his total cost can be expressed as a function of his output level. In the short run, the cost of his fixed inputs must be paid, regardless of his output level. The first-order condition for profit maximization requires the entrepreneur to equate his marginal cost to the selling price of his output. The second-order condition requires that marginal cost be increasing. The entrepreneur is able to vary the levels of his fixed inputs in the long run and therefore is able to select a particular short-run cost function. His long-run total cost function is the envelope of his alternative short-run total cost functions. Long-run profit maximization requires that long-run marginal cost be equated to selling price and that long-run marginal cost be increasing.

A number of interesting results arise if the entrepreneur's production function is homogeneous of degree one. A proportionate variation of all input levels results in a proportionate change of output level and leaves the marginal productivities of the inputs unchanged. Euler's theorem has been utilized to demonstrate that total output is just exhausted if each input is paid its marginal physical productivity. However, the assumptions of competitive profit maximization break down if the entrepreneur's long-run production function is homogeneous of degree one.

Two or more outputs are often produced jointly in a single production process. In the simplest case the quantities of two outputs can be expressed as a function of the quantity of a single input. A product transformation curve is the locus of all output combinations that can be secured from a given input level. The entrepreneur may desire to maximize the revenue he obtains from a given input level. First-order conditions require that he equate the rate of product transformation to the ratio of his output prices. In diagrammatic terms he will operate at a point at which an isorevenue line is tangent to a particular product transformation curve. If he desires to maximize profit, he must equate the value of the marginal productivity of the input with respect to each output to its price.

In the general case n inputs are used for the production of s outputs, and the production function is stated in implicit form. The first-order conditions for profit maximization require that: (1) the rate of product transformation between every pair of outputs equal their price ratio, (2) the value of the marginal productivity of each input with respect to each output equal the input price, and (3) the rate of technical substitution between every pair of inputs equal their price ratio. Substitution effects with respect to price variations can be computed, but there is no counterpart of the consumer's nonsymmetric income effect.

Linear programming encompasses problems in which a linear function is maximized (or minimized) subject to a system of linear inequalities. Many production problems may be placed within this format. An example is provided by the entrepreneur who possesses fixed endowments of inputs and desires to maximize revenue. His production possibilities are described by a number of independent linear activities. The inequality restraints state that he cannot use more than his endowment of any input and that his output levels must be nonnegative. An iterative solution method allows the determination of optimum output levels in a finite number of steps. A dual problem exists for every meaningful linear-programming problem. In the present example the optimum values for the variables of the dual are the imputed prices of the entrepreneur's inputs.

SELECTED REFERENCES

Allen, R. G. D., *Mathematical Economics* (London: Macmillan, 1956). Chapter 18 contains a mathematical statement of the theory of the firm. The necessary algebra is developed in the text.

Bronfenbrenner, M., and Paul H. Douglas, "Cross-Section Studies in the Cobb-Douglas Function," *Journal of Political Economy*, vol. 47 (December, 1939), pp. 761–785. A general discussion of the Cobb-Douglas production function.

Carlson, Sune, *A Study on the Theory of Production* (New York: Kelley & Millman, 1956). An exposition of the theory of the firm in terms of simple mathematics.

Dorfman, Robert, *Application of Linear Programming to the Theory of the Firm* (Berkeley, Calif.: University of California Press, 1951). The optimization problems of the firm are placed within the linear-programming format. A knowledge of matrix algebra is required.

Douglas, Paul H., *The Theory of Wages* (New York: Macmillan, 1934). Includes empirical applications of the Cobb-Douglas production function.

Hicks, J. R., *Value and Capital* (2d ed.; Oxford: Clarendon Press, 1946). The theory of the firm is developed in chaps. VI–VII. The mathematical analysis is contained in an appendix.

Koopmans, Tjalling C. (ed.), *Activity Analysis of Production and Allocation* (New York: Wiley, 1951). A series of essays covering advanced mathematical aspects of linear programming and input-output analysis.

Menger, K., "The Laws of Return," in O. Morgenstern (ed.), *Economic Activity Analysis* (New York: Wiley, 1954), pp. 419–482. A mathematical study of alternative formulations of the law of diminishing returns.

Samuelson, Paul A., *Foundations of Economic Analysis* (Cambridge, Mass.: Harvard University Press, 1948). Chapter 4 contains a mathematical statement of the theory of the firm.

CHAPTER 4

MARKET EQUILIBRIUM

The behavior of consumers and entrepreneurs has been analyzed on the assumption that they are unable to affect the prices at which they buy and sell. The isolated consumer is confronted with given prices, and he purchases the commodity combination that maximizes his utility. The entrepreneur faces given output and input prices and decides to produce the output level for which his profit is maximized. Each must solve a maximum problem. The individual actions of all consumers and entrepreneurs together determine the prices which are considered parameters by each one alone. Prices are determined in the market where consumers and entrepreneurs meet and exchange commodities. The consumer is the buyer and the entrepreneur the seller in the market for a final good. Their roles are reversed in a market for a primary input such as labor. Some inputs are outputs of other firms. Wheat is an input for the milling industry, but an output of agriculture. Both buyers and sellers are entrepreneurs in the markets for such intermediate goods. The analysis of market equilibrium seeks to describe the determination of the market price and the quantity bought and sold. The present chapter is limited to behavior in a single market.

The basic assumptions and characteristics of a perfectly competitive market are outlined in Sec. 4-1. Aggregate demand functions are derived in Sec. 4-2. Aggregate supply functions are derived for the very short, short-run, and long-run periods in Sec. 4-3. This section also contains a discussion of external economies and diseconomies. Demand and supply functions are used for the determination of product-market equilibria in Sec. 4-4. The analysis is applied to the case of spatially separated firms and a problem in taxation in Sec. 4-5. The static market equilibrium analysis is extended to factor markets in Sec. 4-6. The static and dynamic stability of equilibrium is considered in Sec. 4-7, and finally, the properties of equilibrium in markets with lagged supply reactions are discussed in Sec. 4-8. Throughout this chapter it is assumed that the market under consideration is perfectly competitive and that prices remain unchanged in all other markets.

85

4-1. The Assumptions of Perfect Competition

A perfectly competitive commodity market satisfies the following conditions: (1) firms produce a homogeneous commodity, and consumers are identical from the sellers' point of view, in that there are no advantages or disadvantages associated with selling to a particular consumer; (2) both firms and consumers are numerous, and the sales or purchases of each individual unit are small in relation to the aggregate volume of transactions; (3) both firms and consumers possess perfect information about the prevailing price and current bids, and they take advantage of every opportunity to increase profits and utility respectively; (4) entry into and exit from the market is free for both firms and consumers.

Condition (1) ensures the anonymity of firms and consumers. With regard to the firm, it is equivalent to the statement that the product of the firm is indistinguishable from products of others: trade-marks, patents, special brand labels, etc., do not exist. Consumers have no reason to prefer the product of one firm to that of another. The uniformity of consumers ensures that an entrepreneur will sell to the highest bidder. Custom and other institutional rules of the thumb (such as the "first-come-first-served" rule) for distributing output among consumers are nonexistent.

Condition (2) ensures that many sellers face many buyers. If firms are numerous, an individual entrepreneur can increase or reduce his output level without noticeably altering the market price. An individual consumer's demand for the commodity may rise or fall without any perceptible influence on the price. The individual buyer or seller acts as if he had no influence on price and merely adjusts to what he considers a given market situation.

Condition (3) guarantees perfect information on both sides of the market. Buyers and sellers possess complete information with respect to the quality and nature of the product and the prevailing price. Since there are no uninformed buyers, entrepreneurs cannot attempt to charge more than the prevailing price. Consumers cannot buy from some entrepreneurs at less than the prevailing price for analogous reasons. Since the product is homogeneous and everybody possesses perfect information, a single price must prevail in a perfectly competitive market. This can be proved by assuming on the contrary that the commodity is sold at two different prices. By hypothesis, consumers are aware of the facts that (1) the commodity can be bought at two different prices, (2) one unit of the commodity is exactly the same as any other. Since consumers are utility maximizers, they will not buy the commodity at the higher price. Therefore a single price must prevail.

The last condition ensures the unimpeded flow of resources between alternative occupations in the long run. It assumes that resources are mobile and always move into occupations from which they derive the greatest advantage. Firms move into markets in which they can make profits and leave those in which they incur losses. Resources such as labor tend to be attracted to industries the products of which are in great demand. Inefficient firms are eliminated from the market and are replaced by efficient ones.

Perfect competition among sellers prevails if an individual seller has only an imperceptible influence on the market price and on the actions of others. Each seller acts as if he had no influence. Analogous conditions must hold for perfect competition among buyers. A market is perfectly competitive if perfect competition prevails on both the sellers' and the buyers' sides of the market. The market price which was considered a parameter in previous chapters is now a variable, and its magnitude is determined jointly by the actions of buyers and sellers.

4-2. Demand Functions

In general, the ith consumer's demand for Q_j depends upon the price of Q_j, the prices of all other commodities, and his income:

$$D_{ij} = D_{ij}(p_1, p_2, \ldots, p_m, y_i) \tag{4-1}$$

His demand for Q_j may vary as a result of a change in p_k ($k \neq j$), even though p_j remains unchanged, or in response to changes in his income, all prices remaining constant. All other prices and the consumer's income are assumed constant in order to isolate behavior in the jth market. His demand for Q_j is then a function of p_j alone:

$$D_{ij} = D_{ij}(p_j) \tag{4-2}$$

The quantity demanded still depends upon the prices of other commodities and the consumer's income, but these variables are now treated as parameters. Omitting the commodity subscript j in (4-2),

$$D_i = D_i(p) \qquad (i = 1, 2, \ldots, n) \tag{4-3}$$

The aggregate demand for Q at any price is the sum of the quantities demanded by the n individual consumers at that price:

$$D = \sum_{i-1}^{n} D_i(p) = D(p) \tag{4-4}$$

where D is the aggregate demand. The form of (4-4) is the result of the assumptions that all other prices and the incomes of all n consumers are constant. Since the demand functions of the individual consumers are

monotonically decreasing, the aggregate demand function is also monotonically decreasing (see Sec. 2-4). The shape and position of the aggregate demand curve may change with the distribution of income, without
any variation in aggregate income. If one consumer's income is reduced
and another's increased by exactly the same amount, the corresponding
individual demand curves are likely to shift, and the aggregate demand
curve will be affected unless the shifts compensate each other.

In terms of the conventional diagrams the aggregate demand curve is
the horizontal sum of the individual demand curves. Parts (a) and
(b) of Fig. 4-1 represent the demand curves of the only two consumers in a
hypothetical market. Part (c) is their aggregate demand curve which is
constructed by letting the distance OL equal the sum of the distances OM
and ON.

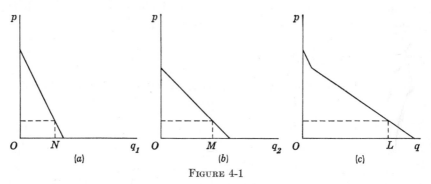

FIGURE 4-1

The aggregate or market demand function confronts the aggregate of
all sellers. The individual entrepreneur considers himself incapable of
influencing market price. A change in his output results in an imperceptible movement along the market demand curve, and he believes that
he can sell any quantity that he is able to produce at the prevailing price.
The demand curve for the output of an individual entrepreneur appears to
him as a horizontal line given by

$$p = \text{constant} \tag{4-5}$$

The market demand curve is not the horizontal sum of the demand curves
faced by individual firms.

The firm's total revenue is

$$R = pq$$

Marginal revenue is the rate at which total revenue increases as a result
of a small increase in sales. In mathematical terms,

$$\frac{dR}{dq} = p$$

since p is a constant. The marginal revenue curve faced by the individual firm is identical with its demand curve.

4-3. The Derivation of Supply Functions

The cost functions of individual firms can be defined for (1) a very short period during which output level cannot vary, (2) a short run during which output level can be varied but plant size cannot, and (3) a long run in which all factors are variable.

The Very Short Period. Assume that the entrepreneur decides every morning how much to produce that day. His output decision is instantly implemented, and he spends the rest of the day trying to sell his output at the highest possible price. He cannot increase his output during the day and sells a given stock of the commodity.[1] Since an output q^0 has already been produced, the marginal cost of any output less than q^0 is zero. Output cannot be increased beyond this point in the very short period, and the marginal cost of higher outputs may be considered infinite. The marginal cost curve is represented by a vertical line at this point.

The firm maximizes profit by selling a quantity for which $MC = p$. Since the MC of any output less than q^0 is zero and the MC of any output greater than q^0 is infinite, the equality $MC = p$ cannot be satisfied, and the firm will expand sales to the point at which price ceases to exceed MC. Therefore, it will sell its entire output (i.e., its entire stock of the commodity) at the prevailing price.[2] This maximizes profit, because the prevailing price is the highest price at which the output can be sold. Quantity sold does not respond to price changes. In general, the aggregate supply function states the quantity that will be supplied by all producers as a function of the price. Since the output of each firm is fixed, the aggregate supply of the commodity is also given and does not depend upon the price. The supply curve is a vertical line, and its distance from the price axis is equal to the sum of the outputs of the individual firms.

The Short Run. The supply function of a perfectly competitive firm states the quantity that it will produce as a function of market price and can be derived from the first-order condition for profit maximization. The horizontal coordinate of a point on the rising portion of the MC curve corresponding to a given price measures the quantity that the firm would

---

[1] The present analysis is simplified by assuming that production and all other adjustments occur instantaneously. It may be more realistic to assume that output is produced as a continuous and steady stream. If production is a time-consuming process, a change in the level of output cannot be realized immediately. The very short period is then any length of time shorter than the period which elapses between the change in the level of inputs and the corresponding change in the output level.

[2] Since the present analysis is static, the costs of holding inventories are neglected.

supply at that price.   The firm's short-run supply curve is identical with
that portion of the short-run MC curve which lies above the AVC curve.

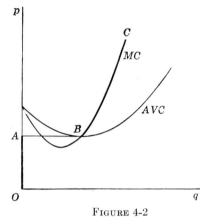

Its supply function is not defined for
outputs less than the abscissa of the
intersection of the MC and AVC
curves.   Quantity supplied would be
zero at all prices less than the ordinate of this point.   The firm's supply
curve consists of the shaded segments OA and BC in Fig. 4-2.

The ith firm's short-run MC is a
function of its output:

$$\mathrm{MC}_i = \Phi_i'(q_i) \qquad (4\text{-}6)$$

FIGURE 4-2

The supply function of the ith firm
is obtained from its first-order con-
dition for profit maximization by letting $p = $ MC and solving (4-6) for
$q_i = S_i$:

$$
\begin{array}{lll}
S_i = S_i(p) & \quad \text{for } p \geqq \text{ minimum AVC} \\
S_i = 0 & \quad \text{for } p < \text{ minimum AVC}
\end{array}
\qquad (4\text{-}7)
$$

The aggregate supply function for Q is obtained by summing the n
individual supply functions.   The aggregate supply is

$$S = \sum_{i=1}^{n} S_i(p) = S(p) \qquad (4\text{-}8)$$

The aggregate supply curve is the horizontal sum of the individual supply
curves.

The second-order condition for maximum profit requires the MC
curve to be rising.   The firm's supply function is therefore monotonically
increasing.[1]   The horizontal sum of monotonically increasing functions is
itself monotonically increasing, and the short-run aggregate supply
function has a positive slope.

Let the total cost curve be

$$C_i = 0.1q_i^3 - 2q_i^2 + 15q_i + 10$$

Then
$$\mathrm{MC}_i = 0.3q_i^2 - 4q_i + 15$$

Setting $\mathrm{MC}_i = p$ and solving for q_i,†

[1] The MC curves of individual firms may have negatively sloped portions in the
relevant range where MC $>$ AVC.   The individual firm's supply function will then
be discontinuous.   In exceptional cases the aggregate supply function need not be
monotonically increasing.

† The mathematical solution (4-9) describes a curve with two branches corresponding to the $+$ and $-$ signs before the square root.   The branch corresponding to the
$-$ sign has a negative slope and can be disregarded, since the second-order condition
requires MC to be rising.

$$q_i = S_i = \frac{4 \pm \sqrt{1.2p - 2}}{0.6} \qquad (4\text{-}9)$$

The individual supply function is relevant for all prices greater than, or equal to, minimum AVC. The AVC function is

$$AVC_i = 0.1q_i^2 - 2q_i + 15$$

The minimum point on the AVC function is located by setting the derivative with respect to q_i equal to zero and solving for q_i:†

$$\frac{d(AVC_i)}{dq_i} = 0.2q_i - 2 = 0 \qquad q_i = 10$$

Substituting $q_i = 10$ in the AVC function gives the value 5. When the price is less than 5 dollars, the firm will find it most profitable to produce no output. The firm's supply function is

$$S_i = \frac{4 + \sqrt{1.2p - 2}}{0.6} \qquad \text{if } p \geqq 5$$
$$S_i = 0 \qquad \text{if } p < 5$$

Assuming that the industry consists of one hundred identical firms, the aggregate supply function is

$$S = 100 \frac{4 + \sqrt{1.2p - 2}}{0.6} \qquad \text{if } p \geqq 5$$
$$S = 0 \qquad \text{if } p < 5$$

At a price of 22.50 dollars the aggregate supply will be 1500 units.

The Long Run. The firm's long-run optimal output is determined by the equality of price and long-run MC. Zero output is produced at prices less than AC and the firm's long-run supply function consists of that portion of its long-run MC function for which MC exceeds AC. The mathematical derivation of the long-run aggregate supply function is similar to the derivation of the short-run supply function. The MC function of the ith firm is

$$MC_i = \Phi_i'(q_i) \qquad (i = 1, \ldots, n) \qquad (4\text{-}10)$$

Setting $p = MC_i$ and solving for $q_i = S_i$

$$S_i = S_i(p) \qquad (i = 1, \ldots, n) \qquad (4\text{-}11)$$

The aggregate supply function is then obtained by adding the n individual supply functions in (4-11). The long-run supply function is positively sloped for the same reason as the short-run supply function.

† The reader may verify that the second-order condition for a minimum is satisfied.

External Economies and Diseconomies.   The individual firm's total costs have been assumed to be a function of only its output level.   However, the firm's total costs may frequently depend upon the output levels of other firms as well.   External economies are realized if an expansion of the jth firm's output lowers the total cost curve of the ith firm. External diseconomies are realized if an expansion of the jth firm's output raises the total cost curve of the ith firm.[1]   External economies or diseconomies may be caused by many factors.   An expansion of the industry's output may lead to the discovery of new and cheaper sources of raw materials and to the diffusion of new technical knowledge.   These phenomena will generally reduce the costs of the ith firm without any diminution of its own output.   Conversely, an increase in the industry's output as a whole may drive up the prices of raw materials and thus increase the total costs of the ith firm.

Assume in general that the long-run costs of the ith firm depend upon the output levels of all n firms:

$$C_i = \Phi_i(q_1, q_2, \ldots, q_n) \qquad (i = 1, 2, \ldots, n) \qquad (4\text{-}12)$$

where q_i is the output of the ith firm.   Each entrepreneur maximizes profit with respect to his own output.   The profit functions are

$$\pi_i = R_i - C_i \qquad (i = 1, 2, \ldots, n) \qquad (4\text{-}13)$$

where $R_i = pq_i$.   Differentiate π_1 with respect to q_1 (considering all other variables constant), π_2 with respect to q_2, etc., and set the resulting partial derivatives equal to zero:

$$
\begin{aligned}
\frac{\partial \pi_1}{\partial q_1} &= p - \frac{\partial \Phi_1(q_1, \ldots, q_n)}{\partial q_1} = 0 \\
\frac{\partial \pi_2}{\partial q_2} &= p - \frac{\partial \Phi_2(q_1, \ldots, q_n)}{\partial q_2} = 0 \\
&\cdots\cdots\cdots\cdots\cdots\cdots \\
\frac{\partial \pi_n}{\partial q_n} &= p - \frac{\partial \Phi_n(q_1, \ldots, q_n)}{\partial q_n} = 0
\end{aligned}
\qquad (4\text{-}14)
$$

The second-order conditions require that $\partial^2 \Phi_i(q_1, \ldots, q_n)/\partial q_i^2 > 0$ for all $(i = 1, 2, \ldots, n)$.   Solving the system of n equations given by (4-14) for $q_1, q_2, \ldots, q_n$, and writing S_i for q_i,

$$
\begin{aligned}
S_1 &= S_1(p) \\
S_2 &= S_2(p) \\
&\cdots\cdots\cdots \\
S_n &= S_n(p)
\end{aligned}
\qquad (4\text{-}15)
$$

[1] Alternative definitions could be stated in terms of the effect of an increase in aggregate output upon the ith firm's (1) marginal cost, its own output level remaining constant, or (2) output level, its use of inputs remaining constant.

Each entrepreneur bases his behavior on his own MC function. The first entrepreneur observes the outputs of all other firms $(q_2^0, q_3^0, \ldots, q_n^0)$ and selects that value of q_1 for his output for which

$$ p - \frac{\partial \Phi_1(q_1, q_2^0, \ldots, q_n^0)}{\partial q_1} = 0 $$

is satisfied. The corresponding optimal value of q_1 may require the other entrepreneurs to adjust their outputs in accordance with their MC functions. This in turn will change the first entrepreneur's optimal output.

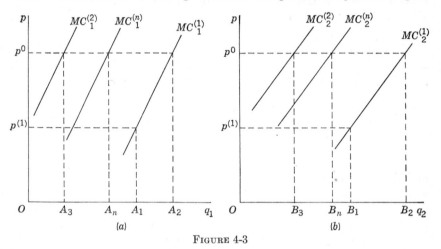

(a)   (b)

FIGURE 4-3

The supply functions (4-15) state each firm's optimal supply as a function of the price after all these adjustments have taken place. The aggregate supply function is obtained as before by adding the individual supply functions (4-15):

$$ S = \sum_{i=1}^{n} S_i(p) = S(p) \tag{4-16} $$

The aggregate supply function may have positive or negative slope in the presence of external economies or diseconomies. The second-order conditions require that the individual MC curves be rising when the outputs of other firms are assumed to be given parameters. However, an expansion of the industry's output not only changes the total costs of individual firms, but may shift the individual MC functions as well. Whether firms in the industry realize external economies or diseconomies, the relevant (positively sloped) portions of their MC curves may shift up or down as a result of an expansion in the industry's output. Figure 4-3 represents the MC curves of two typical firms in the industry. If the price is $p^{(1)}$, the firms' relevant MC functions are $MC_1^{(1)}$ and $MC_2^{(1)}$, and their outputs are OA_1 and OB_1. Assume that the price rises to p^0. Firm

I (Fig. 4-3a) will want to produce OA_2 and firm II (Fig. 4-3b), OB_2. However, the rise of I's output by A_1A_2 units shifts II's MC curve to $MC_2^{(2)}$, and the rise in II's output shifts I's MC curve to $MC_1^{(2)}$. The two firms would seem to produce OA_3 and OB_3 respectively. The diminution of their outputs as compared to their initial output levels will tend to lower their MC curves. The shifting of the MC curves comes to a stop, and the industry's equilibrium output is determined if $MC_1^{(n)}$ is the relevant MC curve for I when II produces OB_n units and if simultaneously $MC_2^{(n)}$ is II's relevant MC curve for an output of OA_n units by I. The final result shows a smaller aggregate output at a higher price. Therefore the aggregate supply curve is negatively sloped in this case.

The fact that the firms are realizing external economies is not sufficient to allow the inference that the slope of the aggregate supply function is negative. Assume that the cost functions of the n firms are

$$C_1 = a_{11}q_1^2 + a_{12}q_2^2 + \cdots + a_{1n}q_n^2$$
$$C_2 = a_{21}q_1^2 + a_{22}q_2^2 + \cdots + a_{2n}q_n^2$$
$$\cdots \cdots \cdots \cdots \cdots \cdots \cdots \cdots \cdots$$
$$C_n = a_{n1}q_1^2 + a_{n2}q_2^2 + \cdots + a_{nn}q_n^2$$

and that the coefficients $a_{11}, a_{22}, \ldots, a_{nn}$ are all positive. If external economies prevail throughout the industry, all a_{ij} $(i \neq j)$ must be negative. Forming the profit functions (4-13) and setting the appropriate partial derivatives equal to zero,

$$p - 2a_{11}q_1 = 0$$
$$p - 2a_{22}q_2 = 0$$
$$\cdots \cdots \cdots \cdots \cdots$$
$$p - 2a_{nn}q_n = 0$$

Solving these equations for the qs and setting $q_i = S_i$,

$$S_1 = \frac{p}{2a_{11}}$$

$$S_2 = \frac{p}{2a_{22}}$$

$$\cdots \cdots \cdots$$

$$S_n = \frac{p}{2a_{nn}}$$

Therefore the aggregate supply function is

$$S = \sum_{i=1}^{n} S_i = \frac{p}{2}\left(\frac{1}{a_{11}} + \frac{1}{a_{22}} + \cdots + \frac{1}{a_{nn}}\right)$$

This function has a positive slope in spite of external economies.

4-4. The Equilibrium of a Commodity Market

Short-run Equilibrium. The market forces which determine the price and the quantity sold can be regarded as manifesting themselves through the aggregate demand and supply functions. The slope of the demand function $[D'(p)]$ is always negative. The slope of the supply function $[S'(p)]$ is always positive in the absence of external economies. $S'(p)$ will be assumed to be positive, unless otherwise specified.

Imagine that buyers and sellers arrive in the market without any foreknowledge as to what will become the going price. Since the commodity is homogeneous, a single price must prevail. The quantity demanded must equal the quantity supplied at the equilibrium price:

$$D(p) - S(p) = 0 \qquad (4\text{-}17)$$

If the equality does not hold for some $p = p^0$, buyers' and sellers' desires are inconsistent: either buyers want to purchase more than sellers are supplying, or sellers are supplying more than buyers wish to purchase. The equality in (4-17) is necessary and sufficient for the buyers' and sellers' desires to be consistent.

Assume that production is instantaneous and producers arrive in the market without any actual output. When the market is open for trading, buyers and sellers begin to bid and attempt to enter into contracts that are favorable to them. Whenever a buyer and seller enter into a contract, they both reserve themselves the right to *recontract* with any person who makes a more favorable offer. It is thus permitted to break existing contracts. Assume that some consumer makes an initial bid and offers a price of p^0 dollars for the commodity. This price is recorded and made public by an auctioneer who is an impartial observer of the trading process. Imagine that the initial price is lower than the equilibrium price. Buyers and sellers will attempt to enter into contracts with each other at the price p^0. Consumers who are willing to buy at this price find that the quantity offered is not sufficient to satisfy their desires, i.e., sellers are not willing to contract for as large a quantity as buyers desire. Some of the consumers who have not been able to satisfy their demand will be induced to raise their bids in the hope of tempting sellers away from other consumers. As soon as this higher price $p^{(1)}$ is recorded and made public by the auctioneer, sellers break their old contracts and recontract at the higher price. As higher prices are offered, the quantity demanded declines, since marginal consumers are driven out of the market and each consumer demands less. Simultaneously the quantity offered by sellers increases. The process of recontracting continues as long as the price announced by the auctioneer is below the equilibrium price, i.e., as long as the quantity demanded exceeds the

quantity supplied.   When the equilibrium price is reached, neither consumers nor producers have an incentive to recontract any further.
Recontracting is discontinued, entrepreneurs instantaneously produce
and deliver the output for which they have contracted, and the exchange

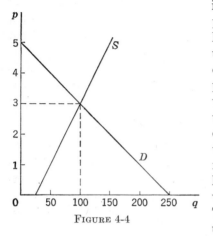

FIGURE 4-4

is completed.   If the arbitrary initial
price p^0 happens to exceed p^e (equilibrium price), some producers will be
unable to sell the quantity which is the
optimal quantity for them at that
price.   They cannot find consumers
who want to enter into contracts with
them.   In order to avoid such an outcome, the sellers who have been unable
to find buyers at the initial price will
reduce the price.   Consumers who
have contracted at the higher price
will find it advantageous to recontract.
The process of recontracting continues
until the equilibrium price is reached.

When p^e is established, both buyers' and sellers' desires are satisfied,
and no one can benefit from further recontracting.

The equilibrium price-quantity combination must satisfy both the
demand and supply functions.   This is the only price-quantity combination for which the desires of buyers and sellers are consistent with each
other.   The equilibrium price is determined by solving the *equilibrium
condition* (4-17) for p.   The equilibrium quantity is determined by substituting the equilibrium price in either the demand or the supply function.   Since the equilibrium price-quantity combination satisfies both
the demand curve and the supply curve, the above operation is equivalent
to finding the coordinates of the intersection point of the demand and
supply curves.

Assume that the demand and supply curves are

$$D = -50p + 250 \qquad S = 25p + 25$$

Setting $D - S = 0$,

$$-50p + 250 - 25p - 25 = 0$$

and therefore $\qquad p = 3 \qquad D = S = 100$

These functions are illustrated in Fig. 4-4.

Long-run Equilibrium.   If plant size is variable, the equilibrium of the
existing firms in the market is given by the intersection of the long-run
supply curve with the corresponding demand curve.   The long-run
cost and supply curves include "normal profit," i.e., the minimum remu-

neration necessary for the firm to remain in existence. It is the profit that accrues to the entrepreneur as payment for managerial services, for providing organization, for risk-bearing, etc. If the intersection of the demand curve and the long-run supply curve occurs at a price at which firms in the industry earn more than normal profit, new entrepreneurs will be induced to enter. The assumption of free entry guarantees that they are able to enter the industry, produce the same homogeneous product, and possess the same complete information as the old firms. The new producers will add their supplies to the already existing supply, and as a result the long-run supply curve will shift to the right. New producers will continue to enter as long as positive profits are made, and the supply curve will continue to shift to the right until its intersection with the demand curve determines a price for which profits are zero.

The converse argument can be made for the case in which existing firms make losses. Some firms will withdraw from the industry, and the aggregate supply will diminish; the supply curve will shift to the left. Firms will continue to leave the industry until the intersection of the demand curve with the supply curve determines a price for which losses (and therefore profits) are zero.

Demand must equal supply, and profits must equal zero for long-run equilibrium. The supply function of the ith firm is $S_i = S_i(p)$. Let n be the number of firms in the industry. Assuming that all firms are identical with respect to their cost functions, the aggregate supply function is

$$S = nS_i(p) = S(p) \tag{4-18}$$

As before, the aggregate demand function is

$$D = D(p) \tag{4-19}$$

In addition to the equality of demand and supply, long-run equilibrium requires that total profit equal zero:

$$\pi = pS - n\Phi_i\left(\frac{S}{n}\right) = 0 \tag{4-20}$$

where $\Phi_i(S/n)$ is the long-run total cost of the ith firm for an output $q_i = S_i = S/n$. The equations (4-17) to (4-20) can generally be solved for the four variables (D, S, p, n). In the long run the forces of perfect competition determine not only the price and the quantity, but the number of firms within the industry as well.

The argument is illustrated in Fig. 4-5. The left-hand side of the diagram shows the cost curves of a typical or "representative" firm. The right-hand side shows the market demand and supply curves with the horizontal scale compressed. The final equilibrium from the industry's point of view is at the intersection of the demand and supply curves, provided that profits are zero. From the entrepreneur's point of view, equilibrium is attained when price equals MC and AC. Optimality is ensured by $p = $ MC, and zero profits by $p = $ AC. Every firm operates at the minimum point of its AC curve in long-run equilibrium, since MC $= $ AC at the minimum point of the AC curve.

The long-run supply curve S is defined to include the supplies offered by firms already in the market, but not the supplies of potential producers. Firms are making positive profits in the situation characterized by the supply curve S (Fig. 4-5). New firms enter, and the supply curve shifts to S'. If the supply curve had been defined to include all supplies (by actual and potential producers, as in S^*), the intersection of the demand and supply curves would have determined the final equilibrium

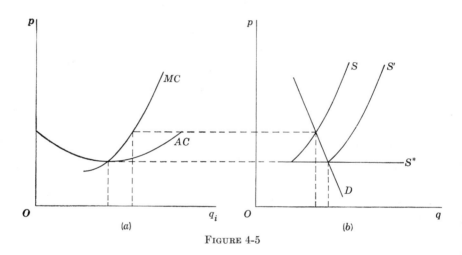

FIGURE 4-5

without any shifting. The supply curve S is given for fixed n in (4-18). S^* is obtained by solving (4-20) for n, substituting this value of n in (4-18), and then solving for S. It is horizontal in the present example, but may be upward sloping if firms do not possess identical cost functions. Since profits are zero for any point on S^*, the ordinate of any point on S^* (the price) is the average cost of producing the output to which it corresponds. S^* is therefore the industry's AC curve.

Differential Cost Conditions and Rent. The symmetry assumption is convenient for purposes of exposition, but is not necessary for the attainment of equilibrium. Firms may choose their own technology, entrepreneurs may differ with respect to organizing ability, and they may have built plants of different size as a result of divergent price expectations. Some entrepreneurs may possess scarce factors such as fertile land that are not available to others. Under any of these conditions the cost functions of all firms will not be identical.

Assume that there are two distinct type of firms. Their long-run AC and MC curves are shown in parts (a) and (b) of Fig. 4-6. Part (c) shows the industry supply curve and five hypothetical demand curves. The supply curve is based on the assumption that there are fifty firms in each category. Assume that the number of firms in each category cannot be increased. For example, the number of low-cost producers (category I) may be unalterably given by the quantity of some scarce resource such as fertile land. New firms are unable to enter category I even though the firms in this category are making profits.

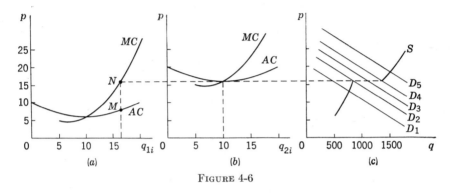

FIGURE 4-6

Consider the demand curve D_4. Each low-cost firm produces an output of 16 units, and each of the other firms produces an output of 10 units. The latter operate at the minimum point of their AC curves and earn normal profits. Each low-cost firm earns a unit profit of NM above normal. If the demand curve shifted to D_2, all high-cost firms (category II) would leave the industry, but each low-cost firm would still earn the same positive profit. They would earn positive profits even if the demand curve were D_1. With D_3 some, but not all, of the high-cost firms would leave the industry. Those remaining would earn a normal profit. If the demand curve were D_5, all firms in the industry would earn profits in excess of normal, and a third group of firms (not shown in Fig. 4-6) might find it profitable to enter the industry. The low-cost firms would still be in the more favorable position.

Assume that the total cost functions of representative firms in the two categories are

$$C_{1i} = 0.04q_{1i}^3 - 0.8q_{1i}^2 + 10q_{1i} \qquad C_{2i} = 0.04_{2i}^3 - 0.8q_{2i}^2 + 20q_{2i}$$

The corresponding average and marginal cost functions are

$$MC_{1i} = 0.12q_{1i}^2 - 1.6q_{1i} + 10 \qquad MC_{2i} = 0.12q_{2i}^2 - 1.6q_{2i} + 20$$
$$AC_{1i} = 0.04q_{1i}^2 - 0.8q_{1i} + 10 \qquad AC_{2i} = 0.04q_{2i}^2 - 0.8q_{2i} + 20$$

The minimum points of the respective average cost curves are at the points $q_{1i} = 10$, $p = 6$ and $q_{2i} = 10$, $p = 16$. The supply curve of an individual low-cost firm is derived by setting $MC_{1i} = p$:

$$p = 0.12q_{1i}^2 - 1.6q_{1i} + 10$$

Solving this quadratic equation for q_{1i},

$$q_{1i} = \frac{1.6 \pm \sqrt{2.56 - 0.48(10 - p)}}{0.24}$$

The minus sign preceding the square root must be disregarded because it corresponds to the situation in which the individual firm's second-order condition for maximization is not fulfilled. Substituting S_{1i} for q_{1i}, the supply curve is

$$S_{1i} = 0 \qquad\qquad\qquad\qquad\qquad \text{if } p < 6$$
$$S_{1i} = \frac{1.6 + \sqrt{2.56 - 0.48(10 - p)}}{0.24} \qquad \text{if } p \geq 6$$

By analogous reasoning the supply curve of the representative high-cost firm is

$$S_{2i} = 0 \qquad\qquad\qquad\qquad\qquad \text{if } p < 16$$
$$S_{2i} = \frac{1.6 + \sqrt{2.56 - 0.48(20 - p)}}{0.24} \qquad \text{if } p \geq 16$$

Maintaining the assumption that there are fifty firms in each category, the aggregate supply function is described by the following set of three equations:

$$S = 0 \qquad\qquad\qquad\qquad\qquad\qquad\qquad \text{if } 0 \leq p < 6$$
$$S = 50\,\frac{1.6 + \sqrt{2.56 - 0.48(10 - p)}}{0.24} \qquad\qquad \text{if } 6 \leq p < 16$$
$$S = \frac{160}{0.24} + \frac{50}{0.24}\,[\sqrt{2.56 - 0.48(10 - p)}$$
$$+ \sqrt{2.56 - 0.48(20 - p)}] \qquad \text{if } p \geq 16$$

Assume that the relevant demand curve is D_1 which has the equation

$$D = -100p + 2050$$

The relevant segment of the supply curve is given by

$$S = 50\,\frac{1.6 + \sqrt{2.56 - 0.48(10 - p)}}{0.24}$$

Setting $D = S$ and solving for p and S gives $p = 13$, $S = 750$.†   If

† If it is not obvious by inspection which supply-curve segment is the relevant one, let $D = S$ for each of the three supply-curve segments separately and solve for the price. Only one of the three prices calculated will be in the range that is appropriate for the particular supply-curve segment used. This segment is the relevant one.

$p = 13$, each low-cost firm will produce 15 units at an average cost of 7 dollars. The high-cost firms produce nothing. The total quantity is, as determined by solving the demand and supply relations, $(50)(15) = 750$ units. Each low-cost firm earns a 90-dollar profit.

Low-cost firms can produce at a lower AC than the others because they possess some scarce factor, such as fertile land, which is not available to the latter. If the demand curve intersects the supply curve at a point at which some firms earn more than normal profit, a considerable profit advantage is enjoyed by those who possess the scarce resource. Some (potential) producers, seeing the large profits made by the low-cost firms, would want to persuade the owners of the fertile land (landlords) to hire it out to them rather than to the firms currently employing it. They would try to accomplish this by offering to pay more for the use of the land than existing firms are paying. The present users would match these offers until competition drove up the amount paid for the use of fertile land to the point where no differential profit advantage could be derived from employing it. The owners will thus be able to exact from the firms using the scarce resource their entire profit in excess of normal. The sums thus exacted are the *rent* paid by the entrepreneur for the use of the scarce resource. One may conclude that no advantage can be derived from being a more efficient (low-cost) producer: the differential profit advantage is wiped out by the extra rent that the low-cost producer must pay. In the present example, the scarce resources employed by each low-cost firm earn a rent of 90 dollars. If an entrepreneur happened to own the scarce resource himself, no actual payment would take place, and the rent would accrue to him. Otherwise the entrepreneur would have to pay 90 dollars for renting the land. Rent is thus defined to be that part of a person's or firm's income which is above the minimum amount necessary to keep that person or firm in its given occupation. Whether it is actually paid to the owner of the scarce resource is immaterial. Distributive shares are distinguished by function, and not by the individual to whom they accrue.

4-5. Applications of the Analysis

The theory of perfect competition can be applied to numerous special cases. Two examples are considered in the present section. The first is an extension of the analysis to the case of spatially distributed firms. The second contains an analysis of the effects of taxation on perfectly competitive output.

Spatially Distributed Firms. Production and consumption are generally assumed to take place at a single point in space. In reality there are many markets in which producers and consumers are spatially separated.

Geographic locations and transport costs are frequently factors of considerable importance.   It is illustrated below how the theory of perfectly competitive markets can be extended to the case in which producers are spatially separated.

Many central markets are supplied by a number of firms located at some distance from them.   Examples are provided by city milk markets. Farmers from the surrounding area supply a central market at varying unit transport costs.   If an entrepreneur produces at any distance from his market, his total cost consists of production and transportation costs:

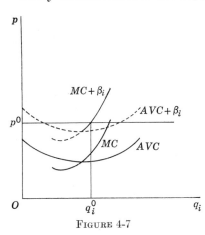

FIGURE 4-7

$$C_i = \phi_i(q_i) + b_i + \beta_i q_i \quad (4\text{-}21)$$

where β_i is the cost of transporting 1 unit of his product to the central market.   His profit is the difference between his total revenue and his total cost of production and transportation:

$$\pi_i = pq_i - \phi_i(q_i) - b_i - \beta_i q_i \tag{4-22}$$

Setting the derivative of (4-22) equal to zero,

$$\frac{d\pi_i}{dq_i} = p - \phi_i'(q_i) - \beta_i = 0$$

or

$$p = \phi_i'(q_i) + \beta_i \tag{4-23}$$

The first-order condition for profit maximization requires that the entrepreneur equate his marginal cost of production plus his unit transport cost to the market price of his product.   The second-order condition, as before, requires that his marginal cost of production be increasing.

The entrepreneur's MC and AVC curves are raised vertically by a distance equal to the amount of his unit transport cost (see Fig. 4-7). His output is determined by the intersection of the rising portion of his $MC + \beta_i$ curve and the horizontal demand curve.   Since the entrepreneur will not supply at prices less than $AVC + \beta_i$, his supply curve coincides with the rising portion of his $MC + \beta_i$ curve which lies above his $AVC + \beta_i$ curve.   An entrepreneur who is not located at the market will supply less at every price (at which he supplies a nonzero amount) than one who is.

The aggregate supply function for the central market is the horizontal sum of the supply curves of the n individual producers:

$$S = \sum_{i=1}^{n} S_i(p) = S(p)$$

where $S_i(p)$ is the supply function of the ith producer. Market equilibrium is attained when supply equals demand.

Assume that fifty of the one hundred firms supplying commodity Q are at location I and the other fifty at location II. It costs 6 dollars to transport to the market a unit of Q from I and 10 dollars from II. All firms possess the same production cost functions, and the total costs of representative firms are

$$C_1 = 0.5q_1{}^2 + 6q_1 \qquad C_2 = 0.5q_2{}^2 + 10q_2$$

where the subscripts 1 and 2 denote firms at locations I and II respectively. The first-order conditions for profit maximization are $p = q_1 + 6$ and $p = q_2 + 10$. Supply functions are obtained by substituting $q_1 = S_1$ and $q_2 = S_2$ into the first-order conditions and invoking the condition that $S_i = 0$ unless $p = AVC + \beta_i$:

$$
\begin{array}{lll}
S_1 = 0 & \text{if } 0 \leq p < 6 & \\
S_1 = p - 6 & \text{if } 6 \leq p & \\
S_2 = 0 & \text{if } 0 \leq p < 10 & (4\text{-}24) \\
S_2 = p - 10 & \text{if } 10 \leq p &
\end{array}
$$

An entrepreneur at I will supply no output if the market price is less than 6 dollars, and an entrepreneur at II will not supply if the market price is less than 10 dollars. The $MC + \beta_i$ curve for an entrepreneur at I is given by $q_1 + 6$, and his $AVC + \beta_i$ by $0.5q_1 + 6$. His supply curve coincides with his $MC + \beta_i$ curve for prices of 6 dollars or more.

The aggregate supply for the central market is given by the following three equations:

$$
\begin{array}{lll}
S = 0 & \text{if } 0 \leq p < 6 & \\
S = 50(p - 6) = 50p - 300 & \text{if } 6 \leq p < 10 & (4\text{-}25) \\
S = 50(p - 6) + 50(p - 10) = 100p - 800 & \text{if } 10 \leq p &
\end{array}
$$

Aggregate supply is zero if price is less than 6 dollars. The fifty entrepreneurs at I will supply a positive amount if the price exceeds 6 dollars, and the fifty entrepreneurs at II will supply if it exceeds 10.

Assume that the aggregate demand function is

$$D = -20p + 1600$$

The appropriate segment of the supply function is given by the third equation of (4-25). Setting $D = S$,

$$-20p + 1600 = 100p - 800$$
$$p = 20 \qquad S = D = 1200$$

From (4-24), each entrepreneur at I supplies 14 units and earns a 98-dollar profit, and each entrepreneur at II supplies 10 units and earns a 50-dollar profit.   In general, if all entrepreneurs produce under the same cost conditions, output and profit are inversely related to the level of unit transport cost.

The existence of more favorable locations may give rise in the long run to rent payments if sites are scarce in the more favorable locations. Competition for the more favorable sites will enable the owners of these sites to charge entrepreneurs a rent which exceeds the rent in the less advantageous location by an amount equal to the profit difference between the two locations, i.e., by 48 dollars.†

Taxation and Perfectly Competitive Output.   A sales tax generally changes the individual entrepreneur's optimum output level.   It shifts the individual supply curve and therefore also the aggregate supply curve. This alters the equilibrium price-quantity combination.   Sales taxes are either *specific* or *ad valorem*.   A specific tax is stated in terms of the number of dollars which the entrepreneur has to pay per unit sold.   An ad valorem tax is stated in terms of a percentage of the sales price.

Assume that the sales tax is a specific tax of t dollars per unit.   The total costs of the representative entrepreneur are

$$C_i = \phi(q_i) + b_i + tq_i \tag{4-26}$$

The first-order condition for profit maximization requires him to produce the output level for which $MC = p$:

$$\phi'(q_i) + t = p$$
or $$\phi'(q_i) = p - t \tag{4-27}$$

The entrepreneur equates the marginal cost of production plus the unit tax to the price.   The second-order condition requires that the MC curve be rising.   The entrepreneur's supply function is obtained by solving (4-27) for q_i and setting $q_i = S_i$ for all prices greater than, or equal to, minimum AVC:

$$S_i = S_i(p - t) \tag{4-28}$$

The aggregate supply function is obtained by summing the individual supply functions:

$$S = \sum_{i=1}^{n} S_i(p - t) = S(p - t) \tag{4-29}$$

† The analysis can be easily extended to the case in which consumers are spatially distributed.

The aggregate supply is a function of the net price $(p - t)$ received by sellers. If, in the absence of a sales tax, aggregate supply is S^0 units at the price of p^0 dollars, entrepreneurs will supply the same quantity S^0 with a sales tax of 1 dollar if the price paid by consumers is $p^0 + 1$ dollars. This is equivalent to a vertical upward shift of the supply curve by 1 dollar. Entrepreneurs are willing to supply less than before at every price. In order to determine the equilibrium price-quantity combination, set demand equal to supply,

$$D(p) - S(p - t) = 0$$

and solve for p.

Let the ad valorem tax rate be v per cent of the sales price. Total costs are

$$C_i = \phi(q_i) + b + vpq_i \tag{4-30}$$

Setting MC equal to price,

$$\phi'(q_i) + vp = p$$
or $\qquad \phi'(q_i) = p(1 - v) \tag{4-31}$

Therefore the individual supply function is

$$S_i = S_i[p(1 - v)]$$

and the aggregate supply function is

$$S = \sum_{i=1}^{n} S_i[p(1 - v)] = S[p(1 - v)] \tag{4-32}$$

Aggregate supply is a function of the net price, and the sales tax involves an upward shift of the supply curve which is proportional to the height of the original supply curve above the quantity axis. The equilibrium price-quantity combination is again determined by setting demand equal to supply.

Let the industry consist of 100 firms with identical cost functions

$$C_i = 0.1q_i^2 + q_i + 10$$

Setting MC equal to price, solving for q_i, and setting $q_i = S_i$,

$$\begin{aligned} S_i &= 0 && \text{if } p < 1 \\ S_i &= 5p - 5 && \text{if } p \geq 1 \end{aligned}$$

The aggregate supply function is

$$\begin{aligned} S &= 0 && \text{if } p < 1 \\ S &= 500p - 500 && \text{if } p \geq 1 \end{aligned}$$

Assume that the demand function is

$$D = -400p + 4,000$$

Setting demand equal to supply, the equilibrium price-quantity combination is

$$p = 5 \qquad D = S = 2,000$$

Assume now that a specific tax of t dollars is imposed. The representative total cost function becomes

$$C_i = 0.1q_i{}^2 + (1 + t)q_i + 10$$

Setting MC equal to price and solving for $q_i = S_i$,

$$S_i = 0 \qquad\qquad \text{if } p < 1 + t$$
$$S_i = 5(p - t) - 5 \qquad \text{if } p \geqq 1 + t$$

Hence the aggregate supply function is

$$S = 0 \qquad\qquad\qquad \text{if } p < 1 + t$$
$$S = 500(p - t) - 500 \qquad \text{if } p \geqq 1 + t$$

Setting demand equal to supply and solving for p,

$$p = 5 + \tfrac{5}{9}\, t$$

If the tax rate is 90 cents per unit of sales, the equilibrium price-quantity combination is

$$p = 5.50 \qquad D = S = 1,800$$

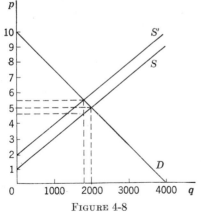

FIGURE 4-8

The price rises and the quantity sold diminishes as a result of the tax. The price rise is less than the amount of the unit tax. The 50-cent increase in the price represents that portion of the unit tax that is passed on to the consumer; the remainder of 40 cents is the burden on the entrepreneur. The example is pictured in Fig. 4-8. The supply curve is S before and S' after the tax is imposed. The tax is 90 cents, the vertical distance between S and S'. The price paid rises from 5 dollars to 5.50, and the price received by entrepreneurs falls to 4.60. The reader may verify that the proportion of the unit tax passed on to the consumer is the greater, the smaller are the slopes (algebraically) of the demand and supply curves. *Ceteris paribus*, the price varies directly, and the quantity inversely with the tax rate.[1]

4-6. Factor-market Equilibrium

The foregoing sections are limited to perfectly competitive commodity markets. Analogous conclusions can be reached with respect to markets for inputs (factors of production). A factor market is perfectly competitive if (1) the input is homogeneous and the buyers are uniform from the sellers' point of view, (2) buyers and sellers are numerous, (3) both buyers and sellers possess perfect information, (4) both buyers and sellers are free to enter or leave the market. Consumers purchase commodities because they derive satisfaction from them. Inputs are purchased for the sake of the contribution they make to production. The demand curves for final products are derived from the consumers' utility functions on the assumption of utility maximization. The demand curves for inputs are derived from production functions on the assumption of profit maximization.

The Demand Function. A rational entrepreneur's optimum input combination satisfies the condition that the price of each input equals the value of its marginal product. Assume that the ith firm's production function is

$$q = f(x_1, x_2) \tag{4-33}$$

Its profit function is

$$\pi = pf(x_1, x_2) - r_1 x_1 - r_2 x_2 \tag{4-34}$$

Setting the partial derivatives of (4-34) equal to zero,

$$pf_1(x_1, x_2) - r_1 = 0$$
$$pf_2(x_1, x_2) - r_2 = 0 \tag{4-35}$$

Solving system (4-35) for x_1 and x_2 and setting $x_1 = D_{i1}$ and $x_2 = D_{i2}$ gives the demand functions of the ith firm for the two inputs:[2]

$$D_{i1} = D_{i1}(r_1, r_2, p)$$
$$D_{i2} = D_{i2}(r_1, r_2, p) \tag{4-36}$$

The demand for an input generally depends upon its price, the prices of

---

[1] The analysis can be used to show the effects of subsidies by treating a subsidy as a negative tax.

[2] A solution exists if the Jacobian of (4-35) is nonvanishing. The reader may verify that the Jacobian is nonzero if the second-order conditions for a maximum are fulfilled.

all other inputs, and the price of the output.   The demand for an input is a *derived demand*, since it depends upon the price of the product and is thus derived indirectly from the demand for the product.   Assuming that all other prices are constant, and neglecting the factor subscripts, the ith firm's demand function for a particular factor is

$$D_i = D_i(r) \qquad (4\text{-}37)$$

where r is the price of the factor.   The aggregate demand function is obtained by summing the individual demand functions.   If there are m firms demanding the input,

$$D = \sum_{i=1}^{m} D_i(r) = D(r) \qquad (4\text{-}38)$$

The Supply Function.   Inputs are either primary or produced.   Produced inputs are the outputs of some other firms.   The supply function of a produced input is the aggregate supply function of the firms which produce it.   Such functions have been derived in Sec. 4-3.   A different procedure is employed in the case of primary inputs such as labor.   It was assumed in Sec. 2-5 that utility is a function of leisure and income:

$$U = g(T - W, y)$$

where T is the total amount of available time (the length of the period for which the utility function is defined) and W the amount of work performed in terms of hours.   It was shown that the utility-maximizing individual allocates his time between work and leisure in such fashion that

$$\frac{g_1}{g_2} = r \qquad (4\text{-}39)$$

where r is the wage rate and g_i is the partial derivative of the utility function with respect to its ith argument.   The g_i's depend upon income and the amount of work performed.   Since $y = rW$, (4-39) contains only the variables r and W.   Solving (4-39) for W and setting $W = S_i$, the labor supply function of the ith individual is

$$S_i = S_i(r) \qquad (4\text{-}40)$$

The supply function states the amounts of work that the individual is willing to perform as a function of the wage rate.   The aggregate supply function is obtained by summing the individual supply functions.   If there are n individuals who are willing to supply labor at some wage rate, the aggregate supply function is

$$S = \sum_{i=1}^{n} S_i(r) = S(r) \qquad (4\text{-}41)$$

The supply function may have either negative or positive slope. If individuals value leisure highly and are more concerned with increasing their time for leisure than raising their incomes, the supply curve of labor may be negatively sloped: the higher the wage, the less work is performed.

Market Equilibrium. Given the demand and supply functions for an input the equilibrium price-quantity combination is determined by invoking the equilibrium condition $D = S$. Market forces similar to those discussed in Sec. 4-4 will change the existing situation whenever the actual price differs from the equilibrium price. Equilibrium is reached only when the quantity demanded equals the quantity supplied. As in product markets, no participant can improve his position by recontracting after equilibrium has been reached.

Since the equilibrium price-quantity combination must lie on the demand curve, it must also satisfy conditions (4-35) from which the demand curve is derived. The equilibrium price of an input is always equal to the value of its marginal product, i.e., the value of the marginal dollar spent on inputs is the same in every use.[1] This equality is a necessary condition for profit maximization, and every entrepreneur can reach his optimum point in a perfectly competitive market if his second-order conditions for maximization are fulfilled.

4-7. The Stability of Equilibrium

Equilibrium price and quantity are determined by the equality of demand and supply. Equilibrium is characterized by the acquiescence of buyers and sellers in the *status quo*: no participant in the market has an incentive to modify his behavior. However, the existence of an equilibrium point does not guarantee that it will be attained. There is no guarantee that the equilibrium price will be established if the market is not in equilibrium when the contracting begins. There is also no reason to assume that the initial price will happen to be the equilibrium price. Moreover, changes in consumer preferences will generally shift the demand curve, and innovations will shift the supply curve. Both factors tend to disturb an established equilibrium situation. The change defines

---

[1] This has an analogue in the theory of consumer behavior. Recall that $f_1 = \lambda p_1$ is one of the equilibrium conditions for the consumer, where f_1 is the marginal utility of the first good and λ is the marginal utility of money. Then $f_1(1/\lambda) = p_1$, or the price of the commodity must equal its marginal utility multiplied by the additional amount of money that has to be paid per unit of additional utility $(1/\lambda)$.

a new equilibrium, but there is again no guarantee that it will be attained.

In general, a disturbance denotes a situation in which the actual price is different from the equilibrium price. An equilibrium is *stable* if a disturbance results in a return to equilibrium and *unstable* if it does not.[1] It was implicitly assumed in the discussion of equilibrium in Sec. 4-4 that the market equilibrium was stable.

Static Stability. A disturbance usually creates an adjustment process in the market. For example, if the actual price is less than the equilibrium price, the adjustment may consist of some buyers raising their bids for the commodity. Static analysis abstracts from the time path of the adjustment process and considers only the nature of the change, i.e., whether it is toward, or away from, equilibrium.

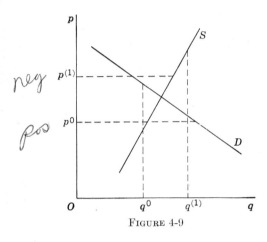

FIGURE 4-9

Define

$$E(p) = D(p) - S(p) \quad (4\text{-}42)$$

as the excess demand at price p. In Fig. 4-9 excess demand is positive at the price p^0, negative at the price $p^{(1)}$. Stability conditions are derived from assumptions about the market behavior of buyers and sellers. The *Walrasian stability condition* is based on the assumption that buyers tend to raise their bids if excess demand is positive and sellers tend to lower their prices if it is negative. If this behavior assumption is correct, a market is stable if a price rise diminishes excess demand, i.e., if

$$\frac{dE(p)}{dp} = E'(p) = D'(p) - S'(p) < 0 \quad (4\text{-}43)$$

Writing p_d for the price at which a given quantity is demanded, p_s for the price at which that same quantity is supplied, and setting $D = S = q$, the demand and supply functions can be solved for the demand price p_d and the supply price p_s:

$$p_d = D^{-1}(q)$$
$$p_s = S^{-1}(q)$$

[1] This is not a rigorous definition of stability and is only one of several alternative definitions. See P. A. Samuelson, *Foundations of Economic Analysis* (Cambridge, Mass.: Harvard University Press, 1948), pp. 260–262.

where D^{-1} and S^{-1} are the inverses of the functions D and S.† The excess demand price is defined as

$$F(q) = D^{-1}(q) - S^{-1}(q) \qquad (4\text{-}44)$$

It is the difference between the price that buyers are willing to pay and the price that sellers are charging for a given quantity. In Fig. 4-9 there is a positive excess demand price at q^0 and a negative excess demand price at $q^{(1)}$. The behavior assumption underlying the *Marshallian stability condition* for a market states that producers will tend to raise their output when the excess demand price is positive and lower it when it is negative. If excess demand price is positive, the producer realizes that consumers are offering a higher price than he is charging and concludes that he can profitably increase the quantity supplied. Analogous reasoning holds for the converse case. Equilibrium is stable in the Marshallian sense if an increase in quantity reduces the excess demand price, i.e., if

$$\frac{dF(q)}{dq} = F'(q) = D^{-1\prime}(q) - S^{-1\prime}(q) < 0 \qquad (4\text{-}45)$$

Since the demand curve is negatively sloped, (4-43) and (4-45) are both satisfied if the supply curve has positive slope.[1] The ordinary supply-demand situation is therefore stable according to both the Walrasian and Marshallian definitions.

If the supply curve is negatively sloped, an equilibrium cannot be stable according to both definitions.[2] Dividing both sides of (4-45) by $D^{-1\prime}(q) \cdot S^{-1\prime}(q)$,

$$\frac{1}{S^{-1\prime}(q)} - \frac{1}{D^{-1\prime}(q)} < 0 \qquad (4\text{-}46)$$

In the usual diagram in which quantity is plotted along the horizontal axis, $D^{-1\prime}(q)$ and $S^{-1\prime}(q)$ are the slopes of the demand and supply curves. By the inverse-function rule,

$$\frac{1}{D^{-1\prime}(q)} = D'(p) \qquad \frac{1}{S^{-1\prime}(q)} = S'(p)$$

Substituting these values into (4-46),

$$S'(p) - D'(p) < 0 \qquad (4\text{-}47)$$

Conditions (4-43) and (4-47) cannot be fulfilled simultaneously. If an

† If $y = f(x)$ can be solved for x, the solution is written as $x = f^{-1}(y)$. The function denoted by f^{-1} is the *inverse* of the function $f(x)$.

[1] The sign of $D'(p)$ is the same as the sign of $D^{-1\prime}(q)$; the sign of $S'(p)$ is the same as that of $S^{-1\prime}(q)$. See the inverse-function rule, Sec. A-2.

[2] The supply curves which may have negative slope are the supply curve for primary inputs such as labor and product supply curves in the presence of external economies or diseconomies. Unstable equilibria may occur only in these cases.

equilibrium is stable in the Walrasian sense, (4-43) holds, and the equilibrium is unstable in the Marshallian sense. The converse statement holds if (4-47) is fulfilled.[1]

It follows from (4-43) and (4-47) that equilibrium is stable in the Walrasian sense if the supply curve is steeper than the demand curve

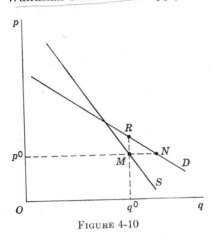

FIGURE 4-10

$[S^{-1\prime}(q) > D^{-1\prime}(q)$ or $D'(p) > S'(p)]$ and unstable in the opposite case. Equilibrium is stable in the Marshallian sense if the supply curve is less steep than the demand curve and unstable in the opposite case. These concepts are illustrated in Fig. 4-10. At the price p^0 the excess demand is MN; therefore competition among consumers will tend to raise the price, and excess demand diminishes. However, the quantity supplied at the price of p^0 is q^0; the corresponding excess demand price RM is positive. The quantity produced will tend to increase, but the excess demand price increases too. The actual price and quantity move farther away from equilibrium.

A negatively sloped supply curve may intersect the demand curve at several points. Such a case is depicted in Fig. 4-11a. Each intersection defines an equilibrium. The successive equilibrium points A, B, C are alternately stable and unstable.[2] The supply curve is steeper than the demand curve at A, and the equilibrium is stable at this point. Another intersection B can exist only if the supply curve becomes less steep than the demand curve; B is therefore unstable. By similar reasoning, C is again stable.

The stability condition (4-43) is no longer sufficient in unusual cases such as the equilibrium point B in Fig. 4-11b. Excess demand is positive at prices less than p^0 and also at prices higher than p^0. The price will tend to rise for downward or upward deviations from equilibrium. Point B is therefore stable for downward and unstable for upward price deviations. Point A is stable, B semistable, and C unstable.

Assertions about the stability of equilibrium depend upon the assump-

[1] No contradiction exists between the two conditions if the supply curve has positive slope. When (4-45) is divided by $D^{-1\prime}(q) \cdot S^{-1\prime}(q)$ the direction of the inequality in (4-46) and (4-47) is reversed because of the division by a negative number. Inequality (4-47) becomes $S'(p) - D'(p) > 0$, which is the same as (4-43).

[2] The argument is based on the Walrasian behavior assumption. An analogous argument can be made in terms of the Marshallian assumption.

tions made concerning the mechanism of the market and the behavior of the participants. One cannot say a priori whether the Walrasian or Marshallian condition is more plausible in reality. In any concrete situation stability of equilibrium can be assessed only after empirical information has been gathered concerning the behavior patterns of the participants in the market.

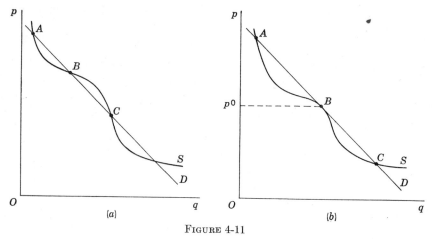

FIGURE 4-11

Dynamic Stability. The static stability conditions are stated in terms of the rate of change of excess demand with respect to price or the rate of change of excess demand price with respect to quantity. The static analysis of stability makes no attempt to investigate the time path of the adjustment process. One would not expect instantaneous adjustments in the present model. If the initial price is not equal to the equilibrium price, it changes, and recontracting takes place. If the new price is still different from the equilibrium price, it is again forced to change. The dynamic nature of the recontracting model may be formally stated as follows. When the market opens some consumer makes an initial bid. This bid is recorded and made public by the auctioneer. After this price is announced, the participants have a specified amount of time (say, one hour) to enter into favorable contracts with each other at this price. After one hour new bids are permitted. The first new bids are recorded and made public by the auctioneer, and a one-hour period of recontracting begins. This process continues until equilibrium is reached. A price is observed in each one-hour period, and the analysis of dynamic stability investigates the course of price over time, i.e., from period to period.[1] Equilibrium is stable in the dynamic sense if the price con-

[1] The prices which are recorded from period to period are potential, rather than realized, prices until equilibrium is reached. As long as $D \neq S$, none of the contracts is executed, and recontracting continues.

verges to (or approaches) the equilibrium price over time; it is unstable if the price change is away from equilibrium. Dynamic stability can also be defined in terms of the convergence of the quantity supplied to the equilibrium quantity. The former definition corresponds to the Walrasian and the latter to the Marshallian definition of stability.

Assuming the Walrasian mechanism to operate in the market, a positive excess demand tends to raise the price. This is expressed mathematically as

$$p_t - p_{t-1} = kE(p_{t-1}) \tag{4-48}$$

where p_t is the price in period t and k a positive constant. Equation (4-48) expresses one possible type of behavior for buyers and sellers. Assuming that there is a positive excess demand $E(p_{t-1})$ in period $(t-1)$, it expresses the assumption that an excess demand of $E(p_{t-1})$ induces buyers to bid a price $p_t = p_{t-1} + kE(p_{t-1}) > p_{t-1}$ in the following period. Assume that the demand and supply functions are

$$D_t = ap_t + b \tag{4-49}$$
$$S_t = Ap_t + B \tag{4-50}$$

Excess demand in period $(t-1)$ is

$$E(p_{t-1}) = (a - A)p_{t-1} + b - B$$

Substituting this into (4-48),

$$p_t - p_{t-1} = k[(a - A)p_{t-1} + b - B]$$
or
$$p_t = [1 + k(a - A)]p_{t-1} + k(b - B) \tag{4-51}$$

The first-order difference equation (4-51) describes the time path of price on the basis of the behavior assumption contained in (4-48). Given the initial condition $p = p_0$ when $t = 0$, its solution is

$$p_t = \left(p_0 - \frac{b - B}{A - a}\right)[1 + k(a - A)]^t + \frac{b - B}{A - a} \tag{4-52}$$

Excess demand is zero in equilibrium. The equilibrium price p^e can be found from (4-49) and (4-50) by setting $D_t - S_t = 0$. Solving for $p_t = p^e$,

$$p^e = \frac{b - B}{A - a}$$

Therefore the constant term in (4-52) is the equilibrium price. The equilibrium is stable if the actual price level approaches the equilibrium level as t increases. The price level converges to p^e without oscillations if $0 < 1 + k(a - A) < 1$. The right-hand side of this inequality holds if

$$a < A \tag{4-53}$$

The left-hand side holds if

$$k < \frac{1}{A - a} \qquad (4\text{-}54)$$

Condition (4-53) is automatically fulfilled if the supply curve has positive slope ($A > 0$). The price level moves upward over time if the initial price is less than the equilibrium price: $[p_0 - (b - B)/(A - a) < 0]$, and downward if it is greater. If the slope of the supply curve is negative, stability requires that the slope of the demand curve ($1/a$) be algebraically greater than the slope of the supply curve ($1/A$); i.e., the supply curve must cut the demand curve from above.[1] Equilibrium is unstable if the supply curve cuts the demand curve from below, and any deviation from equilibrium is followed by increasing deviations from it. If k is sufficiently large and $a - A$ is negative, $1 + k(a - A)$ is also negative, and the price level must oscillate over time.[2]

Both static and dynamic stability depend upon the slopes of the demand and supply curves. Dynamic stability depends in addition on the magnitude of the parameter k which indicates the extent to which the market adjusts to a discrepancy between the quantities demanded and supplied per unit of time. A large k indicates that buyers and sellers tend to "over-adjust": if excess demand is positive, bidding by buyers is sufficiently active to raise the price above the equilibrium level. For example, assume that the equilibrium price is 5 dollars and the actual price bid by buyers is 3 dollars in a given period. Buyers realize that there is an excess demand, but overestimate the adjustment necessary to equilibrate the market and bid 6 dollars in the following period. Sellers become aware of the excess supply and lower their price, but also overestimate the extent of the required adjustment: the price falls to 4 dollars. Each adjustment is in the right direction, but is exaggerated in magnitude. Dynamic analysis thus takes into account the strength of reactions to disturbances.

The dynamic stability of equilibrium can be analyzed diagrammatically in the following fashion. Plotting price along the horizontal axis, the dotted line in Fig. 4-12a represents the excess demand function. Assuming that $k < 1$, the solid line represents $kE(p_{t-1})$. The 45-degree line in Fig. 4-12b represents the locus of points defined by $p_t = p_{t-1}$. The

---

[1] Equations (4-49) and (4-50) state the demand and supply functions with price as the independent variable. Quantity is measured along the horizontal axis and price along the vertical in the customary diagram. Thus the slope of the demand curve is $1/a$, and the slope of the supply curve, $1/A$.

[2] If $1 + k(a - A)$ is greater than -1 (but less than zero), the amplitude of the oscillations decreases over time, and the time path approaches the equilibrium level. If it is less than -1, the market is subject to increasing price fluctuations.

function

$$p_t = p_{t-1} + kE(p_{t-1}) = f(p_{t-1}) \tag{4-55}$$

is obtained by adding the ordinates (corresponding to the same abscissa) of the solid lines in Figs. 4-12a and 4-12b. The result is shown in Fig. 4-12c. Assume that the initial price is p_0. The price in the following period, p_1, is given by the ordinate of the point on $f(p_{t-1})$ directly above p_0. In order to calculate the price in the following period, p_1 is transferred to the horizontal axis by drawing a horizontal line from K to L.

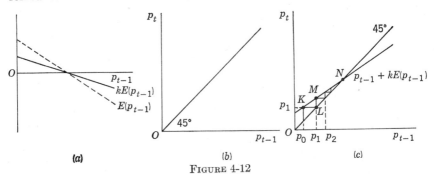

FIGURE 4-12

L lies on a 45-degree line, and the abscissa of each point on it equals its ordinate. The price p_2 is found by moving vertically to M on $f(p_{t-1})$. All subsequent prices are found in this manner. The price level converges in the present example to the equilibrium price given by the intersection of $f(p_{t-1})$ and the 45-degree line.[1] The stability of equilibrium depends upon the slope of the excess demand function and the magnitude of k. If the excess demand function in Fig. 4-12a were positively sloped, the function $f(p_{t-1})$ would cut the 45-degree line from below, and the equilibrium would be unstable. If the excess demand function had negative slope, as in Fig. 4-12a, but k were very large, $f(p_{t-1})$ would have negative slope, and the price level would oscillate.

A dynamic statement of the Marshallian stability condition can be formulated in similar fashion. The conclusions of the static analysis of stability are maintained: equilibrium is dynamically stable in both the Marshallian and Walrasian senses if the supply function has positive slope; equilibrium is stable according to one and unstable according to the other definition if the supply function has negative slope.

The static and dynamic approaches to stability are fundamentally

---

[1] It can be easily verified that point N is the equilibrium point. At N, $p_t = p_{t-1}$ (for the 45-degree line) and $p_t = p_{t-1} + kE(p_{t-1})$. Substituting p_{t-1} for p_t,

$$p_{t-1} = p_{t-1} + kE(p_{t-1})$$

or $kE(p_{t-1}) = 0$. Excess demand equals zero at point N.

different.   Static stability need not imply dynamic stability, but dynamic stability implies static stability.   The reason for this discrepancy is that dynamic analysis is a more inclusive tool for investigating the properties of equilibrium.   Static analysis concerns itself only with the direction of the adjustment and neglects the magnitude of the adjustment from period to period.

Let

$$D_t = -0.5p_t + 100$$
$$S_t = -0.1p_t + 50$$

and let $k = 6$.† The equilibrium is stable in the static Walrasian sense if $D'(p) - S'(p) < 0$.   Substituting from the demand and supply functions, $-0.5 - (-0.1) = -0.4 < 0$.   Dynamic stability requires $-1 < 1 + k(a - A) < 1$.   Substituting the appropriate values gives

$$1 + k(a - A) = -1.4$$

and the required left-hand inequality does not hold.   The market will exhibit explosive oscillations.

4-8. Dynamic Equilibrium with Lagged Adjustment

Producers' supply functions show how they adjust their outputs to the prevailing price.   Since production takes time, the adjustment may not be instantaneous, but may become perceptible in the market only after a period of time.   Agricultural commodities often provide good examples of lagged supply.   An individual farmer may base his production plans on the market price in the fall; the output materializes only during the following summer.

Lagged Adjustment in a Single Market.   Consider the market for winter wheat as an example of a market with lagged supply reaction.   Production plans are made after the harvest.   The output corresponding to these production plans appears on the market a year later.   Assume that the demand and supply functions are

$$D_t = ap_t + b \tag{4-56}$$
$$S_t = Ap_{t-1} + B \tag{4-57}$$

The quantity demanded in any period depends upon the price in that period, but the quantity supplied depends upon the price in the previous period.   It is assumed that the quantity supplied in period t is always equal to the quantity demanded in that period; i.e., p_t adjusts to bring about the equality of D_t and S_t as soon as S_t appears on the market.

† The high value for k indicates that buyers and sellers react violently to disturbances.

This implies that no producer is left with unsold stocks and no consumer with an unsatisfied demand. Therefore

$$D_t - S_t = 0$$

Substituting from (4-56) and (4-57),

$$ap_t + b - Ap_{t-1} - B = 0$$

Solving for p_t,

$$p_t = \frac{A}{a} p_{t-1} + \frac{B - b}{a} \tag{4-58}$$

Assuming that the initial condition is given by $p = p_0$ when $t = 0$, the solution of the first-order difference equation (4-58) is

$$p_t = \left(p_0 - \frac{B - b}{a - A}\right)\left(\frac{A}{a}\right)^t + \frac{B - b}{a - A} \tag{4-59}$$

The solution (4-59) describes the path of the price as a function of time. Some of the possible time paths are illustrated in Figs. 4-13a and 4-13b.

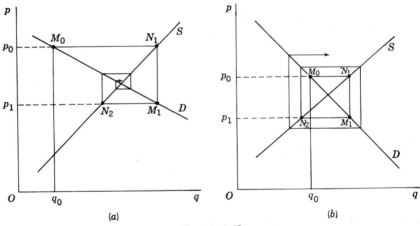

(a)   (b)

FIGURE 4-13

Assume that the initial supply does not equal the equilibrium amount as a result of a disturbance such as a drought. Let the initial supply equal q_0 in Fig. 4-13a. The corresponding initial price is p_0. Consumers demand $p_0 M_0$, and this quantity equals the initial supply. The price p_0 induces entrepreneurs to supply the quantity $p_0 N_1$ in the next period. The price falls instantaneously to p_1. The quantity demanded is then $p_1 M_1$ (which equals $p_0 N_1$, the quantity supplied in that period). In the following period the price p_1 induces a supply of $p_1 N_2$. This process continues indefinitely, producing a cobweb pattern. The price level fluctuates, but converges to the equilibrium level indicated by the intersection of the demand and supply curves. The same mechanism operates in Fig. 4-13b, but the price fluctuations tend to become larger and larger: the market is subject to explosive oscillations.

The conditions for convergence to an equilibrium price can be ascertained from (4-59). The market is in dynamic equilibrium if the price is stable from period to period, i.e., if $p_t = p_{t-1}$. The constant term $(B - b)/(a - A)$ in (4-59) is the equilibrium price.[1] The slope of the demand curve $(1/a)$ is always negative. If the supply curve is positively sloped, A/a is negative, and the price level will fluctuate. The oscillations will decrease in amplitude, have constant amplitude, or increase in amplitude according to whether $|A/a| \lesseqgtr 1$. Therefore the oscillations will increase in amplitude if $|A| > |a|$ or if $\dfrac{1}{|a|} > \dfrac{1}{|A|}$. The oscillations will increase if the slope of the demand curve has greater absolute value than the slope of the supply curve.
The oscillations decrease in the opposite case and are of constant magnitude if the absolute values of the slopes are equal. In the special case in which the supply curve is negatively sloped, A/a is positive, and the price level will not oscillate, but will either increase or decrease continually.[2] The same conditions hold as above: the price will converge to its equilibrium value if the supply curve is steeper than the demand curve (Fig. 4-14), and it will be explosive upward or downward if it is less steep.

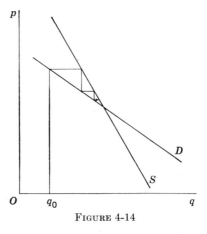

FIGURE 4-14

The conditions for dynamic stability are not the same as in the simple dynamic case where stability depends on the parameter k in addition to the slopes of the demand and supply curves. Buyers and sellers react to excess demand in the simple dynamic case. Excess demand is zero in cobweb situations. Buyers react to given supplies in terms of the prices they offer. Sellers respond to given prices in terms of the quantities they supply in the following period.

Lagged Adjustment in Two Interrelated Markets. Interesting oscillatory behavior can be obtained in the case of two interrelated markets. A case in point is the noted "corn-hog" cycle. A simplified version of this

---

[1] Set $D_t = S_t$ and $p_{t-1} = p_t$ in (4-56) and (4-57) and solve for p_t.

[2] The price may remain constant if the demand and supply curves coincide. No unique equilibrium is defined in this case.

type of market is discussed below. The complete solution is not derived, and the discussion is confined to developing the conditions under which the two markets are stable or unstable.

Let the subscripts c and h refer to corn and hogs respectively. The demand and supply functions for corn are

$$D_{ct} = a_{11}p_{ct} + b_1 \tag{4-60}$$
$$S_{ct} = a_{21}p_{c,t-1} + b_2 \tag{4-61}$$

The corn market possesses the same characteristics which were assumed for the winter wheat market. The demand for corn in any period depends upon the price of corn in the same period, and the corn supply is lagged and depends upon the corn price in the previous period. The demand and supply functions for hogs are

$$D_{ht} = a_{31}p_{ht} + b_3 \tag{4-62}$$
$$S_{ht} = a_{41}p_{h,t-1} + a_{42}p_{c,t-1} + b_4 \tag{4-63}$$

The demand for hogs is a function of the price of hogs in the same period. The supply of hogs depends both upon the price of hogs and the price of corn in the previous period. Equation (4-63) contains two assumptions concerning the behavior of hog producers: their production plans for any period t depend upon (1) the price of their output at time $(t-1)$, and (2) the price of corn at time $(t-1)$. The second assumption reflects the fact that corn is an important input in producing hogs. The price of corn thus tends to affect the hog producers' production plans. A change of $p_{c,t-1}$ results in a shift of the conventional hog supply function.

Equations (4-60) to (4-63) are a system of four simultaneous difference equations which must be solved in order to derive the conditions under which p_{ct} and p_{ht} approach their equilibrium values. Equating aggregate supply and demand in each market,

$$D_{ct} - S_{ct} = 0$$
$$D_{ht} - S_{ht} = 0$$

Substituting from (4-60) − (4-63),

$$a_{11}p_{ct} - a_{21}p_{c,t-1} = b_2 - b_1 \tag{4-64}$$
$$a_{31}p_{ht} - a_{41}p_{h,t-1} - a_{42}p_{c,t-1} = b_4 - b_3 \tag{4-65}$$

Equations (4-64) and (4-65) describe the behavior of prices in the corn and hog markets respectively. The behavior of the corn price is independent of the hog price, since the latter does not enter (4-64). The corn cycle is self-contained and independent of whatever fluctuations may exist in the movement of the hog price. However, the hog price in period t depends upon the corn price in period $(t-1)$. The hog cycle is not independent of the corn cycle. In order to find a solution for p_{ht}, one must

derive an equation which does not contain the price of corn. Solving
(4-65) for $p_{c,t-1}$,

$$p_{c,t-1} = \frac{a_{31}p_{ht} - a_{41}p_{h,t-1} - b_4 + b_3}{a_{42}} \qquad (4\text{-}66)$$

Equation (4-66) holds for any value of t; thus,

$$p_{ct} = \frac{a_{31}p_{h,t+1} - a_{41}p_{ht} - b_4 + b_3}{a_{42}} \qquad (4\text{-}67)$$

Substituting (4-66) and (4-67) into (4-64),

$$p_{ht} - \left(\frac{a_{41}}{a_{31}} + \frac{a_{21}}{a_{11}}\right) p_{h,t-1} + \frac{a_{21}a_{41}}{a_{11}a_{31}} p_{h,t-2} = K \qquad (4\text{-}68)$$

where $K = [(b_2 - b_1)a_{42} + (b_4 - b_3)(a_{11} - a_{21})]/a_{11}a_{31}$. The behavior
of price in the hog market is described by a second-order difference equation, and two initial conditions are necessary to obtain a general solution.
The general solution of (4-68) is of the form

$$p_{ht} = c_1 x_1{}^t + c_2 x_2{}^t + Q \qquad (4\text{-}69)$$

where c_1 and c_2 are constants determined in accordance with the initial
conditions and where Q is the particular solution (see Sec. A-5). Whether
the time path is explosive or convergent depends upon the magnitudes of
x_1 and x_2 which are the roots of the quadratic equation derived from (4-68)
by neglecting the constant term on the right-hand side. The homogeneous equation corresponding to (4-68) is

$$p_{ht} - \left(\frac{a_{41}}{a_{31}} + \frac{a_{21}}{a_{11}}\right) p_{h,t-1} + \frac{a_{21}a_{41}}{a_{11}a_{31}} p_{h,t-2} = 0 \qquad (4\text{-}70)$$

Assume that the solution is of the form x^t. Setting $p_{ht} = x^t$ in (4-70)
and dividing through by x^{t-2},

$$x^2 - \left(\frac{a_{41}}{a_{31}} + \frac{a_{21}}{a_{11}}\right) x + \frac{a_{21}a_{41}}{a_{11}a_{31}} = 0 \qquad (4\text{-}71)$$

The solution of the quadratic equation (4-71) is

$$x = \frac{\dfrac{a_{41}}{a_{31}} + \dfrac{a_{21}}{a_{11}} \pm \sqrt{\left(\dfrac{a_{41}}{a_{31}} + \dfrac{a_{21}}{a_{11}}\right)^2 - 4\dfrac{a_{21}a_{41}}{a_{11}a_{31}}}}{2}$$

$$= \frac{\dfrac{a_{41}}{a_{31}} + \dfrac{a_{21}}{a_{11}} \pm \left(\dfrac{a_{41}}{a_{31}} - \dfrac{a_{21}}{a_{11}}\right)}{2}$$

Therefore

$$x_1 = \frac{a_{41}}{a_{31}} \qquad x_2 = \frac{a_{21}}{a_{11}}$$

The time path of the hog price will converge if both roots are less than unity in absolute value. This requirement is fulfilled if the demand curve is less steep than the supply curve in both markets. Consequently the time paths of prices in the two markets *taken separately* must converge. The assertion that $|x_2| < 1$ is a necessary condition for dynamic stability in the corn market. The assertion that $|x_1| < 1$ is a necessary condition for dynamic stability in the hog market, considering corn prices to be constant. The two assertions together are necessary for stability in the hog market if the effect of changes in corn prices is considered. Stability

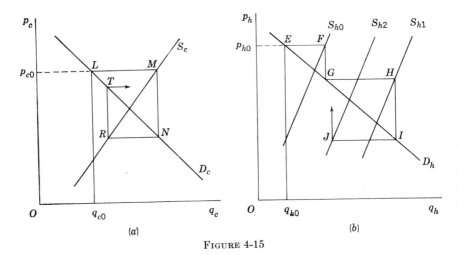

FIGURE 4-15

in the two interrelated markets taken together implies stability in each of them separately, but stability in the corn market alone does not imply stability in both.

A diagrammatic representation may clarify the analysis. Let Fig. 4-15a represent the corn market and Fig. 4-15b the hog market. A change in the price of corn shifts the supply curve for hogs according to (4-63). Denote the initial quantities in the corn and hog markets by q_{c0} and q_{h0} and the initial prices by p_{c0} and p_{h0} respectively. Assume that the relevant supply curve for hogs is S_{h0} if the price of corn is p_{c0}. The movement in the corn market is traced out by the lines LM and MN in Fig. 4-15a. The corresponding movement in the hog market is EF, FG. But the price of corn has fallen by the amount MN. The supply curve for hogs is therefore shifted to the position S_{h1}, and the subsequent movement in the hog market is from G to H and from H to I. During the same time, the supply of corn is reduced by RN, and the corn price is raised by RT. This increase in the price of corn shifts the hog supply curve in the reverse direction to position S_{h2}, and the hog supply is reduced by the amount IJ. These results are based on the assumption that a_{42} in (4-63) is negative, i.e., the higher the price of corn in period $(t - 1)$, the lower the supply of hogs in period t. The conclusion that over-all stability requires both markets to be stable separately is now clear: if the corn market were unstable, fluctuations in the price of corn would tend to become larger and larger, and the hog supply curve would also shift by larger and larger amounts in subsequent periods. The hog market could not be stable. Even if the corn market were stable, and consequently the successive shifts in the supply curve for hogs were of decreasing magnitude, the price of hogs would still exhibit increasing oscillations if the demand curve for hogs were steeper than the supply curve.

If hog producers purchased a sizeable portion of the total corn supply, it might be reasonable to assume that the demand for corn depended upon the prices of both corn and hogs. This assumption would increase the complexity of the model, but would not alter the basic tools of analysis.[1]

4-9. Summary

The theory of perfect competition analyzes the factors that determine price and quantity in markets in which (1) the product is homogeneous and buyers are uniform, (2) buyers and sellers are numerous, (3) buyers and sellers possess perfect information, (4) there are free entry and exit for both buyers and sellers. The participants in the market act as if they had no influence on the price, and each individual regards it as a given parameter.

The price and the quantity bought and sold are determined by supply and demand. The aggregate demand function is derived from the demand functions of individual consumers, which, in turn, are derived from the individual consumers' first-order conditions for utility maximization. The aggregate supply function is derived from individual supply functions which are based on the individual firms' first-order conditions for profit maximization. Equilibrium is attained when demand equals supply. The equality of demand and supply guarantees that buyers' and sellers' desires are consistent. The analysis of a perfectly competitive market is extended to spatially distributed firms and some problems of taxation.

The analysis of perfectly competitive factor markets is similar to the

---

[1] The results of Sec. 4-8 are based on the assumption that the demand and supply functions are linear. If this assumption is relaxed, the variety of possible results increases considerably. The analytical techniques necessary to handle nonlinear cases are correspondingly more difficult and cannot be discussed within the confines of this chapter.

analysis of commodity markets. The equilibrium price-quantity combination is determined by demand and supply, and the equality of demand and supply ensures the consistency of buyers' and sellers' desires. The demand function for a factor is derived from the individual firms' first-order conditions for profit maximization. The supply function for a primary input such as labor is derived from the individual laborers' first-order conditions for utility maximization. Equilibrium in a factor market ensures that the price of a factor equals the value of its marginal product.

The existence of an equilibrium point does not guarantee its attainment. The analysis of the stability of equilibrium is concerned with the effects of disturbances. Equilibrium is stable if a disturbance is followed by a return to equilibrium and unstable if it is not. The static analysis of stability considers merely the direction of the adjustment which follows the disturbance; dynamic analysis considers the degree or strength of the adjustments as well. The conclusions of static and dynamic analysis differ to the extent that a market which is stable according to static analysis may be dynamically unstable. Both analyses make assumptions about the behavior of buyers and sellers. According to the assumption of the Walrasian stability condition buyers and sellers react to excess demand. According to the Marshallian assumption, sellers react to excess demand price. These assumptions are not generally equivalent, and their plausibility must be verified empirically. Special dynamic problems arise in markets in which supply reactions are lagged. In markets of this type both buyers and sellers are assumed to react to price. The time path of the market price oscillates and produces a cobweblike pattern if the supply function has positive slope; an equilibrium is stable if the supply curve is more nearly vertical than the demand curve. The analysis can also be extended to special cases in which two markets are interrelated, and stability conditions can be derived in analogous fashion.

SELECTED REFERENCES

Baumol, W. J., *Economic Dynamics* (New York: Macmillan, 1951). Chapter VII contains a nonmathematical discussion of comparative statics, dynamics, and the cobweb theorem.

Boulding, K. E., *Economic Analysis* (rev. ed.; New York: Harper, 1948). The model of a perfectly competitive economy is developed in nonmathematical terms in parts I and III.

Buchanan, N. S., "A Reconsideration of the Cobweb Theorem," *Journal of Political Economy*, vol. 47 (February, 1939), pp. 67–81. An extension of the cobweb theorem with the use of geometry.

Ellis, H. S., and William Fellner, "External Economies and Diseconomies," *American Economic Review*, vol. 33 (September, 1943), pp. 493–511. Also reprinted in American Economic Association, *Readings in Price Theory* (Chicago: Irwin, 1952), pp. 242–263. A geometric elucidation of these concepts.

Knight, F. H., *Risk, Uncertainty and Profit* (Boston: Houghton Mifflin, 1921). Also reprinted by the London School of Economics in 1937. A nonmathematical analysis of a perfectly competitive economy with emphasis on the effect of uncertainty on profits.

Marshall, Alfred, *Principles of Economics* (8th ed.; London: Macmillan, 1920). Book V contains a nonmathematical analysis of supply and demand and the determination of market equilibrium.

Samuelson, Paul A., *Foundations of Economic Analysis* (Cambridge, Mass.: Harvard University Press, 1948). Chapter IX contains a discussion of market stability. A knowledge of advanced calculus is necessary.

Schneider, Erich, *Pricing and Equilibrium* (London: William Hodge, 1952). Chapter 4 contains a discussion of equilibrium in a single perfectly competitive market in geometric terms.

Stigler, George J., *The Theory of Price* (rev. ed.; New York: Macmillan, 1952). Theories of perfect competition are developed in chaps. 9 and 10 without the use of mathematics.

CHAPTER 5

MULTIMARKET EQUILIBRIUM

The analysis of price determination and allocation can be performed on three levels of increasing generality: (1) the equilibrium of an individual consumer or producer, (2) the equilibrium of a single market, and (3) the simultaneous equilibrium of all markets. The first type of analysis is the subject of Chapters 2 and 3, and the second is the subject of Chapter 4. The present chapter is devoted to the third.

A theoretical analysis contains data, variables, and behavior assumptions that allow the determination of specific values for the variables once the data are known. Consider the analysis of an individual consumer. The data are his utility function, his income, and the prices of all commodities and factors. The variables are the quantities of the commodities he purchases and consumes, and the basic behavior assumption is his desire to maximize utility. The analysis of an individual producer is similar. The data are his production function and the prices of all commodities and factors. The variables are the quantities of the inputs he purchases and the quantity of the output he produces and sells. The behavior assumption is his desire to maximize profit. The analysis of an individual unit sheds no light upon the determination of perfectly competitive prices, however, since all prices are considered parameters.

The analysis of equilibrium in a single market is somewhat more general. A single price is determined as the result of optimizing behavior on the part of a large number of consumers and a large number of producers. The data for the analysis of equilibrium in a commodity market are the utility and production functions of all consumers and producers, the incomes of all consumers, the prices of all factors, and the prices of all commodities other than the one under consideration. The explicit variables are the price of the commodity and the purchases and sales of each consumer and producer. The condition that the market must be cleared, i.e., aggregate demand must equal aggregate supply, is added to the assumptions of utility and profit maximization. The analysis of a single factor market is similar except that the consumers' incomes are determined by their factor sales.

A consumer's demand functions are derived from his equilibrium conditions for utility maximization. If he purchases and consumes two commodities, his demand for each is a function of both prices and his income:

$$D_1 = D_1(p_1,p_2,y) \qquad D_2 = D_2(p_1,p_2,y)$$

In a single-market equilibrium analysis for Q_1, p_2 and y become parameters, and D_1 becomes a function of p_1 alone:

$$D_1 = D_1(p_1,p_2^0,y^0) \qquad D_2 = D_2(p_1,p_2^0,y^0)$$

As a result of these assumptions D_2 also becomes a function of p_1 alone, though this relation is seldom explicit. If the consumer increases his expenditure on Q_1, he must reduce his expenditure on Q_2 by virtue of his budget constraint. The quantities that the consumer purchases of all commodities other than the one under consideration are implicit variables for the equilibrium analysis of a single market. Similar considerations apply to producers. The quantities of the inputs a producer employs become functions of his output price alone.

Every factor and commodity price is a variable for the analysis of its own market and a parameter for the analysis of all other markets. There is no assurance that a consistent set of prices will result from a piecemeal solution, taking one market at a time. It is only by chance that the price assumed for Q_j in the analysis of the market for Q_k will be the same as the price determined in the analysis of the market for Q_j in isolation.

All markets are interrelated. Consumers spend their incomes for all commodities, and the demand for each commodity depends upon all prices. If the goods Q_1 and Q_2 are gross substitutes, an increase in the price of Q_1 will induce consumers as a whole to substitute Q_2 for Q_1. If they are complements, an increase in the price of Q_1 will induce consumers to restrict their consumption of both goods (see Sec. 2-6). Pairs of inputs may also be defined as substitutes or complements. Furthermore, production and consumption are not independent. Consumers earn their incomes from the sale of labor services and other productive factors to producers. As a result of these interrelationships, equilibria for all product and factor markets must be determined simultaneously in order to secure a consistent set of prices.

The data for the determination of a general multimarket equilibrium are the utility and production functions of all producers and consumers and their initial endowments of factors and/or commodities. The variables are the prices of all factors and commodities and the quantities purchased and sold by each consumer and producer. The behavior assumptions require utility and profit maximization together with the condition that every market be cleared.

A multimarket equilibrium analysis is developed for a pure-exchange system in Sec. 5-1 and then extended to include production in Sec. 5-2.

The problems of absolute price determination and the choice of a standard of value are considered in Sec. 5-3. Static and dynamic stability conditions are extended to the multimarket system in Sec. 5-4. Sec. 5-5 contains a brief discussion of the existence and uniqueness of equilibrium solutions, and the empirically oriented input-output system is described in Sec. 5-6.

5-1. Pure Exchange

Pure exchange deals with the pricing and allocation problems of a society in which n individuals exchange and consume fixed quantities of m commodities. Each individual possesses an initial endowment of one or more of the commodities and is free to buy and sell at the prevailing market prices. Purchases and sales may be interpreted as barter transactions. Imagine a consumer whose initial endowment consists of twenty pears and three apples and assume that there are no other commodities. The prevailing market prices determine the terms on which he can barter pears for apples or apples for pears. If the prices are 5 cents for pears and 10 cents for apples, he can obtain one apple by selling two pears or two pears by selling one apple. Given market prices and initial endowments, each consumer's trading will be determined by his ordinal utility function. It would be a rare case if none of the consumers was able to increase his satisfaction level through exchange. A consumer will desire to sell a portion of his initial endowment of some commodities and add to his stocks of others as long as he is able to increase his utility index.

Equilibrium of the ith Consumer. The excess demand of the ith consumer for the jth commodity (E_{ij}) is defined as the difference between the quantity he consumes (q_{ij}) and his initial endowment (q_{ij}^0):

$$E_{ij} = q_{ij} - q_{ij}^0 \qquad (j = 1, \ldots , m) \tag{5-1}$$

If his consumption of Q_j exceeds his initial endowment, his excess demand is positive; he purchases Q_j in the market. If his consumption is less than his initial endowment, his excess demand is negative; he sells Q_j in the market. It is not possible to determine the signs of his excess demands a priori. He may either sell or buy Q_j. The sharp distinction between buyers and sellers used throughout Chapter 4 is no longer possible.

The consumer's income equals the value of his initial endowment:

$$y_i = \sum_{j=1}^{m} p_j q_{ij}^0 \tag{5-2}$$

This is the amount of purchasing power that he would obtain if he sold his entire endowment. In order to relate the present analysis to that of

Chapter 2, assume for the moment that he sells his entire endowment, and uses the proceeds to purchase commodities at the prevailing market prices. The value of the commodities that he purchases and consumes equals his income as given by (5-2):

$$y_i = \sum_{j=1}^{m} p_j q_{ij} \tag{5-3}$$

His purchases will most likely include some of the commodities that he sold, but this does not matter since the acts of buying and selling are assumed costless. The self-canceling transactions can be omitted without affecting the analysis. Therefore, it is henceforth assumed that the consumer does not both buy and sell the same commodity. His budget constraint can be expressed in terms of his excess demands. Subtracting (5-2) from (5-3) and substituting from (5-1),

$$\sum_{j=1}^{m} p_j(q_{ij} - q_{ij}^0) = \sum_{j=1}^{m} p_j E_{ij} = 0 \tag{5-4}$$

The net value of the consumer's excess demands must equal zero. His budget constraint in this form states that the value of the commodities he buys must equal the value of the commodities he sells.

The equilibrium analysis of the consumer as developed in Chapter 2 needs slight modification to be applicable to a consumer in a pure-exchange economy. The consumer's utility index is a function of the quantities of the commodities he consumes, but can be stated as a function of his excess demands and initial endowments by substituting $q_{ij} = E_{ij} + q_{ij}^0$ from (5-1):

$$U_i = U_i(q_{i1}, \ldots, q_{im}) = U_i(E_{i1} + q_{i1}^0, \ldots, E_{im} + q_{im}^0) \tag{5-5}$$

The consumer desires to maximize the value of his utility index subject to a budget constraint. Using the form of the utility function given by (5-5) and the budget constraint (5-4), form the function

$$V_i = U_i(E_{i1} + q_{i1}^0, \ldots, E_{im} + q_{im}^0) - \lambda \left(\sum_{j=1}^{m} p_j E_{ij} \right) \tag{5-6}$$

and set the partial derivatives of V_i with respect to the excess demands and λ equal to zero:

$$\frac{\partial V_i}{\partial E_{ij}} = \frac{\partial U_i}{\partial E_{ij}} - \lambda p_j = 0 \qquad (j = 1, \ldots, m)$$

$$\frac{\partial V_i}{\partial \lambda} = - \left(\sum_{j=1}^{m} p_j E_{ij} \right) = 0 \tag{5-7}$$

Since $dE_{ij}/dq_{ij} = 1$, the first set of equations of (5-7) can be expressed in terms of the utility-index increments:

$$\frac{\partial U_i}{\partial E_{ij}}\frac{dE_{ij}}{dq_{ij}} - \lambda p_j = \frac{\partial U_i}{\partial q_{ij}} - \lambda p_j = 0 \qquad (j = 1, \ldots , m)$$

The first-order conditions for the individual consumer are the familiar ones developed in Chapter 2.   He buys and sells commodities until the rate of commodity substitution for every pair of commodities (the ratio of their utility-index increments) equals their price ratio.   Second-order conditions require that the relevant bordered Hessian determinants alternate in sign (see Sec. 2-7).

If the second-order conditions are satisfied, the ith consumer's excess demand functions can be derived from the first-order conditions.   Use one equation of (5-7) to eliminate λ and solve the remaining m for the excess demands as functions of commodity prices:

$$E_{ij} = E_{ij}(p_1, \ldots ,p_m) \qquad (j = 1, \ldots , m) \tag{5-8}$$

The consumer's excess demands depend upon the prices of all commodities.   If his endowment of Q_j is not zero, his excess demand may be positive for some sets of prices and negative for others.

It was proved in Sec. 2-4 that consumer demand functions are homogeneous of degree zero in income and prices.   A similar theorem can be proved for the pure-exchange barter economy: the consumer's excess demand functions are homogeneous of degree zero in prices, i.e., the excess demands will remain unchanged if all prices are increased or decreased by the same proportion.[1]   A doubling of all prices would double both the value of the consumer's initial endowment and the cost of the commodities he purchases.   If the consumer's endowment consisted of pears and apples and their prices increased from 5 and 10 cents to 10 and 20 respectively, he could still obtain one apple for two pears or two pears for one apple.   In a barter economy of this type the consumer is interested in market exchange ratios rather than absolute price levels.

A graphic description of an individual consumer's equilibrium is contained in Fig. 5-1.   His initial endowment is given by the coordinates of R.   His income line is the locus of all quantity combinations with the same market value as his initial endowment.   If $y_i^{(1)}$ is his income line, he will maximize utility by moving to T.   He will sell RS units of Q_2 and purchase ST units of Q_1 in moving from R to T.   His excess demand for Q_1 is positive, and his excess demand for Q_2 negative.

---

[1] The proof is similar to that used in Sec. 2-4.   Substitute kp_j into the budget constraint in (5-6), set its partial derivates equal to zero to obtain a system similar to (5-7), divide the first $(m - 1)$ equations by the mth to eliminate λ and k, and factor k out of the $(m + 1)$th.

Assume that the price of Q_1 increases relative to the price of Q_2 and that the consumer's new income line is $y_i^{(2)}$. Point L is the position of maximum utility on this income line. The consumer will sell MR units of Q_1 and purchase ML units of Q_2 in moving from R to L. A price change has resulted in a change of the signs of his excess demands. His excess demand for Q_1 is now negative, and his excess demand for Q_2 positive.

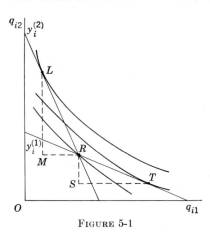

FIGURE 5-1

The irrelevance of absolute price levels is obvious in the graphic analysis. The consumer's initial endowment is given by a point representing physical quantities. His income line is drawn through this point with a slope equal to the negative of the ratio of commodity prices. A proportionate change of both prices will leave their ratio unaffected, and neither the slope nor the position of the income line will change.

Market Equilibrium. An aggregate excess demand function for Q_j is constructed by summing the individual excess demand functions of the n consumers:

$$E_j = \sum_{i=1}^{n} E_{ij}(p_1, \ldots, p_j, \ldots, p_m) = E_j(p_1, \ldots, p_j, \ldots, p_m)$$

Aggregate excess demand is also a function of the m commodity prices. Partial equilibrium is attained in the jth market if the excess demand for Q_j equals zero when the remaining $(m - 1)$ prices are assigned fixed values:

$$E_j(p_1^0, \ldots, p_j, \ldots, p_m^0) = 0 \qquad (5\text{-}9)$$

Condition (5-9) is equivalent to the condition that supply equal demand. The equilibrium price for Q_j is obtained by solving (5-9) for p_j and depends upon the prices assigned to the other $(m - 1)$ commodities. The purchases and sales of the individual consumers are determined by substituting the equilibrium price into the individual excess demand functions.

Multimarket Equilibrium. Now treat all prices as variables and consider the simultaneous equilibrium of all m markets. Aggregate excess demand must equal zero in every market:

$$E_j(p_1, \ldots, p_m) = 0 \qquad (j = 1, \ldots, m) \qquad (5\text{-}10)$$

The equilibrium conditions form a system of m equations in m variables. However, (5-10) contains only $(m - 1)$ independent equations and cannot be solved for the absolute values of the m prices.

The budget constraints of each of the n consumers are not equilibrium conditions, but are identities satisfied for any set of prices. Summing the budget constraints given by (5-4) for all consumers:

$$\sum_{i=1}^{n} \sum_{j=1}^{m} p_j E_{ij} = \sum_{j=1}^{m} p_j E_j = 0 \qquad (5\text{-}11)$$

since $E_j = \sum_{i=1}^{n} E_{ij}$. The aggregate form of the budget constraint is also an identity satisfied for any set of prices. The equilibrium conditions require that every aggregate excess demand equal zero. Clearly if $E_j = 0$, the value of the excess demand for Q_j ($p_j E_j$) must also equal zero. If the first $(m - 1)$ markets are in equilibrium, the aggregate value of their excess demands equals zero:

$$\sum_{j=1}^{m-1} p_j E_j = 0 \qquad (5\text{-}12)$$

Subtracting (5-12) from (5-11),

$$\sum_{j=1}^{m} p_j E_j - \sum_{j=1}^{m-1} p_j E_j = p_m E_m = 0$$

It follows that $E_m = 0$, since $p_m \neq 0$. If equilibrium is attained in $(m - 1)$ markets, it is automatically attained in the mth.

Multimarket equilibrium is completely described by any $(m - 1)$ equations of (5-10). The addition of an mth equation which is dependent upon the other $(m - 1)$ adds no new information. The absolute values of the m commodity prices cannot be determined from the $(m - 1)$ independent equations. The inability to determine absolute price levels should not be a surprising result if it is remembered that consumers are interested only in exchange ratios in a barter-type economy.

Since the excess demand functions are homogeneous of degree zero in prices, the number of variables can be reduced to $(m - 1)$ by dividing the m absolute prices by the price of an arbitrarily selected commodity. If Q_1 is selected, (5-10) may be rewritten as

$$E_j = E_j \left(1, \frac{p_2}{p_1}, \ldots, \frac{p_m}{p_1} \right) \qquad (j = 1, \ldots, m) \qquad (5\text{-}13)$$

The variables of (5-13) are the prices of Q_j ($j \neq 1$) relative to the price of Q_1, i.e., the exchange ratios relative to Q_1. This system of $(m - 1)$

independent equations can generally be solved for the $(m - 1)$ exchange ratios relative to any arbitrarily selected commodity.[1] In Sec. 5-3 it is demonstrated that these $(m - 1)$ exchange ratios are sufficient to determine the barter terms of trade between every pair of commodities.

Once the equilibrium exchange ratios are determined from (5-13), the purchases and sales of each individual can be determined by substituting into the individual excess demand functions. However, a multimarket equilibrium can be determined directly without recourse to aggregate excess demand functions. The individual excess demand functions are homogeneous of degree zero in prices and can be written in the same form as (5-13):

$$E_{ij} = E_{ij}\left(1, \frac{p_2}{p_1}, \ldots, \frac{p_m}{p_1}\right) \qquad \begin{array}{l} (i = 1, \ldots, n) \\ (j = 1, \ldots, m) \end{array} \qquad (5\text{-}14)$$

Now add the condition that every market must be cleared:

$$\sum_{i=1}^{n} E_{ij} = 0 \qquad (j = 1, \ldots, m) \qquad (5\text{-}15)$$

The system formed by (5-14) and (5-15) contains $(mn + m)$ equations with the mn individual excess demands and the $(m - 1)$ exchange ratios as variables. Again one of the equations is functionally dependent upon the others, and the system cannot be solved for absolute price levels.

Two-commodity Exchange. The analysis of pure exchange can be illustrated through an example in which two commodities are exchanged by two individuals. Assume that individual I is endowed with 78 units of Q_1 and no Q_2, and that his utility function is

$$U_1 = q_{11}q_{12} + 2q_{11} + 5q_{12}$$

Substitute $q_{11} = E_{11} + 78$ and $q_{12} = E_{12}$ into his utility function and form the function

$$V_1 = (E_{11} + 78)E_{12} + 2(E_{11} + 78) + 5E_{12} - \lambda(p_1 E_{11} + p_2 E_{12})$$

Set the partial derivatives of V_1 equal to zero:

$$\frac{\partial V_1}{\partial E_{11}} = E_{12} + 2 - \lambda p_1 = 0$$

$$\frac{\partial V_1}{\partial E_{12}} = E_{11} + 83 - \lambda p_2 = 0$$

$$\frac{\partial V_1}{\partial \lambda} = -(p_1 E_{11} + p_2 E_{12}) = 0$$

The reader can verify that the second-order condition presented in Sec. 2-2 is satisfied.

[1] This is not always true (see Sec. 5-5 below).

Eliminating λ and solving the first-order conditions for E_{11} and E_{12}, I's excess demand functions are

$$E_{11} = \frac{p_2}{p_1} - 41.5 \qquad E_{12} = 41.5 \frac{p_1}{p_2} - 1$$

His excess demands are functions of the commodity price ratio and are homogeneous of degree zero in prices. I's budget constraint is satisfied for any set of prices:

$$p_1 \left(\frac{p_2}{p_1} - 41.5 \right) + p_2 \left(41.5 \frac{p_1}{p_2} - 1 \right) = 0$$

The excess demand functions possess the usual properties. An increase of p_1 relative to p_2 will decrease E_{11} and increase E_{12}. An increase of p_2 relative to p_1 will increase E_{11} and decrease E_{12}.

Assume that II's utility function is

$$U_2 = q_{21}q_{22} + 4q_{21} + 2q_{22}$$

and that his endowment consists of 164 units of Q_2 and no Q_1. A derivation similar to that employed for I yields the excess demand functions

$$E_{21} = 84 \frac{p_2}{p_1} - 1 \qquad E_{22} = \frac{p_1}{p_2} - 84$$

II's budget constraint is always fulfilled, and his excess demands are homogeneous of degree zero in prices.

Invoking the condition that each market must be cleared

$$E_1 = E_{11} + E_{21} = 85 \frac{p_2}{p_1} - 42.5 = 0$$

$$E_2 = E_{12} + E_{22} = 42.5 \frac{p_1}{p_2} - 85 = 0$$

Either equation is sufficient for the determination of the equilibrium exchange ratio. Solving the first equation, $p_2/p_1 = 0.5$. Solving the second, $p_1/p_2 = 2$. The solutions are identical. In equilibrium 1 unit of Q_1 can be exchanged for 2 units of Q_2.

Substituting the equilibrium price ratio into the individual excess demand functions,

$$E_{11} = -41 \qquad E_{12} = 82 \qquad E_{21} = 41 \qquad E_{22} = -82$$

I gives 41 units of Q_1 to II in exchange for 82 units of Q_2.

5-2. Production and Exchange

The multimarket equilibrium analysis is now extended to an economy in which goods are both produced and exchanged. The consumers' initial endowments consist of primary factors such as land and labor power. A consumer generally sells factors and uses the proceeds to purchase produced commodities, but may withhold a portion of his initial endowment for direct consumption without further processing. Labor power provides an example. The consumer will seldom supply the full amount of his labor power, but will generally reserve a portion for final consumption in the form of leisure. If a consumer possesses a factor from which he derives no utility, he will supply his entire endowment of that factor regardless of commodity and factor prices. Some consumers may sell one factor and purchase another. An example is provided by a landlord who employs domestic servants. Entrepreneurs use both factors and produced goods for the production of commodities. The produced commodities are useful both as inputs and final consumption goods.[1]

Equilibrium of the ith Consumer. Each of the n consumers is endowed with initial stocks of one or more of s primary goods. The initial endowment of the ith consumer is denoted by $(q_{i1}^0, q_{i2}^0, \ldots, q_{is}^0)$. He may sell (and buy) at the prevailing market prices, $(p_1, p_2, \ldots, p_s)$. The consumer derives utility from the quantities of the primary factors he retains and the quantities of the $(m - s)$ produced commodities he purchases:

$$U_i = U_i(q_{i1}, q_{i2}, \ldots, q_{im}) \tag{5-16}$$

where the produced commodities are numbered from $(s + 1)$ through m.

The consumer's excess demand for a factor equals the quantity he consumes less his initial stock, and his excess demand for a commodity equals the quantity he consumes:

$$
\begin{aligned}
E_{ij} &= q_{ij} - q_{ij}^0 & (j = 1, \ldots, s) \\
E_{ij} &= q_{ij} & (j = s + 1, \ldots, m)
\end{aligned}
\tag{5-17}
$$

The excess demand for a factor may be positive, negative, or zero, but will most often be negative, since the consumer generally sells factors in order to buy commodities. His excess demands for commodities must be positive or zero.

The consumer's income equals the value of his stock of factors:

$$y_i = \sum_{j=1}^{s} p_j q_{ij}^0 \tag{5-18}$$

He is free to sell from this stock in order to purchase commodities and factors. The value of the factors and commodities he consumes must also

---

[1] It is sometimes necessary to distinguish pure intermediate goods which are not desired by consumers. They are produced by entrepreneurs and used as inputs.

equal his income:

$$y_i = \sum_{j=1}^{m} p_j q_{ij} \tag{5-19}$$

The consumer's budget constraint is obtained by subtracting (5-18) from (5-19) and substituting from (5-17):

$$\sum_{j=1}^{m} p_j E_{ij} = 0 \tag{5-20}$$

The net value of his excess demands for factors and commodities must equal zero.

The consumer again desires to maximize his utility level subject to his budget constraint. Form the function

$$Z_i = U_i(E_{i1} + q_{i1}^0, \ldots, E_{is} + q_{is}^0, E_{i,s+1}, \ldots, E_{im}) - \mu \left(\sum_{j=1}^{m} p_j E_{ij} \right)$$

and set the partial derivatives of Z_i equal to zero:

$$\frac{\partial Z_i}{\partial E_{ij}} = \frac{\partial U_i}{\partial E_{ij}} - \mu p_j = 0 \qquad (j = 1, \ldots, m)$$

$$\frac{\partial Z_i}{\partial \mu} = - \sum_{j=1}^{m} p_j E_{ij} = 0 \tag{5-21}$$

First-order conditions require that the consumer equate the RCS for every pair of goods to their price ratio.

If second-order conditions are satisfied, the consumer's excess demand functions are obtained by solving (5-21) for the m excess demands as functions of the m prices:

$$E_{ij} = E_{ij}(p_1, \ldots, p_m) \qquad (j = 1, \ldots, m) \tag{5-22}$$

His excess demands for factors and commodities depend upon the prices of all factors and commodities and are homogeneous of degree zero with respect to the prices of all factors and commodities.

Equilibrium of the hth Firm in the jth Industry. Each firm combines inputs for the production of a single commodity according to the technical rules specified in its production function:[1]

$$\bar{q}_{hj} = f_{hj}(q_{hj1}^*, \ldots, q_{hjm}^*) \tag{5-23}$$

where $\bar{q}_{hj}$ is the output level of the hth firm in the jth industry and q_{hjk}^* is the quantity of the kth good which the entrepreneur uses as an input. Both the s factors and $(m - s)$ commodities serve as inputs.

[1] Production is sometimes introduced with the alternative assumption that each firm jointly produces all commodities.

The entrepreneur's profit is his competitive revenue less the costs of his inputs:

$$\pi_{hj} = p_j f_{hj}(q^*_{hj1}, \ldots, q^*_{hjm}) - \sum_{k=1}^{m} p_k q^*_{hjk} \qquad (5\text{-}24)$$

Setting the partial derivatives of profit with respect to each of the inputs equal to zero,

$$\frac{\partial \pi_{hj}}{\partial q^*_{hjk}} = p_j \frac{\partial \bar{q}_{hj}}{\partial q^*_{hjk}} - p_k = 0 \qquad (k = 1, \ldots, m) \qquad (5\text{-}25)$$

The entrepreneur will utilize each input up to a point at which the value of its marginal physical productivity equals its price. The second-order conditions require that the principal minors of the relevant Hessian determinant alternate in sign (see Sec. 3-2) and imply that the marginal physical productivity of every input is decreasing.

Conditions (5-25) imply that $\partial q_{hj}/\partial q^*_{hjj} = 1$. If the entrepreneur utilizes his own output as an input—as a wheat farmer utilizes wheat for seed—he will utilize it up to a point at which its marginal physical productivity equals unity.

The entrepreneur's excess demand functions for his inputs are obtained by solving the m equations of (5-25) for $q^*_{hjk} = E^*_{hjk}$:

$$E^*_{hjk} = E^*_{hjk}(p_1, \ldots, p_m) \qquad (k = 1, \ldots, m) \qquad (5\text{-}26)$$

The quantity of each input he purchases is a function of all prices. Since the entrepreneur never supplies (sells) inputs, his excess demands are always nonnegative.

If the jth industry contains N_j identical firms, its aggregate excess demand for the kth input equals the excess demand of a representative firm multiplied by the number of firms within the industry:

$$E^*_{jk} = N_j E^*_{hjk}(p_1, \ldots, p_m) = E^*_{jk}(p_1, \ldots, p_m, N_j) \qquad (5\text{-}27)$$

An industry's excess demand for an input is a function of all prices and the number of firms within the industry.

The entrepreneur's excess demand for (supply of) his own output is determined by substituting the excess demand functions for his inputs (5-26) into his production function (5-23) and letting $\bar{E}_{hj} = -\bar{q}_{hj}$:†

$$\bar{E}_{hj} = -f_{hj}[E^*_{hj1}(p_1, \ldots, p_m), \ldots, E^*_{hjm}(p_1, \ldots, p_m)]$$

† Separate excess demand functions are defined for Q_j as an output and as an input. The two could be combined into a single net excess demand without affecting the analysis.

or more simply

$$\bar{E}_{hj} = \bar{E}_{hj}(p_1, \ldots ,p_m)$$

The excess demand for the industry as a whole equals the excess demand of a representative firm multiplied by the number of firms:

$$\bar{E}_j = N_j \bar{E}_{hj}(p_1, \ldots ,p_m) = \bar{E}_j(p_1, \ldots ,p_m,N_j) \qquad (5\text{-}28)$$

The industry's excess demand depends upon the prices of all goods and the number of firms within the industry.

The entrepreneur's excess demand functions for his output and inputs are homogeneous of degree zero in all prices. If all prices are changed by the factor $t > 0$, (5-24) becomes

$$\pi_{hj} = (tp_j)f_{hj}(q^*_{hj1}, \ldots ,q^*_{hjm}) - \sum_{k=1}^{m} (tp_k)q^*_{hjk}$$

Setting the partial derivatives equal to zero,

$$\frac{\partial \pi_{hj}}{\partial q^*_{hjk}} = tp_j \frac{\partial \bar{q}_{hj}}{\partial q^*_{hjk}} - tp_k = 0 \qquad (k = 1, \ldots , m)$$

or

$$t\left(p_j \frac{\partial \bar{q}_{hj}}{\partial q^*_{hjk}} - p_k\right) = 0 \qquad (k = 1, \ldots , m)$$

Since $t \neq 0$,

$$p_j \frac{\partial \bar{q}_{hj}}{\partial q^*_{hjk}} - p_k = 0 \qquad (k = 1, \ldots , m)$$

The first-order conditions from which the excess demands are obtained can be stated in a form identical with (5-25). Since the second-order conditions also remain unchanged, the excess demands are unaffected by a proportionate change of all prices.

Market Equilibrium. The excess demand functions of the consumers and entrepreneurs can be aggregated for both types of goods. The aggregate excess demand for a factor is the sum of the excess demands of the n consumers (5-22) and the $(m - s)$ industries on input account (5-27):

$$E_j = \sum_{i=1}^{n} E_{ij}(p_1, \ldots ,p_m)$$
$$+ \sum_{k=s+1}^{m} E^*_{kj}(p_1, \ldots ,p_m,N_k) \qquad (j = 1, \ldots , s) \quad (5\text{-}29)$$

The aggregate excess demand for a commodity is the sum of the excess demands by the n consumers (5-22), the $(m - s)$ industries on input account (5-27), and its producers (5-28):

$$E_j = \sum_{i=1}^{n} E_{ij}(p_1, \ldots ,p_m) + \sum_{k=s+1}^{m} E^*_{kj}(p_1, \ldots ,p_m,N_k)$$
$$+ \bar{E}_j(p_1, \ldots ,p_m,N_j) \qquad (j = s + 1, \ldots , m) \quad (5\text{-}30)$$

The aggregate excess demands given by (5-29) and (5-30) can be stated simply as

$$E_j = E_j(p_1, \ldots ,p_m, N_{s+1}, \ldots ,N_m) \qquad (j = 1, \ldots , m) \quad (5\text{-}31)$$

The excess demand for each good is a function of the m prices and the numbers of firms within the $(m - s)$ producing industries.

Short-run and long-run partial equilibria can be determined for any of the m markets considered in isolation from the other $(m - 1)$. A short-run equilibrium price is determined by setting the aggregate excess demand for the good under consideration equal to zero. The prices of the other $(m - 1)$ goods and the numbers of firms within the $(m - s)$ producing industries are treated as parameters. The only difference between a short-run and long-run equilibrium analysis for a factor market is the period of time for which the excess demand function is defined. The number of firms within the industry becomes a variable in the determination of a long-run equilibrium for a commodity market.

Multimarket Equilibrium. A long-run multimarket equilibrium requires that every market be cleared and that profit equal zero in every industry:[1,2]

$$E_j(p_1, \ldots ,p_m, N_{s+1}, \ldots ,N_m) = 0 \qquad (j = 1, \ldots , m)$$
$$\pi_j(p_1, \ldots ,p_m) = 0 \qquad (j = s + 1, \ldots , m) \qquad (5\text{-}32)$$

where π_j is the profit of a representative firm in the jth industry. Again one of the market-clearing equations can be expressed as a linear function of the others. The $(2m - s)$ equilibrium conditions given by (5-32) represent only $(2m - s - 1)$ independent equations.

[1] The numbers of firms within the producing industries cannot change during a short-run period. Since the entrepreneurs are also consumers, their profits and losses must be included in their budget constraints. Once this is done, short-run multimarket equilibrium is attained by requiring that every market be cleared.

[2] The market-clearing equations of (5-32) are formulated on the assumption that every good is scarce in relation to the demand for it. The system can be extended to allow for the possibility of free goods by stating the market-clearing equations for the primary factors as weak inequalities:

$$E_j(p_1, \ldots ,p_m, N_{s+1}, \ldots ,N_m) \leqq 0 \qquad (j = 1, \ldots , s)$$

Following the Walrasian behavior assumption, if excess demand is negative, competition among sellers will lower price. Generally, price cannot fall below zero since consumers will refuse to supply a factor at a negative price. If $E_j < 0$ when $p_j = 0$, Q_j is a free good, i.e., sellers will offer a larger quantity than buyers desire to purchase at a zero price. The price of a free good equals zero, and the inequality holds for its market-clearing equation. A zero price situation is stable in the sense that the market will return to it following a disturbance. If price increases above zero, competition among sellers will force it down. If it should fall below zero, supply would equal zero. The inequality formulation allows the pricing mechanism to determine which goods are free and which are scarce.

Equilibrium again depends upon relative, rather than absolute, prices. Since the excess demands of every consumer and entrepreneur are homogeneous of degree zero in prices, the aggregate excess demands are homogeneous of degree zero in prices. The profit functions [see (5-24)] are homogeneous of degree one in prices. If all prices are doubled, the entrepreneur's input and output levels will remain unchanged, but his total revenue and total cost, and hence his profit, will be doubled. However, if a long-run equilibrium is established for one set of prices, the system will remain in equilibrium if all prices are changed by the same proportion. A doubling of all prices will leave the excess demands equal to zero. The representative firms' revenues and costs will be doubled, but profit levels will remain equal to zero, and no new firms will be induced to enter any industry.

The number of variables in (5-32) can be reduced by one by dividing the m absolute prices by the price of an arbitrarily selected commodity. If Q_1 is selected, (5-32) can be rewritten as

$$E_j\left(1, \frac{p_2}{p_1}, \ldots, \frac{p_m}{p_1}, N_{s+1}, \ldots, N_m\right) = 0 \qquad (j = 1, \ldots, m)$$

$$(5\text{-}33)$$

$$\pi_j\left(1, \frac{p_2}{p_1}, \ldots, \frac{p_m}{p_1}\right) = 0 \qquad (j = s+1, \ldots, m)$$

This system of $(2m - s - 1)$ independent equations can generally be solved for the equilibrium values of the $(m - 1)$ exchange ratios relative to Q_1 and the $(m - s)$ firm numbers.

Once the equilibrium exchange ratios and firm numbers are determined, the excess demands of every consumer and entrepreneur can be computed by substituting their values into the individual excess demand functions. A long-run equilibrium solution satisfies the following conditions: (1) every consumer maximizes utility, (2) every entrepreneur maximizes profit, (3) every market is cleared, and (4) every entrepreneur earns a zero profit.

5-3. The Numéraire, Money, and Say's Law

General equilibrium has been established in Secs. 5-1 and 5-2 for barter-type economies in which circulating money is nonexistent. Commodities and factors are exchanged for other commodities and factors, and the conditions of exchange are completely described by exchange ratios. These systems have been solved for the $(m - 1)$ exchange ratios relative to an arbitrarily selected good, generally called the *numéraire*. Any set of absolute prices that yields the equilibrium exchange ratios is an equilibrium solution. If there is one such solution, there is an infinite number.

A number of different kinds of money can be introduced into a general equilibrium system. One good may be selected as a standard of value and serve as money in the sense that all prices are expressed in terms of its units. Money can be established as an abstract unit of account which serves as a standard of value but does not circulate. Under some circumstances circulating paper money can be introduced. Under different circumstances an attempt to introduce paper money leads to a contradiction.

The Numéraire. For m goods there are m^2 exchange ratios taking two commodities at a time: p_j/p_k $(j,\ k = 1,\ \ldots,\ m)$. Of these m are identities which state that the exchange ratio of a good for itself equals unity: $p_j/p_k = 1$ for $j = k$. These m^2 exchange ratios are not independent. Consider the identity and the $(m - 1)$ exchange ratios with Q_1 as *numéraire*. The other $m(m - 1)$ exchange ratios and identities can be derived from these:

$$\frac{p_j}{p_k} = \frac{p_j}{p_1} : \frac{p_k}{p_1} \qquad (j,\ k = 1,\ \ldots,\ m) \qquad (5\text{-}34)$$

Imagine that Q_1 is pears, Q_2 oranges, and Q_3 apples, and that two oranges exchange for one pear $(p_2/p_1 = 0.5)$ and one apple for two pears $(p_3/p_1 = 2)$. Utilizing (5-34), four oranges will exchange for one apple: $p_3/p_2 = 4$. The complete set of exchange ratios is given either directly or indirectly by the $(m - 1)$ exchange ratios and the identity for the *numéraire*.

The *numéraire* can be changed from Q_1 to Q_k by dividing the exchange ratios and identity for Q_1 by p_k/p_1:

$$\frac{1}{p_k/p_1}\left(1, \frac{p_2}{p_1},\ \ldots,\ \frac{p_k}{p_1},\ \ldots,\ \frac{p_m}{p_1}\right) = \left(\frac{p_1}{p_k}, \frac{p_2}{p_k},\ \ldots,\ 1,\ \ldots,\ \frac{p_m}{p_k}\right)$$

The exchange ratios are unaffected by this transformation, and the selection of the *numéraire* is truly arbitrary.

The *numéraire* can also serve as a standard of value. Setting its price identically equal to unity, the exchange ratios become $p_j/p_1 = p_j$. The equilibrium exchange ratios are unaffected by this transformation. The equilibrium price of each good is expressed as the number of units of the *numéraire* which must be exchanged to obtain 1 unit of that good. The price of oranges becomes 0.5 pears per orange, and the price of apples 2 pears per apple. The price of apples is four times as great as the price of oranges, and one apple still exchanges for four oranges in equilibrium. The *numéraire* has become money in the sense that its units serve as a standard of value. However, it does not serve as a store of value, since it is desired only as a productive factor or consumable commodity on the same basis as all other goods. Any good may serve as a standard of value in this sense.

The expression of prices in terms of a good such as pears is not common practice. Prices are generally expressed in terms of a monetary unit such as dollars. An accounting money is easily introduced into the framework of a general equilibrium system. There is no reason why the price of the *numéraire* should equal unity. It could be set equal to 2, $\sqrt{2}$, 25, or 200 million. The equilibrium exchange ratios would be unaffected. Accounting money can be introduced by setting the price of the *numéraire* (or any other good) equal to a specified number of monetary units. Money prices can then be derived for all other goods. If Q_1 is *numéraire* and p_1 is set equal to β dollars, the dollar price of Q_k (ρ_k) is

$$\rho_k = \beta \frac{p_k}{p_1} \qquad (k = 2, \ldots, m)$$

If the price of a pear is set equal to 2 dollars, the price of an orange is 1 dollar and the price of an apple 4 dollars. In this case money only serves as an abstract unit of account. It does not exist in a physical sense. Goods still exchange for goods. No one holds money, and no one desires to hold money. Accounting money serves as a standard, but not a store, of value.[1]

Monetary Equilibrium. Commodity money and accounting money are quite different from circulating money which serves as a store of value. The classical economists of the nineteenth century frequently divided the economy into two sectors with regard to equilibrium price determination: the real sector in which exchange ratios are determined, and the monetary sector in which absolute money prices are determined by the quantity of money in existence. The real sector is described in Secs. 5-1 and 5-2. The present task is to add the monetary sector to this analysis. For simplicity the analysis is developed for the case of pure exchange though it is easily extended to cover production and exchange.

Assume that the n consumers also possess initial stocks of paper money denoted by the subscript $(m + 1)$: $(q^0_{1,m+1}, \ldots, q^0_{n,m+1})$. Paper money serves as a store of value, but does not enter the consumers' utility functions. The ith consumer's excess demand for paper money is defined as the stock he desires to hold less his initial stock:

$$E_{i,m+1} = q_{i,m+1} - q^0_{i,m+1} \qquad (5\text{-}35)$$

His excess demand is positive if he adds to his initial stock of money and negative if he reduces it. The consumer's budget constraint (5-4)

---

[1] The assumption that money is only a unit of account is implicit throughout the analyses of the consumer and entrepreneur. The consumer's income may be expressed in monetary units, but he spends his entire income and does not desire to hold money. The entrepreneur maximizes his money profit, but he also has no desire to hold money. If he earns a positive profit, he will spend it in his role as a consumer.

must be redefined to include money:

$$\sum_{j=1}^{m+1} p_j E_{ij} = 0 \tag{5-36}$$

where p_j is the price of the jth commodity. The price of money p_{m+1} equals unity by definition. The consumer may exchange money for commodities or commodities for money. If his excess demand for money is positive, the value of the commodities he sells is greater than the value of those he buys, and he is exchanging commodities for money.

Since money does not enter the consumer's utility function, his excess demand for money cannot be determined by the principles of utility maximization. It is usually assumed that the consumer finds it convenient to hold money in order to facilitate commodity transactions. Assume that the ith consumer desires to hold a quantity of money which is a fixed proportion of the monetary value of his initial endowment of commodities:

$$q_{i,m+1} = \alpha_i \sum_{j=1}^{m} p_j q_{ij}^0 \tag{5-37}$$

where α_i is a constant. Substituting (5-37) into (5-35),

$$E_{i,m+1} = \alpha_i \sum_{j=1}^{m} p_j q_{ij}^0 - q_{i,m+1}^0 \tag{5-38}$$

The aggregate excess demand for money is obtained by summing (5-38) for all n consumers:

$$E_{m+1} = \alpha \sum_{i=1}^{n} \sum_{j=1}^{m} p_j q_{ij}^0 - \sum_{i=1}^{n} q_{i,m+1}^0 = E_{m+1}(p_1, \ldots, p_m) \tag{5-39}$$

No essentials are lost by assuming that $\alpha_i = \alpha$ for $(i = 1, \ldots, n)$. If the initial endowments of commodities and money are fixed, the excess demand for money is a function of the m commodity prices.

The excess demand functions for the m commodities are determined by maximizing utility for each consumer subject to his budget constraint, including money, solving the first-order conditions in order to obtain individual excess demand functions, and then summing for all consumers. A general equilibrium is established if the excess demand for each commodity and money equals zero:

$$E_j(p_1, \ldots, p_m) = 0 \qquad (j = 1, \ldots, m+1) \tag{5-40}$$

This gives a system of $(m + 1)$ equations in the m variable commodity prices. Since the aggregate budget constraint including money is always satisfied, only m of these equations are independent. Therefore, if the m commodity markets are in equilibrium, the money market is also in equilibrium, i.e., consumers as a whole do not desire to exchange commodities for money or money for commodities. The quantity of money that consumers desire to hold equals the quantity in existence. The m independent equations of (5-40) can generally be solved for the money prices of the m commodities.

The excess demands for commodities and money are not homogeneous of degree zero in commodity prices. If all commodity prices are increased by the factor $t > 0$, the excess demand for money (5-39) becomes

$$E_{m+1} = \alpha \sum_{i=1}^{n} \sum_{j=1}^{m} (tp_j) q_{ij}^0 - \sum_{i=1}^{n} q_{i,m+1}^0 \qquad (5\text{-}41)$$

The partial derivative of (5-41) with respect to t is

$$\frac{\partial E_{m+1}}{\partial t} = \alpha \sum_{i=1}^{n} \sum_{j=1}^{m} p_j q_{ij}^0 > 0$$

A proportionate increase of all commodity prices will increase the excess demand for money. If the system is in equilibrium before the price increase, consumers will desire to exchange commodities for money in order to bring their monetary stocks into the desired relation with the monetary values of their initial endowments of commodities. However, there will not be a corresponding negative excess demand for commodities. Any proportionate change of the equilibrium commodity prices will throw the system out of equilibrium.

The excess demands for commodities and money are homogeneous of degree zero in commodity prices and initial money stocks. The excess demand for money becomes

$$E_{m+1} = \alpha \sum_{i=1}^{n} \sum_{j=1}^{m} (tp_j) q_{ij}^0 - \sum_{i=1}^{n} (tq_{i,m+1}^0)$$

and
$$\frac{\partial E_{m+1}}{\partial t} = \alpha \sum_{i=1}^{n} \sum_{j=1}^{m} p_j q_{ij}^0 - \sum_{i=1}^{n} q_{i,m+1}^0$$

which equals zero if the money market was in equilibrium before the price change. Each consumer's money stock retains the desired relation to the value of his commodity endowment, and he will not desire to exchange commodities for money or money for commodities.

It can also be demonstrated that a change of the money stock of each consumer by the factor t will result in a change of the money price of each commodity by the same factor, but will leave the real sector unaffected.

If equilibrium has been established and then each money stock is increased by the factor t, each consumer will desire to exchange money for commodities, but no one will desire to exchange commodities for money. As a result commodity prices will increase until the existing stocks of money no longer exceed the stocks that consumers desire to hold.

Monetary equilibrium will be reestablished when the values of all commodity stocks are increased by the factor t

$$\sum_{i=1}^{n} \sum_{j=1}^{m} \rho_j q_{ij}^0 = t \sum_{i=1}^{n} \sum_{j=1}^{m} p_j q_{ij}^0 \qquad (5\text{-}42)$$

where ρ_j is the price of the jth commodity after equilibrium has been reestablished. Proportionate increases of all commodity prices: $\rho_j = tp_j$ $(j = 1, \ldots, m)$, will satisfy (5-42), but so will many other price constellations. Consider a nonproportionate set of price changes which satisfies (5-42). It follows that $\rho_h = up_h$ and $\rho_k = vp_k$ where $u > t > v$ for some h and k. The exchange ratio between Q_h and Q_k is now $up_h/vp_k > p_h/p_k$. The price of Q_h has increased relative to the price of Q_k, and consumers will desire to exchange Q_h for Q_k. If the system was in equilibrium at the initial exchange ratio, the new exchange ratio will result in a positive aggregate excess demand for Q_k and a negative aggregate excess demand for Q_h. The aggregate excess demands for all commodities will equal zero if and only if $\rho_h/\rho_k = p_h/p_k$ for $(h, k = 1, \ldots, m)$. This is consistent with monetary equilibrium if and only if $\rho_j = tp_j$ $(j = 1, \ldots, m)$. The dichotomization of equilibrium price determination is complete. Equilibrium exchange ratios are determined by the consumers' utility functions and the real values of their initial endowments. Money prices are determined by the quantity of money.

The introduction of circulating paper money into a static general equilibrium system is possible, but rather artificial. Equation (5-37) postulates a mode of behavior that is logically, though not mathematically, inconsistent with utility maximization: the consumer desires to hold a stock of money from which he derives no utility rather than spend it on commodities from which he does. It is difficult to find motives for holding money in a static system that is in no way connected with preceding or succeeding points in time. The interesting problems of money only arise in a dynamic analysis where behavior is considered over time.

Say's Law. The classical economists frequently denied the possibility of a positive excess demand for all commodities. In terms of the present analysis this can be interpreted as the statement that

$$\sum_{j=1}^{m} p_j E_j = 0 \qquad (5\text{-}43)$$

where the excess demand for all commodities is measured in monetary terms.   This proposition has becomes known as Say's law in honor of its promulgator, the nineteenth-century French economist Jean Baptiste Say.   Unfortunately, Say did not use mathematics and was vague regarding the conditions under which his law applies.   Some twentieth-century economists have interpreted it as an equilibrium condition, and others as an identity that holds regardless of whether or not the system is in equilibrium.   The quantity of money will determine the absolute price level if (5-43) is an equilibrium condition, but will not if it is an identity.

Monetary equilibrium has been established for the case in which the budget constraints are defined to include money.   The relevant identity (5-36) holds for all commodities and money, and (5-43) is an equilibrium condition.   In equilibrium, consumers do not desire to exchange money for commodities or commodities for money.

If (5-43) is an identity, consumers will never desire to exchange money for commodities or commodities for money.   This implies that the excess demand for money is identically equal to zero:

$$E_{m+1} \equiv 0 \tag{5-44}$$

Regardless of commodity prices consumers will never desire to increase or decrease their money stocks.   This implied behavior is inconsistent with the introduction of quantity equations, such as (5-37), which state that the consumers' excess demands for money depend upon commodity prices.   Therefore, the quantity of money cannot serve to determine absolute price levels.   Since (5-43) is an identity, if $(m - 1)$ of the commodity markets are in equilibrium, the mth must also be in equilibrium.   The general equilibrium system contains $(m - 1)$ independent equations which can be solved for $(m - 1)$ exchange ratios.   The statement that the money market is always in equilibrium adds no useful information, and absolute prices are indeterminate.   The crucial point in considering Say's law and money is whether or not money is included in the consumers' budget constraints.   If it is, (5-43) is an equilibrium condition. If it is not, (5-43) is an identity.

5-4. Multimarket Stability

The effects of a disturbance in one market upon the equilibria in other markets are ignored in Sec. 4-6 in accordance with the assumptions of partial equilibrium analysis.   A general equilibrium analysis involves an explicit recognition of the interrelated nature of all markets.   The excess demand for each good is a function of the prices of all goods.   A disturbance in one market will throw other markets out of equilibrium.

The stability of a single market depends upon the adjustments following the induced disturbances in other markets. Both the static and dynamic conditions for stability in a single market are extended to a multimarket system in the present section. The static conditions are often called the *Hicksian* conditions in honor of their formulator, J. R. Hicks. The Walrasian behavior assumptions (see Sec. 4-6) are employed throughout the present section.

Static Stability. Return to the assumption that the multimarket system does not contain money. Let Q_1 serve as *numéraire* and set its price identically equal to unity.

The stability condition for a two-market system is the same as the condition for a single market. There is only one independent equation and only one variable price: $E_1 = E_1(p_2)$ and $E_2 = E_2(p_2)$. The aggregate budget constraint, $E_1 + p_2E_2 = 0$, is always satisfied. A relaxation of the equilibrium condition for Q_2 so that $E_2 \neq 0$ necessarily implies a relaxation of the equilibrium condition for Q_1 such that $dE_1 + p_2\, dE_2 = 0$. The differentials dE_1 and dE_2 and therefore the derivatives dE_1/dp_2 and dE_2/dp_2 must be of opposite sign except for the trivial case in which both equal zero. Equilibrium is stable according to the static Walrasian assumption if $dE_2/dp_2 < 0$ (or equivalently if $dE_1/dp_2 > 0$). If equilibrium is restored in the market for Q_2, equilibrium is automatically restored in the market for the *numéraire*, i.e., if E_2 equals zero, E_1 must also equal zero. The unique problems of multimarket stability arise only for systems with three or more interrelated markets.

If $\partial E_k/\partial p_j \neq 0$, a displacement of equilibrium in the market for Q_j will cause a displacement of equilibrium in the market for Q_k. Walrasian stability for an isolated market requires that $\partial E_j/\partial p_j < 0$ where $\partial E_j/\partial p_j$ is a partial derivative and all other prices are assumed to remain unchanged. The total derivative dE_j/dp_j must be utilized for a multimarket analysis. Its value may be computed under a number of alternative assumptions regarding the adjustment of other markets. One possibility is to assume that equilibrium is restored in all markets other than those for Q_j and the *numéraire*.[1] There are many possible price-adjustment patterns other than the case of complete inflexibility, in which none of the other $(m - 2)$ markets adjusts, and the case of complete flexibility, in which they all adjust. In general, one can imagine a system with M "rigid prices" which will not change from their initial equilibrium values during the period under consideration where M may be any number from one through $(m - 1)$. The price of the *numéraire* is always rigid as a result of its definition.

---

[1] Since the aggregate budget constraint is always satisfied, $p_jE_j + E_1 = 0$ if Q_1 is *numéraire*. The violation of the equilibrium condition for the *numéraire* provides the slack necessary to allow the excess demand for Q_j to take on a nonzero value.

The most stringent stability conditions for the market for Q_j $(j \neq 1)$ require that the total derivative dE_j/dp_j be negative for all possible combinations of rigid and flexible prices. The market for Q_j is perfectly stable by the Hicksian definition if $dE_j/dp_j < 0$ under the following conditions: (1) if all the $(m - 1)$ prices other than p_j are rigid, (2) if $(m - 2)$ of the prices are rigid but p_h is flexible and adjusts so that $E_h = 0$, (3) if $(m - 3)$ of the prices are rigid but p_h and p_k are flexible and adjust so that $E_h = 0$ and $E_k = 0$, and so on up to the final case in which the prices of all goods other than the *numéraire* are flexible. The system as a whole is perfectly stable if the $(m - 1)$ markets for the goods other than the *numéraire* are perfectly stable.

The excess demand functions for a system with m goods are

$$E_j = E_j(p_2, \ldots , p_m) \qquad (j = 2, \ldots , m) \tag{5-45}$$

The excess demand function for the *numéraire* may be omitted, since it can be derived from the other $(m - 1)$. The effects of price changes upon the excess demands are computed by total differentiation of (5-45),

$$
\begin{aligned}
dE_2 &= b_{22}\, dp_2 + b_{23}\, dp_3 + \cdots + b_{2m}\, dp_m \\
dE_3 &= b_{32}\, dp_2 + b_{33}\, dp_3 + \cdots + b_{3m}\, dp_m \\
&\cdot\ \cdot\ \cdot\ \cdot\ \cdot\ \cdot\ \cdot\ \cdot\ \cdot\ \cdot\ \cdot\ \cdot\ \cdot\ \cdot\ \cdot \\
dE_m &= b_{m2}\, dp_2 + b_{m3}\, dp_3 + \cdots + b_{mm}\, dp_m
\end{aligned}
\tag{5-46}
$$

where $b_{jk} = \partial E_j/\partial p_k$. Since b_{jk} may be assumed constant in a small neighborhood about the equilibrium point, (5-46) forms a system of $(m - 1)$ simultaneous linear equations in the $(m - 1)$ variables $(dp_2, \ldots , dp_m)$. The coefficients of (5-46) form the Jacobian (see Sec. A-3) of $(E_2, \ldots , E_m)$ with respect to $(p_2, \ldots , p_m)$.

Consider the case in which equilibrium is displaced in the market for Q_j and all other prices are rigid. Substituting $dp_k = 0$ for $(k = 2, \ldots , m)$ and $(j \neq k)$ into (5-46) the $(j - 1)$th equation becomes[1]

$$dE_j = b_{jj}\, dp_j$$

Dividing through by dp_j, the first condition for the perfect stability of the market for Q_j is

$$\frac{dE_j}{dp_j} = b_{jj} < 0 \tag{5-47}$$

---

[1] A displacement of equilibrium in the market for Q_j will cause displacements of the equilibria in the other markets. The other equations of (5-46) become

$$dE_k = b_{kj}\, dp_j$$

Since the other prices are assumed rigid, these displacements will not react back upon the excess demand for Q_j, and nonzero excess demands will continue to exist in the other markets.

Condition (5-47) is identical with the stability requirement for an isolated market. Perfect stability for the system as a whole requires that (5-47) hold for $(j = 2, \ldots, m)$, and thus the first condition for perfect stability implies the isolated stability of every market in the system.

Now consider the case in which equilibrium is displaced in the market for Q_j, p_h adjusts, and all other prices are rigid. Substituting $dE_h = 0$ and $dp_k = 0$ for $(k \neq j, h)$ into (5-46), the equations for Q_j and Q_h become

$$dE_j = b_{jj}\, dp_j + b_{jh}\, dp_h$$
$$0 = b_{hj}\, dp_j + b_{hh}\, dp_h$$

Using Cramer's rule to solve for dp_j,

$$dp_j = \frac{\begin{vmatrix} dE_j & b_{jh} \\ 0 & b_{hh} \end{vmatrix}}{\begin{vmatrix} b_{jj} & b_{jh} \\ b_{hj} & b_{hh} \end{vmatrix}} = dE_j \frac{b_{hh}}{\begin{vmatrix} b_{jj} & b_{jh} \\ b_{hj} & b_{hh} \end{vmatrix}}$$

Dividing through by the constant term on the right and by dp_j, the second condition for the perfect stability of the market for Q_j is

$$\frac{dE_j}{dp_j} = \frac{\begin{vmatrix} b_{jj} & b_{jh} \\ b_{hj} & b_{hh} \end{vmatrix}}{b_{hh}} < 0 \tag{5-48}$$

Perfect stability of the market for Q_h requires that the denominator of (5-48) be negative. Therefore, perfect stability for the system as a whole requires that the numerator of (5-48) be positive.

Finally, consider the case in which equilibrium is displaced in the market for Q_j, p_h and p_i adjust, and the other $(m - 4)$ prices are rigid. Substituting $dE_h = dE_i = 0$ and $dp_k = 0$ for the other $(m - 4)$ prices into (5-46), the relevant equations become

$$dE_j = b_{jj}\, dp_j + b_{jh}\, dp_h + b_{ji}\, dp_i$$
$$0 = b_{hj}\, dp_j + b_{hh}\, dp_h + b_{hi}\, dp_i$$
$$0 = b_{ij}\, dp_j + b_{ih}\, dp_h + b_{ii}\, dp_i$$

Using Cramer's rule to solve for dp_j,

$$dp_j = \begin{vmatrix} dE_j & b_{jh} & b_{ji} \\ 0 & b_{hh} & b_{hi} \\ 0 & b_{ih} & b_{ii} \end{vmatrix} : \begin{vmatrix} b_{jj} & b_{jh} & b_{ji} \\ b_{hj} & b_{hh} & b_{hi} \\ b_{ij} & b_{ih} & b_{ii} \end{vmatrix}$$

Expanding the numerator by its first column and solving for dE_j/dp_j, the third condition for the perfect stability of the market for Q_j is

$$\frac{dE_j}{dp_j} = \begin{vmatrix} b_{jj} & b_{jh} & b_{ji} \\ b_{hj} & b_{hh} & b_{hi} \\ b_{ij} & b_{ih} & b_{ii} \end{vmatrix} : \begin{vmatrix} b_{hh} & b_{hi} \\ b_{ih} & b_{ii} \end{vmatrix} < 0 \tag{5-49}$$

Letting $j = h$ and $h = i$ in requirement (5-48), perfect stability of the market for Q_h requires that the denominator of (5-49) be positive. Therefore, perfect stability for the system as a whole requires that the numerator of (5-49) be negative.

Perfect stability for the system as a whole requires that the Jacobian determinants of order $[1,2,3, \ldots ,(m-1)]$:

$$b_{jj}, \quad \begin{vmatrix} b_{jj} & b_{jh} \\ b_{hj} & b_{hh} \end{vmatrix}, \quad \begin{vmatrix} b_{jj} & b_{jh} & b_{ji} \\ b_{hj} & b_{hh} & b_{hi} \\ b_{ij} & b_{ih} & b_{ii} \end{vmatrix}, \ldots \tag{5-50}$$

be alternatively negative and positive for all values of $j, h, i, \ldots$.

The conditions for perfect stability are stronger than necessary for the consideration of many multimarket systems. If the system contains no rigid prices, the only relevant value for dE_j/dp_j is the one computed on the assumption that the other $(m-2)$ markets adjust. Following the computational procedure outlined above, the market for Q_2 is stable if

$$\frac{dE_2}{dp_2} = \frac{\mathbf{B}}{\mathbf{B}_{22}} < 0 \tag{5-51}$$

where $\mathbf{B}$ is the Jacobian determinant of the complete system given by (5-46) and $\mathbf{B}_{22}$ is the cofactor of b_{22}. In the Hicksian terminology the system as a whole is *imperfectly stable* if a condition similar to (5-51) holds for all goods other than the *numéraire*. It is interesting to note that imperfect stability does not necessarily imply the isolated stability of each market.

Consider the following excess demand functions for three-commodity systems:

(1) $E_2 = -2p_2 + 3p_3 - 5$ $E_3 = 4p_2 - 8p_3 + 16$
(2) $E_2 = 2p_2 - 3p_3 + 5$ $E_3 = -4p_2 + 4p_3 - 4$
(3) $E_2 = 2p_2 + 3p_3 - 13$ $E_3 = 4p_2 - 8p_3 + 16$

The equilibrium prices are $p_2 = 2$ and $p_3 = 3$ for all three examples. System (1) satisfies all the conditions for perfect stability:

$$\frac{dE_2}{dp_2} = \frac{\partial E_2}{\partial p_2} = -2 < 0 \qquad \frac{dE_2}{dp_2} = \frac{\begin{vmatrix} -2 & 3 \\ 4 & -8 \end{vmatrix}}{-8} = -0.5 < 0$$

$$\frac{dE_3}{dp_3} = \frac{\partial E_3}{\partial p_3} = -8 < 0 \qquad \frac{dE_3}{dp_3} = \frac{\begin{vmatrix} -2 & 3 \\ 4 & -8 \end{vmatrix}}{-2} = -2 < 0$$

System (2) fails to satisfy the conditions for perfect stability, but satisfies the conditions for imperfect stability:

$$\frac{dE_2}{dp_2} = \frac{\begin{vmatrix} 2 & -3 \\ -4 & 4 \end{vmatrix}}{4} = -1 < 0 \qquad \frac{dE_3}{dp_3} = \frac{\begin{vmatrix} 2 & -3 \\ -4 & 4 \end{vmatrix}}{2} = -2 < 0$$

The markets for both Q_2 and Q_3 are unstable when considered in isolation, but the system as a whole is stable if both prices adjust. System (3) fails to satisfy the conditions for either perfect or imperfect stability.

Dynamic Stability. The conditions for the dynamic stability of a multimarket system represent a generalization of the condition for the dynamic stability of a single market. An explicit statement of the laws of price change is introduced, and the time paths of the prices following a disturbance are investigated. Many different types of dynamic adjustment processes may be introduced to describe the behavior of the participants in particular systems. In general, a multimarket equilibrium is dynamically stable if every price approaches its equilibrium level over time following a slight displacement from equilibrium, i.e., if

$$\lim_{t \to \infty} p_{jt} = p_j^e \qquad (j = 2, \ldots, m) \tag{5-52}$$

where p_{jt} is the price of Q_j at time t and p_j^e is the equilibrium price of Q_j.

Much of the mathematics necessary for a full development of dynamic stability is beyond the scope of the present volume, but the general nature of the analysis can be indicated with the aid of a linear example for a three-commodity system:

$$\begin{aligned} E_{2t} &= a_{22}p_{2t} + a_{23}p_{3t} + a_{20} \\ E_{3t} &= a_{32}p_{2t} + a_{33}p_{3t} + a_{30} \end{aligned} \tag{5-53}$$

Equilibrium prices can be computed by setting E_{2t} and E_{3t} equal to zero and solving for p_{2t} and p_{3t}:

$$p_2^e = \frac{a_{23}a_{30} - a_{33}a_{20}}{a_{22}a_{33} - a_{23}a_{32}} \qquad p_3^e = \frac{a_{32}a_{20} - a_{22}a_{30}}{a_{22}a_{33} - a_{23}a_{32}} \tag{5-54}$$

Assume that the dynamic laws of price adjustment are given by the linear equations

$$\begin{aligned} p_{2,t+1} - p_{2t} &= kE_{2t} \\ p_{3,t+1} - p_{3t} &= kE_{3t} \end{aligned} \tag{5-55}$$

where $k > 0$ is the "speed of adjustment," i.e., the amount that price will increase (or decrease) per unit of excess demand. The price-adjustment process which is described by (5-55) follows the Walrasian behavior assumptions. A positive excess demand means that buyers desire to purchase more than is being offered at the current price. Competition among buyers will then lead to an increase of price. A negative excess demand means that sellers offer more than buyers desire to purchase at the current price. Competition among sellers will then lead to a decrease of price. Neither price will change if both markets are in equilibrium, i.e., if the excess demand for each good equals zero. The "speed of adjustment" need not be the same for both markets, but no generality is lost by assuming that it is, since the units in which the goods are measured are arbitrary.

Substitute the values of the excess demands from (5-53) into (5-55) and write the equations in implicit form:

$$p_{2,t+1} - (1 + ka_{22})p_{2t} - ka_{23}p_{3t} - ka_{20} = 0$$
$$p_{3,t+1} - (1 + ka_{33})p_{3t} - ka_{32}p_{2t} - ka_{30} = 0$$

$$(5\text{-}56)$$

Solve the second equation of (5-56) for p_{2t}:

$$p_{2t} = \frac{1}{ka_{32}} p_{3,t+1} - \frac{1 + ka_{33}}{ka_{32}} p_{3t} - \frac{a_{30}}{a_{32}} \qquad (5\text{-}57)$$

Now substitute the values of p_{2t} and $p_{2,t+1}$ given by (5-57) into the first equation of (5-56):

$$p_{3,t+2} + \alpha_3 p_{3,t+1} + \beta_3 p_{3t} + \gamma_3 = 0 \qquad (5\text{-}58)$$

where $\alpha_3 = -(2 + ka_{33} + ka_{22})$
$\beta_3 = 1 + ka_{33} + ka_{22} + k^2 a_{22} a_{33} - k^2 a_{23} a_{32}$
$\gamma_3 = k^2 a_{22} a_{30} - k^2 a_{32} a_{20}$

The time path of the price of Q_3 is described by a second-order, non-homogeneous difference equation with constant coefficients. The solution of (5-58) (see Sec. A-6) is

$$p_{3t} = A_3 \sigma_{31}{}^t + B_3 \sigma_{32}{}^t + \frac{a_{32} a_{20} - a_{22} a_{30}}{a_{22} a_{33} - a_{23} a_{32}} \qquad (5\text{-}59)$$

where σ_{31} and σ_{32} are the roots of the homogeneous part of (5-58), and A_3 and B_3 are constants determined by the initial conditions. The constant term of (5-59) is the equilibrium price of Q_3 as given by (5-54).†

The time path of p_{2t} can be described by an equation similar to (5-59). Substituting $p_3{}^e$ for the constant term in (5-59) and writing a similar equation for the price of Q_2,

$$p_{2t} = A_2 \sigma_{21}{}^t + B_2 \sigma_{22}{}^t + p_2{}^e$$
$$p_{3t} = A_3 \sigma_{31}{}^t + B_3 \sigma_{32}{}^t + p_3{}^e$$

$$(5\text{-}60)$$

The system is dynamically stable and p_{2t} and p_{3t} will approach their equilibrium values over time if $-1 < \sigma_{ij} < 1$ $(i = 2, 3)$ and $(j = 1, 2)$.

† The reader can verify this by substituting $p_{3t} = K$ into (5-58) and solving

$$K + \alpha_3 K + \beta_3 K + \gamma_3 = 0$$

for K.

The absolute values of the roots of the homogeneous parts of (5-58) and the corresponding equation for Q_2 must be less than unity.

The roots σ_{ij}, and therefore dynamic stability, depend upon the "speed of adjustment" as well as the coefficients of the excess demand equations. Hicksian stability depends only upon the values of the coefficients. A system which satisfies the Hicksian conditions for perfect stability will prove dynamically unstable for some values of k. Consider the system given by

$$E_2 = -2p_2 + 3p_3 - 5$$
$$E_3 = 4p_2 - 8p_3 + 16$$

which was demonstrated to satisfy the Hicksian conditions for perfect stability. Assume the dynamic adjustment process is described by (5-55). For this example (5-58) becomes

$$p_{3,t+2} + (10k - 2)p_{3,t+1} + (4k^2 - 10k + 1)p_{3t} - 12k^2 = 0$$

The roots of the homogeneous part are

$$\sigma_{31} = -0.41k + 1 \qquad \sigma_{32} = -9.58k + 1$$

Since $k > 0$, σ_{31} and $\sigma_{32} < 1$ for all admissible speeds of adjustment, and the market for Q_3 is dynamically stable if the value of k is such that both roots are greater than -1. Since $\sigma_{32} < \sigma_{31}$, dynamic stability requires that $\sigma_{32} > -1$, or equivalently that $k < 0.21$. If k were greater than 0.21, the market for Q_3 would be characterized by overadjustment on the part of buyers and sellers, and p_{3t} would exhibit ever-increasing fluctuations about p_3^e.

5-5. Solutions

The mere formulation of a multimarket system gives no assurance of the existence of an equilibrium solution. Some systems have no mathematical solution; others have many. The existence of a mathematical solution may not be adequate. Economics places bounds upon the admissible values for the variables. Prices must be given by nonnegative,[1] real numbers. Furthermore, the consumption levels of each con-

---

[1] If the price of a commodity were negative, purchasing power would be transferred from sellers to buyers rather than from buyers to sellers. Negative prices are not always nonsensical. The possession of discommodities such as garbage will reduce a consumer's utility level, and he will generally be willing to pay for their removal. The possibility of meaningful negative prices is eliminated by centering attention upon the commodity counterparts of discommodities. The consumer may be considered to buy garbage-removal service rather than sell garbage, and the garbage collector may be considered to sell garbage-removal service rather than buy garbage. The price of garbage-removal service is positive and equal in absolute value to the negative price of garbage.

sumer and the input and output levels of each firm must be nonnegative. A mathematical solution which contains, for example, negative consumption levels is meaningless.

The question of the existence of an admissible solution may be considered on two different levels. One may desire to determine whether or not a particular numerically implemented multimarket system possesses an admissible solution. On a more general level one may desire to prove an existence theorem which states that admissible solutions exist for all multimarket systems that satisfy a number of general conditions.

Solutions for Particular Systems. In general, a solution for N equations in N variables exists if its Jacobian does not vanish in a small neighborhood (see Sec. A-3). The system of m equations obtained by setting the excess demands equal to zero cannot be solved for the absolute values of the m prices. Since the aggregate budget constraint is always satisfied, the excess demands are functionally dependent, and their Jacobian vanishes identically. The nonexistence of a solution for absolute prices is meaningful from the economic viewpoint, since the excess demands are homogeneous of degree zero in all prices.

By letting $p_1 = 1$ and omitting the excess demand equation for Q_1 the system is reduced to $(m - 1)$ equations in $(m - 1)$ variable prices. Thus far, it has been assumed that these equations are independent and a solution exists for the reduced system. This assumption is not necessarily true. Consider the three-commodity reduced system given by

$$E_2 = -2p_2 - 4p_3 + 10 = 0$$
$$E_3 = -3p_2 - 6p_3 + 15 = 0$$

The Jacobian of this system vanishes identically, and it cannot be solved for p_2 and p_3. The excess demand functions for Q_2 and Q_3 are not independent. The functional dependence in this case is $E_3 = 1.5E_2$. Society as a whole always demands and supplies Q_2 and Q_3 in a fixed proportion. Any set of values for p_2 and p_3 which satisfies $p_2 = 5 - 2p_3$ will result in multimarket equilibrium. Examples are ($p_2 = 1$, $p_3 = 2$) and ($p_2 = 3$, $p_3 = 1$).

Each numerical multimarket system may be treated individually. First apply the nonvanishing Jacobian condition to determine whether a mathematical solution exists. If one does, solve the system and examine its solution(s) from the viewpoint of admissibility.

Existence Theorems. The individual-solution method is not helpful if one wishes to consider the existence problem for abstract multimarket systems which are not numerically implemented. One must prove a general existence theorem. Existence theorems have been proved for a number of types of multimarket systems, including systems in which the production functions are formulated as combinations of linear activities[1] and the input-output system.[2]

Arrow and Debreu have considered the problem of existence for abstract multimarket systems similar to the one presented in Sec. 5-2.[3] Their analysis differs from that of Sec. 5-2 in that they employ set-theoretical techniques rather than differential calculus. Their assumptions for the first of the two cases which they consider are approximately as follows: (1) no firm realizes increasing returns to scale, (2) at least one primary factor is necessary for the production of each commodity, (3) the quantity of a primary factor supplied by a consumer cannot exceed his initial endowment, (4) each consumer's ordinal utility function is continuous, (5) consumers' wants cannot be saturated, (6) indifference surfaces are convex with respect to the origin, and (7) each consumer is capable of supplying all primary factors. Arrow and Debreu have proved that competitive equilibrium solutions exist for all systems that satisfy these assumptions. They weaken assumption (7) in the second of their existence proofs.

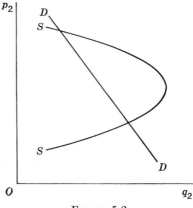

FIGURE 5-2

An existence theorem is based upon a sufficiency rather than a necessity argument. All systems that satisfy these conditions possess equilibrium solutions, but one could construct examples of systems that do not satisfy these conditions and yet possess equilibrium solutions.

Multiple Solutions. An existence theorem does not prove uniqueness. A multimarket system may possess more than one admissible solution. Some of the consequences of multiple solutions can be illustrated by a second-degree excess demand function for a two-commodity system. Second-degree functions may arise under a variety of circumstances. The supply curve for a factor such as labor may be backward-bending, as illustrated in Fig. 5-2. At low wage rates the supply curve for labor is positively sloped. An increase of the wage rate would induce consumers to increase their offering of labor and thereby increase their incomes in

---

[1] See R. Dorfman, P. Samuelson, and R. Solow, *Linear Programming and Economic Analysis* (New York: McGraw-Hill, 1958), chap. XIII.

[2] An input-output existence theorem is proved for the two-commodity case in Sec. 5-6 below.

[3] Kenneth J. Arrow and Gerard Debreu, "Existence of an Equilibrium for a Competitive Economy," *Econometrica*, vol. 22 (July, 1954), pp. 265–290.

terms of commodities. At higher wage rates the supply curve will turn back and become negatively sloped. A high wage rate and correspondingly high income in terms of commodities will induce consumers to decrease their offering of labor and increase their consumption of leisure. The demand and supply curves pictured in Fig. 5-2 yield the excess demand curve for labor pictured in Fig. 5-3a.

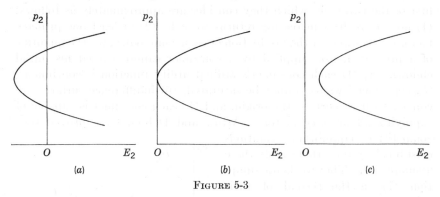

FIGURE 5-3

Consider a two-commodity system in which a consumption good, Q_1, serves as *numéraire* and Q_2 is labor. The excess demand function for labor corresponding to Fig. 5-3a is

$$p_2{}^2 - 14p_2 + 40 = 0$$

with the roots $p_2 = 4$ and $p_2 = 10$. Both roots are real, positive numbers which satisfy the requirements for a competitive equilibrium. As is generally true, stable and unstable equilibria alternate (see Sec. 4-6). The solution $p_2 = 4$ is stable and $p_2 = 10$ unstable: $E_2'(4) = -6$ and $E_2'(10) = 6$.

The excess demand function for labor corresponding to Fig. 5-3b is

$$p_2{}^2 - 14p_2{}^2 + 49 = 0$$

with the identical roots $p_2 = 7$. There is a unique multimarket equilibrium point. The excess demand curve is tangent to the vertical axis at $p_2 - 7$ and lies to the right for all other values of p_2. The stability of this unique solution is in question since $E_2'(7) = 0$. The graphic presentation suggests that it is stable for downward and unstable for upward price disturbances.

Finally, the excess demand function for labor corresponding to Fig. 5-3c is

$$p_2{}^2 - 14p_2 + 53 = 0$$

The roots of this function are the complex conjugates $p_2 = 7 \pm 4 \sqrt{-1}$. Prices with imaginary components are meaningless, and there is no admissible solution for the system. The excess demand curve for labor lies to the right of the vertical axis. The quantity of labor that consumers offer is less than the quantity that entrepreneurs demand at every wage rate. Equilibrium cannot be achieved in such a market.

The problems of multiple solutions are similar for systems containing more than two commodities. Consider the three-commodity system given by

$$E_2 = 2p_2{}^2 + 22p_2 - 13p_2p_3 - 64p_3 + 20p_3{}^2 + 48 = 0$$
$$E_3 = p_2 - 2p_3 + 2 = 0$$

This system has two solutions: $(p_2 = 4,\ p_3 = 3)$ and $(p_2 = 2,\ p_3 = 2)$. The rule of alternating stable and unstable equilibria applies. Equilibrium in the market for Q_2 considered in isolation is stable for $p_2 = 4$ and unstable for $p_2 = 2$. The solution $(p_2 = 4,\ p_3 = 3)$ satisfies the conditions for Hicksian perfect stability. The solution $(p_2 = 2, p_3 = 2)$ fails to satisfy the conditions for either perfect or imperfect stability.

Empirical Applications. A multimarket equilibrium analysis presents a very general picture of the interrelationships of markets throughout the economy, but it is so general as to be of little use for empirical studies in its pure form. A simple system with 2 factors, 50 commodities, 10,000 consumers, and 2,000 firms involves more than 200,000 individual excess demand functions. Numerical solutions are out of the question for systems of this size even if the necessary data could be obtained. If the economist desires to make empirical applications, he must deal with a somewhat simplified version of the partial equilibrium analysis or a greatly simplified version of the general equilibrium analysis.

5-6. The Input-Output System

The input-output system as developed by Wassily W. Leontief is an empirically oriented multimarket analysis. Its assumptions represent a considerable simplification of the general multimarket equilibrium analysis. Utility functions are omitted, and consumer demands are stated on the basis of outside information without regard to the equilibrium of individual consumers. The industry, rather than the firm, is the unit of production. The production function for each industry is of the constant-coefficient type, and there are no optimization problems in the productive sphere. In general, input-output analysis assumes away the problems of equilibrium. However, its simplifying assumptions are not without reward. The very general, but empirically sterile, multimarket equilibrium analysis is transformed into a model capable of empirical implementation. The input-output system provides numerical answers for a number of interesting problems which involve the economy as a whole.

Interindustry Flows.   The first step for input-output analysis is to obtain a detailed statement of the flows of goods and services during some base year.   Economic activity is classified into endogenous and exogenous sectors.   The endogenous sectors are the m producing industries which use primary factors and their own outputs as inputs.   The exogenous sectors supply primary factors and consume the outputs of the producing industries.   It is sometimes convenient to lump all the exogenous sectors together into a single *final demand* sector for an analysis of their consumption.   The final demand sector is not uniquely defined.   It generally includes households, government, and foreign trade.   Since the model is static, investment and inventory change are also included. One or more of these sectors might be considered endogenous for specific applications.[1]

The gross output (q_i) of the produced good Q_i equals the sum of the flows of Q_i to the producing industries and to final demand:

$$q_i = q_{i1} + \cdots + q_{im} + \alpha_i \qquad (i = 1, \ldots, m) \qquad (5\text{-}61)$$

where q_{ij} is the flow of Q_i to the jth industry and α_i is the flow to final demand.   Each industry is assumed to produce a single homogeneous output, and the flows can be measured in either physical units or base-year values.   Leontief's practice of defining a physical unit as a dollar's worth in the base year is employed throughout the present discussion.

The r primary factors are also used as inputs.   The total quantity of the ith primary factor used during the base year is the sum of the quantities used by each of the m industries:

$$q_i = q_{i1} + \cdots + q_{im} \qquad (i = m + 1, \ldots, m + r) \qquad (5\text{-}62)$$

Factor quantities are also measured in base-year values.

The base-year flows for a hypothetical system containing two endogenous industries and one factor are presented in Table 5-1.   An industry's output distribution is described by its row, and its input purchases by its column.   Reading across the first row, industry 1 used 2,000 dollars worth of its output as an intraindustry input, delivered 6,400 to industry 2 and 1,600 to final demand.   Reading down the first column, the inputs of industry 1 consisted of 2,000 dollars worth of its own output,

---

[1] An "open" input-output system contains one or more exogenous sectors.   All sectors are endogenous in a "closed" system.   Nearly all current analysis is for "open" systems, and the description in the text is limited to these.   The reader interested in the properties of a closed system is referred to Wassily W. Leontief, *The Structure of American Economy, 1919–1939* (2d ed.; New York: Oxford University Press, 1951).

6,000 of the output of industry 2, and 2,000 of the factor. The economy is assumed to be in long-run equilibrium, and the costs of each industry including normal profits equal its revenues. Therefore, the gross output of an industry can also be obtained by summing the values of its inputs, including the primary factor, entrepreneurship.

TABLE 5-1. BASE-YEAR FLOWS

Industry	1	2	Final demands	Gross outputs
1	$2,000	$6,400	$1,600	$10,000
2	6,000	4,800	5,200	16,000
3	2,000	4,800		

Analytical Aspects. Inputs are assumed to be combined in fixed proportions for the production of each of the m endogenous outputs:

$$q_{ij} = a_{ij}q_j \qquad \begin{aligned} &(i = 1, \ldots, m + r) \\ &(j = 1, \ldots, m) \end{aligned} \qquad (5\text{-}63)$$

where a_{ij} is the quantity of Q_i necessary for the production of a unit of Q_j. The production coefficients can be obtained from the base-year-flow table by dividing the components of each column for an endogenous industry by the industry's gross output. Table 5-2 contains the coefficients for

TABLE 5-2. INPUT-OUTPUT COEFFICIENTS

Industry	1	2
1	0.2	0.4
2	0.6	0.3
3	0.2	0.3

the hypothetical system. If the assumption of constant coefficients is correct, 0.2 units (2,000/10,000) of Q_1, 0.6 of Q_2, and 0.2 of Q_3 are needed to produce 1 unit of Q_1.

Substituting the production relations of (5-63) into the flow equations (5-61),

$$q_i - a_{i1}q_1 - \cdots - a_{ii}q_i - \cdots - a_{im}q_m = \alpha_i \qquad (i = 1, \ldots, m)$$

Collecting terms,

$$-a_{i1}q_1 - \cdots + (1 - a_{ii})q_i - \cdots - a_{im}q_m$$
$$= \alpha_i \qquad (i = 1, \ldots, m) \quad (5\text{-}64)$$

which gives a system of m nonhomogeneous linear equations with the m gross outputs as variables and the m final demands as constants.

Using Cramer's rule to solve (5-64) for q_j,

$$q_j = \frac{\mathbf{A}_j}{\mathbf{A}} \qquad (j = 1, \ldots, m)$$

where
$$\mathbf{A} = \begin{vmatrix} (1 - a_{11}) & -a_{12} & \cdots & -a_{1m} \\ -a_{21} & (1 - a_{22}) & \cdots & -a_{2m} \\ \cdots & \cdots & \cdots & \cdots \\ -a_{m1} & -a_{m2} & \cdots & (1 - a_{mm}) \end{vmatrix}$$

and $\mathbf{A}_j$ is $\mathbf{A}$ with the jth column replaced by the final demands. The solution of the input-output system can be generalized by expanding $\mathbf{A}_j$ by its jth column:

$$q_j = \frac{\mathbf{A}_{1j}}{\mathbf{A}} \alpha_1 + \frac{\mathbf{A}_{2j}}{\mathbf{A}} \alpha_2 + \cdots + \frac{\mathbf{A}_{mj}}{\mathbf{A}} \alpha_m \qquad (j = 1, \ldots, m) \quad (5\text{-}65)$$

where $\mathbf{A}_{ij}$ is the cofactor of the element in the ith row and jth column of $\mathbf{A}$. The system can be solved for the gross outputs corresponding to any set of final demands if $\mathbf{A} \neq 0$, i.e., if the equations of (5-64) are independent. The quantities of the r factors necessary to support a particular set of final demands are easily computed from (5-62) and (5-63) once the gross outputs have been determined.

The system for the two-industry example is

$$(1 - a_{11})q_1 - a_{12}q_2 = \alpha_1$$
$$-a_{21}q_1 + (1 - a_{22})q_2 = \alpha_2$$

or substituting the values of the coefficients from Table 5-2,

$$0.8q_1 - 0.4q_2 = \alpha_1$$
$$-0.6q_1 + 0.7q_2 = \alpha_2$$

Evaluating the determinant of the coefficients,

$$\mathbf{A} = (1 - a_{11})(1 - a_{22}) - a_{12}a_{21} = 0.56 - 0.24 = 0.32$$

Solving by Cramer's rule,

$$q_1 = \frac{0.7}{0.32} \alpha_1 + \frac{0.4}{0.32} \alpha_2 = 2.1875\alpha_1 + 1.2500\alpha_2$$

$$q_2 = \frac{0.6}{0.32} \alpha_1 + \frac{0.8}{0.32} \alpha_2 = 1.8750\alpha_1 + 2.5000\alpha_2$$

The solution states that 2.1875 units of Q_1 and 1.8750 units of Q_2 are necessary to support the delivery of 1 unit of Q_1 to final demand.

Since the final demands are restricted to nonnegative values, the gross outputs will be nonnegative for all admissible sets of final demands if and only if all the coefficients of (5-65) are nonnegative. It is easily proved that the coefficients of (5-65) are nonnegative in the two-industry case if at least one factor is required for the production of each commodity. By the definition of dollar's worth units

$$a_{11} + a_{21} + a_{31} = 1 \quad \text{and} \quad a_{12} + a_{22} + a_{32} = 1$$

Since a_{31}, $a_{32} \neq 0$,

$$1 - a_{11} - a_{21} > 0 \quad \text{and} \quad 1 - a_{12} - a_{22} > 0$$
and
$$1 - a_{11} > a_{21} \quad \text{and} \quad 1 - a_{22} > a_{12}$$

Taken together these inequalities imply

$$\mathbf{A} = (1 - a_{11})(1 - a_{22}) - a_{12}a_{21} > 0$$

All the cofactors of $\mathbf{A}$ are nonnegative:

$$\mathbf{A}_{11} = (1 - a_{22}) \geq 0 \qquad \mathbf{A}_{12} = a_{21} \geq 0$$
$$\mathbf{A}_{21} = a_{12} \geq 0 \qquad \mathbf{A}_{22} = (1 - a_{11}) \geq 0$$

The coefficients of (5-65) are ratios of nonnegative and positive numbers and are therefore nonnegative. This existence theorem can be proved by advanced methods for systems containing more than two industries.

5-7. Summary

A multimarket equilibrium analysis allows the determination of a consistent set of prices for all goods. In a pure-exchange system individuals are endowed with commodity stocks. Each is free to buy and sell commodities at prevailing prices subject to his budget constraint, which states that the value of his sales must equal the value of his purchases. Individual excess demand functions are derived from the first-order conditions for utility maximization. Aggregate functions are obtained by summing the individual functions for each commodity. All the individual, and therefore the aggregate, functions are homogeneous of degree zero in prices. Consumer behavior is determined by exchange ratios rather than absolute prices. Multimarket equilibrium requires that the excess demand for every commodity equal zero. Only $(m - 1)$ of the m market-clearing equations are independent, and the system is solved for the exchange ratio of each commodity relative to an arbitrarily selected *numéraire*.

Production is introduced in the second stage of the analysis. The consumers' endowments are assumed to consist of primary factors which they generally sell to entrepreneurs in order to be able to purchase produced commodities. The consumer's excess demand functions for factors and commodities are derived from his first-order conditions for utility maximization. Each entrepreneur uses both factors and commodities as inputs for the production of a single commodity. An entrepreneur's excess demand functions for his inputs are derived from his first-order conditions for profit maximization.   The excess demand for his output is obtained by substituting the input values into his production function. The entrepreneur's excess demands are also homogeneous of degree zero in prices.   Aggregate excess demand functions for each factor and commodity are obtained by summing the functions of the individual consumers and entrepreneurs.   The symmetry assumption is introduced, and the aggregate excess demands become functions of prices and the number of firms in each industry.   Long-run equilibrium requires that every market be cleared and that the profit of the representative firm in each industry equal zero.   Again, one of the market-clearing equations is redundant, and the system is solved for exchange ratios and the number of firms in each industry.

The exchange ratios between every pair of commodities can be determined from the exchange ratios relative to the *numéraire*.   The *numéraire* can serve as money in the standard-of-value sense.   Its price can be set equal to unity, and all prices expressed in terms of its units.   Abstract accounting money can serve as a standard of value.   Circulating paper money can be introduced, and its quantity will determine the level of absolute prices if Say's law is interpreted as an equilibrium condition and money is included in the budget constraints.   The quantity of money cannot determine the level of absolute prices if Say's law is interpreted as an identity and money is excluded from the budget constraints.

The static and dynamic conditions for multimarket stability represent a generalization of the Walrasian condition for a single market.   Perfect stability in the static Hicksian sense requires that the total derivatives dE_j/dp_j $(j = 2, \ldots, m)$ be negative for all possible combinations of rigid and flexible prices.   Imperfect stability requires that the total derivatives be negative, given the assumption that all prices are flexible. An analysis of dynamic stability requires an explicit statement of the laws of price adjustment over time.   A multimarket system is dynamically stable if all prices approach their equilibrium values over time following a disturbance.

The mere formulation of a multimarket system gives no assurance that an equilibrium solution exists.   Particular numerical systems may be examined individually to determine existence.   An existence theorem states that systems which satisfy a number of general conditions possess equilibrium solutions.   A multimarket system may possess more than one equilibrium solution.   The multimarket equilibrium analysis in its pure form is far too complicated to be a useful tool for empirical applications.

The input-output system represents an empirical application of multimarket analysis.   The equilibrium aspects are omitted.   The economy is divided into producing and final demand sectors.   Constant-coefficient-type production functions are postulated for the producing sectors.   The values of the production coefficients are computed from a numerical flow table for some base year.   The system is solved for the outputs of the producing sectors in terms of their deliveries to the final demand sectors, and it is possible to determine the output levels necessary to support any set of deliveries to final demand.

SELECTED REFERENCES

Allen, R. G. D., *Mathematical Economics* (London: Macmillan, 1956).   Multimarket equilibrium is covered in chap. 10, input-output system in chap. 11, and multimarket stability in chap. 13.   The necessary mathematical concepts beyond the calculus are developed in the text.

Arrow, Kenneth J., and Gerard Debreu, "Existence of an Equilibrium for a Competitive Economy," *Econometrica*, vol. 22 (July, 1954), pp. 265–290.   Two existence theorems for perfectly competitive multimarket equilibrium are proved with the use of advanced mathematics.

Hicks, J. R., *Value and Capital* (2d ed.; Oxford: Clarendon Press, 1946).   Multimarket equilibrium is covered in chaps. IV–VIII.   The mathematical development is contained in an appendix.

Lange, Oscar, *Price Flexibility and Employment* (Bloomington, Ind.: Principia Press, 1945).   The nonmathematical text contains a multimarket equilibrium approach to some problems of economic policy.   A mathematical analysis of multimarket stability is contained in an appendix.

———, "Say's Law: A Restatement and Criticism," in Lange, McIntyre, and Yntema (eds.), *Studies in Mathematical Economics and Econometrics* (Chicago: University of Chicago Press, 1942), pp. 49–68.   A mathematical statement of alternative versions of Say's law and the possibility of introducing money into a multimarket equilibrium system.

Leontief, Wassily W., *The Structure of American Economy, 1919–1939* (2d ed.; New York: Oxford University Press, 1951).   A description of the input-output system by its originator.

Metzler, Lloyd A., "Stability of Multiple Markets: The Hicks Conditions," *Econometrica*, vol. 13 (October, 1945), pp. 277–292.   An advanced mathematical discussion of the Hicksian and dynamic multimarket stability conditions.

Mosak, Jacob L., *General Equilibrium Theory in International Trade* (Bloomington, Ind.: Principia Press, 1944).   A mathematical theory of multimarket equilibrium for a closed economy is developed in the first two chapters.

Patinkin, Don, *Money, Interest, and Prices* (Evanston, Ill.: Row, Peterson, 1956).   An attempt to integrate multimarket equilibrium and monetary theory.   The mathematical analysis is an appendix.

Samuelson, Paul A., *Foundations of Economic Analysis* (Cambridge, Mass.: Harvard University Press, 1948).   Dynamic multimarket stability is discussed in chap. IX.

Walras, Léon, *Elements of Pure Economics*, trans. by William Jaffé (Homewood, Ill.: Irwin, 1954).   The original statement of multimarket equilibrium theory.

CHAPTER 6

MONOPOLISTIC COMPETITION

Thus far, conditions of perfect competition have been assumed to prevail in all markets. A perfectly competitive industry contains a large number of firms selling a homogeneous product. Input and output prices are unaffected by the actions of any individual firm. Each firm faces a horizontal demand curve and maximizes profit by selecting an output level at which marginal cost equals market price.

A market is monopolistically competitive if the actions of one or more buyers or sellers have a perceptible influence on price. This broad definition of monopolistic competition encompasses markets of many different types, which can be distinguished by further classification. Product and input markets are frequently classified according to the numbers of sellers and buyers which they contain. A market with a single seller is a *monopoly*, one with two a *duopoly*, and one with a small number greater than two an *oligopoly*. A market with a single buyer is a *monopsony*, one with two a *duopsony*, and one with a small number greater than two an *oligopsony*. Any combination of buyer and seller relationships is possible. A firm might be a perfect competitor in the markets for its inputs and a monopolist in the market for its output. Another firm might be a duopsonist in the markets for its inputs and an oligopolist in the market for its output. In fact, a single firm might purchase its various inputs in markets of quite different organization.

Product markets can be further classified with regard to differentiation. The theory of perfect competition is based upon the assumption that all firms within an industry produce a single homogeneous product and that buyers do not distinguish between the outputs of the various firms. However, the reader need not look far to discover industries in which the products of the various firms are close substitutes but differentiated in the eyes of the buyers. The cigarette industry provides a good example. Camels and Chesterfields are not the same product, though they satisfy the same need, and the demand for one depends upon the price of the other. The cigarette industry is an oligopoly *with product differentiation*.

Monopolistic competition is not limited to markets with small numbers of buyers and sellers. Product differentiation alone is sufficient for its existence. An industry with a large number of firms selling closely related, but differentiated, products is monopolistically competitive, since each firm, though small in relation to the market as a whole, possesses some control over the price at which it sells.

The market demand curve for a commodity gives consumers' purchases as a function of price on the assumption that the prices of all other commodities remain unchanged. The relation between price and sales for an individual seller depends upon the organization of the market in which he sells. A monopolist's demand curve is the same as the corresponding market demand curve. A perfect competitor's demand curve is not directly related to the market demand curve for his output, since he is unable to influence price. His price-sales relationship is represented by a horizontal line at the going market price. His sales would fall off to zero if he attempted to charge more than the going price. He is able to sell his entire output at this price and would not be acting rationally if he lowered it. As a result, the individual seller's demand curve is constructed on the assumption that all sellers charge the same price.

The construction of individual demand curves for duopolists and oligopolists presents a number of new problems. First, consider the market for a homogeneous product. Competition among buyers will result in a single price for all sellers, but each seller is sufficiently large in relation to the market so that his actions will have noticeable effects upon his rivals. An output change on the part of one seller will affect the price received by all. The consequences of attempted price variations on the part of an individual seller are uncertain. His rivals may follow his change, or they may not, but he can no longer assume that they will not notice it. The results of any move on the part of a duopolist or oligopolist depend upon the reactions of his rivals. Since, in general, reaction patterns are uncertain, general price-sales relationships cannot be defined for an individual firm.

The scope for individual action is greater if the product is differentiated. An individual seller will not lose all his sales if he charges a higher price than his competitors. Some former buyers will switch to his competitors, but some of his more loyal customers will continue to purchase his differentiated product at a higher price because of their relatively strong preference for it. A market demand curve covering the entire industry cannot be defined, since each member of the market produces a commodity which is distinct in the eyes of consumers. Each producer faces a separate demand curve. The quantity sold by an individual producer is a function of his price and the prices of all his competitors. His actions are generally governed by the actions and reactions of his competitors.

A profit-maximizing monopolist operates unfettered by the competition of close rivals. An individual producer in a large group selling a differentiated product knows that his actions will have a negligible effect upon each of his competitors, and he is able to maximize his profit in a manner similar to that of an individual producer under conditions of perfect competition. The actions of individual sellers (or buyers) are highly interdependent in all other forms of monopolistic competition. The actions of one firm have significant effects upon the quantities, prices, and profits of the others.   Unqualified profit maximization is not possible, since an individual firm does not have control over all the variables which affect its profit.   If an entrepreneur desires to maximize profit, he must take account of the reactions of his rivals to his decisions.   There is a very large number of possible reaction patterns for duopolistic and oligopolistic markets, and as a result there is a very large number of theories of duopoly and oligopoly.   Only a few of the many possible reaction patterns can be presented within the confines of the present chapter.

The traditional theory of monopoly, the one-firm industry, is developed in Sec. 6-1. Turning to the problems of industries containing a small number of firms, product differentiation and six different theories of duopoly and oligopoly are discussed in Sec. 6-2. The many-sellers case of monopolistic competition is described in Sec. 6-3, and monopsonistic behavior is briefly outlined in Sec. 6-4.

6-1. Monopoly

There is no distinction between the industry and the firm in a monopolistic market. The monopolistic firm is the industry; it has no competitors.[1]   A monopolist's individual demand curve possesses the same general properties as the industry demand curve for a perfectly competitive market.   It is an aggregate of the demand curves of individual consumers and is therefore negatively sloped.   The quantity of his sales is a single-valued function of the price which he charges:

$$q = f(p) \qquad (6\text{-}1)$$

where $dq/dp < 0$.   The demand curve has a unique inverse, and price may be expressed as a single-valued function of quantity:

$$p = F(q) \qquad (6\text{-}2)$$

---

[1] In a broad sense all products compete for the limited incomes of consumers.   The term monopoly defines a situation in which a single firm produces a commodity for which there are no *close* substitutes.   The prices of all other commodities are assumed constant, as is always the case for the analysis of a single market, and the competition of other commodities for the consumer's income is reflected in the position and shape of the monopolist's demand curve.

where $dp/dq < 0$. A major difference between a monopolist and a perfect competitor is that the monopolist's price decreases as he increases his sales. A perfect competitor accepts price as a parameter and maximizes profit with respect to variations of his output level; a monopolist may maximize profit with respect to variations of either output or price. Of course, he cannot set both independently since his price (output level) is uniquely determined by his demand curve once he has selected his output level (price). The price-quantity combination which maximizes profit is invariant with respect to the choice of the independent variable.

The monopolist's total revenue (R) is price multiplied by quantity sold:

$$R = pq \tag{6-3}$$

His marginal revenue (MR) is the derivative of his total revenue with respect to his output level. Differentiating (6-3) with respect to q,

$$\text{MR} = \frac{dR}{dq} = p + q\frac{dp}{dq} \tag{6-4}$$

Since $dp/dq < 0$, MR is less than price. The MR of a perfect competitor is also defined by (6-4). His MR equals price since $dp/dq = 0$. The monopolist's MR equals price less the rate of change of price with respect to quantity multiplied by quantity. If the perfect competitor expands his sales by 1 unit, his revenue will increase by the market value of the additional unit. The monopolist must decrease the price he receives for every unit in order to sell an additional unit.

Linear demand and MR curves are pictured in Fig. 6-1. Demand is monotonically decreasing, and

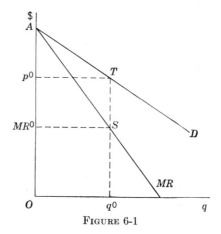

FIGURE 6-1

MR is less than price for every output greater than zero. The rate of decline of MR is twice the rate of decline of price:

$$p = a - bq \qquad R = aq - bq^2 \qquad \text{MR} = \frac{dR}{dq} = a - 2bp$$

Since $dp/dq = -b$ is a constant, the distance between the two curves $\left(q\dfrac{dp}{dq} = bq\right)$ is a linear function of output. Total revenue for the price-quantity combination (p^0, q^0) equals the area of the rectangle Op^0Tq^0.

The area $OASq^0$ which lies under the MR curve also equals total revenue:

$$\int_0^q (a - 2bq)\, dq = aq - bq^2 = R$$

This result is applicable to demand curves which are not linear. In general

$$\int_0^q \left(p + q\frac{dp}{dq}\right) dq = pq = R$$

since the integration constant always equals zero. Total revenue is always given by the area lying under the MR curve.

The elasticity of demand (e) at a point on a demand curve is defined as the absolute value of the rate of percentage change of output divided by the rate of percentage change of price:

$$e = -\frac{d(\log q)}{d(\log p)} = -\frac{p}{q}\frac{dq}{dp} \tag{6-5}$$

MR as given by (6-4) can be expressed in terms of price and demand elasticity:

$$\mathrm{MR} = p\left(1 + \frac{q}{p}\frac{dp}{dq}\right) = p\left(1 - \frac{1}{e}\right) \tag{6-6}$$

MR is positive if $e > 1$, zero if $e = 1$, and negative if $e < 1$. The difference between MR and price decreases as demand elasticity increases, and MR approaches price as demand elasticity approaches infinity.

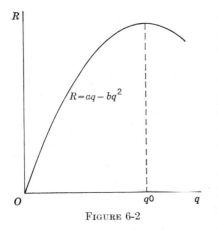

FIGURE 6-2

A parabolic total revenue curve which corresponds to the linear demand curve of Fig. 6-1 is presented in Fig. 6-2. The first derivative of total revenue (MR) is monotonically decreasing and reaches zero at the output level q^0. Total revenue is increasing and $e > 1$ for $q < q^0$, is at a maximum and $e = 1$ for $q = q^0$, and is declining and $e < 1$ for $q > q^0$.

The monopolist's total revenue and total cost can both be expressed as functions of output:

$$R = R(q) \qquad C = C(q)$$

His profit is the difference between his total revenue and total cost:

$$\pi = R(q) - C(q) \tag{6-7}$$

To maximize profit set the derivative of (6-7) with respect to q equal to zero:

$$\frac{d\pi}{dq} = R'(q) - C'(q) = 0$$

or $$R'(q) = C'(q) \qquad (6\text{-}8)$$

MR must equal MC for profit maximization. The monopolist can increase his profit by expanding (or contracting) his output, as long as the addition to his revenue (MR) exceeds (or is less than) the addition to his cost (MC).

The second-order condition for profit maximization requires that

$$\frac{d^2\pi}{dq^2} = R''(q) - C''(q) < 0$$

or adding $C''(q)$ to both sides of the inequality,

$$R''(q) < C''(q) \qquad (6\text{-}9)$$

The rate of increase of MR must be less than the rate of increase of MC. The second-order condition is *a fortiori* satisfied if MR is decreasing and MC increasing, as is generally assumed. If MC is decreasing, (6-9) requires that MR be decreasing at a more rapid rate. If both conditions for profit maximization are satisfied for more than one output level, the one which yields the greatest profit can be selected by inspection.

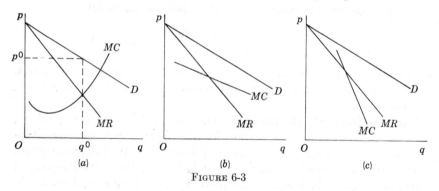

FIGURE 6-3

The first-order condition can be satisfied in each of the three cases presented in Fig. 6-3. The equalization of MR and MC for (a) determines a quantity of q^0 and a price of p^0. The monopolist can set the price p^0 and allow the consumers to purchase q^0, or he can offer q^0 for sale and allow the consumers to determine a price of p^0. The second-order condition requires that the algebraic value of the slope of the MC curve exceed that of the MR curve, i.e., the MC curve must cut the MR curve from below. This condition is satisfied at the intersection points in (a) and (b). There is no point of maximum profit in (c) since the MC curve cuts the MR curve from above at their only point of intersection. The first-order condition can be satisfied, but the second-order condition cannot.

If a monopolist followed the rule of a perfect competitor and equated MC to price, he would produce a greater output and charge a lower price. This is obvious by Fig. 6-3a. The coordinates of the intersection point of the MC and demand curves give a price less than p^0 and a quantity greater than q^0.

Consider a monopolist who faces a linear demand curve:

$$p = 100 - 4q \qquad R = pq = 100q - 4q^2 \qquad (6\text{-}10)$$

and produces at a constant MC of 20 dollars. His total cost is a linear function of his output level:

$$C = 50 + 20q \qquad (6\text{-}11)$$

His profit is

$$\pi = (100q - 4q^2) - (50 + 20q)$$

Setting MR equal to MC,

$$100 - 8q = 20$$
$$q = 10 \qquad p = 60 \qquad \pi = 350$$

The second-order condition is satisfied: the rate of change of MC (zero) exceeds the rate of change of MR (-8). If the monopolist were to follow the rule of the perfect competitor and set price equal to MC:

$$100 - 4q = 20$$
$$q = 20 \qquad p = 20 \qquad \pi = -50$$

he would sell a larger quantity at a lower price and earn a smaller profit. In this example the monopolist's 350 dollar profit would be reduced to a 50 dollar loss.

The Discriminating Monopolist. The monopolist need not always sell his entire output in a single market for a uniform price. In some situations he is able to sell in two or more distinct markets at different prices and thereby increase his profit. Price discrimination is feasible only if buyers are unable to purchase the product in one market and resell it in another. Otherwise, speculators would buy in a low-price market and resell in a high-price market at a profit, and thereby equalize price in all markets. Personal services are seldom transferable, and their sale frequently provides an opportunity for price discrimination. The resale of such commodities as electricity, gas, and water, which require physical connections between the facilities of the producer and consumer, is extremely difficult, and price discrimination is widely followed in setting utility rates. Price discrimination is often possible in spatially separated markets such as the "home" and "foreign" markets of a monopolist who sells abroad; resale can be prevented by a sufficiently high tariff.

If a monopolist practices price discrimination in two distinct markets, his profit is the difference between his total revenue from both markets and his total cost of production:

$$\pi = R_1(q_1) + R_2(q_2) - C(q_1 + q_2) \tag{6-12}$$

where q_1 and q_2 are the quantities which he sells in the two markets, $R_1(q_1)$ and $R_2(q_2)$ are his revenue functions, and $C(q_1 + q_2)$ is his cost function. Setting the partial derivatives of (6-12) equal to zero,

$$\frac{\partial \pi}{\partial q_1} = R_1'(q_1) - C'(q_1 + q_2) = 0$$

$$\frac{\partial \pi}{\partial q_2} = R_2'(q_2) - C'(q_1 + q_2) = 0$$

or $\qquad R_1'(q_1) = R_2'(q_2) = C'(q_1 + q_2) \tag{6-13}$

The MR in each market must equal the MC of the output as a whole. If the MRs were not equal, the monopolist could increase total revenue without affecting total cost by shifting sales from the low MR market to the high one. The equality of the MRs does not necessarily imply the equality of prices in the two markets. Denoting the prices and the demand elasticities in the two markets by p_1, p_2, e_1 and e_2 and utilizing (6-6), the equality of the MRs implies

$$p_1 \left(1 - \frac{1}{e_1} \right) = p_2 \left(1 - \frac{1}{e_2} \right)$$

and $\qquad \dfrac{p_1}{p_2} = \dfrac{1 - 1/e_2}{1 - 1/e_1}$

Price will be lower in the market with the greater demand elasticity. The prices will be equal if and only if the demand elasticities are equal.

Second-order conditions require that the principal minors of the relevant Hessian determinant

$$\begin{vmatrix} R_1'' - C'' & -C'' \\ -C'' & R_2'' - C'' \end{vmatrix}$$

alternate in sign beginning with the negative sign. Expanding the principal minors,

$$R_1'' - C'' < 0 \qquad (R_1'' - C'')(R_2'' - C'') - (C'')^2 > 0$$

These imply that $(R_2'' - C'') < 0$. The MR in each market must be increasing less rapidly than the MC for the output as a whole.

Assume that the monopolist whose demand and cost functions are given by (6-10) and (6-11) is able to separate his consumers into two distinct markets:[1]

$$p_1 = 80 - 5q_1 \qquad R_1 = 80q_1 - 5q_1{}^2$$
$$p_2 = 180 - 20q_2 \qquad R_2 = 180q_2 - 20q_2{}^2$$
$$C = 50 + 20(q_1 + q_2)$$

Setting the MR in each market equal to the MC of the output as a whole,

$$80 - 10q_1 = 20 \qquad 180 - 40q_2 = 20$$

Solving for q_1 and q_2 and substituting into the demand, profit, and elasticity equations,

$$q_1 = 6 \qquad p_1 = 50 \qquad e_1 = 1.67$$
$$q_2 = 4 \qquad p_2 = 100 \qquad e_2 = 1.25$$
$$\pi = 450$$

Second-order conditions are satisfied:

$$-10 < 0; \quad \begin{vmatrix} -10 & 0 \\ 0 & -40 \end{vmatrix} = 400 > 0$$

The monopolist has increased his profit from 350 to 450 dollars through discrimination. Price is lower in the market with the greater demand elasticity. Further discrimination would be profitable if the monopolist were able to subdivide his consumers into a larger number of groups with different demand elasticities.

The Multiple-plant Monopolist. Consider a monopolist selling in a single market, who can produce his output in two separate plants. His profit is the difference between his total revenue and his total production costs for both plants:

$$\pi = R(q_1 + q_2) - C_1(q_1) - C_2(q_2) \tag{6-14}$$

where q_1 and q_2 are the quantities which he produces in the two plants, $R(q_1 + q_2)$ is his revenue function, and $C_1(q_1)$ and $C_2(q_2)$ are his cost

---

[1] His aggregate demand curve remains unchanged. Solving the demand equations for q_1 and q_2,

$$q_1 = 16 - 0.2p_1 \qquad q_2 = 9 - 0.05p_2$$

The total demand at any price (p) is the sum of the demands in the two markets:

$$q = q_1 + q_2 = 16 - 0.2p + 9 - 0.05p = 25 - 0.25p$$

Solving for p,

$$p = 100 - 4q$$

which is the demand function (6-10).

functions. Setting the partial derivatives of (6-14) equal to zero,

$$\frac{\partial \pi}{\partial q_1} = R'(q_1 + q_2) - C_1'(q_1) = 0$$

$$\frac{\partial \pi}{\partial q_2} = R'(q_1 + q_2) - C_2'(q_2) = 0$$

or
$$R'(q_1 + q_2) = C_1'(q_1) = C_2'(q_2) \qquad (6\text{-}15)$$

The MC in each plant must equal the MR of the output as a whole. Second-order conditions require that the principal minors of the relevant Hessian determinant

$$\begin{vmatrix} R'' - C_1'' & R'' \\ R'' & R'' - C_2'' \end{vmatrix} \qquad (6\text{-}16)$$

alternate in sign beginning with the negative sign. The reader can verify that (6-16) requires that the MC in each plant must be increasing more rapidly than the MR of the output as a whole.

Taxation and Monopoly Output. A lump-sum or a profit tax (with a marginal rate less than 100 per cent) will reduce the profit after taxes of a profit-maximizing monopolist, but will not affect his optimum price-quantity combination. A sales tax, whether based upon quantity sold or value of sales, will reduce his profit and output level and increase his price.

The monopolist cannot avoid a lump-sum tax. It must be paid regardless of the physical quantity or value of his sales or the amount of his profit. His profit becomes

$$\pi = R(q) - C(q) - T \qquad (6\text{-}17)$$

where T is the amount of the lump-sum tax and π is his profit after the tax payment. Setting the derivative of (6-17) equal to zero,

$$\frac{d\pi}{dq} = R'(q) - C'(q) = 0 \qquad R'(q) = C'(q)$$

Since T is a constant, it vanishes upon differentiation, and the monopolist's output level and price are determined by the equality of MR and MC as would be the case if no tax were imposed.[1]

A profit tax requires that the monopolist pay the government a specified proportion of the difference between his total revenue and total cost. If the tax is a flat rate (constant proportion), his profit after tax payment is

$$\pi = R(q) - C(q) - t[R(q) - C(q)] = (1 - t)[R(q) - C(q)] \qquad (6\text{-}18)$$

---

[1] Second-order conditions are henceforth assumed to be satisfied unless otherwise stated.

where $0 < t < 1$.   Setting the derivative of (6-18) equal to zero,

$$\frac{d\pi}{dq} = (1 - t)[R'(q) - C'(q)] = 0$$

Since $(1 - t) \neq 0$,

$$R'(q) - C'(q) = 0 \qquad R'(q) = C'(q)$$

Since the first-order condition is the same as (6-8), output level and price are unaffected.   The only way a monopolist can avoid a profit tax is to reduce his profit before taxes.   If he is able to keep a fraction of an increase of profit before taxes, he will maximize his profit after taxes by equating MR and MC.

If a specific sales tax of α dollars per unit of output is imposed,

$$\pi = R(q) - C(q) - \alpha q \tag{6-19}$$

and $\qquad \dfrac{d\pi}{dq} = R'(q) - C'(q) - \alpha = 0 \qquad R'(q) = C'(q) + \alpha \tag{6-20}$

The monopolist maximizes profit after tax payment by equating MR with MC plus the unit tax.   Taking the total differential of (6-20),

$$R''(q)\, dq = C''(q)\, dq + d\alpha$$

and $\qquad \dfrac{dq}{d\alpha} = \dfrac{1}{R''(q) - C''(q)} \tag{6-21}$

Since $R''(q) - C''(q) < 0$ by the assumption that the second-order condition is fulfilled, $dq/d\alpha < 0$, and the optimum output level declines as the tax rate increases.   The imposition of a specific sales tax results in a smaller quantity sold and a higher price.

Return to the example given by (6-10) and (6-11) and assume that the government imposes a tax of 8 dollars per unit upon the monopolist's output:

$$\pi = (100q - 4q^2) - (50 + 20q) - 8q$$

$$\frac{d\pi}{dq} = 72 - 8q = 0 \qquad q = 9 \qquad p = 64 \qquad \pi = 274$$

Sales diminish by 1 unit, price increases by 4 dollars, and the monopolist's profit diminishes by 76 dollars as a result of the imposition of the tax. Price increases by less than the unit tax, but the monopolist's profit decreases by more than the 72 dollar tax revenue.   If the government imposed a 72 dollar lump-sum tax upon the monopolist, it would receive the same revenue, the monopolist's profit would be decreased by 4 dollars less, and the consumers would not have to pay a higher price for the product.   As a result it is frequently argued that a lump-sum tax is preferable to a sales tax.

The results are similar if the sales tax is a proportion of the value of sales (total revenue),

$$\pi = R(q) - C(q) - sR(q) = (1 - s)R(q) - C(q)$$
$$\frac{d\pi}{dq} = (1 - s)R'(q) - C'(q) = 0 \qquad (1 - s)R'(q) = C'(q) \quad (6\text{-}22)$$

where $0 < s < 1$. Profits are maximized by equating MC to the portion of the MR that the monopolist is allowed to retain. Taking the total differential of (6-22),

$$(1 - s)R''(q)\,dq - R'(q)\,ds = C''(q)\,dq$$

and
$$\frac{dq}{ds} = \frac{R'(q)}{(1 - s)R''(q) - C''(q)} \qquad (6\text{-}23)$$

Since the first-order condition requires that MR be positive and the second-order condition requires that the denominator of (6-23) be negative, $dq/ds < 0$. The imposition of an ad valorem sales tax also results in a reduced output level and an increased price.

6-2. Duopoly and Oligopoly

A duopolistic industry contains two sellers. An oligopolistic industry contains a number sufficiently small so that the actions of any individual seller have a perceptible influence upon his rivals. It is not sufficient to distinguish oligopoly from perfect competition for a homogeneous product or from the many-sellers case of monopolistic competition for a differentiated product on the basis of the number of sellers alone. The essential distinguishing feature is the interdependence of the various sellers' actions. If the influence of one seller's quantity decision upon the profit of another, $\partial \pi_i/\partial q_j$, is imperceptible, the industry satisfies the basic requirement for either perfect competition or the many-sellers case of monopolistic competition. If $\partial \pi_i/\partial q_j$ is of a noticeable order of magnitude, it is duopolistic or oligopolistic.[1]

[1] Market symmetry is assumed throughout the present chapter, in the sense that the partial derivatives $\partial \pi_i/\partial q_j$ are assumed to be of the same order of magnitude for all i and j except $i = j$. Many asymmetric market situations can be analyzed by modifying and combining the analyses for symmetric markets. Consider the case of partial monopoly, i.e., a market containing one large seller and a large number of small ones. The partial derivatives $\partial \pi_i/\partial q_j$ are of an imperceptible order of magnitude for $(i = 1, \ldots, n)$, $(j = 2, \ldots, n)$, and $i \neq j$, and $\partial \pi_i/\partial q_1$ is of a noticeable order of magnitude for all i where the subscript 1 denotes the large seller.

A theory of partial monopoly can be formulated by combining the theories of pure monopoly and perfect competition. The small firms will accept the going price and adjust their output levels to maximize profit in the same manner as a perfect competitor. The partial monopolist's effective demand function is obtained by subtracting the supply of the small firms, a function of price, from the market demand curve, also a function of price. Using this demand function, the partial monopolist maximizes profit by selecting either a price or output level in the same manner as a pure monopolist.

The price-quantity combination and profit of a duopolist or oligopolist depend upon the actions of all members of his market.   He can control his own output level (or price, if his product is differentiated), but he has no direct control over the other variables which affect his profit.   The profit of each seller is the result of the interaction of the decisions of all market members.   There are no generally accepted behavior assumptions for oligopolists and duopolists as there are for perfect competitors and monopolists.   There are many different solutions for duopolistic and oligopolistic markets.   Each solution is based upon a different set of behavior assumptions.   Six of the more interesting solutions are described in the present section.   Each is developed for a duopolistic market, but all except the Stackelberg and theory-of-games solutions are easily generalized for oligopolistic markets.   The Cournot, collusion, and Stackelberg solutions are developed for markets with homogeneous products, but are easily extended to cover markets with differentiated products.   The market shares and kinked-demand-curve solutions are developed for differentiated products, but can be modified to cover homogeneous products.   The theory-of-games solution is developed for application to either type of market.

The Cournot Solution.   The classical solution of the duopoly (and oligopoly) problem is associated with the name of Augustin Cournot, an early-nineteenth-century French economist.   Two firms are assumed to produce a homogeneous product.   The inverse demand function states price as a function of the aggregate quantity sold:

$$p = F(q_1 + q_2) \qquad (6\text{-}24)$$

where q_1 and q_2 are the levels of the duopolists' outputs.   The total revenue of each duopolist depends upon his own output level and that of his rival:

$$R_1 = q_1 F(q_1 + q_2) = R_1(q_1, q_2)$$
$$R_2 = q_2 F(q_1 + q_2) = R_2(q_1, q_2) \qquad (6\text{-}25)$$

The profit of each equals his total revenue less his cost, which depends upon his output level alone:

$$\pi_1 = R_1(q_1, q_2) - C_1(q_1)$$
$$\pi_2 = R_2(q_1, q_2) - C_2(q_2) \qquad (6\text{-}26)$$

The basic behavior assumption of the Cournot solution is that each duopolist maximizes his profit on the assumption that the quantity produced by his rival is invariant with respect to his own quantity decision.   The first duopolist (I for short) maximizes π_1 with respect to q_1, treating q_2 as a parameter, and the second (II for short) maximizes π_2 with respect to q_2, treating q_1 as a parameter.

Setting the appropriate partial derivates of (6-26) equal to zero,

$$\frac{\partial \pi_1}{\partial q_1} = \frac{\partial R_1}{\partial q_1} - \frac{dC_1}{dq_1} = 0 \qquad \frac{\partial R_1}{\partial q_1} = \frac{dC_1}{dq_1}$$

$$\frac{\partial \pi_2}{\partial q_2} = \frac{\partial R_2}{\partial q_2} - \frac{dC_2}{dq_2} = 0 \qquad \frac{\partial R_2}{\partial q_2} = \frac{dC_2}{dq_2} \qquad (6\text{-}27)$$

First-order conditions require that each duopolist equate his MC to his MR. The MRs of the duopolists are not necessarily equal. Let $q = q_1 + q_2$ and $\partial q/\partial q_1 = \partial q/\partial q_2 = 1$. The MRs of the duopolists are

$$\frac{\partial R_i}{\partial q} = p + q_i \frac{dp}{dq} \qquad (i = 1, 2)$$

The duopolist with the greater output will have the smaller MR. An increase of output by either duopolist acting alone will result in a reduction of price, i.e., a movement down the market demand curve, and the total revenues of both will be affected. The rates of change of the total revenues depend upon the output levels. Imagine that price decreases at the rate of 1 dollar per unit increase of aggregate sales, and that $q_1 = 100$ and $q_2 = 200$. If I increases his output to 101 units, he will receive 100 dollars less for the 100 units he had previously sold at a higher price. If II's output remains unchanged, he will lose 200 dollars of revenue as a result of I's action, but this is of no concern to I within the framework of the Cournot assumptions. If II increases his output by 1 unit, with I's output level unchanged, he will receive 200 dollars less for the units he had previously sold.

The second-order condition for each duopolist requires that

$$\frac{\partial^2 \pi_i}{\partial q_i{}^2} = \frac{\partial^2 R_i}{\partial q_i{}^2} - \frac{d^2 C_i}{dq_i{}^2} < 0 \qquad (i = 1, 2)$$

or

$$\frac{\partial^2 R_i}{\partial q_i{}^2} < \frac{d^2 C_i}{dq_i{}^2} \qquad (i = 1, 2) \qquad (6\text{-}28)$$

Each duopolist's MR must be increasing less rapidly than his MC. The maximization process for the Cournot solution is not the same as in the case of the two-plant monopolist, where a single individual controls the values of both output levels. Here each duopolist maximizes his profit with respect to the single variable under his control.

The duopolistic market is in equilibrium if the values of q_1 and q_2 are such that each duopolist maximizes his profit, given the output of the other, and neither desires to alter his output. The equilibrium solution can be obtained by solving (6-27) for q_1 and q_2 if (6-28) is satisfied. The market process can be described more fully by introducing an additional step before solving for the equilibrium output levels. Reaction functions which express the output of each duopolist as a function of his rival's output are determined by solving the first equation of (6-27) for q_1 and the second for q_2:

$$q_1 = \Psi_1(q_2)$$
$$q_2 = \Psi_2(q_1) \qquad (6\text{-}29)$$

I's reaction function gives a relationship between q_1 and q_2 with the property that for any specified value of q_2 the corresponding value of q_1 maximizes π_1.   II's reaction function gives the value of q_2 which maximizes π_2 for any specified value of q_1.   An equilibrium solution is a pair of values for q_1 and q_2 which satisfy both reaction functions.

If the demand and cost functions are

$$p = 100 - 0.5(q_1 + q_2) \qquad C_1 = 5q_1 \qquad C_2 = 0.5q_2{}^2 \qquad (6\text{-}30)$$

the profits of the duopolists are

$$\pi_1 = 100q_1 - 0.5q_1{}^2 - 0.5q_1q_2 - 5q_1$$
$$\pi_2 = 100q_2 - 0.5q_2{}^2 - 0.5q_1q_2 - 0.5q_2{}^2 \qquad (6\text{-}31)$$

Setting the appropriate partial derivates equal to zero,

$$\frac{\partial \pi_1}{\partial q_1} = 95 - q_1 - 0.5q_2 = 0$$

$$\frac{\partial \pi_2}{\partial q_2} = 100 - 0.5q_1 - 2q_2 = 0$$

The corresponding reaction functions are

$$q_1 = 95 - 0.5q_2 \qquad q_2 = 50 - 0.25q_1 \qquad (6\text{-}32)$$

A rise of either duopolist's output level will cause a reduction of the other's optimum output.   The reaction functions are of the shapes pictured in Fig. 6-4.   The equilibrium solution is given by their point of intersection. Solving (6-32) for q_1 and q_2 and substituting in the demand and profit functions,

$$q_1 = 80 \qquad q_2 = 30 \qquad p = 45$$
$$\pi_1 = 3,200 \qquad \pi_2 = 900 \qquad (6\text{-}33)$$

The second-order conditions are satisfied for this solution:

$$\frac{\partial^2 \pi_1}{\partial q_1{}^2} = -1 < 0 \qquad \frac{\partial^2 \pi_2}{\partial q_2{}^2} = -2 < 0$$

The basic behavior assumption of the Cournot solution is rather weak. Each duopolist acts as if his rival's output were fixed.   However, this is not the case.   Equilibrium is reached through a sequence of instantaneous adjustments.   One sets an output; this induces the other to adjust his output, which in turn induces the first to adjust his, and so on. It is rather unlikely that each will assume that his quantity decisions do not affect his rival's quantity decision if each of his adjustments is immediately followed by a reaction on the part of his rival. Others have assumed that each maximizes his profit on the assumption that his rival's price remains unchanged, but this is an even more unrealistic assumption if the product is homogeneous. Duopolists and oligopolists generally recognize the mutual interdependence of their decisions and those of their rivals.

The Cournot solution is easily extended to markets containing more than two sellers. As the number of sellers is increased, the output of each represents a progressively smaller proportion of the industry total, and the effects of an individual seller's actions upon his rivals become less and less noticeable. In the limit the Cournot solution approaches the perfectly competitive result. An individual seller will be unable to influence price, his MR will equal the market price, and his actions will not induce reactions on the part of his rivals.

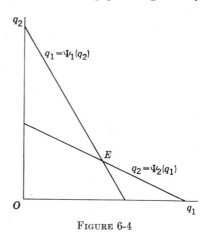

FIGURE 6-4

The Collusion Solution. Duopolists (or oligopolists) may recognize their mutual interdependence and agree to act in unison in order to maximize the total profit of the industry. Both variables are then under a single control, and the industry is, in effect, a monopoly. Maximization proceeds in the same manner as for the two-plant monopolist.

Returning to the example given by (6-30), industry profit is

$$\pi = \pi_1 + \pi_2 = 100(q_1 + q_2) - 0.5(q_1 + q_2)^2 - 5q_1 - 0.5q_2^2$$

Setting the partial derivatives of π equal to zero,

$$\frac{\partial \pi}{\partial q_1} = 95 - q_1 - q_2 = 0 \qquad \frac{\partial \pi}{\partial q_2} = 100 - q_1 - 2q_2 = 0$$

Solving for q_1 and q_2 and substituting in the profit and demand equations,

$$q_1 = 90 \qquad q_2 = 5 \qquad \pi = 4,525 \qquad p = 52.5$$

Comparison with (6-33) shows that the colluding duopolists produce a smaller total output at a higher price for a larger total profit than in the Cournot case. From the viewpoint of the industry as a whole, it is advantageous for the firm with the less rapidly increasing MC (I in this example) to increase its relative share of total output. The equilibrium MCs of the two firms are equal for the collusion solution.

Industry profit is increased from 4,100 to 4,525 dollars. I's profit is increased from 3,200 to 4,275 dollars, and II's reduced from 900 to 250 dollars. I's increase exceeds II's reduction, and collusion is profitable to both if I compensates II by a payment which is greater than II's reduction (650 dollars) but less than I's increase (1,075 dollars).

The Stackelberg Solution. Generally, the profit of each duopolist is a function of the ouput levels of both:

$$\pi_1 = h_1(q_1,q_2) \qquad \pi_2 = h_2(q_1,q_2) \qquad (6\text{-}34)$$

The Cournot solution is obtained by maximizing π_1 with respect to q_1 and π_2 with respect to q_2. The collusion solution is obtained by maximizing $(\pi_1 + \pi_2)$ with respect to both q_1 and q_2. Many other modes of maximizing behavior are possible for the duopolists whose profit functions are given by (6-34). One of the more interesting is the analysis of leadership and followership formulated by the German economist Heinrich von Stackelberg.

A follower observes his reaction function (6-29) and adjusts his output level to maximize his profit, given the quantity decision of his rival, whom he assumes to be a leader. A leader does not observe his reaction function. He assumes that his rival acts as a follower, and maximizes his profit, given his rival's reaction function. If I desires to play the role of a leader, he assumes that II's reaction function is valid and substitutes this relation into his profit function:

$$\pi_1 = h_1[q_1,\Psi(q_1)]$$

I's profit is now a function of q_1 alone and can be maximized with respect to this single variable. II can also determine his maximum profit from leadership on the assumption that I observes his reaction function and acts as a follower. I's maximum profit from followership is determined by substituting II's optimum leadership output level in I's reaction function, and II's maximum profit from followership is determined by substituting I's optimum leadership output level in II's reaction function.

Each duopolist determines his maximum profit levels from both leadership and followership and desires to play the role which yields the larger maximum. Four outcomes are possible: (1) I desires to be a leader, and II a follower; (2) II desires to be a leader, and I a follower; (3) both desire to be leaders; or (4) both desire to be followers. Outcome (1) results in consistent behavior patterns and therefore a determinate equilibrium.[1] I assumes that II will act as a follower, and he does; II assumes that I will act as a leader, and he does. Likewise (2) results in a determinate equi-

---

[1] The first- and second-order conditions for maxima are assumed to be fulfilled in all cases.

librium. If both desire to be followers, their expectations are not realized, since each assumes that the other will act as a leader. The duopolists must revise their expectations. Under the Stackelberg assumptions, the Cournot solution is achieved if each desires to act as a follower, knowing that the other will also act as a follower. Otherwise, one must change his behavior pattern and act as a leader before equilibrium can be achieved.

If both desire to be leaders, each assumes that the other's behavior is governed by his reaction function, but, in fact, neither of the reaction functions is observed, and a *Stackelberg disequilibrium* is encountered. Stackelberg believed that this disequilibrium is the most frequent outcome. The final result of a Stackelberg disequilibrium cannot be predicted a priori. If Stackelberg was correct, this situation will result in economic warfare, and equilibrium will not be achieved until one has succumbed to the leadership of the other or a collusive agreement has been reached.

Return again to the example given by (6-30). The maximum leadership profit of I is obtained by substituting II's reaction function (6-32) into I's profit equation (6-31):

$$\pi_1 = 100q_1 - 0.5q_1{}^2 - 0.5q_1(50 - 0.25q_1) - 5q_1$$
$$= 70q_1 - 0.375q_1{}^2$$

Maximizing with respect to q_1,

$$\frac{d\pi_1}{dq_1} = 70 - 0.75q_1 = 0 \qquad q_1 = 93\frac{1}{3} \qquad \pi_1 = 3,266\frac{2}{3}$$

Likewise for II,

$$\pi_2 = 100q_2 - 0.5q_2{}^2 - 0.5q_2(95 - 0.5q_2) - 0.5q_2{}^2$$
$$= 52.5q_2 - 0.75q_2{}^2$$
$$\frac{d\pi_2}{dq_2} = 52.5 - 1.5q_2 = 0 \qquad q_2 = 35 \qquad \pi_2 = 918.75$$

To determine I's maximum followership profit, first determine his output by substituting the leadership output of II (35 units) into his reaction function (6-32), and then compute his profit from the first equation of (6-31):

$$q_1 = 95 - 0.5q_2 = 77.5 \qquad \pi_1 = 3,003.125$$

Likewise substitute $93\frac{1}{3}$ into II's reaction function and then compute his profit from the second equation of (6-31):

$$q_2 = 50 - 0.25q_1 = 26\frac{2}{3} \qquad \pi_2 = 1555\frac{5}{9}$$

Each duopolist receives a greater profit from leadership, and both desire to act as leaders. An example in which the Cournot solution is easily determined has become a Stackelberg disequilibrium as the result of an alteration of the basic behavior assumptions.

Product Differentiation. The individual producer of a differentiated product in an oligopolistic market faces his own distinct demand curve. The quantity which he can sell depends upon the price decisions of all members of the industry:

$$q_i = f_i(p_1, p_2, \ldots, p_n) \qquad (i = 1, \ldots, n) \qquad (6\text{-}35)$$

where $\partial q_i / \partial p_i < 0$ and $\partial q_i / \partial p_j > 0$ for all $i \neq j$. An increase of price on the part of the ith seller with all other prices remaining unchanged results in a reduction of his output level. Some of his customers will turn to his competitors. If some other seller should increase his price, the ith seller can sell a larger quantity at a fixed price. Some of his competitor's customers will turn to him.

Individual producers can set either price or quantity. Demand functions may be expressed in inverse form with output levels as independent variables:[1]

$$p_i = F_i(q_1, q_2, \ldots, q_n) \qquad (i = 1, \ldots, n) \qquad (6\text{-}36)$$

All partial derivatives of (6-36) are negative. If the ith seller increases his output level, with all other output levels constant, p_i will decline, since a larger quantity always brings a lower price. If some other seller increases his output level, his price will decline, and the price of the ith firm must also decline in order to maintain q_i at a constant level. Otherwise some of his customers would turn to the firm with the lowered price.

The Cournot, collusion, and Stackelberg solutions are easily modified for product differentiation by replacing $p = F(q_1 + q_2)$ with individual demand functions:

$$p_1 = F_1(q_1, q_2) \qquad p_2 = F_2(q_1, q_2)$$

The analysis can also be extended to cases in which prices are the independent variables:

$$q_1 = f_1(p_1, p_2) \qquad q_2 = f_2(p_1, p_2)$$

Profits were expressed as functions of quantities:

$$\pi_1 = h_1(q_1, q_2) \qquad \pi_2 = h_2(q_1, q_2)$$

---

[1] The demand functions may be constructed to describe a situation in which price is the independent variable for some sellers and quantity for others. The dependent variable of each seller is then expressed as a function of the independent variables of all sellers.

By substitution,

$$\pi_1 = h_1[f_1(p_1,p_2), f_2(p_1,p_2)] = H_1(p_1,p_2)$$
$$\pi_2 = h_2[f_1(p_1,p_2), f_2(p_1,p_2)] = H_2(p_1,p_2)$$

The profit of each duopolist is a function of both prices, and maximization may proceed with respect to prices.

In the case of differentiated products the duopolists' profits may also depend upon the amounts of their advertising expenditures. If advertising is effective, it allows the firm to sell a larger quantity at a given price or a given quantity at a higher price. The demand curves are

$$p_1 = F_1(q_1,q_2,A_1,A_2) \qquad p_2 = F_2(q_1,q_2,A_1,A_2)$$

where A_1 and A_2 are the amounts of advertising expenditure by I and II respectively. The profit functions become

$$\pi_1 = q_1 F_1(q_1,q_2,A_1,A_2) - C_1(q_1) - A_1$$
$$\pi_2 = q_2 F_2(q_1,q_2,A_1,A_2) - C_2(q_2) - A_2$$

Each duopolist must now maximize his profit with respect to his advertising expenditure as well as his output level.

The Market-shares Solution. Assume that II desires to maintain a fixed share of the total sales of a differentiated product, regardless of the effects of his actions on his short-run profits. His major concern is with the long-run advantages that are derived from maintaining a given market share. A quantity change on the part of I will be immediately followed by a proportionate change on the part of II. The relation

$$\frac{q_2}{q_1 + q_2} = k \qquad q_2 = \frac{kq_1}{1-k} \tag{6-37}$$

where k is II's desired market share, will always hold. I is a market leader in the sense that his actions will always be followed by II in a predetermined manner.

I's demand function is $p_1 = F_1(q_1,q_2)$, and his profit function is

$$\pi_1 = q_1 F_1(q_1,q_2) - C_1(q_1)$$

Substituting from (6-37) for q_2,

$$\pi_1 = q_1 F_1\left(q_1, \frac{kq_1}{1-k}\right) - C_1(q_1)$$

I's profit is a function of q_1 alone and may be maximized with respect to this single variable as long as II reacts to maintain his market share.

Let I's demand and cost functions be

$$p_1 = 100 - 2q_1 - q_2 \qquad C_1 = 2.5q_1{}^2 \tag{6-38}$$

Let $k = \frac{1}{3}$, and therefore $q_2 = 0.5q_1$. I's profit is

$$\pi_1 = q_1(100 - 2q_1 - 0.5q_1) - 2.5q_1{}^2 = 100q_1 - 5q_1{}^2 \tag{6-39}$$

Setting the first derivative of (6-39) equal to zero, solving for q_1, and substituting in the above relations,

$$\frac{d\pi_1}{dq_1} = 100 - 10q_1 = 0 \tag{6-40}$$

$$q_1 = 10 \qquad q_2 = 5 \qquad p_1 = 75 \qquad \pi_1 = 500$$

I maximizes his profit at an output of 10 units, and II reacts by producing 5 units.

The Kinked-demand-curve Solution. Duopolistic and oligopolistic markets are characterized by infrequent price changes. Firms usually do not change their price-quantity combinations in response to small shifts of their cost curves as the foregoing market analyses would suggest. The kinked-demand-curve solution presents a theoretical analysis which is consistent with this observed behavior. Starting from predetermined price-quantity combinations, if one of the duopolists lowers his price (increases his quantity), the other is assumed to react by lowering his price (increasing his quantity) in order to maintain his market share. If one of the duopolists raises his price, his rival is assumed to leave his own price unchanged and thereby increase his market share. Price decreases will be followed, but price increases will not.

Assume that the demand and cost functions of the duopolists are

$$p_1 = 100 - 2q_1 - q_2 \qquad C_1 = 2.5q_1{}^2$$
$$p_2 = 95 - q_1 - 3q_2 \qquad C_2 = 25q_2 \tag{6-41}$$

and that the currently established prices and quantities are $p_1 = 70$, $q_1 = 10$, $p_2 = 55$, and $q_2 = 10$.† If I increased his price, II would leave his own price unchanged at 55 dollars. Substituting $p_2 = 55$ into II's demand function (6-41) and solving for q_2,

$$q_2 = \frac{40 - q_1}{3} \tag{6-42}$$

† The reader can verify that these price-quantity combinations represent a Cournot solution. MC equals MR for each duopolist, on the assumption that his rival's output level remains unchanged. The method by which the initial price-quantity combinations were achieved is of no concern for the kinked-demand-curve analysis.

II's output level and market share will increase as I increases his price and thereby decreases his output level. Substituting the value for q_2 given by (6-42) into I's demand function (6-41),

$$p_1 = \frac{260 - 5q_1}{3} \tag{6-43}$$

I's price is a function of q_1 alone given the assumption that II maintains his price at 55 dollars. Starting from the initial position, (6-43) is only valid for $p_1 > 70$ and $q_1 < 10$. I's MR function for price increases can be derived by forming his total revenue function from (6-43):

$$R_1 = q_1 \left(\frac{260 - 5q_1}{3} \right)$$

and $$\frac{dR_1}{dq_1} = \frac{260 - 10q_1}{3} \tag{6-44}$$

At $q_1 = 10$, I's MR for a price increase is $53\frac{1}{3}$ dollars.

The demand and MR functions given by (6-43) and (6-44) are not valid if I reduces his price. In this case, II will follow by lowering his price by an amount sufficient to allow him to retain half the total volume of sales. II must increase his output level by the same amount as I in order to maintain his market share: $q_2 = q_1$. Substituting $q_2 = q_1$ into I's demand function (6-41),

$$p_1 = 100 - 3q_1 \tag{6-45}$$

I's price is a function of q_1 alone given the fact that II maintains his market share. The demand function given by (6-45) is valid for $p_1 < 70$ and $q_1 > 10$. I's MR function for price decreases can be derived by forming a total revenue function from (6-45):

$$R_1 = q_1(100 - 3q_1)$$

and $$\frac{dR_1}{dq_1} = 100 - 6q_1 \tag{6-46}$$

At $q_1 = 10$, I's MR for a price decrease is 40 dollars.

The initial position represents a maximum-profit point for I. His MC for an output of 10 units is 50 dollars. He cannot increase his profit by increasing his price (reducing his output level), since MR exceeds MC ($53\frac{1}{3} > 50$) and this difference would be increased by a price increase. He cannot increase his profit by reducing his price (increasing his output level), since MR is less than MC ($40 < 50$) and this difference would be increased by a price reduction. His initial price-quantity combination is optimal for any value of MC from $53\frac{1}{3}$ to 40 dollars. A reduction of his MC by an amount not greater than 10 dollars would not induce him to lower his price and expand his sales.   Likewise, an increase of MC by an amount not greater than $3\frac{1}{3}$ dollars would not induce him to increase his price and contract his sales.

Graphically, I's effective demand curve is "kinked" and his effective MR curve discontinuous at his initial output level.   His demand curve

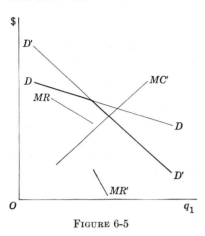

is $D'D'$ (see Fig. 6-5) if II reacts by maintaining his market share and DD if II reacts by maintaining his price. The shaded portions of these demand curves give his effective demand curve; DD is valid for price increases, and $D'D'$ for price decreases.   His effective MR curve follows the MR curve corresponding to DD to the left of his initial output level and the MR curve corresponding to $D'D'$ to the right of his initial output level. I is unable to equate MR and MC.

FIGURE 6-5

The Theory-of-games Solution. The mathematical theory of games has been applied to market situations in which the outcome depends upon the actions of participants with conflicting interests.   Situations of duopoly, oligopoly, and bilateral monopoly (a market with a single seller and a single buyer) often fit into this category.   Duopolists are in conflict if a move by one results in a diminution of the profit of the other.   The theory of games provides specific behavior assumptions which result in an equilibrium for such a market, though the equilibrium is quite different from those provided by the other solutions.

A game may consist of a sequence of moves as in chess, or it may consist of a single move on the part of each of its participants.   The present analysis is limited to single-move games.   In this context, a *strategy* is the specification of a particular move for one of the participants.   A duopolist's strategy consists of selecting a particular value for each of the variables under his control.   If price is his only variable, a strategy consists of selecting a particular price.   If price and advertising expenditure are both variables, a strategy consists of selecting particular values for both price and advertising expenditure.   Each participant is assumed to possess a finite number of strategies though the number may be very large.   This assumption rules out the possibility of continuous variation of the action variables.   The outcome of the duopolistic game, i.e., the profit earned by each of the participants, is determined from the relevant cost and demand relations once each of the duopolists has selected a strategy.

Games are classified on the basis of two criteria: (1) the number of participants and (2) the net outcome. The first merely involves a counting of the number of participants with conflicting interests. There are one-person, two-person, three-person, and in the general case, n-person games. The second criterion allows a distinction between zero-sum and non-zero-sum games. A zero-sum game is one in which the algebraic sum of the outcomes, e.g. profits, for all the participants equals zero for every possible combination of strategies. If the net outcome of a game is different from zero for at least one strategy combination, it is classified as a non-zero-sum game.

A one-person, zero-sum game is uninteresting, since the player gains nothing, regardless of his strategy choice. A monopolist or a monopsonist might be considered as the sole participant in a one-person, non-zero-sum game. The present analysis is restricted to two-person, zero-sum games and can be applied to a duopolistic market in which one participant's gain always equals the absolute value of the other's loss. In general, if I has m and II has n strategies, the possible outcomes of the game are given by the profit matrix

$$\begin{bmatrix} a_{11} & a_{12} & \cdots & a_{1n} \\ a_{21} & a_{22} & \cdots & a_{2n} \\ \cdots & \cdots & \cdots & \cdots \\ a_{m1} & a_{m2} & \cdots & a_{mn} \end{bmatrix} \tag{6-47}$$

where a_{ij} is I's profit if I employs his ith strategy and II employs his jth. Since the game is zero-sum, the corresponding profit earned by II is $-a_{ij}$.

For a specific example consider the profit matrix

$$\begin{bmatrix} 8 & 40 & 20 & 5 \\ 10 & 30 & -10 & -8 \end{bmatrix} \tag{6-48}$$

If I employs his first strategy and II employs his second, I's profit is 40, and II's is -40. If I employs his second strategy and II employs his third, I's profit is -10, and II's is 10.

The duopolist's decision problem consists of choosing an optimal strategy. I desires the outcome (40) in the first row and second column of (6-48), and II desires the outcome (-10) is the second row and third column. The final outcome depends upon the strategies of both duopolists, and neither has the power to enforce his desires. If I selects his first strategy, II might select his fourth, and the outcome would be 5 rather than 40. If II selects his third strategy, I might select his first, and the outcome would be 20 rather than -10. The theory of games postulates behavior patterns which allow the determination of equilibrium in these situations. I fears that II might discover his choice of strategy and desires to "play it safe." If I selects his ith strategy, his minimum profit, and hence II's maximum, is given by the smallest element in the ith row of the profit matrix: $\min_j a_{ij}$. This is his expected profit from the employment of his ith strategy if his fears regarding II's knowledge and behavior are realized. I's profit will be greater than this amount if II fails to select his appropriate strategy. I desires to maximize his minimum expected profit. Therefore, he selects the strategy i for which $\min_j a_{ij}$ is the largest. His expected outcome is $\max_i \min_j a_{ij}$. He cannot earn a smaller profit and may earn a larger one.

II possesses the same fears regarding I's information and behavior. If II employs his jth strategy, he fears that I may employ the strategy corresponding to the largest element in the jth column of the profit matrix: $\max_i a_{ij}$. Therefore, II selects the strategy j for which $\max_i a_{ij}$ is the smallest, and his expected profit is $-\min_j \max_i a_{ij}$. The decisions of the duopolists are consistent and equilibrium is achieved if

$$\max_i \min_j a_{ij} = \min_j \max_i a_{ij}$$

Returning to the example given by (6-48), I will employ his first strategy. If II anticipates his choice, I's profit will be 5. If I employed his second strategy, and II anticipated his choice, his profit would be -10. II will employ his fourth strategy and limit his loss to 5. Every other column of (6-48) has a maximum greater than 5. In this case

$$\max_i \min_j a_{ij} = \min_j \max_i a_{ij} = a_{14} = 5$$

The duopolists' decisions are consistent, and an equilibrium is established. Neither of the duopolists can increase his profit by changing his strategy if his opponent's strategy remains unchanged.

Assume that the profit matrix is

$$\begin{bmatrix} -2 & 4 & -1 & 6 \\ 3 & -1 & 5 & 10 \end{bmatrix} \qquad (6\text{-}49)$$

where I has two strategies and II has four. This profit matrix and its corresponding game problem can be simplified by introducing the concept of dominance. An inspection of (6-49) reveals that II will never employ his third strategy since he can always do better by employing his first, regardless of I's strategy choice. Each element in the third column is larger, and therefore represents a greater loss for II, than the corresponding element in the first. In general, the jth column dominates the kth if $a_{ij} \leq a_{ik}$ for all i and $a_{ij} < a_{ik}$ for at least one i. The fourth column of (6-49) is dominated by both the first and second columns. Dominance can also be defined with regard to I's strategies. In general, the ith row dominates the hth if $a_{ij} \geqq a_{hj}$ for all j and $a_{ij} > a_{hj}$ for at least one j. Neither row of (6-49) dominates the other. A rational player will never employ a dominated strategy. Therefore, the profit matrix can be simplified by the removal of all dominated strategies.

Eliminating the third and fourth columns of (6-49), the profit matrix becomes

$$\begin{bmatrix} -2 & 4 \\ 3 & -1 \end{bmatrix} \tag{6-50}$$

Following the rules established above, I will desire to employ his second strategy, and II will desire to employ his first. These decisions are not consistent:

$$\max_{i} \min_{j} a_{ij} = a_{22} = -1 \neq 3 = a_{21} = \min_{j} \max_{i} a_{ij}$$

If the duopolists employ these strategies, the initial outcome would be $a_{21} = 3$. If II employs his first strategy, I cannot increase his profit by changing strategies. However, if I employs his second strategy, II can decrease his loss from 3 to -1 by switching to his second strategy. I can then increase his profit from -1 to 4 by switching to his first. II can then decrease his loss from 4 to -2 by switching to his first. The assumptions which lead to an equilibrium position for (6-48) result in endless fluctuations for (6-50).

The game problem given by (6-50) can be solved by allowing the duopolists to select their strategies on a probabilistic basis. Let the probabilities of I's employing his first and second strategies be r and $(1 - r)$ respectively where $0 \leqq r \leqq 1$. If he selected probabilities of 0.5 for each strategy, he could flip a coin and employ his first strategy if it fell "heads" and his second if it fell "tails." Such a random selection will not allow II to anticipate I's choice even if he knows the probabilities assigned to I's strategies. II can randomize his strategy selection by assigning the probabilities s and $(1 - s)$ to his strategies where $0 \leqq s \leqq 1$. The duopolists are now concerned with expected, rather than actual, profits. A duopolist's expected profit equals the sum of the possible outcomes, each multiplied by the probability of its occurrence. For example, if II employs his first strategy with a probability of one and I selects the probabilities r and $(1 - r)$, I's expected profit is $ra_{11} + (1 - r)a_{21}$. If II employs his second strategy with a probability of one, I's expected profit is $ra_{21} + (1 - r)a_{22}$.

The decision problem of each duopolist is to select an optimal set of probabilities. The probabilities which they employ are defined as optimal if

$$ra_{11} + (1 - r)a_{21} \geqq V$$
$$ra_{12} + (1 - r)a_{22} \geqq V \tag{6-51}$$

and
$$sa_{11} + (1 - s)a_{12} \leqq V$$
$$sa_{21} + (1 - s)a_{22} \leqq V \tag{6-52}$$

where V is defined as the *value of the game*. The relations of (6-51) state that I's expected profit is at least as great as V if II employs either of his pure strategies with a probability of one. The relations of (6-52) state that II's expected loss is at least as small as V if I employs either of his pure strategies with a probability of one. It can be proved that values for r and s always exist such that (6-51) and (6-52) are satisfied and that V is unique.

If both duopolists select their strategies on a probabilistic basis, I's expected profit can be determined from (6-51):

$$E_1 = s[ra_{11} + (1 - r)a_{21}] + (1 - s)[ra_{12} + (1 - r)a_{22}] \geqq sV + (1 - s)V$$
or
$$E_1 = sra_{11} + s(1 - r)a_{21} + (1 - s)ra_{12}$$
$$+ (1 - r)(1 - s)a_{22} \geqq V \quad (6\text{-}53)$$

II's expected loss can be determined from (6-52):

$$E_2 = r[sa_{11} + (1 - s)a_{12}] + (1 - r)[sa_{21} + (1 - s)a_{22}] \leqq rV + (1 - r)V$$
or
$$E_2 = rsa_{11} + r(1 - s)a_{12} + (1 - r)sa_{21}$$
$$+ (1 - r)(1 - s)a_{22} \leqq V \quad (6\text{-}54)$$

The left-hand sides of (6-53) and (6-54) are identical: I's expected profit equals II's expected loss. Combining (6-53) and (6-54):

$$V \leqq E_1 = E_2 \leqq V$$

which proves that

$$E_1 = E_2 = V$$

The expected outcome is the same for each of the duopolists and equals the value of the game if both employ their optimal probabilities. If I employs his optimal probabilities, his expected profit cannot be less than V, regardless of II's strategy choice. It will be greater than V if II employs a nonoptimal set of probabilities. Likewise, if II employs his optimal probabilities, his expected loss cannot be greater than V, regardless of I's strategy choice. It will be less if I employs a nonoptimal set of probabilities.

I's optimal probabilities can be determined by reducing the theoretical game problem to a linear-programming problem (see Sec. 3-7). Define the variables

$$z_1 = \frac{r}{V} \quad \text{and} \quad z_2 = \frac{1 - r}{V} \tag{6-55}$$

By this definition

$$\frac{1}{V} = z_1 + z_2 \qquad (6\text{-}56)$$

I desires to make his expected profit as large as possible, or equivalently, he desires to make $1/V$ as small as possible. His programming problem is to find values for z_1 and z_2 which minimize (6-56) subject to

$$\begin{aligned} a_{11}z_1 + a_{21}z_2 &\geq 1 \\ a_{12}z_1 + a_{22}z_2 &\geq 1 \end{aligned} \qquad (6\text{-}57)$$

such that $z_1, z_2 \geq 0$.† The relations of (6-57) are derived by substituting (6-55) into (6-51). Using the solution method described in Sec. 3-7, the optimum solution for the game problem given by (6-50) is $z_1 = 0.4$, $z_2 = 0.6$, and $1/V = 1$. By (6-55), $r = 0.4$, and $(1 - r) = 0.6$.

The dual for I's linear-programming problem is to find values for w_1 and w_2 that maximize

$$w_1 + w_2$$

subject to

$$\begin{aligned} a_{11}w_1 + a_{12}w_2 &\leq 1 \\ a_{21}w_2 + a_{22}w_2 &\leq 1 \end{aligned}$$

such that $w_1, w_2 \geq 0$. Letting $w_1 = s/V$ and $w_2 = (1 - s)/V$, the dual problem allows the determination of II's optimal probabilities. The solution of the dual for the game problem given by (6-50) is $w_1 = 0.5$, $w_2 = 0.5$, and $1/V = 1$. II's optimum probabilities are $s = 0.5$ and $(1 - s) = 0.5$.

An extension of the analysis to more complicated games is possible, but requires the use of mathematics beyond the scope of the present volume. An extension is a necessity for economic applications since the zero-sum requirement is seldom fulfilled in an actual market situation. The duopoly problem might be extended to a two-person, non-zero-sum game, or equivalently, to a three-person, zero-sum game in which the third person is an artificial entity—"Nature"—with outcomes equal to the negative of the combined outcomes of the duopolists. The possibility of coalitions arises in games containing three or more persons. For example, the duopolists may act together in order to maximize industry profit. In an oligopolistic market two or more of the participants may join together to the detriment of their rivals.

† The value of the game need not be positive. It may be negative or zero. To ensure that $V > 0$, and therefore z_1, $z_2 \geq 0$, select a number U with the property that $a_{ij} + U > 0$ for all i and j and add U to every element of the profit matrix. This operation increases the value of the game by U, but it does not change the optimal probabilities. See J. G. Kemeny, J. L. Snell, and G. L. Thompson, *Introduction to Finite Mathematics* (Englewood Cliffs, N.J.: Prentice-Hall, 1957), p. 291.

6-3. Product Differentiation: Many Sellers

The many-sellers case of monopolistic competition contains elements of both monopoly and perfect competition.[1]   It is akin to perfect competition in that the number of sellers is sufficiently large so that the actions of an individual seller have no perceptible influence· upon his competitors. It is akin to monopoly and differentiated oligopoly in that each seller possesses a negatively sloped demand curve for his distinct product.

Assuming linear demand curves, the price received by each seller is a function of the quantities sold by each of the n firms within the industry:

$$p_k = A_k - a_{kk}q_k - \sum_{\substack{i=1 \\ i \neq k}}^{n} b_{ki}q_i \qquad (k = 1, \ldots, n) \qquad (6\text{-}58)$$

where $\partial p_k / \partial q_i = -b_{ki}$ is negative, but numerically small.   To facilitate exposition, assume that all firms have identical demand and cost functions, i.e., $b_{ki} = b$ for all k and i except $k = i$, $a_{kk} = a$, $A_k = A$, and $C_k(q_k) = C(q_k)$ for all k.   Assuming initial price-quantity combinations which are the same for all firms, the industry can be described in terms of the actions of a "representative" firm.   The revenue and cost functions of all firms and their maximizing behavior are identical, though their products are differentiated in the eyes of consumers.   The demand curve facing the representative firm becomes

$$p_k = A - aq_k - b \sum_{\substack{i=1 \\ i \neq k}}^{n} q_i \qquad (6\text{-}59)$$

The profit of the representative firm is

$$\pi_k = q_k \left(A - aq_k - b \sum_{\substack{i=1 \\ i \neq k}}^{n} q_i \right) - C(q_k) \qquad (6\text{-}60)$$

Since b is numerically small and a quantity change on the part of the representative firm affects each of its $(n-1)$ competitors to the same degree, the effects of his movements upon the price of any particular competitor are negligible.   Therefore, the entrepreneur of the representative firm acts as if his actions had no effects upon his competitors.   Equating his MR and MC on the assumption that the output levels of his competitors remain unchanged:

$$A - 2aq_k - b \sum_{\substack{i=1 \\ i \neq k}}^{n} q_i = C'(q_k) \qquad (6\text{-}61)$$

[1] See Edward H. Chamberlin, *The Theory of Monopolistic Competition* (7th ed.; Cambridge, Mass.: Harvard University Press, 1956).

The second-order condition requires that his MC be increasing more rapidly than his MR. The optimum output level for the kth firm depends upon the current output levels of all its competitors.

The symmetry assumption ensures that if it is profitable for the representative firm to make a particular move, it is profitable for all other firms to make the same move. All firms will attempt to maximize profit simultaneously, and quantity variations by the kth firm will be accompanied by identical variations on the part of all the other firms within the industry. The representative firm will not move along the demand curve (6-59) which is constructed upon the assumption that the output levels of the other firms remain unchanged. Its effective demand curve is constructed by substituting $q_k = q_i$ into (6-59):

$$p_k = A - [a + (n - 1)b]q_k \qquad (6\text{-}62)$$

The number $(n - 1)$ is not of a negligible order of magnitude. A 1 per cent increase in the output level of one competitor may cause p_k to decrease by 0.02 per cent, but a simultaneous 1 per cent increase on the part of 1,000 firms may decrease p_k by 20 per cent or more. The effective demand curve (6-62) which accounts for simultaneous and identical movements on the part of all sellers has a steeper slope than (6-59). The entrepreneur of the representative firm may realize that he is unable to move along his individual demand curve, but this information is of no use to him, since he has no control over the output levels of his competitors. The other firms change their output levels because they can increase their profits. Their actions are not governed by the actions of the representative firm. The representative firm must take advantage of its opportunity to increase profit and act in the same manner as the other firms.

The representative firm starting from some arbitrary initial price-quantity combination faces two separate demand curves. In Fig. 6-6a, DD is its demand curve for variations of its output level alone, and $D'D'$ is its effective demand curve for identical variations of the output levels of all firms within the industry. The two intersect at the initial price-quantity combination. As all firms increase their output levels, the shape and position of $D'D'$, which is a function of q_k alone [see (6-62)], remain unchanged, and DD, the position of which is dependent upon the outputs of all firms [see (6-59)], "slides" along $D'D'$, always intersecting it at the current output level of the representative firm.

The industry reaches an equilibrium when MR equals MC for all firms. The n simultaneous equations of (6-61) must be solved for the n unknown quantities. It can be proved by advanced methods that the symmetry assumption guarantees that (6-61) will result in equal output levels for all n firms. Therefore, the solution can be obtained by substituting $q_k = q_i$

in (6-61) and solving

$$A - [2a + (n - 1)b]q_k = C'(q_k) \tag{6-63}$$

for q_k.† The latter formulation involves only one equation and one variable. The maximum profit and optimum price-quantity combination are the same for all firms. A graphic description of short-run equilibrium is presented in Fig. 6-6b. MR equals MC, and DD intersects $D'D'$ at the equilibrium price-quantity combination.

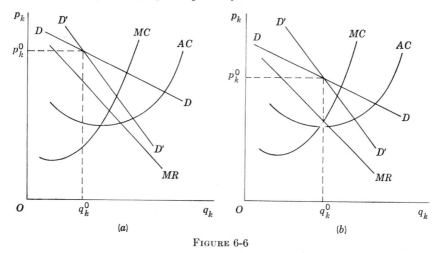

FIGURE 6-6

Free entry and exit drive pure profit to zero in a perfectly competitive industry and can have the same effect in the many-sellers case of monopolistic competition. The profit of the representative firm can be expressed as a function of its output and the number of firms within the industry if $q_k = q_i$ is substituted in (6-60):

$$\pi_k = Aq_k - [a + (n - 1)b]q_k{}^2 - C(q_k) \tag{6-64}$$

Setting π_k equal to zero, (6-63) and (6-64) are a system of two equations in the two variables q_k and n. The solution of these equations gives the long-run equilibrium values for the output level of the representative firm and the number of firms.

The long-run equilibrium position of the representative firm is pictured in Fig. 6-7. New firms will be induced to enter the industry if the pure profit of the representative firm is greater than zero. As the num-

---

† This solution is not the same as that for an oligopolistic market in which one of the entrepreneurs knows that (6-62) is his effective demand curve. MR is $A - [2a + 2(n - 1)b]q_k$ in this case, or $(n - 1)bq_k$ dollars less for every output level. The output level at which MR and MC are equated is smaller than that obtained from a solution of (6-63).

ber of firms increases, the representative firm can sell a smaller output at any given price, i.e., both DD and $D'D'$ are shifted to the left. Long-run equilibrium is attained when MR equals MC, DD is tangent to the average cost curve (indicating that total revenue equals total cost and therefore profit equals zero), and the tangency point is intersected by $D'D'$.

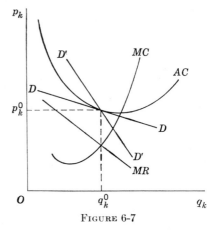

FIGURE 6-7

The long-run equilibrium point for the representative firm is to the left of the minimum point on its average total cost curve. Price equals average cost, as is true for the representative firm in perfect competition, but price does not equal MC. Contrasted with the results of perfect competition, the representative firm produces a smaller output at a greater average total cost.

6-4. Monopsony

The preceding sections deal with entrepreneurs who purchase their inputs in perfectly competitive markets. Input prices are invariant with respect to the quantities which they buy. The entrepreneur who is the sole purchaser of a particular input, the *monopsonist*, is considered in the present section. A monopsonist cannot purchase an unlimited amount of an input at a uniform price; the price which he must pay for each quantity purchased is given by the market supply curve for the input. Since the supply curves for most inputs are positively sloped, the price which the monopsonist must pay is generally an increasing function of the quantity he purchases.

First consider the case of a monopsonist who uses a single input, which we shall call labor, for the production of a commodity which he sells in a perfectly competitive market. An example might be provided by a producer who is the sole purchaser in a local labor market and sells his output in a competitive national or international market. His production function states output as a function of the quantity of labor (x) employed:

$$q = h(x) \tag{6-65}$$

The cost equation and revenue function are, as before:

$$R = pq \qquad C = rx$$

where r is the price of labor. However, the price of labor is now an increasing function of the amount employed:

$$r = g(x) \tag{6-66}$$

where $dr/dx > 0$. The *marginal cost of labor* is the rate of change of its cost with respect to the quantity employed:[1]

$$\frac{dC}{dx} = r + xg'(x) \tag{6-67}$$

Since $g'(x) > 0$, the marginal cost of labor exceeds its price for $x > 0$.

The monopsonist's profit can be expressed as a function of the amount of labor which he employs:

$$\pi = R - C = ph(x) - rx \tag{6-68}$$

Setting the derivative of (6-68) with respect to x equal to zero,

$$\frac{d\pi}{dx} = ph'(x) - r - xg'(x) = 0$$

$$ph'(x) = r + xg'(x) \tag{6-69}$$

The first-order condition for profit maximization requires that labor be employed up to a point at which the value of its marginal product equals its marginal cost. The second-order condition requires that the rate of change of the value of the marginal product of labor be less than the rate of change of its marginal cost:

$$\frac{d^2\pi}{dx^2} = ph''(x) - 2g'(x) - xg''(x) < 0$$

$$ph''(x) < 2g'(x) + xg''(x) \tag{6-70}$$

The monopsonist's optimum output and the price of labor are determined by solving (6-69) for x and substituting the value for which the second-order condition is satisfied into (6-65) and (6-66).

The profit-maximizing monopsonist (see Fig. 6-8) will employ x^0 units of labor at a wage rate of r^0 dollars. The equality of the price of labor with the value of its marginal product, the equilibrium point for an entrepreneur who purchases labor in a perfectly competitive market, would result in the employment of $x^{(1)}$ units of labor at a wage rate of $r^{(1)}$. The monopsonist employs a smaller quantity of labor at a lower wage rate.

---

[1] The reader should note that marginal cost is here defined with respect to the quantity of labor employed rather than the quantity of output produced. The abbreviated form (MC) is reserved for marginal cost with respect to output level.

If the monopsonist's production and labor supply functions are

$$q = 15x^2 - 0.2x^3 \qquad r = 144 + 23.4x$$

and he sells his output in a perfectly competitive market at a price of

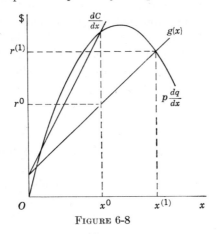

FIGURE 6-8

3 dollars, his total revenue function and cost equation are

$$R = 45x^2 - 0.6x^3 \qquad C = 144x + 23.4x^2$$

Setting the value of the marginal product of labor equal to its marginal cost,

$$90x - 1.8x^2 = 144 + 46.8x$$

which yields the quadratic equation:

$$1.8x^2 - 43.2x + 144 = 0$$

with the roots $x = 4$ and $x = 20$. The second-order condition

$$90 - 3.6x < 46.8$$

is satisfied for $x = 20$. The solution $x = 4$ is a minimum-profit position. Substituting $x = 20$ into the appropriate functions,

$$q = 4,400 \qquad r = 612 \qquad \pi = 960$$

If a monopsonist is also a monopolist in the market for his output, the price he receives is a function of the quantity which he sells:

$$p = F(q)$$

His profit may again be expressed as a function of the quantity of labor which he employs:

$$\pi = pq - rx = F[h(x)]h(x) - rx$$

or more simply,

$$\pi = R(x) - C(x) \tag{6-71}$$

where total revenue and total cost are expressed as functions of the quantity of labor employed. Setting the derivative of (6-71) equal to zero yields the first-order condition that the rate of increase of total revenue from the employment of another unit of labor (the marginal-revenue product of labor) must equal its marginal cost. The second-order condition requires that the marginal-revenue product of labor increase less rapidly than its marginal cost.

6-5. Summary

A monopolistic firm constitutes an industry and is unfettered by the competition of close rivals. A monopolist is free to select any price-quantity combination which lies on his negatively sloped demand curve. Since an expansion of his output results in a reduction of his price, his MR is less than his price. His first-order condition for profit maximization requires the equality of MR and MC. His second-order condition requires that MC be increasing more rapidly than MR.

If second-order conditions are satisfied, a discriminating monopolist maximizes his profit by equating the MR in each of his markets to the MC for his output as a whole. Similarly, a multiple-plant monopolist maximizes his profit by equating the MC in each of his plants to the MR for his output as a whole.

Neither a lump-sum nor a profit tax will affect the optimum price-quantity combination for a profit-maximizing monopolist. The imposition of either a specific or an ad valorem sales tax will result in a reduction of his output and an increase of his price.

The profit of a duopolist or an oligopolist depends upon the actions and reactions of his rivals. Different theories are based upon different assumptions regarding market behavior. The Cournot solution is realized if each market participant maximizes his profit on the assumption that his rivals' output levels are unaffected by his actions. The collusion solution is realized if the market participants join together to maximize total industry profit. The Stackelberg solution is based upon the assumption that duopolists explicitly recognize the interdependence of their actions. Each desires to assume the role of either a leader or a follower, and market equilibrium is achieved if their desires are consistent. These three solutions are applicable for both homogeneous and differentiated products. The producers of differentiated products may find advertising profitable.

The market-shares solution is realized if a market participant follows the moves of his rivals in such a way as to maintain his historical share of total industry sales. The kinked-demand-curve solution is realized if a seller assumes that his rivals will follow his price reductions, but leave their prices unchanged in response to his price increases. In the two-person, zero-sum case, the theory-of-games solution is based upon the assumption that each duopolist desires to "play it safe" and selects a strategy or combination of strategies to maximize his profit, given the most unfavorable strategy choice on the part of his rival.

In the many-sellers case of monopolistic competition an individual seller possesses a negatively sloped demand curve for his distinct product, but his output constitutes such a small part of the total market that his actions do not have perceptible effects upon his rivals. However, simultaneous movements on the part of all sellers cause shifts of the individual demand curves. Short-run equilibrium is achieved when each seller has equated MR and MC. The number of firms within the industry increases or decreases sufficiently to drive the pure profit of the representative firm to zero in the long run.

A monopsonist faces a rising supply curve for an input. He may be the sole purchaser of a particular type of labor. The monopsonist's marginal cost of labor exceeds the wage rate, since he must increase the wage rate for all his employees in order to expand employment. The first-order condition for profit maximization requires that he employ labor up to the point at which the value of its marginal productivity equals its marginal cost. If the monopsonist is also a monopolist in his product market, the first-order condition requires that he equate the marginal-revenue productivity of labor to its marginal cost.

SELECTED REFERENCES

Buchanan, Norman S., "Advertising Expenditures: A Suggested Treatment," *Journal of Political Economy*, vol. 50 (August, 1942), pp. 537–557. Also reprinted in R. V. Clemence (ed.), *Readings in Economic Analysis* (Cambridge, Mass.: Addison-Wesley, 1950), vol. 2, pp. 230–250. A geometric determination of the optimum advertising expenditure for a firm.

Chamberlin, E. H., *The Theory of Monopolistic Competition* (7th ed.; Cambridge, Mass: Harvard University Press, 1956). The first statement of the problems of monopolistic competition and product differentiation. Geometry is used.

Cournot, Augustin, *Researches into the Mathematical Principles of the Theory of Wealth*, trans. by Nathaniel T. Bacon (New York: Macmillan, 1897). The original statement of the Cournot solution. Also one of the first applications of mathematics to economics.

Efroymson, Clarence W., "A Note on Kinked Demand Curves," *American Ecnomic Review*, vol. 33 (March, 1943), pp. 98–109. Also reprinted in Clemence, *Readings in Economic Analysis*, vol. 2, pp. 218–229. A nonmathematical discussion of kinked demand curves and full-cost pricing.

Fellner, William, *Competition Among the Few* (New York: Knopf, 1949). A nonmathematical discussion of oligopoly and bilateral monopoly. Contains an exposition of the Stackelberg solution.

Hicks, J. R., "Annual Survey of Economic Theory: The Theory of Monopoly," *Econometrica*, vol. 3 (January, 1935), pp. 1–20. Also reprinted in American Economic Association, *Readings in Price Theory* (Homewood, Ill.: Irwin, 1952), pp. 361–383. A survey of the theories of monopolistic competition developed during the late twenties and early thirties.

McKinsey, J. C. C., *Introduction to the Theory of Games* (New York: McGraw-Hill, 1952). A textbook. A knowledge of advanced calculus is required.

Neumann, J. von, and O. Morgenstern, *The Theory of Games and Economic Behavior* (2d ed.; Princeton, N.J.: Princeton University Press, 1947). The original application of the theory of games to economic problems. Mathematical concepts are developed as needed.

Nicholls, William H., *A Theoretical Analysis of Imperfect Competition with Special Application to the Agricultural Industries* (Ames, Iowa: Iowa State College Press, 1941). Contains largely nonmathematical descriptions of many different forms of monopolistic competition. Particularly useful for the analysis of oligopsony.

Robinson, Joan, *The Economics of Imperfect Competition* (London: Macmillan, 1933). A pioneer study of monopoly, price discrimination, and monopsony in which many modern concepts were developed. The analysis is generally limited to geometry.

Triffin, Robert, *Monopolistic Competition and General Equilibrium Theory* (Cambridge, Mass: Harvard University Press, 1940). A survey of monopolistic competition theories and an attempt to classify markets on the basis of demand cross elasticities.

CHAPTER 7

WELFARE ECONOMICS

The objective of welfare economics is the evaluation of the social desirability of alternative economic states. An economic state is a particular arrangement of economic activities and of the resources of the economy. States of the economy may differ in many respects: (1) markets may be perfectly competitive or monopolistic; (2) markets may be in equilibrium or disequilibrium; (3) there may be several multimarket equilibrium positions, and the economy may have attained one of them. Each state is characterized by a different allocation of resources and a different distribution of the rewards for economic activity. Although the economist may not always be able to prescribe a method by which one state of the economy can be transformed into another, policy measures frequently will be available for changing an existing situation. It is important to know in such cases whether the contemplated change is desirable. Imagine, for example, that the economy can attain multimarket equilibrium at two different sets of commodity and factor prices. Since the desires of consumers and entrepreneurs are consistent at both equilibria, society can choose between them, if at all, only on welfare grounds. The principles by which such problems can be solved fall within the domain of welfare economics.

The welfare of a society depends, in the broadest sense, upon the satisfaction levels of all its consumers.[1] But almost every alternative to be judged by welfare economists will have favorable effects on some people and unfavorable effects on others. Welfare comparisons would be simple if it were possible to aggregate the utilities of individuals into a single utility function. Unfortunately this operation cannot be performed. Interpersonal comparisons of utility are not possible. There is no obvious way to determine whether individual I or individual II derives more satisfaction from the consumption of a given bundle of goods.[2]

[1] Statements of this kind are based on ethical beliefs or value judgments and cannot be proved. It is reasonable to postulate that the concept of social welfare transcends the more restricted notion of economic welfare. For obvious reasons the present analysis deals only with the latter.

[2] Ordinal utility functions are assumed throughout this chapter. The difficulty would not be eliminated by assuming cardinal functions, since measurability for

Welfare comparisons on the basis of individual utilities are possible only in a very restricted sense. As a result the conclusions of welfare economics are not so widely applicable as would be desirable.

The Pareto conditions for maximum welfare and the fulfillment of these conditions in perfect competition are discussed in Sec. 7-1. The welfare implications of monopolistic competition are outlined in Sec. 7-2. The argument for the optimality of perfect competition is qualified by introducing interdependent utility functions and external economies and diseconomies in Sec. 7-3. Finally, social welfare functions and alternative criteria for judging improvements in social welfare are considered in Sec. 7-4.

7-1. The Efficiency of Perfect Competition

Economic efficiency, often called Pareto optimality, is defined in terms of the outcome of one or more economic activities. The distribution of consumer goods (including leisure and other withheld primary factors) among consumers is efficient if every possible reallocation of goods among consumers results in the reduction of the satisfaction of at least one. Production is efficient if every feasible reallocation of inputs among (within) firms diminishes the output level of at least one firm (commodity). It will be shown that—in the absence of external economies and diseconomies—a perfectly competitive equilibrium satisfies the conditions of Pareto optimality.

Since individual utility levels cannot be compared, changes which improve the positions of some individuals but cause a deterioration in those of others cannot be evaluated in terms of efficiency; the net effects of the moves may or may not be beneficial.   However, welfare can be said to increase (diminish) if at least one person's position improves (deteriorates) with no change in the positions of others.   Clearly no situation can be optimal unless all possible improvements of this variety have been made.   Perfect competition is an optimum and a welfare ideal in this sense.[1]

The Consuming Sector.   According to the hypothesis of perfect competition among consumers, the price of a commodity is not altered by variations in the consumption level of an individual consumer.   Similarly, the prices of labor and other primary factors are independent of the sales by any single consumer.

---

individual consumers is neither necessary nor sufficient for interpersonal utility comparisons.

[1] The present discussion is limited to static efficiency.   No attention is paid to the welfare aspects of resource allocation over time, the time path of welfare, or the welfare aspects of alternative time paths for the economy.

The utility function of the ith consumer is

$$U_i = U_i(q_{i1}, \ldots, q_{im}) \tag{7-1}$$

where q_{ik} is the quantity of Q_k which he consumes. The goods consumed include the quantities of primary factors which he retains, such as labor (see Sec. 5-2). Primary factors retained are indicated by the subscript $(k = 1, \ldots, s)$, and produced commodities by $(k = s + 1, \ldots, m)$. If there is perfect competition among consumers, a consumer maximizes his satisfaction if his RCS (rate of commodity substitution) between any pair of goods equals their price ratio:[1]

$$-\frac{\partial q_{ik}}{\partial q_{ij}} = \frac{p_j}{p_k} \qquad (j, k = 1, \ldots, m) \tag{7-2}$$

Since prices are the same for all consumers, perfect competition implies that the rates of commodity substitution between Q_k and Q_j are the same for all n consumers:

$$-\frac{\partial q_{ik}}{\partial q_{ij}} = -\frac{\partial q_{hk}}{\partial q_{hj}} \qquad \begin{matrix} (i, h = 1, \ldots, n) \\ (j, k = 1, \ldots, m) \end{matrix} \tag{7-3}$$

These equalities are necessary for the realization of Pareto optimality in consumption. For illustration assume that there are only two consumers denoted by the first subscripts 1 and 2 and only two goods Q_1 and Q_2. The utility functions of the consumers are $U_1(q_{11}, q_{12})$ and $U_2(q_{21}, q_{22})$ where $q_{11} + q_{21} = q_1^0$ and $q_{12} + q_{22} = q_2^0$. Now assume that consumer II enjoys the level of satisfaction $U_2^0 = $ constant. In order to maximize the utility of consumer I subject to this constraint, form the function

$$U_1^* = U_1(q_{11}, q_{12}) + \lambda[U_2(q_1^0 - q_{11}, q_2^0 - q_{12}) - U_2^0]$$

where λ is a Lagrange multiplier, and set its partial derivatives equal to zero:

$$\frac{\partial U_1^*}{\partial q_{11}} = \frac{\partial U_1}{\partial q_{11}} - \lambda \frac{\partial U_2}{\partial q_{11}} = 0$$

$$\frac{\partial U_1^*}{\partial q_{12}} = \frac{\partial U_1}{\partial q_{12}} - \lambda \frac{\partial U_2}{\partial q_{12}} = 0 \tag{7-4}$$

$$\frac{\partial U_1^*}{\partial \lambda} = U_2(q_1^0 - q_{11}, q_2^0 - q_{12}) - U_2^0 = 0$$

and

$$\frac{\partial U_1/\partial q_{11}}{\partial U_1/\partial q_{12}} = \frac{\partial U_2/\partial q_{11}}{\partial U_2/\partial q_{12}} \tag{7-5}$$

---

[1] Of course, the second-order conditions must also be fulfilled. It is postulated throughout the remainder of this section that the second-order conditions are fulfilled.

The left-hand side of (7-5) is consumer I's RCS, and the right-hand side is II's. If (7-5) were not fulfilled, it would be possible to increase I's satisfaction without diminishing II's. The equality of the RCSs resulting from perfect competition ensures that the distribution of goods (including leisure) among consumers is Pareto-optimal. The mathematical analysis for the two-consumer case is easily generalized for any number of consumers.

The argument can be presented in terms of an Edgeworth box diagram. The dimensions of the rectangle in Fig. 7-1 represent the total available quantities of Q_1 and Q_2 in a pure-exchange economy. Any point in the box represents a particular distribution of the commodities between the two consumers. For example, if the distribution of commodities is given by point A, the quantities of Q_1 and Q_2 consumed by I are measured by the coordinates of A, using the southwest corner O as the origin; the quantities consumed by II are measured by the coordinates of point A, using the northeast corner O' as the origin. The indifference map of I is drawn, using O as the origin, and the indifference map of II, using O' as the origin. The RCSs of the two consumers are equal where an indifference curve of I is tangent to an indifference curve of II. The locus of all such points is the *contract curve CC*. The mathematical form of the contract curve is given by (7-5), which is a function of q_{11} and q_{12}.

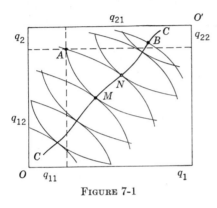

FIGURE 7-1

The rates of commodity substitution are unequal at point A, and it is possible to increase the utility levels of both consumers by altering the existing distribution. For example, if the final position (after a redistribution of Q_1 and Q_2) is between M and N, both consumers would have gained, since both would be on higher indifference curves than at A. If the final point is at M or N, one consumer will have gained without any deterioration in the other's position. If a point on the contract curve is reached, it is not possible to improve further the position of either consumer without a deterioration in the position of the other. According to the conditions of Pareto optimality any point between M and N is unambiguously superior to A. However, the evaluation of alternative points on the contract curve would involve an interpersonal comparison of utilities and is therefore not possible without an explicit ethical belief in one's ability to make such comparisons.

The Producing Sector. In perfect competition among producers in commodity markets the price of a commodity is not altered by variations of the individual firm's output level. Perfect competition among producers in input markets requires that the prices that the firm pays for inputs do not change in response to variations in the levels of its purchases.

Let the hth firm's production function be given by the implicit function

$$F_h(q_{h1}, \ldots, q_{hm}) = 0 \qquad (7\text{-}6)$$

where q_{hk} $(k = 1, \ldots, s)$ is an input and is defined as $q_{hk} = -x_{hk}$ and q_{hk} $(k = s + 1, \ldots, m)$ an output. It was shown (see Sec. 3-6) that profit maximization under conditions of perfect competition requires that

$$-\frac{\partial q_{hk}}{\partial q_{hj}} = \frac{p_j}{p_k} \qquad (7\text{-}7)$$

If both subscripts j and k refer to inputs, (7-7) states that the RTS (rate of technical substitution) must equal the ratio of the input prices. If the subscripts refer to two outputs, it states that the RPT (rate of product transformation) must equal the ratio of output prices. If q_{hk} is an output and q_{hj} an input, (7-7) states that the rate at which an input can be transformed into an output (MP, or marginal product) must equal the ratio of the prices of the input and output.

Conditions (7-7) ensure Pareto optimality in the producing sector. The argument is analogous to that employed for the consumer. Since each entrepreneur adjusts to the prices that confront him in the market without noticeably affecting them, each pays the same price for a given type of input and receives the same price for a given type of output, and the corresponding RTSs, RPTs, and MPs are the same for all N firms:

$$-\frac{\partial q_{hk}}{\partial q_{hj}} = -\frac{\partial q_{ik}}{\partial q_{ij}} \qquad \begin{array}{l} (i, h = 1, \ldots, N) \\ (j, k = 1, \ldots, m) \end{array} \qquad (7\text{-}8)$$

These equalities imply Pareto optimality in the following senses: (1) if inputs are reallocated among firms so that the output level of one firm is increased, the output level of some other firm must decrease, and (2) if inputs are reallocated among uses within firms so that the aggregate output level of one commodity is increased, the aggregate output level of some other commodity must decrease.

Only the proof of the first statement is given here.[1] Assume that there are two producers using the primary inputs X_1 and X_2 with the explicit production functions $q_1 = f_1(x_{11}, x_{12})$ and $q_2 = f_2(x_{21}, x_{22})$, where $x_{11} + x_{21} = x_1^0$ and $x_{12} + x_{22} = x_2^0$ are the total quantities of the two inputs and $q_1 + q_2 = q$ is the aggregate output of commodity Q. Maximize the out-

---

[1] The reader may verify the proof of the other statement.

put of entrepreneur I subject to the constraint that the output of II is at the predetermined level q_2^0. Form the function

$$L = f_1(x_{11}, x_{12}) + \lambda[f_2(x_1^0 - x_{11}, x_2^0 - x_{12}) - q_2^0]$$

and set the partial derivatives equal to zero:

$$\frac{\partial L}{\partial x_{11}} = \frac{\partial f_1}{\partial x_{11}} - \lambda \frac{\partial f_2}{\partial x_{11}} = 0$$

$$\frac{\partial L}{\partial x_{12}} = \frac{\partial f_1}{\partial x_{12}} - \lambda \frac{\partial f_2}{\partial x_{12}} = 0$$

$$\frac{\partial L}{\partial \lambda} = f_2(x_1^0 - x_{11}, x_2^0 - x_{12}) - q_2^0 = 0$$

and
$$\frac{\partial f_1/\partial x_{11}}{\partial f_1/\partial x_{12}} = \frac{\partial f_2/\partial x_{11}}{\partial f_2/\partial x_{12}} \tag{7-9}$$

which proves that the equality of the RTSs is necessary for Pareto optimality.

General Pareto Optimality. Efficiency in the consuming and producing sectors implies that the allocation of resources is Pareto-optimal throughout the economy. Consider the consumers' RCSs between Q_k and Q_j. All these RCSs equal p_j/p_k. This price ratio also equals all producers' RPTs between Q_k and Q_j. Therefore RCS = RPT for all consumers, firms, and commodities. Similar conditions can be derived if either j or k or both refer to primary factors: the consumers' RCS between a factor which they retain and a commodity which they consume must equal (by an analogous argument) the producers' corresponding rate of transforming the factor into the commodity (MP). The equality of the various rates of substitution and transformation ensures Pareto optimality throughout the economy. For example assume that RCS = $\frac{1}{3}$ and RPT = $\frac{2}{3}$. Three units of Q_j could be transformed into two units of Q_k by moving along a producer's transformation function. A consumer who surrenders three units of Q_j (the position of all other consumers remaining unchanged) would require only one unit of Q_k in exchange in order to remain on the same indifference curve and avoid a diminution of utility. The satisfaction level of this consumer could therefore actually be increased by performing the technological transformation of three units of Q_k into two of Q_j. Such an improvement is not possible if the RCSs and RPTs are equal.

The Pareto optimality of perfect competition can be deduced directly from the following argument. The RCS between any two commodities Q_k and Q_j equals their price ratio if there is perfect competition among consumers:

$$\text{RCS} = \frac{p_j}{p_k}$$

If there is perfect competition among entrepreneurs in commodity and factor markets,

$$p_j = \frac{r}{\mathrm{MP}_j} \qquad p_k = \frac{r}{\mathrm{MP}_k} \tag{7-10}$$

where r is the price of factor X and MP_j and MP_k are its marginal products in producing Q_j and Q_k. Therefore

$$\mathrm{RCS} = \frac{p_j}{p_k} = \frac{r/\mathrm{MP}_j}{r/\mathrm{MP}_k} = \frac{1/\mathrm{MP}_j}{1/\mathrm{MP}_k}$$

$$= \frac{\text{marginal cost of } Q_j \text{ in terms of } X}{\text{marginal cost of } Q_k \text{ in terms of } X} = \mathrm{RPT} \tag{7-11}$$

which proves Pareto optimality.

Equation (7-11) would appear to hold even if (7-10) does not, provided that

$$\frac{p_j}{p_k} = \frac{r/\mathrm{MP}_j}{r/\mathrm{MP}_k} \tag{7-12}$$

But (7-12) can hold without (7-10) only if

$$p_j = k \frac{r}{\mathrm{MP}_j} \qquad (j = 1, \ldots, m) \tag{7-13}$$

where $k \neq 1$ is a factor of proportionality, i.e., if prices are proportional to marginal cost $(= r/\mathrm{MP})$. Equation (7-13) becomes

$$\frac{r}{p_j} = \frac{1}{k} \mathrm{MP}_j \tag{7-14}$$

The left-hand side of (7-14) equals the consumers' rate of substitution between Q_j and X; the right-hand side is $(1/k)$ times the producers' rate of transformation between Q_j and X. Therefore the consumers' and producers' corresponding rates of substitution and transformation are not equal. Consumers do not provide the optimal amount of X (labor), and allocation cannot be Pareto-optimal.[1] Assume, for example, that price is three times MC, i.e., $k = 3$. Let the RCS between labor and commodity Q equal 2 and the MP of labor, 6. A consumer would be willing to surrender an additional hour of leisure (work for an additional hour) if he received 2 more units of Q. But the application of an additional hour of labor would result in the production of 6 more units of Q. Thus the situation is not Pareto-optimal.

---

[1] Since r/MP is the marginal cost of output (MC), (7-12) can be stated as

$$\frac{p_j}{p_k} = \frac{\mathrm{MC}_j}{\mathrm{MC}_k}$$

The above proof also implies that for an optimum, $p = \mathrm{MC}$ for every commodity; the proportionality of prices and marginal costs is not sufficient.

Perfect competition represents a welfare optimum in the narrow sense of fulfilling the requirements of Pareto optimality. Optimality is contingent on the assumption that all second-order conditions are fulfilled. If one should be violated (e.g., if transformation functions were convex or indifference curves and isoquants concave to the origin), the equality of the relevant rates of substitution or transformation would not ensure optimality. In fact, the point at which the rates of substitution and transformation are equal may be a "pessimum" rather than an optimum. The optimum is then represented by a corner solution (see Sec. 2-2).

Corner solutions may result even if indifference curves are convex and transformation curves concave to the origin, provided that their shapes are such that the RCSs are always greater (or smaller) than the corresponding RPTs for any point on a transformation curve. In such cases welfare optima must be described in terms of marginal inequalities.

An additional difficulty is introduced by the fact that the analysis of Pareto optimality accepts the prevailing income distribution, i.e., the prevailing factor endowment. The problem of finding an optimal income distribution is not considered. It is conceivable that the norm of the perfectly competitive economy would lead to a situation in which a majority of individuals lived at a subsistence level or below. At point B in Fig. 7-1, consumer I is very well off, but consumer II is not. Since point B is on the contract curve, one could not improve one consumer's position without causing a deterioration in the position of the other. It is an efficient point and cannot be said to be inferior to any other point, such as A. The analysis of welfare in terms of Pareto optimality leaves a considerable amount of indeterminacy in the solution: there are an infinite number of points in Fig. 7-1 which are Pareto-optimal. The acceptance of the contract curve as representing welfare optima is already a value judgment. In order to judge the relative social desirability of alternative points on the contract curve, society must make additional value judgments which state its preferences among alternative ways of allocating satisfaction to individuals. Value judgments are ethical beliefs and are not the subject of economic analysis. They are taken for granted and can then be incorporated in economic analysis. The indeterminacy is the consequence of considering an increase in welfare to be unambiguously defined only if an improvement in one individual's position is not accompanied by a deterioration of the position of another. This indeterminacy can only be removed by further value judgments.

7-2. The Efficiency of Monopolistic Competition

The conditions for Pareto optimality fail to be realized in a world characterized by monopolistic competition. The efficiency criteria of

Sec. 7-1 are not fulfilled in the presence of monopolies, oligopolies, monopsonies, etc. It was shown in Sec. 7-1 that perfect competition leads to an efficient allocation of resources. It will be shown in the present section that an efficient allocation of resources must be a perfectly competitive one. The argument will parallel the development of Sec. 7-1.

The Consuming Sector. Assume that consumers are not in perfect competition in commodity and factor markets. One or more consumers may be unable to buy as much of a commodity or sell as much of a factor as they desire without noticeably affecting its price. Assume that a consumer must pay a higher price as he increases his purchases.

Assume that there are two consumers with the utility functions

$$U_1 = U_1(q_{11}, q_{12}) \qquad U_2 = U_2(q_{21}, q_{22}) \qquad (7\text{-}15)$$

where q_{ij} is the amount of the jth commodity consumed by the ith consumer. Let the price of each commodity depend upon the aggregate amount demanded:

$$p_1 = g(q_{11} + q_{21}) \qquad p_2 = h(q_{12} + q_{22}) \qquad (7\text{-}16)$$

The budget constraints of the two consumers are

$$\begin{aligned}
y_1^0 - g(q_{11} + q_{21})q_{11} - h(q_{12} + q_{22})q_{12} = 0 \\
y_2^0 - g(q_{11} + q_{21})q_{21} - h(q_{12} + q_{22})q_{22} = 0
\end{aligned} \qquad (7\text{-}17)$$

Each maximizes his utility index subject to his budget constraint. Form the functions

$$\begin{aligned}
U_1^* &= U_1(q_{11}, q_{12}) + \lambda[y_1^0 - g(q_{11} + q_{21})q_{11} - h(q_{12} + q_{22})q_{12}] \\
U_2^* &= U_2(q_{21}, q_{22}) + \mu[y_2^0 - g(q_{11} + q_{21})q_{21} - h(q_{12} + q_{22})q_{22}]
\end{aligned}$$

and set the appropriate partial derivatives equal to zero:

$$\begin{aligned}
\frac{\partial U_1}{\partial q_{11}} - \lambda[g + q_{11}g'] = 0 \qquad & \frac{\partial U_1}{\partial q_{12}} - \lambda[h + q_{12}h'] = 0 \\
\frac{\partial U_2}{\partial q_{21}} - \mu[g + q_{21}g'] = 0 \qquad & \frac{\partial U_2}{\partial q_{22}} - \mu[h + q_{22}h'] = 0
\end{aligned} \qquad (7\text{-}18)$$

and

$$\frac{\partial U_1/\partial q_{11}}{\partial U_1/\partial q_{12}} = \frac{g + q_{11}g'}{h + q_{12}h'} \qquad (7\text{-}19)$$

$$\frac{\partial U_2/\partial q_{21}}{\partial U_2/\partial q_{22}} = \frac{g + q_{21}g'}{h + q_{22}h'} \qquad (7\text{-}20)$$

The individual consumer is in equilibrium if his RCS equals the ratio of the marginal costs of acquiring additional quantities of Q_1 and Q_2.† Under the present assumptions the marginal costs will not equal the commodity prices and will exceed them if g' and h' are positive (see Sec. 6-4).

† Again it is assumed that the second-order conditions are fulfilled.

In general, the right-hand sides of (7-19) and (7-20), and thus the corresponding RCSs, will not be equal.[1] One may conclude that in the absence of perfect competition among consumers the distribution of consumer goods will not generally be Pareto-optimal.

The Producing Sector.   The failure to establish Pareto optimality in the productive sector may be the result of monopolistic competition in product or input markets.   The failure to attain Pareto optimality can be proved by simple extensions of Secs. 3-2, 3-5, and 6-4.

If there is monopolistic competition in the markets for inputs, the price of each input is an (increasing) function of the quantity bought. It is easily seen that each entrepreneur's RTS must equal the ratio of the marginal costs of buying additional units of inputs, not the ratio of their prices.   These ratios will generally differ from entrepreneur to entrepreneur, and their respective RTSs will not be equal.   The production of aggregate output for the commodity in question is not Pareto-optimal, because the divergence between individual entrepreneurs' RTSs implies that they are not on their contract curve: it would be possible to increase some entrepreneurs' output levels without decreasing the output levels of the others by appropriately reallocating inputs among them.[2]

If there is perfect competition in input markets, but monopolistic competition in product markets, the MP of X in producing Q multiplied by the marginal revenue (MR) of Q must equal the price of X.   The rates of product transformation between two given commodities will not necessarily be the same for all producers, and the production of commodities will not be Pareto-optimal: one could find a reallocation of inputs which would increase the output level of a commodity without diminishing the output level of another.

The Absence of Pareto Optimality in General.   Any element of monopolistic competition prevents a Pareto-optimal allocation of resources. This assertion is easily proved by a four-stage argument:

1. Under conditions of monopolistic competition among consumers, the corresponding RCSs of different consumers are not necessarily equal.

2. Under conditions of monopolistic competition among firms in input markets, the corresponding RTSs of different firms are not necessarily equal.

[1] The RCSs will be equal if $q_{11} = q_{12}$ and $q_{21} = q_{22}$. However, the system as a whole will not achieve Pareto optimality even if the RCSs are equal.

[2] The argument can be phrased alternatively as follows. If input markets are monopolistically competitive, the MP of X in producing Q must equal (marginal cost of hiring an extra unit of X)/p, and the RTSs need not be the same for all firms.   Let MP_x and MP_y be the marginal products of inputs X and Y in producing Q, and assume that $MP_x/MP_y = 1\frac{9}{5}$ for firm I and $MP_x/MP_y = \frac{2}{3}$ for firm II.   The output levels of both firms will increase if a unit of X is transferred from II to I and a unit of Y is transferred from I to II.

3. Under conditions of monopolistic competition among firms in product markets, the corresponding RPTs of different firms are not necessarily equal.

4. Assume that 1 and 2 do not hold, i.e., that monopolistic competition exists only among firms in product markets. In addition, postulate that the corresponding RPTs for different firms *are* equal by accident. Then

$$\text{RPT} = \frac{1/\text{MP}_j}{1/\text{MP}_k} = \frac{r/\text{MP}_j}{r/\text{MP}_k} = \frac{\text{MR}_j}{\text{MR}_k} \qquad (7\text{-}21)$$

RPT = RCS is a necessary, but insufficient, condition for Pareto optimality. This necessary condition is fulfilled if and only if

$$\frac{\text{MR}_j}{\text{MR}_k} = \frac{p_j}{p_k}$$

i.e., if the elasticity of demand for Q_j equals the elasticity of demand for Q_k, since $\text{MR} = p[1 - (1/e)]$. The insufficiency of this condition is proved by assuming that RCS = RPT for every pair of commodities and showing that the allocation of resources cannot be Pareto-optimal. Equation (7-21) can hold only if

$$\frac{r/\text{MP}_j}{r/\text{MP}_k} = \frac{p_j}{p_k} \qquad (7\text{-}22)$$

The existence of monopolistic competition implies that only the ratios are equal, but not the numerators (or denominators) taken in pairs. It was shown [Eqs. (7-12) to (7-14)] that the consumer's rates of substitution between commodities and primary factors, then, do not equal the corresponding MPs (the producers' rate of transforming labor into output). Therefore the over-all allocation of resources is not Pareto-optimal.

It was proved in Sec. 7-1 that perfect competition results in Pareto-optimal allocation. One may now add the even stronger conclusion that every Pareto-optimal allocation must be a perfectly competitive one, since Pareto optimality cannot be obtained under conditions of monopolistic competition. It is therefore necessary and sufficient for an efficient allocation of resources that all markets be perfectly competitive. This is intuitively clear from the fact that price exceeds MC in the absence of perfect competition. MC is a measure of the cost to society of using resources in the production of an additional unit of commodity Q; its price is a measure of the benefit to society from producing an additional unit of Q. The net benefit to society can be increased as long as $p > \text{MC}$, and imperfect competition violates the criteria of efficiency by not producing sufficiently large quantities of commodities.

7-3. External Effects in Consumption and Production

The conclusions of the foregoing analysis are not universally valid. They are contingent upon the assumption that there are no external effects in consumption and production, i.e., that the utility level of a consumer does not depend upon the consumption levels of others and that the total cost of an entrepreneur does not depend upon the output levels of others. Pareto optimality may not be realized under conditions of perfect competition if there are external effects in consumption and production.

Interdependent Utility Functions. Assume that the utility level of one consumer depends upon the consumption of another. Extreme altruism may increase the satisfaction of the ith consumer if the consumption level of the jth consumer is raised. The desire to "keep up with the Joneses" may have the opposite effect.

Assume that there are two consumers with the utility functions

$$U_1 = U_1(q_{11}, q_{12}, q_{21}, q_{22})$$
$$U_2 = U_2(q_{11}, q_{12}, q_{21}, q_{22}) \tag{7-23}$$

where $q_{11} + q_{21} = q_1^0$, $q_{12} + q_{22} = q_2^0$. In order to maximize the utility of I subject to the constraint that the utility of II is at the predetermined level $U_2^0 = \text{constant}$, form the function

$$U_1^* = U_1(q_{11}, q_{12}, q_1^0 - q_{11}, q_2^0 - q_{12})$$
$$+ \lambda[U_2(q_{11}, q_{12}, q_1^0 - q_{11}, q_2^0 - q_{12}) - U_2^0]$$

and set the partial derivatives equal to zero:

$$\frac{\partial U_1^*}{\partial q_{11}} = \frac{\partial U_1}{\partial q_{11}} - \frac{\partial U_1}{\partial q_{21}} + \lambda\left[\frac{\partial U_2}{\partial q_{11}} - \frac{\partial U_2}{\partial q_{21}}\right] = 0$$

$$\frac{\partial U_1^*}{\partial q_{12}} = \frac{\partial U_1}{\partial q_{12}} - \frac{\partial U_1}{\partial q_{22}} + \lambda\left[\frac{\partial U_2}{\partial q_{12}} - \frac{\partial U_2}{\partial q_{22}}\right] = 0 \tag{7-24}$$

$$\frac{\partial U_1^*}{\partial \lambda} = U_2(q_{11}, q_{12}, q_1^0 - q_{11}, q_2^0 - q_{12}) - U_2^0 = 0$$

and

$$\frac{\partial U_1/\partial q_{11} - \partial U_1/\partial q_{21}}{\partial U_1/\partial q_{12} - \partial U_1/\partial q_{22}} = \frac{\partial U_2/\partial q_{11} - \partial U_2/\partial q_{21}}{\partial U_2/\partial q_{12} - \partial U_2/\partial q_{22}} \tag{7-25}$$

Equation (7-25) is the necessary condition for Pareto optimality. It generally differs from (7-3) [or (7-5)], which states that I's RCS must equal II's. Perfect competition results in the attainment of (7-3), but not of (7-25). Since the partial derivatives of the utility functions are functions of all variables, the optimum position of each consumer depends upon the consumption level of the other. For example, assume that the only external effect present in the two-consumer system is $\partial U_2/\partial q_{11} < 0$.

Equation (7-25) becomes

$$\frac{\partial U_1/\partial q_{11}}{\partial U_1/\partial q_{12}} = \frac{\partial U_2/\partial q_{11} - \partial U_2/\partial q_{21}}{-\partial U_2/\partial q_{22}} \tag{7-26}$$

The RCS of consumer II must be smaller for an optimal distribution than it would be in the absence of external effects.

It can be shown diagrammatically that condition (7-3) does not necessarily ensure Pareto optimality in the presence of external effects. Figures 7-2a and 7-2b give the indifference maps of consumers I and II

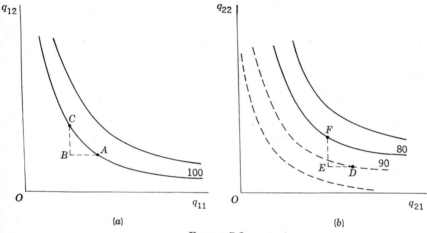

FIGURE 7-2

respectively. Assume that in the initial situation I consumes the commodity batch represented by A and II consumes the batch represented by F. These points—at which their RCSs are equal—are reached by utility maximization carried out individually by the two consumers with no regard for possible external effects. Assume that I is not affected by II's consumption, and II's utility level is reduced by I's consumption of Q_1 (but not of Q_2). II's indifference map (solid curves) is drawn on the assumption that I's consumption is given by A. In their individual equilibrium situations I's utility index is 100, and II's, 80. Let the distribution of commodities be altered by some authority in such a way that the aggregate quantities consumed remain unchanged and that I moves to C and II to D. The utility level of consumer I has not been changed by this reallocation. However, the diminution of his consumption of Q_1 changes II's utility level for every commodity combination consumed by the latter: II's relevant indifference curves after the change in I's consumption are given by the dotted curves in Fig. 7-2b. Consumer II's utility level is increased to 90 since his new position is at D. One can conclude that II's utility level can be increased without diminishing I's utility level; hence the equality of the RCSs does not ensure Pareto optimality.

External Economies and Diseconomies. It was shown that the $p = $ MC criterion is necessary for Pareto optimality in the producing sector. The equality of price and marginal cost for all commodities and firms implies that the corresponding RPTs of different firms are the same. The RPT (the slope of the transformation curve) measures the opportunity cost or the real sacrifice, in terms of opportunities foregone, of producing an additional unit of a commodity.   Until now this opportunity cost has been considered internal to the firm: in order to produce an additional unit of Q_j it has to sacrifice the production of a certain number of units of Q_k.   The relevant measure of the sacrifice from society's point of view is the number of units of Q_k that society has to give up in order to produce an additional unit of Q_j.   The opportunity cost is the same from the private and social points of view in the absence of external economies and diseconomies.   If such external effects are present in the productive sphere, one must take into account the interdependence between the costs of the ith firm and the output of the hth (see Sec. 4-3).

Assume for simplicity's sake that there are only two firms with the cost functions

$$C_1 = C_1(q_1,q_2) \qquad C_2 = C_2(q_1,q_2) \qquad (7\text{-}27)$$

where q_1 and q_2 are the output levels.   The cost functions (7-27) express the existence of external effects.   If each firm maximizes its profit individually, price will equal MC or

$$p = \frac{\partial C_1}{\partial q_1} \qquad p = \frac{\partial C_2}{\partial q_2} \qquad (7\text{-}28)$$

The profit of each firm depends upon the output level of the other, but neither can affect the output of the other, and thus each firm maximizes its profit with respect to the variable under its control.

The welfare associated with production can be measured by the difference between the social benefit created and the social cost incurred. The social benefit derived from $q_1 + q_2$ units of the commodity can be measured by the total revenue $p(q_1 + q_2)$, i.e., by the amount that consumers are willing to pay for the output.   The social costs are measured by the sum of the costs incurred by both entrepreneurs producing the commodity, $C_1(q_1,q_2) + C_2(q_1,q_2)$. In order to maximize welfare, one must maximize the entrepreneurs' joint profits:

$$\pi = \pi_1 + \pi_2 = p(q_1 + q_2) - C_1(q_1,q_2) - C_2(q_1,q_2) \qquad (7\text{-}29)$$

Setting the partial derivatives equal to zero,

$$\frac{\partial \pi}{\partial q_1} = p - \frac{\partial C_1}{\partial q_1} - \frac{\partial C_2}{\partial q_1} = 0$$

$$\frac{\partial \pi}{\partial q_2} = p - \frac{\partial C_1}{\partial q_2} - \frac{\partial C_2}{\partial q_2} = 0$$

(7-30)

The second-order conditions require that the principal minors of the relevant Hessian

$$\begin{vmatrix} - \dfrac{\partial^2 C_1}{\partial q_1^2} - \dfrac{\partial^2 C_2}{\partial q_1^2} & - \dfrac{\partial^2 C_1}{\partial q_1 \, \partial q_2} - \dfrac{\partial^2 C_2}{\partial q_1 \, \partial q_2} \\ - \dfrac{\partial^2 C_1}{\partial q_1 \, \partial q_2} - \dfrac{\partial^2 C_2}{\partial q_1 \, \partial q_2} & - \dfrac{\partial^2 C_1}{\partial q_2^2} - \dfrac{\partial^2 C_2}{\partial q_2^2} \end{vmatrix}$$

alternate in sign, or that

$$- \frac{\partial^2 C_1}{\partial q_1^2} - \frac{\partial^2 C_2}{\partial q_1^2} < 0 \tag{7-31}$$

and $\left(- \dfrac{\partial^2 C_1}{\partial q_1^2} - \dfrac{\partial^2 C_2}{\partial q_1^2} \right)\left(- \dfrac{\partial^2 C_1}{\partial q_2^2} - \dfrac{\partial^2 C_2}{\partial q_2^2} \right)$

$$- \left(\frac{\partial^2 C_1}{\partial q_1 \, \partial q_2} + \frac{\partial^2 C_2}{\partial q_1 \, \partial q_2} \right)^2 > 0 \quad (7\text{-}32)$$

Inequalities (7-31) and (7-32) together imply

$$\frac{\partial^2 C_1}{\partial q_1^2} + \frac{\partial^2 C_2}{\partial q_1^2} > 0 \qquad \frac{\partial^2 C_1}{\partial q_2^2} + \frac{\partial^2 C_2}{\partial q_2^2} > 0 \tag{7-33}$$

The partial derivatives $\partial C_1/\partial q_1$ and $\partial C_2/\partial q_2$ are the *private* marginal costs because they measure the rate of increase of an individual entrepreneur's total cost as his output level rises. Individual maximization requires that price equal private marginal cost and that private marginal cost be increasing. The sums $\partial C_1/\partial q_1 + \partial C_2/\partial q_1$ and $\partial C_1/\partial q_2 + \partial C_2/\partial q_2$ are *social* marginal costs because they measure the rate of increase of the industry's costs as the output level of a particular firm increases. Welfare maximization requires that price equal the *social marginal cost* of each entrepreneur and that *social marginal cost be increasing*. The equality of price and social marginal cost guarantees that the consumers' RCS will equal not the individual firms' RPTs but society's RPT, since the ratio of the social marginal costs measures, from society's point of view, the alternatives foregone by producing an additional unit of a commodity.

Assume that firm I experiences external economies and firm II experiences external diseconomies. Then $\partial C_1/\partial q_2 < 0$ and $\partial C_2/\partial q_1 > 0$. As a result, $\partial C_1/\partial q_1 + \partial C_2/\partial q_1$ in (7-30) can be made to equal price only if $\partial C_1/\partial q_1$ is smaller than under individual profit maximization.   With increasing MC this means that the firm which is the cause of external diseconomies should produce a lower level of output for welfare maximization than in the case of individual maximization.   By analogous reasoning the firm which is the cause of external economies should increase its output.   This can generally be accomplished by appropriate taxation and subsidization of the output levels of the firms concerned.

Assume that the cost functions of the two firms are

$$C_1 = 0.1q_1{}^2 + 5q_1 - 0.1q_2{}^2 \qquad C_2 = 0.2q_2{}^2 + 7q_2 + 0.025q_1{}^2$$

Firm I experiences external economies and is the cause of external diseconomies; the converse holds for firm II.   Assuming that the price is 15 dollars and setting it equal to MC for both firms,

$$15 = 0.2q_1 + 5 \qquad q_1 = 50 \qquad \pi_1 = 290$$
$$15 = 0.4q_2 + 7 \qquad q_2 = 20 \qquad \pi_2 = 17.5$$

In order to maximize welfare, form the joint profit function

$$\pi = 15(q_1 + q_2) - 0.125q_1{}^2 - 5q_1 - 0.1q_2{}^2 - 7q_2$$

and set the partial derivatives equal to zero:

$$\frac{\partial \pi}{\partial q_1} = 15 - 0.25q_1 - 5 = 0$$

$$\frac{\partial \pi}{\partial q_2} = 15 - 0.20q_2 - 7 = 0$$

Hence $q_1 = 40$, $q_2 = 40$, and $\pi = 360$.   The reader may verify that the second-order conditions are satisfied.   Total profits are greater under welfare maximization than under individual maximization

$$290 + 17.5 = 307.5 < 360$$

Individual maximization does not ensure Pareto optimality.   Pareto optimality requires that the RCS equal the rate at which society can transform one commodity into another.   In the absence of external effects, the private and social rates of product transformation are identical.   In the presence of external economies or diseconomies individual maximization results in the fulfillment of the socially "wrong" or irrelevant marginal conditions.   Of course, aggregate profits *have* to be redistributed among the individual firms.   Without such redistribution, some firms would experience a diminution in their profits, and the resulting position could not be said to be socially preferable.   In the present example, 400 dollars accrue to firm I and -40 dollars to firm II as a result of welfare maximization.   A redistribution of any amount greater than

57.5, but less than 110, dollars from firm I to firm II will leave each better off than under individual maximization.

The quantities that would be produced under joint profit maximization can be enforced by appropriately taxing and subsidizing producers if they maximize profits individually. The magnitude of the necessary taxes can be calculated from the demand and supply functions. Let the aggregate demand function be $D = D(p)$, the aggregate supply function with individual profit maximization $S = \Sigma S_i(p)$, and the supply function derived on the assumption of joint profit maximization $S^* = \Sigma S_i^*(p)$. The equality $S^* = D$ determines a price p^* and the quantities sold $S_i^*(p^*)$. To achieve this price and these quantities under individual profit maximization, one must impose unit taxes (or subsidies) t_i such that

$$S_i(p^* - t_i) = S_i^*(p^*)$$

The taxes can be determined by solving for the t_is:

$$t_i = h_i(p^*)$$

Finally, it follows that the profits of at least one entrepreneur can be increased without reducing the profits of the others, if the amount collected by taxation is appropriately redistributed among entrepreneurs as lump-sum payments.

7-4. Social Welfare Functions

The indeterminacy which remains if Pareto optimality is the only requirement for welfare optimization can be removed through the introduction of a social welfare function. A social welfare function is an ordinal index of society's welfare and is a function of the utility levels of all individuals. It is not unique, and its form depends upon the value judgments of the person for whom it is a desirable welfare function. In certain cases it may be impossible to decide upon an acceptable form for the social welfare function by common consensus; it may then have to be imposed in dictatorial fashion. Whatever the case may be, its form depends upon the value judgments of its promulgators, since it expresses their views concerning the effect that the utility level of the ith individual has on the welfare of society. Moreover, the acceptance by an individual of the social welfare function for the purpose of solving the problem of distribution also involves a value judgment. The general form of the social welfare function is

$$W = W(U_1, U_2, \ldots, U_n) \qquad (7\text{-}34)$$

where U_i is the level of the utility index of the ith individual.

Determination of the Welfare Optimum. Assume that society consists of two individuals whose utility functions are

$$U_1 = U_1(q_{11}, q_{12}, x_1) \qquad U_2 = U_2(q_{21}, q_{22}, x_2) \tag{7-35}$$

where q_{ij} is the amount of the jth commodity consumed by the ith individual and x_i the amount of work performed by the ith individual.

Society's aggregate production function states the aggregate amounts of each commodity that can be produced as a function of the aggregate amount of labor and can be stated as an implicit function:

$$F(q_{11} + q_{21},\ q_{12} + q_{22},\ x_1 + x_2) = 0 \tag{7-36}$$

Assume finally that the social welfare function is

$$W = W(U_1, U_2) \tag{7-37}$$

The goal of society is to maximize (7-37) subject to the constraint given by (7-36). Form the function

$$W^* = W[U_1(q_{11}, q_{12}, x_1), U_2(q_{21}, q_{22}, x_2)] + \lambda F(q_{11} + q_{21},\ q_{12} + q_{22},\ x_1 + x_2)$$

and set its partial derivatives equal to zero:

$$\frac{\partial W^*}{\partial q_{11}} = W_1 \frac{\partial U_1}{\partial q_{11}} + \lambda F_1 = 0$$

$$\frac{\partial W^*}{\partial q_{12}} = W_1 \frac{\partial U_1}{\partial q_{12}} + \lambda F_2 = 0$$

$$\frac{\partial W^*}{\partial x_1} = W_1 \frac{\partial U_1}{\partial x_1} + \lambda F_3 = 0$$

$$\frac{\partial W^*}{\partial q_{21}} = W_2 \frac{\partial U_2}{\partial q_{21}} + \lambda F_1 = 0 \tag{7-38}$$

$$\frac{\partial W^*}{\partial q_{22}} = W_2 \frac{\partial U_2}{\partial q_{22}} + \lambda F_2 = 0$$

$$\frac{\partial W^*}{\partial x_2} = W_2 \frac{\partial U_2}{\partial x_2} + \lambda F_3 = 0$$

$$\frac{\partial W^*}{\partial \lambda} = F(q_{11} + q_{21},\ q_{12} + q_{22},\ x_1 + x_2) = 0$$

The system of equations (7-38) consists of seven equations in seven variables and can generally be solved for the unknowns (see Secs. A-3 and 5-5). The welfare optimum is completely determined as a result of the introduction of distributional value judgments in the form of the social welfare function.[1] It can easily be verified that the resulting allocation

---

[1] In terms of the Edgeworth box diagram discussed in Sec. 7-1, the introduction of the social welfare function is equivalent to ranking all points on the contract curve from the point of view of social preferability.

is Pareto-optimal. Move the second terms of the first six equations in (7-38) to the right and then divide the first equation by the second and third and the fourth equation by the fifth and sixth respectively:

$$\frac{\partial U_1/\partial q_{11}}{\partial U_1/\partial q_{12}} = \frac{F_1}{F_2} = \frac{\partial U_2/\partial q_{21}}{\partial U_2/\partial q_{22}} \qquad \frac{\partial U_1/\partial q_{11}}{\partial U_1/\partial x_1} = \frac{F_1}{F_3} = \frac{\partial U_2/\partial q_{21}}{\partial U_2/\partial x_2} \qquad (7\text{-}39)$$

The rates of commodity substitution are the same for all consumers and also equal the corresponding rates of product transformation. Moreover, the rate at which consumers substitute work (or its counterpart, leisure) for commodities equals the marginal product of labor. This proves Pareto optimality if the second-order conditions are also satisfied.[1]

Social Preference and Indifference. Economists have tried to develop criteria by which one can judge whether a given change in the economy is socially preferable to the existing state. Such criteria are usually stated as "compensation criteria":

1. The Kaldor criterion: state A is socially preferable to B if those who gain from A can compensate the losers (i.e., bribe them into accepting state A) and still be in a better position than at B.

2. The Hicks criterion: state A is socially preferable to B if those who would lose from A cannot profitably bribe the gainers into not making the change from B to A.

3. The Scitovsky criterion: state A is socially preferable to B if the gainers can bribe the losers into accepting the change and simultaneously the losers cannot bribe the gainers into not making the change.

The fundamental difficulty of compensation principles is that they refer to potential, rather than actual, welfare since they do not require that compensation actually be paid. In general, nothing can be said about the social preferability of A over B in the absence of actual compensation unless one is willing to make additional value judgments. Consider the case in which a change is contemplated from state A to state B. Some persons are affected unfavorably by the movement, and others benefit. Assume that there exists some redistribution of income (I) which compensates the losers; assume moreover that the losers cannot bribe the gainers to oppose the change from A to B. There is no guarantee, however, that the redistribution that would compensate the losers

---

[1] A social welfare function is analogous to the individual consumer's utility function. It provides a ranking—from society's or a dictator's point of view—of alternative positions in which different individuals enjoy different utility levels. It possesses the property that if a given social welfare function provides an acceptable ranking, so does any monotonic transformation of it. The reader may verify this proposition by proceeding analogously to the analysis in Sec. 2-3. Assume that the welfare function is $S = G(W)$ where $G' > 0$ and derive the first- and second-order conditions for a maximum.

will actually be carried out. The actual redistribution (II) following the establishment of B may be such that the losers are not compensated. In addition, it is possible that the losers could have effectively blocked the move to B (by bribing the gainers) had they known that the actual outcome was going to be given by redistribution II. Under these circumstances it is not legitimate to say that the fulfillment of the Scitovsky criterion implies that state B is socially preferable to A.

In the effort to create a social analogue to individual indifference curves, economists have tried to derive contour lines in the commodity space which represent alternative combinations of aggregate quantities of commodities among which society as a whole is indifferent. *Scitovsky contours* are derived in the following fashion. Assume that all individuals enjoy specified levels of utility and that the outputs of all commodities but one are at specified levels. Then determine the smallest quantity of the remaining commodity necessary to meet the above specifications. The problem is expressed mathematically for a two-person–two-commodity economy as follows:

$$\text{Minimize } q_{11} + q_{21}$$

subject to
$$U_1(q_{11}, q_{12}) - U_1^0 = 0$$
$$U_2(q_{21}, q_{22}) - U_2^0 = 0$$
$$q_{12} + q_{22} = q_2^0$$

This problem can be solved by forming the function

$$V = q_{11} + q_{21} + \lambda_1[U_1(q_{11}, q_{12}) - U_1^0] \\ + \lambda_2[U_2(q_{21}, q_2^0 - q_{12}) - U_2^0] \quad (7\text{-}40)$$

where λ_1 and λ_2 are Lagrange multipliers, and setting the partial derivatives with respect to q_{11}, q_{12}, q_{21}, λ_1, and λ_2 equal to zero. The total minimum quantity of Q_1 necessary to satisfy the conditions of the problem is generally determinate. For each possible value of q_2^0 a different optimal value of q_1^0 $(= q_{11} + q_{21})$ can be determined. The locus of all (q_1^0, q_2^0) points for given values of U_1 and U_2 forms a Scitovsky contour.[1] If the individual indifference curves are convex to the origin, the Scitovsky contours will be convex to the origin. However, these contours are not "social" indifference curves, as it might appear from their shapes alone. A completely different Scitovsky contour is obtained if the specified values of U_1 and U_2 are changed. Take for example point A on the Scitovsky contour S_1 in Fig. 7-3. For any point on S_1 the total quantities of Q_1 and Q_2 must be distributed between the two consumers in such a manner that I enjoys the utility level U_1^0 and II the level U_2^0. But the quantities

---

[1] The reader may verify that points on a Scitovsky contour represent a Pareto-optimal distribution of commodities by finding the partial derivatives of (7-40).

corresponding to A could also be distributed in a different manner, one that results in a utility level $U_1^{(1)}$ for I and $U_2^{(1)}$ for II. By carrying out the maximization process as indicated in (7-40) for these new values of U_1 and U_2, an entirely new set of points is determined, which describe a new Scitovsky contour corresponding to the different utility levels assigned to individuals. This new contour S_2 must have a common point with S_1 at A, but there is clearly no reason to expect that the two contours will coincide throughout their lengths. S_1 and S_2 may therefore either intersect at A (as in Fig. 7-3) or be tangent to each other. Neither case is consistent with the usual properties of indifference curves.

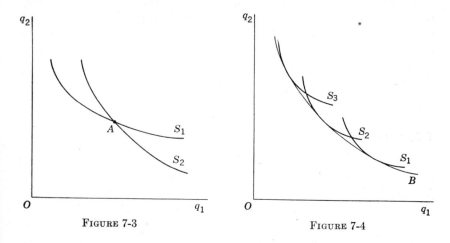

FIGURE 7-3   FIGURE 7-4

The explicit introduction of value judgments in the form of a social welfare function permits the derivation of contours with some desirable properties. Let the social welfare function be $W = W(U_1, U_2)$ in a two-person society. Find the Scitovsky contours corresponding to all distributions of utility (U_1, U_2) for which $W(U_1, U_2) = W^0$. These contours are shown in Fig. 7-4. The least ordinate corresponding to any value of q_1 represents the minimum amount of Q_2 necessary to ensure society the welfare level W^0. Therefore the envelope B of the Scitovsky contours in Fig. 7-4 is the locus of minimal combinations of Q_1 and Q_2 necessary to ensure society the welfare level W^0 and may be called a *Bergson contour*.[1]

The problem of finding the point of maximum welfare can thus be solved in two equivalent ways.

---

[1] See J. de V. Graaff, *Theoretical Welfare Economics* (London: Cambridge University Press, 1957), chap. III. The felicitous terms *Scitovsky contour* and *Bergson contour* are due to Graaff. Bergson contours are nonintersecting in the absence of external effects but do not necessarily possess the "right" convexity.

1. Each point on the aggregate transformation function defines a commodity combination that can be attained with the available resources. Even if only Pareto-optimal distributions of commodities are considered, a contract curve and thus an infinite number of ways in which utility can be distributed among consumers correspond to each point on the aggregate transformation function.[1] Find all possible ways of distributing utility among consumers corresponding to all points satisfying the transformation function. Of all these utility distributions choose the one for which $W(U_1, U_2, \ldots , U_n)$ is a maximum. The solution is obtained by examining points in the utility space.

2. Determine all Bergson contours. Each of these contours corresponds to a different welfare level. Choose that point on the aggregate transformation function which lies on the highest attainable Bergson contour. A solution is thus also obtained by examining points in the commodity space. The equivalence of the two procedures is obvious from the fact that both are equivalent to maximizing $W(U_1, \ldots , U_n)$ subject to the constraint given by the aggregate production function.

7-5. Summary

The purpose of welfare economics is to evaluate the social desirability of alternative allocations of resources. In the absence of elaborate value judgments concerning the desirability of alternative income distributions, a simple value judgment is to consider a reallocation to represent an improvement in welfare if it makes at least one person better off without making anybody worse off. If it is not possible to reallocate resources without making at least one person worse off, the existing allocation is Pareto-optimal. It is necessary for Pareto optimality that (1) the corresponding rates of substitution of all consumers be equal, (2) the corresponding rates of transformation of all producers be equal, (3) the rates of substitution equal the corresponding rates of transformation. The second-order conditions must also be fulfilled for maximum welfare in the Pareto sense.

Perfect competition results in the fulfillment of the first-order conditions for Pareto optimality. It is in this sense that perfect competition represents a welfare optimum. It does not guarantee that the second-order conditions are fulfilled; nor does it ensure that the distribution of income (or of utility) is optimal in any sense. In addition, the definition of optimum welfare in terms of Pareto optimality leaves a certain amount of indeterminacy in the analysis, since every point on a contract curve is

---

[1] The geometric representation of the possible ways of distributing utility among two consumers corresponding to a given point on the aggregate transformation curve is called a *utility possibility curve*.

Pareto-optimal and one cannot choose between them without additional restrictions.

It has been shown that the existence of monopolistic elements in competition among consumers or entrepreneurs in any market precludes the possibility of a Pareto-optimal allocation. Even if, by accident, consumers' rates of commodity substitution were equal to the corresponding rates of product transformation for producers, Pareto optimality would still not be attained as a result of divergences between consumers' rate of substitution between commodities and labor and the producers' corresponding rate of transforming labor into commodities.

The conditions under which Pareto optimality is attained under perfect competition must be modified in the presence of external effects such as interdependent utility functions and external economies and diseconomies. The equality of the rates of commodity substitution is no longer sufficient to ensure Pareto optimality in the consuming sector (even if one postulates that the second-order conditions are fulfilled). Price must equal social marginal cost rather than private marginal cost in the producing sector. A Pareto-optimal allocation can generally be attained by appropriately subsidizing or taxing the sale of commodities the production of which causes external economies or diseconomies respectively.

The indeterminacy which remains in the analysis of Pareto optimality can be removed by explicitly introducing a social welfare function which states society's (or a dictator's) preferences among alternative distributions of utility among individuals. Rather than a single social welfare function there are many, each expressing the evaluations of different groups of people. Which one is chosen for the purpose of solving the problem of allocation depends upon the institutional framework within which society decides upon such matters. Economists have attempted to judge the social preferability of alternative positions in terms of the ability of the gainers to compensate the losers and the inability of the losers to bribe the gainers into not undertaking the reallocation. Such compensation principles are invalid if compensation is potential rather than actual. The desirability of a reorganization of the economy can still be evaluated, however, by translating the social welfare function into the commodity space and finding that point on society's transformation curve which lies on the highest Bergson contour.

SELECTED REFERENCES

Arrow, K. J., *Social Choice and Individual Values* (New York: Wiley, 1951). A treatise on the problems of constructing a social welfare function. Difficult for those unfamiliar with the mathematics of sets.

Bator, F. M., "The Simple Analytics of Welfare Maximization," *American Economic*

Review, vol. 47 (March, 1957), pp. 22–59.   A geometric exposition of some fundamental results of welfare economics.

Baumol, W. J., *Welfare Economics and the Theory of the State* (London: Longmans, 1952).   Contains a discussion of the welfare implications of perfect competition and monopoly and an analysis of some of the nineteenth-century literature on welfare.   Mathematics is in appendixes.

Bergson, A., "A Reformulation of Certain Aspects of Welfare Economics," *Quarterly Journal of Economics*, vol. 52 (February, 1938), pp. 310–334.   Also reprinted in R. V. Clemence (ed.), *Readings in Economic Analysis* (Cambridge, Mass.: Addison-Wesley, 1950), vol. 1, pp. 61–85.   The first modern mathematical treatment of welfare economics.

Graaff, J. de V., *Theoretical Welfare Economics* (London: Cambridge University Press, 1957).   A treatise on welfare incorporating the theories of the last decade.   The mathematics is in appendixes.

Lerner, A. P., *The Economics of Control* (New York: Macmillan, 1944).   A nonmathematical analysis of welfare maximization in a controlled economy.

Little, I. M. D., *A Critique of Welfare Economics* (Oxford: Clarendon Press, 1950).   Contains discussions of value judgments, the conditions for maximum welfare, and some applications of welfare economics.   Geometry is the tool of analysis.

Samuelson, Paul A., *Foundations of Economic Analysis* (Cambridge, Mass.: Harvard University Press, 1948).   Chapter VIII contains a discussion of the social welfare function and the conditions for maximum welfare.   The mathematics is mostly incidental.

Scitovsky, T., *Welfare and Competition* (Homewood, Ill.: Irwin, 1951).   A textbook, a large portion of which is devoted to the welfare implications of different market forms.   Elementary mathematics and geometry are used.

———, "A Reconsideration of the Theory of Tariffs," *Review of Economic Studies*, vol. 9 (1941–1942), pp. 89–110.   Also reprinted in American Economic Association, *Readings in the Theory of International Trade* (New York: Blakiston Division, McGraw-Hill, 1949), pp. 358–389.   The concept of Scitovsky contours was introduced and applied to international trade theory in this article.

CHAPTER 8

OPTIMIZATION OVER TIME

The theories of consumption and production as presented in Chapters 2 and 3 cover optimization for a single time period. In a short-run analysis entrepreneurs are assumed to possess plants of fixed size, but beyond this, the decisions of optimizing units for successive time periods are assumed to be independent. The consumer spends his entire income during the current period and maximizes the level of a utility index defined only for goods consumed during the current period. Similarly, the entrepreneur's production function relates inputs and outputs during the current period, and he maximizes his profit for the current period.

Multiperiod utility and production functions are defined in the present chapter, and the single-period theories of consumption and production are extended to cover optimization over time. The introduction of time is accompanied by a number of simplifying assumptions. Time is divided into periods of equal length, and market transactions are assumed to be limited to the first day of each period. During the remaining days of each period the consumers supply the factors they have sold and consume the commodities they have purchased; entrepreneurs apply the inputs they have purchased and produce commodities for sale on the next marketing date. The consumer's current expenditure is no longer bounded by a single-period budget constraint. He may spend more or less than his current income and borrow or lend the difference. Entrepreneurs also have the option of borrowing and lending.

The bond market and the concepts of compounding and discounting are described in Sec. 8-1. Section 8-2 contains an extension of the theory of the consumer to the multiperiod, multicommodity case. Time preference and the effects of interest rates upon consumption expenditures over time are considered in Sec. 8-3. Section 8-4 contains a brief discussion of how production theory can be extended to the multiperiod case, and an investment theory for the firm is developed in Sec. 8 5. Methods for extending the single and multimarket equilibrium analyses to cover interest rates and multiperiod expectations are indicated in Sec. 8-6. Finally, an appendix contains a discussion of the problems involved in determining the length of investment periods.

8-1. Basic Concepts

Multiperiod analysis requires the introduction of several new concepts to describe the methods and costs of borrowing and lending.

The Bond Market. Borrowing and lending are introduced with the following simplifying assumptions: (1) consumers and entrepreneurs are free to enter into borrowing and lending contracts only on the first day of each period; (2) there is only one type of credit instrument: bonds with a one-period duration; (3) the bond market is perfectly competitive; (4) borrowers sell bonds to lenders in exchange for specified amounts of current purchasing power, expressed in terms of money of account; and (5) loans plus borrowing fees are repaid without default on the following marketing date.

These assumptions represent a considerable simplification of actual credit markets, but they allow the easy derivation of many basic results which can be extended to more complicated markets. Each of the above assumptions may be relaxed, at the cost of complicating the analysis, but without essentially altering the basic results. Assumption (1) follows from the discrete definition of time utilized in multiperiod analyses. As the period is defined to be smaller and smaller, market transactions become more frequent and are continuous in the limit.[1] Assumption (2) could be altered by assuming the existence of different types of credit instruments, e.g., promissory notes and mortgages, with different maturities. Assumption (3) can be relaxed by drawing on the analysis of monopolistic competition given in Chapter 6. Assumptions (4) and (5) can also be altered in a number of ways.

Let b_t be the bond position of some individual at the end of trading on the tth marketing date. The sign of b_t signifies whether he is a borrower or lender. If $b_t < 0$, he is a borrower with bonds outstanding and must repay b_t dollars plus the appropriate borrowing fee on the $(t + 1)$th marketing date. If $b_t > 0$, he is a lender who holds the bonds of others and will receive b_t dollars plus the appropriate borrowing fee on the $(t + 1)$th marketing date.

Since borrowing fees are also expressed in terms of money of account, they may be quoted as proportions of the amounts borrowed. On the $(t + 1)$th marketing date a borrower must repay $(1 + i_t)$ times the amount he borrowed on the tth. The proportion i_t is the market rate of interest connecting the tth and $(t + 1)$th marketing dates. Since the bond market is assumed to be perfectly competitive, the market rate of interest is not affected by the borrowing or lending of any single individual and is the same for all individuals. Interest rates are fre-

---

[1] See the appendix to this chapter for an example of an analysis in which market transactions are assumed to take place continuously.

quently expressed as percentages. If the interest rate is i_t, the borrowing fee is $100i_t$ per cent of the amount borrowed. For example, the borrowing fee is 5 per cent if $i_t = 0.05$.

Market Rates of Return. Individuals desiring to borrow for a duration of more than one period can sell new bonds on successive marketing dates to pay off the principal and interest on their maturing issues. Similarly, lenders may reinvest their principal and interest income. Consider the case of an individual who invests b_t dollars on the tth marketing date and continues to reinvest both principal and interest until the τth marketing date. The value of his investment at the beginning of the $(t + 1)$th marketing date is $b_t(1 + i_t)$. If he invests the entire amount, the value of his investment at the beginning of the $(t + 2)$th marketing date is $b_t(1 + i_t)(1 + i_{t+1})$. The value of his investment at the beginning of the τth marketing date is

$$b_t(1 + i_t)(1 + i_{t+1}) \cdot \cdot \cdot (1 + i_{\tau-1})$$

The total return on this investment is

$$J = b_t(1 + i_t)(1 + i_{t+1}) \cdot \cdot \cdot (1 + i_{\tau-1}) - b_t$$

Since the bond market is perfectly competitive, the average and marginal rates of return $(\xi_{t\tau})$ for this investment are equal and constant:

$$\xi_{t\tau} = \frac{J}{b_t} = \frac{dJ}{db_t} = (1 + i_t)(1 + i_{t+1}) \cdot \cdot \cdot (1 + i_{\tau-1}) - 1 \quad \text{(8-1a)}$$

For example, if $\tau = (t + 2)$, $i_t = 0.10$ and $i_{t+1} = 0.06$,

$$\xi_{t,t+2} = (1.10)(1.06) - 1 = 0.166$$

Since the investor is earning interest on his previous interest income, the compound market rate of return exceeds the sum of the individual interest rates. It is interesting to note that only the levels of the interest rates, and not the order of their sequence, affect the market rate of return. The market rate of return remains 0.166 for $i_t = 0.06$ and $i_{t+1} = 0.10$.

It is convenient to define

$$\xi_{tt} = 0 \quad \text{(8-1b)}$$

which states that an investor will earn a zero rate of return if he buys and sells bonds on the same marketing date. A positive return is earned only if bonds are held until the following marketing date. The market rates of return defined by (8-1) are applicable for borrowing as well as lending.

If the investor expects a constant rate of interest, $i_t = \cdots = i_{\tau-1} = i$, Eqs. (8-1a) and (8-1b) become

$$\xi_{t\tau} = (1 + i)^{\tau-t} - 1$$

which can be evaluated from a compound-interest table for specific values of $(\tau - t)$ and i.

Discount Rates and Present Values.   The existence of a bond market implies that a rational individual will not consider one dollar payable on the current $(t = 1)$ marketing date equivalent to 1 dollar payable on some future marketing date.   If he invests 1 dollar in bonds on the current marketing date, he will receive $(1 + i_1)$ dollars on the second marketing date.   One dollar payable on the second marketing date is the market equivalent of $(1 + i_1)^{-1} = 1/(1 + i_1)$ dollars payable on the first.   It is possible to lend $(1 + i_1)^{-1}$ dollars on the first marketing date and receive 1 dollar on the second, or borrow $(1 + i_1)^{-1}$ dollars on the first and repay 1 dollar on the second.   The ratio $(1 + i_1)^{-1}$ is the *discount rate* for amounts payable on the second marketing date.   The *present value*, sometimes called the discounted value, of y_2 dollars payable on the second marketing date is $y_2(1 + i_1)^{-1}$ dollars.

Discount rates can be defined for amounts payable on any marketing date.   In general, the discount rate for sums payable on the tth marketing date is

$$[(1 + i_1)(1 + i_2) \cdots (1 + i_{t-1})]^{-1} = (1 + \xi_{1t})^{-1}$$

It follows from (8-1) that an investment of $(1 + \xi_{1t})^{-1}$ dollars on the first marketing date will have a value of 1 dollar on the tth.

An entire income or outlay stream can be expressed in terms of its present value, a single number.   Consider the income stream $(y_1, y_2, \ldots, y_\tau)$ where y_t is the income payable on the tth marketing date.   The present value (y) of this stream is

$$y = y_1 + \frac{y_2}{(1 + \xi_{12})} + \cdots + \frac{y_\tau}{(1 + \xi_{1\tau})}.$$

If all interest rates are positive, the discount rate increases and the present value of any fixed amount decreases as τ increases.   If all interest rates are 0.10, the present value of a dollar payable on the second marketing date is approximately 0.91 dollars, a dollar payable on the fifth is approximately 0.68, and a dollar payable on the tenth approximately 0.42.

The computation of present values allows an economically meaningful comparison of alternative income and outlay streams.   Assume that the interest rate is 0.10 and consider two alternative two-period income streams: $(y_1 = 100, y_2 = 330)$ and $(y_1 = 300, y_2 = 121)$.   The first income stream contains 9 dollars more than the second, but the second will always be preferred, since its present value (410 dollars) exceeds the present value of the first (400 dollars). The preferability of the second stream can be demonstrated by transforming it into a stream directly comparable to the first. The second income stream gives its holder 200 dollars more on the first marketing date than the first income stream. Let him invest these 200 dollars in bonds on the first marketing date. This leaves a spendable income of 100 dollars on the first marketing date and adds 220 dollars to his spendable income on the second. The transformed income stream is $(y_1 = 100, y_2 = 341)$, which is clearly preferable to the first income stream. This result can be generalized: regardless of how an income stream is transformed through borrowing and lending, an income stream with a greater present value can be transformed into a preferred stream.

8-2. Multiperiod Consumption

A consumer generally receives income and purchases commodities on each marketing date. His present purchases are influenced by his expectations regarding future price and income levels, and he must tentatively plan purchases for future marketing dates. If his expectations prove correct and his tastes do not differ from the expected pattern, his tentative plans will be carried out on future marketing dates. If his expectations are not realized, he will revise his tentative plans. The present discussion is restricted to a consumer who formulates an integrated plan on the current marketing date for his consumption expenditures on n goods over a horizon containing T periods. His horizon is simply the period of time for which he plans on the current marketing date. It may be of any length, but for simplicity assume that it corresponds to the remainder of his expected lifetime. It is not essential that he actually know how long he will live; it is only necessary that he presently plan as if he did. If his life expectancy should change in the future, he would alter his horizon accordingly and revise his plans.

The Multiperiod Utility Function. In the most general case the consumer's ordinal utility index depends upon his planned consumption of each of the n goods in each of the T time periods:

$$U = U(q_{11}, \ldots, q_{n1}, q_{12}, \ldots, q_{n2}, \ldots, q_{1T}, \ldots, q_{nT}) \quad (8\text{-}2)$$

where q_{jt} is the quantity of Q_j that he purchases on the tth marketing date and consumes during the tth period.

The construction of a single utility index does not imply that the consumer expects his tastes to remain unchanged over time. It only implies that he plans as if he knew the manner in which they will change. For example, he may know that a baby carriage will yield a great deal of satisfaction during the years in which he is raising his family and no satisfaction at all during the years of his retirement. The utility index (8-2) is not necessarily valid for the consumer's entire planning horizon. It merely expresses his present expectations. A change in his objective circumstances or subjective desires may cause him to revise his utility index on some future marketing date. A consumer who formulates his utility index on the expectation that he will become the father of a bouncing baby girl and in fact becomes the father of triplet boys will surely revise his utility index after the event. A consumer who discovers a desirable new commodity will revise his utility index to include this commodity.

The Budget Constraint. The consumer expects to receive the earned-income stream $(y_1, y_2, \ldots, y_T)$ on the marketing dates within his planning horizon. Generally, his expected-income stream is not even over time. One possibility is a relatively low earned income during the early years of the consumer's working life, which increases as he gains training and seniority and reaches a peak during the middle years of his working life. His earned income may then begin to fall and become zero after retirement. Whatever his earned-income stream may be, it will seldom coincide with his desired consumption stream. Through borrowing and lending he is able to reconcile the two streams.

The consumer's total income receipts on the tth marketing date are the sum of his earned income and his interest income from bonds held during the preceding period: $(y_t + i_{t-1}b_{t-1})$. His interest income will be positive if his bond holdings are positive and negative if his bond holdings are negative, i.e., if he is in debt. His expected savings on the tth marketing date, denoted by s_t, are defined as the difference between his expected total income and total consumption expenditures on that date:

$$s_t = y_t + i_{t-1}b_{t-1} - \sum_{j=1}^{n} p_{jt}q_{jt} \qquad (t = 1, \ldots, T) \qquad (8\text{-}3)$$

where p_{j1} is the price of Q_j on the initial marketing date and p_{jt} ($t = 2, \ldots, T$) is the price that he expects to prevail for Q_j on the tth marketing date. Similarly, i_1 is the rate of interest determined on the initial marketing date and i_t ($t = 2, \ldots, T - 1$) is the rate of interest that the consumer expects to prevail on the tth marketing date. The consumer's savings will be negative if his expenditures exceed his total income.

If the consumer is at the beginning of his earning life, his initial bond holdings (b_0) represent his inherited wealth. If he is revising his plans at a date subsequent to the beginning of his earning life, his bond holdings also reflect the results of his past savings decisions. To simplify the present analysis assume that he is at the beginning of his earning life and that $b_0 = 0$. On each marketing date the consumer will increase or decrease the value of his bond holdings by the amount of his savings on that date:

$$b_t = b_{t-1} + s_t \qquad (t = 1, \ldots, T) \qquad (8\text{-}4)$$

A "typical" consumer might dissave and go into debt during the early years of his earning life while he is earning a comparatively low income, buying a home, and raising a family; then save to retire his debts and establish a positive bond position during the remainder of his working life; and finally dissave and liquidate his bonds during retirement.

Taking (8-3) and (8-4) together, the consumer's planned bond holdings after trading on the τth marketing date can be expressed as a function of his earned incomes, his consumption levels, prices and interest rates:

$$b_1 = \left(y_1 - \sum_{j=1}^{n} p_{j1}q_{j1} \right)$$

$$b_2 = \left(y_1 - \sum_{j=1}^{n} p_{j1}q_{j1} \right) (1 + i_1) + \left(y_2 - \sum_{j=1}^{n} p_{j2}q_{j2} \right)$$

$$b_3 = \left(y_1 - \sum_{j=1}^{n} p_{j1}q_{j1} \right) (1 + i_1)(1 + i_2) + \left(y_2 - \sum_{j=1}^{n} p_{j2}q_{j2} \right)(1 + i_2)$$

$$+ \left(y_3 - \sum_{j=1}^{n} p_{j3}q_{j3} \right)$$

and in general, utilizing (8-1a),

$$b_\tau = \sum_{t=1}^{\tau} \left(y_t - \sum_{j=1}^{n} p_{jt}q_{jt} \right) (1 + \xi_{t\tau}) \qquad (\tau = 1, \ldots, T) \qquad (8\text{-}5)$$

The consumer's bond holdings after trade on the τth marketing date equal the algebraic sum of all of his savings, net of interest expense or income, through that date with interest compounded on each.

In the single-period case the optimizing consumer would buy a sufficiently large quantity of each commodity to reach complete satiation if he did not possess a budget constraint. A similar situation would arise in the multiperiod case if there were no limitation upon the amount of debt that he could amass over his lifetime. The budget constraint for a multiperiod analysis can be expressed as a restriction upon the amount of the consumer's terminal bond holdings (b_T). He may plan to leave an estate (or debts) for his heirs, but for simplicity assume that he plans to leave his heirs neither assets nor debts.   Evaluating b_T from (8-5), his budget constraint is:

$$b_T = \sum_{t=1}^{T} \left(y_t - \sum_{j=1}^{n} p_{jt}q_{jt} \right) (1 + \xi_{tT}) = 0$$

Dividing through by the constant $(1 + \xi_{1T})$ and moving the consumption-expenditure terms to the right, the consumer's budget constraint can also be written as

$$\sum_{t=1}^{T} y_t(1 + \xi_{1t})^{-1} = \sum_{t=1}^{T} \sum_{j=1}^{n} p_{jt}q_{jt}(1 + \xi_{1t})^{-1} \qquad (8\text{-}6)$$

since

$$\frac{1 + \xi_{tT}}{1 + \xi_{1T}} = \frac{(1 + i_t) \, \cdots \, (1 + i_{T-1})}{(1 + i_1) \, \cdots \, (1 + i_{T-1})}$$

$$= \frac{1}{(1 + i_1) \, \cdots \, (1 + i_{t-1})} = (1 + \xi_{1t})^{-1}$$

In the form (8-6) the budget constraint states that the consumer equates the present values of his earned income and consumption streams.

Utility Maximization.   The consumer desires to maximize the level of his lifetime utility index (8-2) subject to his budget constraint (8-6). Form the function

$$U^* = U(q_{11}, \, \ldots \, ,q_{nT}) + \lambda \sum_{t=1}^{T} \left(y_t - \sum_{j=1}^{n} p_{jt}q_{jt} \right) (1 + \xi_{1t})^{-1}$$

and set its partial derivatives equal to zero:

$$\frac{\partial U^*}{\partial q_{jt}} = \frac{\partial U}{\partial q_{jt}} - \lambda(1 + \xi_{1t})^{-1} p_{jt} = 0 \qquad \begin{aligned} &(j = 1, \, \ldots \, , n) \\ &(t = 1, \, \ldots \, , T) \end{aligned}$$

$$\frac{\partial U^*}{\partial \lambda} = \sum_{t=1}^{T} \left(y_t - \sum_{j=1}^{n} p_{jt}q_{jt} \right) (1 + \xi_{1t})^{-1} = 0$$

and

$$-\frac{\partial q_{jt}}{\partial q_{kr}} = \frac{\partial U/\partial q_{kr}}{\partial U/\partial q_{jt}} = \frac{p_{kr}(1 + \xi_{1r})^{-1}}{p_{jt}(1 + \xi_{1t})^{-1}} \qquad \begin{aligned} &(j, k = 1, \, \ldots \, , n) \\ &(t, \tau = 1, \, \ldots \, , T) \end{aligned} \quad (8\text{-}7)$$

The consumer must equate the rates of substitution between each pair of commodities in every pair of periods to the ratio of their discounted prices.

The first-order conditions are similar to those for the single-period analysis.   Commodities are now distinguished by time period as well as kind, and discounted prices have replaced simple prices.   Once these modifications have been made, the second-order conditions are the same as those given in Sec. 2-7 for the general one-period analysis. Income and substitution effects can be defined with respect to changes in the discounted prices of the various commodities on the various marketing dates if the interest rates remain unchanged.[1]

Demand Functions. Solving the nT independent equations given by (8-7) and the budget constraint for the consumer's commodity demands,

$$q_{jt} = D_{jt}(p_{11}, \ldots, p_{nT}, i_1, \ldots, i_{T-1}) \qquad \begin{array}{c} (j = 1, \ldots, n) \\ (t = 1, \ldots, T) \end{array}$$

The consumer's demand for the jth commodity on the tth marketing date depends upon the price of each commodity on each marketing date and the interest rates connecting each pair of successive periods. The consumer's demand functions for bonds are obtained by substituting his commodity demand functions for the q_{jt}s in (8-5):

$$b_\tau = \sum_{t=1}^{\tau} \left\{ \left[y_t - \sum_{j=1}^{n} p_{jt} D_{jt}(p_{11}, \ldots, i_{T-1}) \right] (1 + \xi_{t\tau}) \right\}$$
$$= b_\tau(p_{11}, \ldots, i_{T-1}) \qquad\qquad (\tau = 1, \ldots, T)$$

If earned-income levels are treated as parameters, bond purchases are also functions of all prices and all interest rates.

The demand functions for commodities are again homogeneous of degree zero in prices and earned-income levels: if all actual and expected prices and earned-income levels change by the factor $k > 0$ *with all interest rates remaining unchanged*, the consumer's demand for each commodity on each marketing date will remain unchanged.[2] The demand functions for bonds are homogeneous of degree one with respect to prices and earned-income levels. From the zero-degree homogeneity of the commodity demand functions it follows that

$$b_\tau(kp_{11}, \ldots, kp_{nT}, i_1, \ldots, i_{T-1}) = \sum_{t=1}^{\tau} \left[ky \right.$$
$$\left. - \sum_{j=1}^{n} kp_{jt} D_{jt}(kp_{11}, \ldots, kp_{nT}, i_1, \ldots, i_{T-1})(1 + \xi_{t\tau}) \right] = kb_\tau$$

If every element in the consumer's earned-income stream and all prices should double, his planned commodity purchases would remain unchanged,

---

[1] More than one discounted price would change if one of the interest rates changed, since each interest rate enters the discount factors applicable for all prices on all the marketing dates following the date on which it is determined.

[2] The method of proof for this statement is the same as that utilized to prove the similar statement in Sec. 2-4.

and he would double his planned bond purchases. However, since his bond holdings are measured in terms of the monetary unit of account, they will exchange for exactly the same physical quantities of commodities as before the doubling of the values of bond holdings and commodity prices. The interest rates are pure numbers independent of the monetary unit and must remain unchanged if commodity demands are to remain unchanged.

8-3. Time Preference

Though much of the analysis of multiperiod consumption is formally identical with the analysis for a single period, the explicit introduction of time and interest rates presents a number of new problems. Attention is centered upon the unique problems of multiperiod consumption by assuming that actual and expected commodity prices are fixed in value and remain unchanged. The consumer's problem can then be stated as that of selecting an optimal time pattern for his consumption expenditures.

The Consumption-utility Function. For pairs of commodities purchased on a particular marketing date, the first-order conditions given by (8-7) become

$$- \frac{\partial q_{jt}}{\partial q_{kt}} = \frac{p_{kt}}{p_{jt}} \qquad \begin{array}{l} (j, k = 1, \ldots, n) \\ (t = 1, \ldots, T) \end{array} \qquad (8\text{-}8)$$

The consumer equates the rate of commodity substitution (RCS) between every pair of commodities purchased on a single marketing date to their simple price ratio. The intraperiod substitution rates are independent of the interest rates. Thus, with regard to purchases on each marketing date, the consumer satisfies the first-order conditions for single-period utility maximization, with the exception of the single-period budget constraint. The consumer's optimization problem can be separated into two parts: (1) the selection of optimal values for his total consumption expenditures on the various marketing dates, and (2) the selection of optimal commodity combinations corresponding to the planned expenditures on each marketing date. Once the first problem has been solved, the consumer can solve the second by formulating T independent single-period problems with the optimal total consumption expenditures serving as single-period budget constraints.

Define c_t as the consumer's total expenditure for commodities on the tth marketing date:

$$c_t = \sum_{j=1}^{n} p_{jt} q_{jt} \qquad (t = 1, \ldots, T) \qquad (8\text{-}9)$$

The utility function (8-2), together with (8-9) and the $(n - 1)T$ independent equations of (8-8), forms a system of $(nT + 1)$ equations in $(nT + T + 1)$ variables: U, q_{jt} $(j = 1, \ldots , n)$ $(t = 1, \ldots , T)$, and c_t $(t = 1, \ldots , T)$. Generally, nT of these equations can be utilized to eliminate the q_{jt}s, and the consumer's utility index can be expressed as a function of his consumption expenditures:

$$U = V(c_1, \ldots ,c_T) \tag{8-10}$$

Since (8-10) is constructed on the assumption that (8-8) is satisfied, it gives the maximum value of the utility index corresponding to each consumption-expenditure pattern.

The consumer's time-substitution rate:

$$-\frac{\partial c_\tau}{\partial c_t} = \frac{V_t}{V_\tau} \qquad (t, \tau = 1, \ldots , T)$$

is the rate at which consumption expenditure on the τth marketing date must be increased to compensate for a reduction of consumption expenditure on the tth in order to leave the consumer's satisfaction level unchanged. No generality is lost by limiting attention to the cases for which $\tau > t$. If the consumer's time-substitution rate is 1.06, his consumption expenditure on the τth marketing date must be increased at the rate of 1.06 dollars for each dollar of consumption expenditure sacrificed on the tth. In other words he must receive a premium of at least 0.06 dollars before he will postpone a dollar's worth of consumption expenditure from period t to period τ. This minimum premium is defined as the consumer's rate of time preference for consumption in period t rather than period τ and is denoted by $\eta_{t\tau}$:

$$\eta_{t\tau} = -\frac{\partial c_\tau}{\partial c_t} - 1 \qquad (t, \tau = 1, \ldots , T) \quad (\tau > t) \tag{8-11}$$

The consumer's rates of time preference may be negative for some consumption time patterns, i.e., he may be willing to sacrifice a dollar's worth of consumption in period t in order to secure less than a dollar's worth in a later period. If expected consumption expenditures are 10,000 dollars on the tth marketing date and only 1 dollar on the τth, $\eta_{t\tau}$ would most likely be negative. The consumer's subjective rates of time preference are derived from his consumption-utility function and depend upon the levels of his consumption expenditures. They are independent of the market rates of interest and his borrowing and lending opportunities.

The Consumption Plan. The consumer's utility-maximization problem of Sec. 8-2 can now be reformulated using his consumption expenditures as variables. He wants to maximize the level of his consumption-utility index (8-10) subject to his lifetime budget constraint. Form the function

$$V^* = V(c_1, \ldots, c_T) + \mu \sum_{t=1}^{T} (y_t - c_t)(1 + \xi_{1t})^{-1}$$

and set its partial derivatives equal to zero:

$$\frac{\partial V^*}{\partial c_t} = V_t - \mu(1 + \xi_{1t})^{-1} = 0 \qquad (t = 1, \ldots, T)$$

$$\frac{\partial V^*}{\partial \mu} = \sum_{t=1}^{T} (y_t - c_t)(1 + \xi_{1t})^{-1} = 0$$

and $\qquad -\dfrac{\partial c_\tau}{\partial c_t} = \dfrac{(1 + \xi_{1t})^{-1}}{(1 + \xi_{1\tau})^{-1}} = (1 + \xi_{t\tau}) \qquad (t, \tau = 1, \ldots, T)$

$$(\tau > t) \quad (8\text{-}13)$$

and substituting from (8-1a) and (8-11),

$$\eta_{t\tau} = \xi_{t\tau} \qquad (t, \tau = 1, \ldots, T) \quad (\tau > t) \tag{8-14}$$

The consumer in this case adjusts his subjective preferences to his market opportunities by equating his rate of time preference between every pair of periods to the corresponding market rate of return. If $\eta_{t\tau}$ were less than $\xi_{t\tau}$, the consumer could buy bonds and receive a premium greater than necessary to maintain indifference. If $\eta_{t\tau}$ were greater than $\xi_{t\tau}$, he could increase his satisfaction by selling bonds and increasing his consumption in period t at the expense of consumption in period τ. Though $\eta_{t\tau}$ may be negative for some consumption-expenditure patterns, the observed (optimum) values of $\eta_{t\tau}$ will always be positive if the interest rates are positive.

Second-order conditions require that the principal minors of the relevant bordered Hessian determinant alternate in sign:

$$\begin{vmatrix} V_{11} & V_{12} & -1 \\ V_{21} & V_{22} & -(1 + \xi_{12})^{-1} \\ -1 & -(1 + \xi_{12})^{-1} & 0 \end{vmatrix} > 0;$$

$$\begin{vmatrix} V_{11} & V_{12} & V_{13} & -1 \\ V_{21} & V_{22} & V_{23} & -(1 + \xi_{12})^{-1} \\ V_{31} & V_{32} & V_{33} & -(1 + \xi_{13})^{-1} \\ -1 & -(1 + \xi_{12})^{-1} & -(1 + \xi_{13})^{-1} & 0 \end{vmatrix} < 0; \cdots \tag{8-15}$$

The reader may verify that the second-order conditions imply that the rates of time preference be decreasing.

For a numerical example consider a hypothetical consumer with a two-period horizon. Assume that his utility function is $U = c_1 c_2$ and that his actual and expected incomes are $(y_1 = 10{,}000, y_2 = 5{,}250)$. Form the function

$$V^* = c_1 c_2 + \mu[(10{,}000 - c_1) + (5{,}250 - c_2)(1 + i_1)^{-1}]$$

and set its partial derivatives equal to zero:

$$\frac{\partial V^*}{\partial c_1} = c_2 - \mu = 0$$

$$\frac{\partial V^*}{\partial c_2} = c_1 - \mu(1 + i_1)^{-1} = 0$$

$$\frac{\partial V^*}{\partial \mu} = (10{,}000 - c_1) + (5{,}250 - c_2)(1 + i_1)^{-1} = 0$$

If the interest rate is 0.05 (5 per cent), the optimum consumption expenditures are $c_1 = 7{,}500$ and $c_2 = 7{,}875$. The consumer's rate of time preference for these expenditures equals the interest rate (market rate of return):

$$\eta_{12} = -\frac{dc_2}{dc_1} - 1 = \frac{c_2}{c_1} - 1 = \frac{7{,}875}{7{,}500} - 1 = 0.05$$

The second-order condition requires that

$$\begin{vmatrix} 0 & 1 & -1 \\ 1 & 0 & -(1 + i_1)^{-1} \\ -1 & -(1 + i_1)^{-1} & 0 \end{vmatrix} = 2(1 + i_1)^{-1} > 0$$

and is satisfied for $i_1 > -1$.

The two-period horizon case can be described graphically by giving a new interpretation to the conventional indifference-curve diagram. The consumer's earned-income stream is given by the coordinates of point A in Fig. 8-1. Let y^0 be the present value of this income stream. The consumer's budget constraint is

$$y^0 - c_1 - c_2(1 + i_1)^{-1} = 0$$

The locus of all consumption points with a present value of y^0 forms a straight line with negative slope equal to the market exchange rate, $(1 + i_1)$, between consumption expenditures on the first and second marketing dates. One dollar of income on the first marketing date can

FIGURE 8-1

be transformed into $(1 + i_1)$ dollars of consumption expenditure on the second if the consumer lends at the market rate of interest. Likewise,

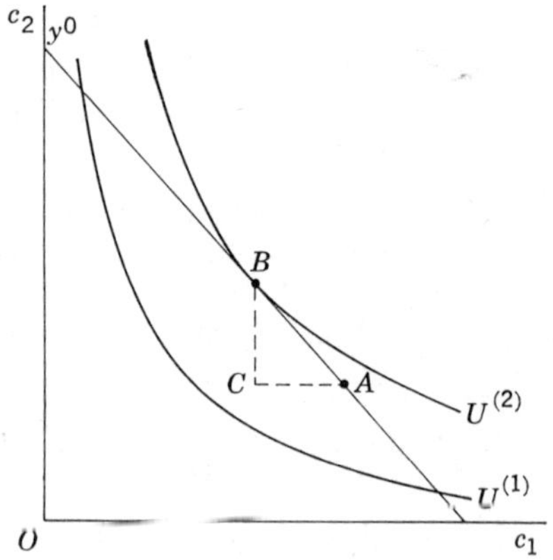

$(1 + i_1)$ dollars of income on the second marketing date can be transformed into 1 dollar of consumption expenditure on the first if the consumer borrows at the market rate of interest. Assume that the consumer's budget constraint is given by the line labeled y^0 in Fig. 8-1. If he borrows on the first marketing date, he will move along his budget line going to the right of point A. If he lends, he will move along his budget line going to the left of point A.

The curves labeled $U^{(1)}$ and $U^{(2)}$ are members of the family of time indifference curves. Each is the locus of consumption expenditures yielding a given level of satisfaction. The slope of a time indifference curve is $-(1 + \eta_{12})$. These curves reflect the assumption that the rate of time preference is decreasing, i.e., the curves are convex with respect to the origin as required by the second-order condition (8-15). The coordinates of the tangency point B give the optimal consumption expenditures. The consumer will buy AC dollars worth of bonds on the first marketing date and will spend the principal and interest, CB, for consumption goods on the second.

Substitution and Income Effects. The effects of a change in the rate of interest upon the consumer's optimal consumption levels can be separated into income and substitution effects by methods similar to those employed in Sec. 2-6.

Assume that the consumer's horizon encompasses two marketing dates. In order to determine the effects of changes in the interest rate and earned-income levels, differentiate the first-order conditions (8-12) totally for $T = 2$:

$$
\begin{aligned}
V_{11}\, dc_1 + & \quad V_{12}\, dc_2 - & du &= 0 \\
V_{21}\, dc_1 + & \quad V_{22}\, dc_2 - (1 + i_1)^{-1}\, d\mu &= -\mu(1 + i_1)^{-2}\, di_1 \\
-dc_1 - & (1 + i_1)^{-1}\, dc_2 - \quad 0 &= -dy_1 - (1 + i_1)^{-1}\, dy_2 \\
& & &\quad + (y_2 - c_2)(1 + i_1)^{-2}\, di_1
\end{aligned}
\tag{8-16}
$$

The array of coefficients on the left-hand side of (8-16) is the same as the array for the last (and for $T = 2$, the only) bordered Hessian determinant of (8-15).

Using Cramer's rule to solve (8-16) for dc_1,

$$
dc_1 = -\mu(1 + i_1)^{-2} \frac{\mathbf{D}_{21}}{\mathbf{D}}\, di_1 + [-dy_1 - (1 + i_1)^{-1}\, dy_2
$$
$$
+ (y_2 - c_2)(1 + i_1)^{-2}\, di_1] \frac{\mathbf{D}_{31}}{\mathbf{D}} \tag{8-17}
$$

where $\mathbf{D}$ is the bordered Hessian determinant and $\mathbf{D}_{tr}$ is the cofactor of the element in its tth row and rth column. Dividing (8-17) through by di_1 and assuming that $dy_1 = dy_2 = 0$,

$$\frac{\partial c_1}{\partial i_1} = -\mu(1 + i_1)^{-2}\frac{\mathbf{D}_{21}}{\mathbf{D}} + (y_2 - c_2)(1 + i_1)^{-2}\frac{\mathbf{D}_{31}}{\mathbf{D}} \qquad (8\text{-}18)$$

Let y denote the present value of the consumer's earned-income stream:

$$y = y_1 + y_2(1 + i_1)^{-1}$$

An increase of y_1 by 1 dollar or of y_2 by $(1 + i_1)$ dollars will each increase y by 1 dollar. The rate of increase of c_1 with respect to a dollar's increase in the present value of the consumer's earned-income stream can be derived from (8-17):

$$\frac{\partial c_1}{\partial y} = \frac{\partial c_1}{\partial y_1} = (1 + i_1)\frac{\partial c_1}{\partial y_2} = -\frac{\mathbf{D}_{31}}{\mathbf{D}} \qquad (8\text{-}19)$$

A change of i_1 will alter the present values of the consumer's earned-income and consumption streams. Consider those changes of i_1 which are accompanied by changes in c_1 and c_2 such that the level of the consumer's utility index remains unchanged: $dU = V_1\,dc_1 + V_2\,dc_2 = 0$. Since (8-13) requires that $V_2/V_1 = (1 + i_1)^{-1}$, it follows that

$$-dc_1 - (1 + i_1)^{-1}\,dc_2 = 0$$

and from (8-16) it follows that

$$-dy_1 - (1 + i_1)^{-1}\,dy_2 + (y_2 - c_2)(1 + i_1)^{-2}\,di_1 = 0$$

Substituting into (8-17)

$$\left(\frac{\partial c_1}{\partial i_1}\right)_{U=\text{const}} = -\mu(1 + i_1)^{-2}\frac{\mathbf{D}_{21}}{\mathbf{D}} \qquad (8\text{-}20)$$

Substituting $-(y_1 - c_1)(1 + i_1)^{-1} = (y_2 - c_2)(1 + i_1)^{-2}$, which follows from the budget constraint, and utilizing (8-18) and (8-19), (8-17) may be written as

$$\frac{\partial c_1}{\partial i_1} = \left(\frac{\partial c_1}{\partial i_1}\right)_{U=\text{const}} + (y_1 - c_1)(1 + i_1)^{-1}\left(\frac{\partial c_1}{\partial y}\right)_{i_1=\text{const}} \qquad (8\text{-}21)$$

The total effect of a change in the rate of interest is the sum of a substitution and an income effect. The income effect equals the rate of change of consumption expenditure with respect to an increase in the present value of the consumer's earned-income stream weighted by his bond holdings multiplied by a discount factor.

The sign of the substitution effect is easily determined. From the first-order conditions $\mu > 0$, and from the second-order condition $\mathbf{D} > 0$.

Evaluating $\mathbf{D}_{21}$,

$$\mathbf{D}_{21} = - \begin{vmatrix} V_{12} & -1 \\ -(1 + i_1)^{-1} & 0 \end{vmatrix} = (1 + i_1)^{-1} > 0$$

Therefore, the substitution effect with respect to c_1 in (8-18) is negative. The substitution effect with respect to c_2 is

$$\left(\frac{\partial c_2}{\partial i_1} \right)_{U = \text{const}} = -\mu(1 + i_1)^{-2} \frac{\mathbf{D}_{22}}{\mathbf{D}}$$

Since $\mathbf{D}_{22} = -1 < 0$, the substitution effect with respect to c_2 is positive. An increase of the interest rate will induce the consumer to substitute consumption in period 2 for consumption in period 1 as he moves along a given time indifference curve.   This follows from the fact that an increase of the interest rate is equivalent to an increase in the prices of commodities on the first marketing date relative to those on the second.   If the consumer reduces consumption in period 1 and purchases bonds, his interest earnings will be greater, and he will be able to purchase a larger quantity of commodities on the second marketing date for each dollar's worth of purchases sacrificed on the first.

Although an increase of income may cause a reduction in the purchases of a particular commodity, it is difficult to imagine a situation in which an increase of income will cause a reduction in the aggregate consumption expenditure on any of the marketing dates.   One can assume that $(\partial c_1/\partial y)_{i_1=\text{const}}$ is positive for all except the most extraordinary cases.   If this is true, the direction of the income effect is determined by the sign of the consumer's bond position $(y_1 - c_1)$ at the end of trading on the first marketing date since the second term of (8-21) is of the same sign as $(y_1 - c_1)$.   If the consumer's bond holdings are positive, an increase of the interest rate will increase his interest income and is equivalent to an increase of his earned income.   If he is in debt, an increase of the interest rate will increase his interest expense and is equivalent to a reduction of his earned income.   In this case both effects are negative, and the total effect, $\partial c_1/\partial i_1$, will therefore be negative.   If his bond position is positive, the total effect will be positive or negative depending upon whether the value of the income effect is larger or smaller than the absolute value of the substitution effect.

8-4. Multiperiod Production

The theory of the firm can also be extended to the multiperiod case. The analysis of the entrepreneur is similar to that of the consumer, as in the single-period case.

The Multiperiod Production Function. Production is seldom instantaneous. Generally, time must elapse between the application of inputs and the securing of outputs. Assume that (1) the entrepreneur buys inputs and sells outputs only on the marketing dates within his horizon, (2) he performs the technical operations of his production process in the time between marketing dates, (3) during the tth period he applies the inputs he purchased on the tth marketing date, and (4) on the $(t + 1)$th marketing date he sells the outputs secured during the tth period. These assumptions serve to define the time sequence of production. The following analysis could be based on many alternative sets of time-sequence assumptions without any major changes of its results.

Consider an entrepreneur who desires to formulate an optimal production plan for a horizon encompassing L complete periods and $(L + 1)$ marketing dates. Following the notation of Sec. 3-6, the entrepreneur's production function can be written in implicit form as

$$F(q_{12}, \ . \ . \ . \ , q_{s,L+1}, q_{s+1,1}, \ . \ . \ . \ , q_{mL}) = 0 \qquad (8\text{-}22)$$

where q_{jt} $(j = 1, \ . \ . \ . \ , s)$ $(t = 2, \ . \ . \ . \ , L + 1)$ is the quantity of the jth output secured during the $(t - 1)$th period and sold on the tth marketing date and $-q_{jt}$ $(j = s + 1, \ . \ . \ . \ , m)$ $(t = 1, \ . \ . \ . \ , L)$ is the quantity of the jth input purchased on the tth marketing date and applied to the production process during the tth period. Any outputs which the entrepreneur may sell on the initial marketing date are the result of past production decisions, and their levels enter (8-22) as constants rather than variables. On the $(L + 1)$th marketing date the entrepreneur plans to sell the outputs secured during the Lth period, but does not plan to purchase inputs, since he does not anticipate production in any period beyond the Lth. The multiperiod production function relates the input and output levels for all periods within the entrepreneur's planning horizon. The inputs applied during each period contribute to the production of outputs during all periods, and it is usually impossible to attribute a particular output to inputs applied during a specific period. However, it is possible to ascertain the effects of marginal variations and compute the marginal productivities of each input applied during each period with respect to each output secured during each period.

Profit Maximization. The entrepreneur also faces a perfectly competitive bond market and is free to borrow and lend on the same terms as consumers. Given these opportunities, he will generally desire to maximize the present value of his net revenues from production subject to the technical constraints imposed by his production function. Form the function

$$\pi^* = \sum_{t=1}^{L+1} \sum_{j=1}^{m} p_{jt}q_{jt}(1 + \xi_{1t})^{-1} + \lambda F(q_{12}, \ . \ . \ . \ , q_{mL})$$

and set its partial derivatives equal to zero:

$$\frac{\partial \pi^*}{\partial q_{jt}} = p_{jt}(1 + \xi_{1t})^{-1} + \lambda \frac{\partial F}{\partial q_{jt}} = 0$$

$$(t = 2, \ldots, L + 1) \quad \text{for } (j = 1, \ldots, s)$$
$$(t = 1, \ldots, L) \qquad \text{for } (j = s + 1, \ldots, m)$$

$$\frac{\partial \pi^*}{\partial \lambda} = F(q_{12}, \ldots, q_{mL}) = 0$$

and

$$-\frac{\partial q_{jt}}{\partial q_{k\tau}} = \frac{\partial F / \partial q_{k\tau}}{\partial F / \partial q_{jt}} = \frac{p_{k\tau}(1 + \xi_{1\tau})^{-1}}{p_{jt}(1 + \xi_{1t})^{-1}}$$

$$(t, \tau = 2, \ldots, L + 1) \quad \text{for } (j, k = 1, \ldots, s)$$
$$(t, \tau = 1, \ldots, L) \qquad \text{for } (j, k = s + 1, \ldots, m) \qquad \text{(8-23)}$$

If Q_j and Q_k are both outputs, (8-23) requires that their rate of product transformation (RPT) equal the ratio of their discounted prices. If both are inputs, it requires that their rate of technical substitution (RTS) equal the ratio of their discounted prices. If Q_j is an output and Q_k an input, let $x_{k\tau} = -q_{k\tau}$ and $r_{k\tau} = p_{k\tau}$ and write (8-23) as

$$\frac{\partial q_{jt}}{\partial x_{k\tau}} p_{jt}(1 + \xi_{1t})^{-1} = r_{k\tau}(1 + \xi_{1\tau})^{-1}$$

$$(j = 1, \ldots, s) \qquad (k = s + 1, \ldots, m)$$
$$(t = 2, \ldots, L + 1) \quad (\tau = 1, \ldots, L)$$

The discounted value of the marginal product of X_k applied during the τth period with respect to each output in each time period must be equated to the discounted price of X_k on the τth marketing date.

The second-order conditions are the same as those presented in Sec. 3-6 if each output and each input on each marketing date is defined as a distinct variable and simple prices are replaced by discounted prices. Substitution effects may be derived for changes in each of the discounted prices, assuming that the interest rates remain unchanged.

An entrepreneur would not undertake single-period production if all inputs were variable and his maximum profit were negative. A similar limitation applies in the multiperiod case. If all inputs are variable, the entrepreneur will not undertake production at all if the discounted value of his net revenues from operations is negative. However, this restriction does not take account of all his options. He may find it most profitable to undertake production, but to cease operations before the end of his planning horizon. The entrepreneur will not operate after the τth marketing date unless the present value of the added net revenues is nonnegative:

$$\sum_{t=\tau+1}^{L+1} \sum_{j=1}^{s} p_{jt}q_{jt}(1 + \xi_{1t})^{-1}$$

$$- \sum_{t=\tau}^{L} \sum_{j=s+1}^{m} r_{jt}x_{jt}(1 + \xi_{1t})^{-1} \geqq 0 \qquad (\tau = 1, \ldots, L) \quad (8\text{-}24)$$

If (8-24) does not hold for some value of τ, the entrepreneur can earn more by investing all his funds in bonds on the τth marketing date than by continuing production. If (8-24) does not hold for $\tau = 1$, he will not undertake production at all.

Demand and supply functions can be derived in a manner similar to that used in Sec. 8-1 to derive consumer demand functions. The entrepreneur's demands for inputs, supplies of outputs, and demands for bonds on each marketing date can be expressed as functions of all prices and interest rates. The demand functions for inputs and supply functions for outputs are homogeneous of degree zero, and the demand functions for bonds are homogeneous of degree one with respect to all input and output prices.

8-5. Investment Theory of the Firm

The multiperiod production decisions of the firm are presented in a very general form in Sec. 8-4. The advantages and disadvantages of this formulation are similar to the advantages and disadvantages of the multiperiod consumption analysis contained in Sec. 8-2. The formal relationships between single-period and multiperiod production decisions are obvious, but many of the new problems arising from the introduction of time and interest rates are obscured by this formulation. Simplifying assumptions similar to those employed in Sec. 8-3 are utilized in the present section in order to bring the new problems to the forefront and derive some of the concepts and results of neoclassical investment theory. Specifically, it is assumed that entrepreneurs consider all current and expected input and output prices as known and constant and perform certain preliminary optimizations. It is then possible to treat the investment expenditures and revenues from sales on each of the marketing dates within the entrepreneur's horizon as the only variables and confine the analysis to an investigation of their interrelationships and the effects of the interest rates.

Special cases have played an important role in the development of microeconomic investment theory. Cases are frequently distinguished on the basis of input and output time structures. The simplest case is *point-input–point-output*, which covers investment in working capital: all inputs are purchased on one marketing date, and all outputs are sold on a subsequent marketing date. Tree growing and wine aging often serve as examples. The *multipoint-input–point-output* case covers the production of an output which requires the application of inputs during a number of successive periods.[1] Shipbuilding might fall into this category. The *point-input–multipoint-output* case covers an investment in a durable good which is purchased on one marketing date and is used for the production of outputs during a number of successive periods. Finally, there is the general *multipoint-input–multipoint-output* case. The first three cases are, of course, embraced by the fourth. In the present section attention is limited to the general and *point-input–point-output* cases.

The Investment-opportunities Function. The entrepreneur's investment expenditure on the tth marketing date, denoted by I_t, equals the value of his input purchases on that date:

$$I_t = - \sum_{j=s+1}^{m} p_{jt} q_{jt} \qquad (t = 1, \ldots, L) \qquad (8\text{-}25)$$

His total revenue from sales on the tth marketing date, denoted by R_t, is

$$R_t = \sum_{j=1}^{s} p_{jt} q_{jt} \qquad (t = 2, \ldots, L + 1) \qquad (8\text{-}26)$$

The definitions (8-25) and (8-26) require $2L$ equations.

Assume that an entrepreneur is given the levels for all his inputs and outputs except the inputs he purchases on the tth marketing date, and desires to minimize the present value of his investment expenditure on that date. To solve his constrained-minimization problem, form the function

$$I_t^* = - \sum_{j=s+1}^{m} p_{jt} q_{jt} (1 + \xi_{1t})^{-1}$$
$$+ \lambda^* F(q_{12}^0, \ldots, q_{s,L+1}^0, q_{s+1,1}^0, \ldots, q_{s+1,t}, \ldots, q_{s+2,t}, \ldots, q_{mL}^0)$$

and set its partial derivatives equal to zero:

$$\frac{\partial I_t^*}{\partial q_{jt}} = -p_{jt}(1 + \xi_{1t})^{-1} + \lambda^* \frac{\partial F}{\partial q_{jt}} = 0 \qquad (j = s + 1, \ldots, m)$$

$$\frac{\partial I_t^*}{\partial \lambda^*} = F(q_{12}^0, \ldots, q_{s,L+1}^0, q_{s+1,1}^0, \ldots, q_{s+1,t}, \ldots, q_{s+2,t}, \ldots, q_{mL}^0) = 0$$

and $\qquad -\dfrac{\partial q_{jt}}{\partial q_{kt}} = \dfrac{p_{kt}}{p_{jt}} \qquad (j, k = s + 1, \ldots, m) \qquad (8\text{-}27)$

---

[1] If time is treated as a continuous variable, the word *continuous* replaces *multipoint* in the titles of the special cases.

The first-order conditions are the familiar ones for single-period constrained cost minimization (see Sec. 3-2): RTSs are equated to fixed price ratios. The optimum intraperiod RTSs are independent of the interest rates. It is assumed that the entrepreneur always allocates his investment expenditure on the tth marketing date so that (8-27) is satisfied. Conditions (8-27) contain $(m - s - 1)$ independent equations for each marketing date, or a total of $L(m - s - 1)$ independent equations.

Now assume that the entrepreneur is given the levels for all his inputs and outputs except the outputs he sells on the tth marketing date, and desires to maximize the present value of his revenue from sales on this date. The first-order conditions for this constrained-maximization problem require that

$$-\frac{\partial q_{jt}}{\partial q_{kt}} = \frac{p_{kt}}{p_{jt}} \qquad (j, k = 1, \ldots, s) \qquad (8\text{-}28)$$

The optimum RPTs for outputs sold on a given marketing date are also constants which are independent of the interest rates. It is assumed that the entrepreneur always adjusts his production so that (8-28) is satisfied. Conditions (8-28) contain a total of $L(s - 1)$ independent equations.

The entrepreneur's investment-opportunities function is constructed with the assumptions that (1) he satisfies his multiperiod production function, (2) he always equates his intraperiod RTSs to the fixed input-price ratios, and (3) he always equates his intraperiod RPTs to the fixed output-price ratios. His investment opportunities therefore are described by his production function (8-22) and Eqs. (8-25) through (8-28). The system as a whole contains $(Lm + 1)$ independent equations and $(Lm + 2L)$ variables. Generally, Lm of the equations can be used to eliminate the Lm q_{jt}s. The revenues and investment expenditures are then related by a single implicit function:

$$H(I_1, \ldots, I_L, R_2, \ldots, R_{L+1}) = 0 \qquad (8\text{-}29)$$

Given all the revenues and all but one of the investment expenditures, (8-29) gives the minimum value for the remaining investment expenditure. Similarly, given all but one of the revenues and all the investment expenditures, (8-29) gives the maximum value for the remaining revenue.

The entrepreneur possesses both external and internal investment opportunities: he can purchase bonds and he can invest in his own firm. His external rates of return are the same as those for consumers, as given by (8-1). In the general case, average internal rates of return cannot be defined in a manner parallel to average market rates of return, since it is not possible to attribute the entire revenue on the τth marketing date to the investment on any particular marketing date. Each revenue depends upon all the investment expenditures. However, marginal internal rates of return can be defined for any investment-revenue pair, assuming that all other investments and revenues remain unchanged. The *marginal internal rate of return*[1] from investment on the tth marketing date with respect to revenue on the τth, denoted by $\rho_{t\tau}$, is

$$\rho_{t\tau} = \frac{\partial R_\tau}{\partial I_t} - 1 = -\frac{\partial H/\partial I_t}{\partial H/\partial R_\tau} - 1$$

$$(t = 1, \ldots, L) \quad (\tau = 2, \ldots, L+1) \quad (8\text{-}30)$$

Each of the marginal internal rates of return depends upon the levels of all the planned revenues and investment expenditures.

The marginal internal rate of return functions given above by (8-30) are independent of the market rates of interest and the entrepreneur's borrowing and lending opportunities. For given input and output price expectations, (8-30) provides a description in marginal terms of the objective technical framework within which the entrepreneur operates. For some investment and revenue combinations $\rho_{t\tau}$ may be negative.

The Investment Plan. The entrepreneur's maximization problem of Sec. 8-4 can now be expressed in terms of investment expenditures and revenues. From the set of investment and revenue streams that satisfy (8-29) he desires to select one that maximizes the present value of his net-revenue stream. Form the function

$$\pi^* = \sum_{t=2}^{L+1} R_t(1 + \xi_{1t})^{-1} - \sum_{t=1}^{L} I_t(1 + \xi_{1t})^{-1} + \mu H(I_1, \ldots, R_{L+1})$$

and set its partial derivates equal to zero:

$$\frac{\partial \pi^*}{\partial R_t} = (1 + \xi_{1t})^{-1} + \mu \frac{\partial H}{\partial R_t} = 0 \quad (t = 2, \ldots, L+1)$$

$$\frac{\partial \pi^*}{\partial I_t} = -(1 + \xi_{1t})^{-1} + \mu \frac{\partial H}{\partial I_t} - 0 \quad (t = 1, \ldots, L)$$

$$\frac{\partial \pi^*}{\partial \mu} = H(I_1, \ldots, R_{L+1}) = 0$$

---

[1] There is no generally accepted name for this concept. Friedrich Lutz and Vera Lutz, *The Theory of Investment of the Firm* (Princeton, N.J.: Princeton University Press, 1951), use "marginal internal rate of return." Irving Fisher, *The Theory of Interest* (New York: Kelly and Millman, 1954), uses "marginal rate of return over cost." Other names for this or closely allied concepts include "marginal productivity of investment," "marginal efficiency of investment," and "marginal efficiency of capital."

where $\mu < 0$.† Substituting from (8-30), the first-order conditions require that

$$\rho_{t\tau} = \xi_{t\tau} \qquad \begin{array}{l} (t = 1, \ldots , L) \\ (\tau = 2, \ldots , L + 1) \end{array} \qquad (8\text{-}31)$$

The entrepreneur must equate each of his marginal internal rates of return to the corresponding market rate of return.

The second-order conditions require that

$$\begin{vmatrix} H_{11} & H_{12} & H_1 \\ H_{21} & H_{22} & H_2 \\ H_1 & H_2 & 0 \end{vmatrix} < 0; \quad \begin{vmatrix} H_{11} & H_{12} & H_{13} & H_1 \\ H_{21} & H_{22} & H_{23} & H_2 \\ H_{31} & H_{32} & H_{33} & H_3 \\ H_1 & H_2 & H_3 & 0 \end{vmatrix} < 0; \cdots \qquad (8\text{-}32)$$

where H_j is the first-order partial derivative of the implicit function (Eq. 8-29) with respect to the jth variable and H_{jk} is the second-order partial derivative with respect to the jth and kth variables. All the above determinants must be negative.[1] These conditions must hold regardless of the order in which the $2L$ investments and revenues are listed.

Expanding the first determinant of (8-32),

$$2H_1 H_2 H_{12} - H_{22}H_1{}^2 - H_{11}H_2{}^2 < 0 \qquad (8\text{-}33)$$

The rate of change of the marginal internal rate of return for investment on the tth marketing date with respect to revenue on the τth is

$$\frac{\partial \rho_{t\tau}}{\partial I_t} = \frac{\partial^2 R_\tau}{\partial I_t{}^2} = -\frac{1}{H_2{}^3}(H_{11}H_2{}^2 - 2H_{12}H_1 H_2 + H_{22}H_1{}^2)$$

where $H_1 = \partial H / \partial I_t$ and $H_2 = \partial H / \partial R_\tau$. Since (8-33) must hold for the variables listed in this order and since $H_2 > 0$, (8-33) implies that

$$\frac{\partial \rho_{t\tau}}{\partial I_t} < 0 \qquad \begin{array}{l} (t = 1, \ldots , L) \\ (\tau = 2, \ldots , L + 1) \end{array} \qquad (8\text{-}34)$$

Thus, the second-order conditions imply that all the marginal internal rates of return be decreasing.

---

† The first-order conditions require that $\partial H / \partial R_t$ and $\partial H / \partial I_t$ be of opposite sign. The investment-opportunities function is assumed to be constructed so that $\partial H / \partial R_t > 0$ and $\partial H / \partial I_t < 0$ for the optimum production plan. If a solution were obtained with the signs reversed, it would only be necessary to redefine (8-29) as $-H$ to obtain the desired form.

[1] Second-order conditions require that the principal minors of the Hessian determinant of the second-order derivatives of π^* bordered by the first-order derivatives of $H(I_1, \ldots , R_{L+1})$ be alternately positive and negative. Conditions (8-32) are obtained by factoring out $\mu < 0$.

If conditions (8-31) and (8-34) were not satisfied, the entrepreneur could increase the present value of his profit by either selling bonds and expanding internal investment or buying bonds and contracting internal investment.

Point-input–Point-output. In the simplest case the entrepreneur invests on one marketing date and receives the resultant revenue on the next. He may repeat the production process over time, but his production on the first marketing date only affects his revenue on the second, and his effective planning horizon includes one full period and two marketing dates.

The entrepreneur's revenue can generally be stated as an explicit function of his investment expenditure:

$$R_2 = h(I_1) \tag{8-35}$$

In this special case all revenues on the second marketing date can be attributed to investment on the first, and it is possible to define an average internal rate of return:

$$\frac{R_2 - I_1}{I_1} = \frac{h(I_1)}{I_1} - 1$$

The average internal rate of return can be compared with the corresponding market rate of return i_1.

The entrepreneur desires to maximize the present value of his net revenues from operation:

$$\pi = R_2(1 + i_1)^{-1} - I_1$$

Substituting from (8-35), π can be stated as a function of I_1 alone:[1]

$$\pi = h(I_1)(1 + i_1)^{-1} - I_1$$

Differentiating,

$$\frac{d\pi}{dI_1} = h'(I_1)(1 + i_1)^{-1} - 1 = 0 \tag{8-36}$$

Rearranging terms and substituting from (8-1) and (8-30), the first-order condition becomes

$$\rho_{12} = i_1 = \xi_{12}$$

The entrepreneur equates his marginal internal rate of return to the corresponding market rate of return—in this case the market rate of interest.

---

[1] Direct substitution and the use of a Lagrange multiplier are equivalent alternatives. The same result is obtained by maximizing

$$\pi^* = R_2(1 + i_1)^{-1} - I_1 + \mu[R_2 - h(I_1)]$$

(see Sec. A-3).

The second-order condition requires that

$$\frac{d^2\pi}{dI_1{}^2} = h''(I_1)(1 + i_1)^{-1} < 0$$

and if $i_1 > -1$,

$$h''(I_1) < 0 \tag{8-37}$$

The marginal internal rate of return must be decreasing.

Imagine that (8-37) is satisfied, but $\rho_{12} > \xi_{12}$. The marginal return from borrowing funds for internal use exceeds their interest cost, and the

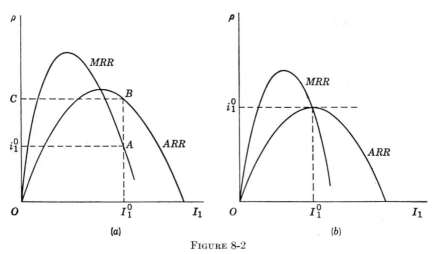

(a)

(b)

FIGURE 8-2

entrepreneur can increase his profit by expanding investment. Conversely, if $\rho_{12} < \xi_{12}$, he is earning less on the marginal dollar of internal investment than he must pay for it and he can increase his profit by contracting investment.

By total differentiation of (8-36),

$$h''(I_1)\, dI_1 = di_1$$

and

$$\frac{dI_1}{di_1} = \frac{1}{h''(I_1)} < 0 \tag{8-38}$$

If the second-order condition is satisfied, (8-38) is negative: an increase in the rate of interest will cause the entrepreneur to reduce his investment expenditure.

Possible shapes for the average and marginal internal return functions, labeled ARR and MRR respectively, are pictured in Fig. 8-2a. Both the average and marginal rates increase, reach a peak, and then decline as investment is increased. These curves possess the normal properties of average and marginal pairs (see Sec. A-2). If the interest rate is

i_1^0, the entrepreneur will invest I_1^0 dollars.   For this level of investment
the marginal internal and market rates of return are equal (first-order
condition), and the marginal internal rate is decreasing (second-order
condition).   The entrepreneur's total interest cost is given by the area
$OI_1^0 A i_1^0$, his total return by $OI_1^0 BC$, and his net return by $i_1^0 ABC$.

In a perfectly competitive system the net return of the representative
firm in each industry will be driven down (or increased) to zero by the
entry (or exit) of firms.   A long-run competitive equilibrium is pictured
in Fig. 8-2b.   The optimal investment of the representative firm is I_1^0.
The average and marginal internal rates of return are equal, and the
average internal rate of return now equals the rate of interest.

8-6. Interest-rate Determination

The methods of Chapters 4 and 5 can be utilized for an analysis of
bond-market equilibrium, and interest-rate determination can be included
within the general pricing process.   A closer analogy with the earlier
analyses of market equilibrium is obtained if the use of loanable funds
rather than bonds is treated as the commodity for sale.[1]   A demand for
(supply of) bonds is equivalent to a supply of (demand for) loanable
funds.   An interest rate is the price of using loanable funds for a specified
period of time.   By convention, interest rates are expressed as proportions of the amounts borrowed, but they can be expressed in terms of
money of account, as are all other prices.   Let 100 dollars serve as a unit
of purchasing power.   An interest rate of i_t is then the equivalent of a
price of $100i_t$ dollars per unit of purchasing power.

First, consider a partial-equilibrium analysis of the loanable-funds
market.   From the individual equilibrium conditions derived in Secs.
8-3 and 8-5 the current excess demand for loanable funds by each consumer and entrepreneur can be expressed as a function of the current and
expected interest rates.   It is convenient to use excess demand functions
rather than demand and supply functions, since individual consumers
and entrepreneurs may demand loanable funds at one interest rate and
supply them at another.

A theory of interest-rate expectations must be formulated before
market equilibrium can be determined.   Many different expectation
theories might be utilized.   One possibility is to assume that individuals
expect future interest rates to be at fixed levels regardless of the current
interest rate; future interest rates then enter the current excess demand
functions as constants rather than variables.   Another possibility is the
expectation that future interest rates will equal the current interest rate:

[1] In the present analysis there is assumed to be no circulating money.   Loanable
funds represent general purchasing power expressed in terms of a money of account.

$i_1 = i_2 = i_3 \cdots$. Still another possibility is the expectation that the current absolute change of the interest rate will be realized in the future: $i_1 - i_0 = i_2 - i_1 = i_3 - i_2 = \cdots$, or in general, $i_t = ti_1 - (t-1)i_0$. Each of these expectation assumptions allows the individual excess demands to be stated as functions of the current interest rate alone. An aggregate excess demand function is constructed by summing the individual functions. Since the individual excess demands are transformed into functions of the current interest rate before aggregation, it is not necessary that all individuals plan for horizons of the same length. An equilibrium current interest rate is one for which the excess demand for current loanable funds equals zero.

The multimarket equilibrium theory of Chapter 5 can also be extended to include the interest rate and multiperiod expectations. Theories of price and interest-rate expectations must be introduced to allow the individual excess demands for each commodity and loanable funds to be expressed as functions of only current prices and the current interest rate.[1] Multimarket equilibrium is then determined by the requirement that the excess demand for every commodity and for loanable funds simultaneously equal zero.

The formulation of the mathematical requirements for specific cases of single-market and multimarket equilibrium is left as an exercise for the reader.

8-7. Summary

Consumers and entrepreneurs are assumed to have free access to a perfectly competitive bond market and may adjust their income and outlay streams over time through borrowing (selling bonds) and lending (buying bonds). An interest rate expresses the cost of borrowing, or income from lending, for a duration of one period, as a proportion of the amount borrowed or lent. Market rates of return for durations longer than one period are defined as compounds of the interest rates connecting pairs of successive periods. Discount rates are defined as the reciprocals of the corresponding market rates of return. An entire income or cost stream can be reduced to a single number, its present value, by multiplying each of its elements by the appropriate discount rate and summing.

The consumer's utility index is defined as a function of the quantities of n goods that he consumes during each of the T periods within his planning horizon. He desires to maximize the level of this index subject to a lifetime budget constraint, which requires the equality of the present values of his consumption and earned-income streams. First-order con-

---

[1] See J. R. Hicks, *Value and Capital* (2d ed.; Oxford: Clarendon Press, 1946), chap. XVI, for a specific theory of price expectations.

ditions require that he equate intraperiod and interperiod RCSs to discounted commodity-price ratios. Second-order conditions follow from those for the n-commodity, single-period analysis. The consumer's present and planned commodity demands are functions of all current and expected prices and interest rates and are homogeneous of degree zero with respect to all prices and earned incomes. His demands for bonds are functions of the same variables, but are homogeneous of degree one with respect to all prices and earned incomes.

If prices are assumed to remain unchanged, the consumer's utility index can be expressed as a function of his consumption expenditures. The consumer's rate of time preference for consumption during period t rather than period τ $(>t)$ is defined as the smallest premium which he will accept as compensation for postponing a marginal dollar's worth of consumption expenditure. The first-order conditions for constrained utility maximization require that the consumer equate his rates of time preference to the corresponding market rates of return. Substitution and income effects with respect to changes in the rate of interest can be defined analogously to the single-period case.

An entrepreneur is assumed to formulate a production plan for a planning horizon encompassing L periods and $(L + 1)$ marketing dates. On the tth marketing date he sells the outputs produced during the $(t - 1)$th period and purchases inputs for application to the production process during the tth period. He desires to maximize the present value of his net operating revenues subject to the technical rules specified in his multiperiod production function. First-order conditions require that he equate input and output substitution rates to discounted price ratios. Second-order conditions again follow from those for the general one-period analysis.

The analysis of the entrepreneur's investment problems can also be simplified by assuming that actual and expected prices remain unchanged and that he always combines inputs and produces outputs so that intraperiod RTSs and RPTs are equated to the appropriate price ratios. The entrepreneur's investment-opportunities function relates his investment expenditures and revenues on the assumption that he performs this preliminary optimization. Marginal internal rates of return are defined for each of the investments with respect to each of the revenues. First-order conditions require that each marginal internal rate of return be equated with the corresponding market rate of return. Second-order conditions imply that each of the marginal internal rates be decreasing. The general analysis is applied to the special case of point-input–point-output.

Single-market and multimarket equilibrium analyses can be extended to include the current interest rate and multiperiod expectations.

Appendix: A Note on the Length of the Investment Period

Capitalistic production is characterized by the fact that time elapses between the application of inputs and the attainment of the resultant outputs. The multiperiod approach tends to obscure some of the time aspects of capitalistic production. Though the variables are dated, entrepreneurs' horizons are assumed to be of fixed length, and time does not enter the analysis as a variable. In the point-input–point-output case the length of time for which inputs are invested by definition always equals one period and is unaffected by changes in the rate of interest. The members of the "Austrian school" of capital theory considered the length of the investment period, or the "period of production," as they called it, to be the crucial variable in the theory of investment and capital.[1]

A consideration of the investment period in the point-input–point-output case requires the adoption of an alternative approach in which time is treated as a continuous variable and purchases and sales may take place at any point in time. A time period, such as a year, is necessary to provide a unit with which to measure time, but it has no other significance. Since elapsed time is now a variable, let $t = 0$ represent the present. The value $t = \tau$ now represents a point in time τ periods hence, where τ no longer need be an integer.

The concepts of Sec. 8-1 do not allow the determination of compound and present values for sums due on dates for which t is not an integer. Since time is assumed a continuous variable, interest is assumed to be compounded continuously. It can be proved with the use of advanced methods[2] that if interest is compounded continuously, the value of principal and compound interest at time t of a present investment of w dollars is

$$we^{it}$$

where the irrational number $e = 2.71828$ apx is the base of the system of natural logarithms and i is the interest rate per year which is assumed to remain unchanged. The present value of u dollars payable at time t is

$$ue^{-it}$$

since a present investment of ue^{-it} dollars in bonds will have a value of u dollars at time t.

---

[1] See Eugen v. Böhm-Bawerk, *The Positive Theory of Capital*, trans. by W. Smart (New York: G. E. Stechert, n.d.), and Knut Wicksell, *Lectures on Political Economy*, trans. by E. Classen (London: Routledge, 1934), vol. I, pp. 144–195.

[2] These methods are described, though not rigorously derived, by R. D. G. Allen, *Mathematical Analysis for Economists* (New York: Macmillan, 1938), pp. 228–232.

Imagine an entrepreneur engaged in the point-input–point-output process of wine aging. He purchases a cask of grape juice for I^0 dollars and waits while it ferments and ages. Assume that fermentation and aging are costless processes so that his only other cost is the interest charge on his initial investment. Further assume that the sales value of the wine is a function of the length of its aging period $[R(t)]$.

The entrepreneur's optimization problem is to select an aging period, i.e., a value for t, that maximizes the present value of his profit:

$$\pi = R(t)e^{-it} - I^0$$

Setting the derivative of π with respect to t equal to zero,

$$\frac{d\pi}{dt} = R'(t)e^{-it} - iR(t)e^{-it} = 0$$

Factoring out $e^{-it} \neq 0$ and rearranging terms,

$$\frac{R'(t)}{R(t)} = i \tag{8A-1}$$

The entrepreneur must equate his marginal rate of return with respect to time $[R'(t)/R(t)]$ to his marginal rate of cost with respect to time (i).

The second-order condition requires that

$$\frac{d^2\pi}{dt^2} = [R''(t) - 2iR'(t) + i^2R(t)]e^{-it} < 0$$

Substituting from (8A-1) for i and i^2 and multiplying through by $e^{it}/R(t) > 0$,

$$\frac{R''(t)R(t) - [R'(t)]^2}{[R(t)]^2} < 0 \tag{8A-2}$$

The marginal rate of return with respect to time must be decreasing, i.e., its derivative must be negative. If (8A-1) and (8A-2) are satisfied for $t = \tau$, the entrepreneur's marginal earnings would be more than the rate of return if his investment period were slightly shorter than τ, and less than the market rate of return if it were slightly longer than τ.

The effect of a change of the rate of interest upon the investment period can be determined by total differentiation of (8A-1):

$$R''(t)\,dt - iR'(t)\,dt - R(t)\,di = 0$$

and
$$\frac{dt}{di} = \frac{R(t)}{R''(t) - iR'(t)} < 0 \tag{8A-3}$$

The numerator of (8A-3) is positive, and (8A-2) requires that its denominator be negative. A decline in the interest rate will lead the entrepreneur to lengthen his investment period.

The investment period is a meaningful concept for point-input–point-output production processes such as wine aging and tree growing. It provides a description of the "method of production" and varies in a known way with the interest rate. Some members of the Austrian school attempted the impossible task of extending the point-input–point-output results to more complex cases by defining average investment periods. Investment periods cannot be defined in the multipoint-input–multipoint-output case, since it is impossible to attribute particular outputs to particular inputs. But this is not the only difficulty. An entire output stream can be attributed to the inputs on a specific date in the point-input–multipoint-output case. There are as many investment periods as there are elements in the output stream. The average investment period must be some weighted average of these periods. The values of the elements in the output stream cannot be used as weights, since dollars at different points in time are not identical. It is necessary to discount intertemporal values if they are to be comparable, but if discounted values are used as weights, the average investment period is not independent of the interest rate.

SELECTED REFERENCES

Carlson, Sune, *A Study on the Pure Theory of Production* (New York: Kelley and Millman, 1956). Chapter VI contains a multiperiod production theory developed with the aid of elementary calculus.

Fisher, Irving, *The Theory of Interest* (New York: Kelley and Millman, 1954). A classic statement of many of the concepts of this chapter which contains verbal, geometric, and mathematical descriptions.

Friedman, Milton, *A Theory of the Consumption Function* (Princeton, N.J.: Princeton University Press, 1957). Chapter II contains a theory of multiperiod consumption. The remainder of the volume is devoted to attempts at its statistical verification.

Hicks, J. R., *Value and Capital* (2d ed.; Oxford: Clarendon Press, 1946). Parts III and IV and the mathematical appendix contain multiperiod analyses.

Lutz, Friedrich and Vera, *The Theory of Investment of the Firm* (Princeton, N.J.: Princeton University Press, 1951). A detailed study of many different investment problems in which time is treated as a continuous variable. A knowledge of differential and integral calculus is helpful, but not absolutely necessary.

Modigliani, Franco, and Richard Brumberg, "Utility Analysis and the Consumption Function," in Kenneth K. Kurihara (ed.), *Post Keynesian Economics* (New Brunswick, N.J.: Rutgers University Press, 1954), pp. 388–436. A theoretical and empirical study of lifetime consumption patterns. Some knowledge of calculus and mathematical statistics is required.

MATHEMATICAL REVIEW

This appendix contains a brief review of some of the mathematical concepts that are used in the text. Rigorous proofs are generally omitted; in fact, many statements are not proved at all.

The major tools of analysis are algebra and differential and integral calculus. The solution of simultaneous equations and the use of determinants are outlined in Sec. A-1. The fundamentals of differential calculus with respect to functions of a single variable are discussed in Sec. A-2. The analysis is extended to functions of many variables, and the applications of partial differentiation are discussed in Sec. A-3. The basic properties of integrals are reviewed in Sec. A-4, and the appendix ends with a discussion of difference equations in Sec. A-5.

A-1. Simultaneous Equations and Determinants

A system of n equations in n variables can be written as

$$
\begin{aligned}
a_{11}x_1 + a_{12}x_2 + \cdots + a_{1n}x_n &= b_1 \\
a_{21}x_1 + a_{22}x_2 + \cdots + a_{2n}x_n &= b_2 \\
&\cdots\cdots\cdots\cdots\cdots\cdots \\
a_{n1}x_1 + a_{n2}x_2 + \cdots + a_{nn}x_n &= b_n
\end{aligned}
\tag{A-1}
$$

where the as are coefficients and the bs constant terms. Any set of n numbers that preserves all n of the equalities in (A-1) when substituted for the xs is a solution for this system. A simple example of a system of simultaneous equations is

$$
\begin{aligned}
3x_1 - 5x_2 &= 11 \\
x_1 + 2x_2 &= 11
\end{aligned}
$$

Its only solution is $x_1 = 7$, $x_2 = 2$.

A determinant is a number derived from a square array of numbers according to rules to be specified. It is denoted either by vertical lines on both sides of the array from which it is calculated or by a boldface letter.   If A denotes the array,[1] $\mathbf{A}$ denotes its determinant:

$$\mathbf{A} = \begin{vmatrix} a_{11} & a_{12} & \cdots & a_{1n} \\ a_{21} & a_{22} & \cdots & a_{2n} \\ \cdot & \cdot & \cdot & \cdot \\ a_{n1} & a_{n2} & \cdots & a_{nn} \end{vmatrix}$$

The *elements* of the matrix A are the coefficients a_{ij} where the first subscript is the *row index* and the second subscript the *column index*.   Thus a_{57} is the element in the fifth row and seventh column of the array.

The rule by which a determinant is calculated from an array is merely stated here.[2]   Products of numbers (or elements) are formed from A such that each product contains one and only one element from each row and one and only one element from each column.   Thus the determinant is defined only for square arrays.   All such products can be written with the row indices in natural order $(1,2,3, \ldots ,n)$.   Examples are the products $a_{11}a_{22} \cdots a_{nn}$ and $a_{12}a_{21}a_{33} \cdots a_{nn}$.   If the number of *inversions*[3] among the column indices is even, the sign of the product is left unchanged.   If the number of inversions among the column indices is odd, it is changed from minus to plus or from plus to minus.   The value of the determinant is the algebraic sum of all such products.   Consider the determinant

$$\mathbf{A} = \begin{vmatrix} a_{11} & a_{12} \\ a_{21} & a_{22} \end{vmatrix} = a_{11}a_{22} - a_{12}a_{21}$$

Only two products can be formed from the matrix A according to the rule stated above.   A negative sign precedes the second term, since it contains one inversion (an odd number) of the column subscripts when the row subscripts are written in natural order.[4]

[1] Any rectangular array of numbers is called a *matrix*.   A matrix with m rows and n columns is of the order $(m \times n)$.   An $(m \times 1)$ matrix is a column vector, and a $(1 \times m)$ matrix is a row vector.   The terms "array" and "matrix" are used interchangeably.

[2] For more extensive discussion see A. C. Aitken, *Determinants and Matrices* (New York: Interscience, 1951), chap. II; S. Perlis, *Theory of Matrices* (Cambridge, Mass.: Addison-Wesley, 1952), chap. IV; or G. Birkhoff and S. MacLane, *A Survey of Modern Algebra* (rev. ed.; New York: Macmillan, 1953), chap. X.

[3] An inversion is an instance in which a lower index follows a higher one.   For example, the indices 1, 2 are in natural order; the sequence 2, 1 contains one inversion. The sequence 1, 3, 2, 5, 4 contains two inversions, since it contains two instances in which a lower index follows a higher one: 3 comes before 2, and 5 before 4.   The sequence 4, 3, 2, 1, 5 contains six inversions.

[4] The same result is obtained by counting the number of inversions among row subscripts when the column subscripts are written in natural order.   The reader may check that if a matrix has n rows and n columns, the number of terms in the expression for its determinant is $n!$ (read "n factorial"), i.e., $n \cdot (n - 1) \cdots 3 \cdot 2 \cdot 1$.   See Aitken, *op. cit.*, pp. 26–36.

If the matrix is[1]

$$\begin{bmatrix} 3 & 2 \\ -1 & 4 \end{bmatrix}$$

the determinant is $12 + 2 = 14$.

The above rule is very cumbersome if the matrix contains a large number of rows and columns. Generally, a determinant is more easily evaluated by an expansion in terms of *cofactors*. For any element a_{ij} of the matrix A form an array by striking out the ith row and the jth column of the original matrix. The determinant of the remaining array, which contains $(n - 1)$ rows and $(n - 1)$ columns, is the *minor* of the element a_{ij}.† The cofactor of this element is its minor multiplied by $+1$ if $(i + j)$ is even and by -1 if $(i + j)$ is odd. The determinant $\mathbf{A}$ can be written as

$$\mathbf{A} = a_{i1}\mathbf{C}_{i1} + a_{i2}\mathbf{C}_{i2} + \cdots + a_{in}\mathbf{C}_{in}$$

for any given row index i where $\mathbf{C}_{ij}$ is the cofactor of the element in the ith row and jth column. Similarly,

$$\mathbf{A} = a_{1j}\mathbf{C}_{1j} + a_{2j}\mathbf{C}_{2j} + \cdots + a_{nj}\mathbf{C}_{nj}$$

for any column index j. Since a determinant can be expanded in terms of any single row or column, the multiplication of any row or column of the array A by a number k changes the value of the determinant by the same multiple.

Imagine that the ith row of the matrix is multiplied by k. Then expanding the new determinant in terms of the ith row and denoting it by $\mathbf{A}^*$,

$$\mathbf{A}^* = ka_{i1}\mathbf{C}_{i1} + ka_{i2}\mathbf{C}_{i2} + \cdots + ka_{in}\mathbf{C}_{in} = k\mathbf{A}$$

The expansion

$$a_{i1}\mathbf{C}_{j1} + a_{i2}\mathbf{C}_{j2} + \cdots + a_{in}\mathbf{C}_{jn} \qquad \text{for } i \neq j$$

is an expansion by *alien cofactors* and equals zero.[2] Using this theorem it can be proved that adding a multiple of any row (or column) to any

---

[1] The matrix or the array itself is written with square or round brackets. The operation of forming the determinant, however, is indicated by vertical bars instead of brackets.

† The diagonal of the array running in northwest-southeast direction is the principal diagonal. Minors of elements on the principal diagonal (i.e., of a_{11}, a_{22}, etc.) are called principal minors. The principal minor of a_{11} in the original determinant $\mathbf{A}$ is a determinant of the order $(n - 1) \times (n - 1)$ and is denoted by $\mathbf{A}_{11}$. The principal minor of a_{22} in the minor $\mathbf{A}_{11}$ is a determinant of order $(n - 2) \times (n - 2)$ and is denoted by $\mathbf{A}_{11,22}$. This $(n - 2) \times (n - 2)$ determinant is itself a principal minor of the original determinant.

[2] See Birkhoff and MacLane, *op. cit.*, p. 286.

other row (or column) leaves the value of the determinant unchanged. For example, multiply the jth row by k, add it to the ith row, and denote the new determinant by $\mathbf{A}^{**}$. Expanding $\mathbf{A}^{**}$ in terms of its ith row:

$$\mathbf{A}^{**} = (a_{i1} + ka_{j1})\mathbf{C}_{i1} + (a_{i2} + ka_{j2})\mathbf{C}_{i2} + \cdots + (a_{in} + ka_{jn})\mathbf{C}_{in}$$
$$= a_{i1}\mathbf{C}_{i1} + a_{i2}\mathbf{C}_{i2} + \cdots + a_{in}\mathbf{C}_{in}$$
$$+ k(a_{j1}\mathbf{C}_{i1} + a_{j2}\mathbf{C}_{i2} + \cdots + a_{jn}\mathbf{C}_{in})$$
$$= \mathbf{A}$$

since the bracketed term in the second line is an expansion by alien cofactors and therefore equals zero.

The system of simultaneous equations in (A-1) can be solved by *Cramer's rule*, which states that the solution for x_j is given by the ratio of two determinants, the denominator being the determinant of the coefficients of the system of equations and the numerator being the determinant of the coefficients with the jth column replaced by the column of constant terms. First applying the rule that multiplying a column of the array multiplies the value of the determinant by the same number and then applying the rule that adding multiples of one column to some other column does not alter the value of the determinant, the solution for x_1 is derived as follows:

$$x_1\mathbf{A} = \begin{vmatrix} a_{11}x_1 & a_{12} & \cdots & a_{1n} \\ a_{21}x_1 & a_{22} & \cdots & a_{2n} \\ \cdots & \cdots & \cdots & \cdots \\ a_{n1}x_1 & a_{n2} & \cdots & a_{nn} \end{vmatrix} = \begin{vmatrix} a_{11}x_1 + a_{12}x_2 & a_{12} & \cdots & a_{1n} \\ a_{21}x_1 + a_{22}x_2 & a_{22} & \cdots & a_{2n} \\ \cdots & \cdots & \cdots & \cdots \\ a_{n1}x_1 + a_{n2}x_2 & a_{n2} & \cdots & a_{nn} \end{vmatrix} = \cdots$$

$$= \begin{vmatrix} a_{11}x_1 + a_{12}x_2 + \cdots + a_{1n}x_n & a_{12} & \cdots & a_{1n} \\ a_{21}x_1 + a_{22}x_2 + \cdots + a_{2n}x_n & a_{22} & \cdots & a_{2n} \\ \cdots & \cdots & \cdots & \cdots \\ a_{n1}x_1 + a_{n2}x_2 + \cdots + a_{nn}x_n & a_{n2} & \cdots & a_{nn} \end{vmatrix}$$

$$= \begin{vmatrix} b_1 & a_{12} & \cdots & a_{1n} \\ b_2 & a_{22} & \cdots & a_{2n} \\ \cdots & \cdots & \cdots & \cdots \\ b_n & a_{n2} & \cdots & a_{nn} \end{vmatrix}$$

by substituting the column of constants from (A-1) for the sums in the first column. Denoting the determinant on the right-hand side by $\mathbf{A}_1$, the solution for x_1 is

$$x_1 = \frac{\mathbf{A}_1}{\mathbf{A}} \tag{A-2}$$

as stated. The expression (A-2) is meaningless if $\mathbf{A} = 0$. In this case no unique solution exists, and the rows of the array are *linearly dependent* or, equivalently, the matrix is *singular*.[1]

If the value of a determinant is zero, one of the equations can be expressed as a linear combination of the remaining ones. For example, the nth equation might then be obtained by multiplying the first equation by 6 and adding 3 times the second to the first. The nth equation contains no new information and can be omitted, because it depends linearly on the first $(n-1)$ equations. For example, assume that the nth equation is a linear combination of the first $(n-1)$ equations. The ith equation is

$$\sum_{j=1}^{n} a_{ij}x_j = b_i$$

and the nth is

$$\sum_{i=1}^{n-1} c_i \sum_{j=1}^{n} a_{ij}x_j = \sum_{i=1}^{n-1} c_i b_i$$

where the cs are constants not all equal to zero. Any set of xs which satisfies the first $(n-1)$ equations necessarily satisfies the nth. The last equation adds no new information. The system is reduced to $(n-1)$ equations in n variables. If no $(n-1)$-rowed minor vanishes, it is possible to solve for any $(n-1)$ variables in terms of the constant terms and the remaining variable.

If the original system of n equations is *homogeneous* (all constant terms equal zero), all the xs are zero if the determinant of the system is non-vanishing. According to Cramer's rule each x is expressed as a fraction. The denominator is nonzero by hypothesis. The numerator vanishes for every x, because all bs equal zero, and the determinant of any array with a column of zeros is itself zero. If the determinant vanishes, it is possible to solve only for the relative values of the variables, and the solution is unique except for a factor of proportionality. For example, if

---

[1] Denote by Σ (the Greek capital letter sigma) the operation of summing such that $\sum_{i=1}^{n} a_i$ is defined to mean $a_1 + a_2 + \cdots + a_n$. The rows of the matrix A are defined to be linearly dependent if it is possible to find a set of numbers $c_1, c_2, \ldots, c_n$ such that $\sum_{i=1}^{n} c_i a_{ij} = 0$ for all values of the index j, provided that the cs are not all equal to zero. It can be proved that the value of the determinant of the array is zero if and only if the rows (or the columns) of the array are linearly dependent. See Aitken, *op. cit.*, pp. 62 and 64.

the system of simultaneous equations is

$$3x_1 - 4x_2 = 0$$
$$6x_1 - 8x_2 = 0$$

the determinant is $(3)(-8) - (6)(-4) = 0$. Hence the two equations are not independent, and the second equation can be omitted.[1] Then

$$3x_1 - 4x_2 = 0$$

or

$$\frac{x_1}{x_2} = \frac{4}{3}$$

Any set of values satisfies the system as long as the relation between x_1 and x_2 is as 4:3.† Numerical values for the variables can only be obtained by choosing an arbitrary value for one of them.

A-2. Calculus: Functions of a Single Variable

Functions, Limits, Continuity. The relation $y = f(x)$ (read "y is a function of x") means that a rule exists by which it is possible to associate values of the variable y with values of the variable x. Examples are $y = 1/x$, $y = 3x^2$, $y = \log \sin x$, and $y = 1$ when x is an odd integer and $y = 0$ for any other value of x. In each case values of y correspond to given values of x according to the rule of association specified in the form of the function. The variable y may be undefined for some values of x; $y = 1/x$ cannot be evaluated for $x = 0$, and $y = \log \sin x$ cannot be evaluated for values of x for which $\sin x$ is negative. The relation $y = f(x)$ is an *explicit* function, since y is expressed in terms of x. If the functional relation between y and x is denoted by $g(y,x) = 0$, y is an *implicit* function of x. Specifying a value of x implicitly defines a value of y such that the expression on the left-hand side reduces to zero when the appropriate values of x and y are substituted in it. The relations $y = x^2$, $y = ax + b$, and $y = \sqrt[3]{x}$ provide examples of explicit functions; the expressions $ax + b - y = 0$, $x^2 - y^2 = 0$, and $e^y + y - x + \log x = 0$ are examples of implicit functions. In order to rewrite an implicit function in explicit form it is necessary to solve the equation $g(y,x) = 0$ for y. This is not always possible. The implicit function $e^y + y - x + \log x = 0$ cannot be written in explicit form because the equation cannot be solved analytically for x or y. An

---

[1] It does not matter which equation is omitted. Discarding the first leads to the same answer.

† The discussion in the previous paragraphs is intentionally not rigorous. Necessary and sufficient conditions for the solubility of a system of simultaneous equations are proved in any textbook on algebra. See Aitken, *op. cit.*, pp. 63–66, 69–71, or Perlis, *op. cit.*, pp. 45–48.

explicit function can always be rewritten in implicit-function form. For example, the explicit function $y = 3x^4 + 2 \sin x - 1$ becomes $y - 3x^4 - 2 \sin x + 1 = 0$ in implicit form.

A sequence of numbers is a list or enumeration of numbers such as $1, 2, 3, 4, 5, \ldots$; or $1, \frac{1}{2}, \frac{1}{3}, \frac{1}{4}, \frac{1}{5}, \ldots$; or $2, 1, \frac{1}{2}, \frac{1}{4}, \frac{1}{8}, \ldots$; or $1, 0, -1, 0, 1, \ldots$. Each number in a sequence can be assigned an index indicating how "far out" the number is in the sequence. Thus in the third sequence above, $x_2 = 1$. The sequence converges to a limit K if there exists a number K with the property that the numerical magnitude of the difference between K and an item in the sequence is arbitrarily small (can be made as small as one desires) if one takes an item in the sequence sufficiently "far out," i.e., an item with sufficiently high index, and if the difference remains at least as small for every item in the sequence with even higher index. The third sequence has the limit zero.

The explicit function $f(x)$ (or, what is the same thing, the variable y) approaches the limit L as x approaches the number a, if the value of the function can be made to be as near the number L as is desired by taking x values which are sufficiently close to a, and if the value of the function remains at least as near L for all x values even closer to a. The process of finding the limit of $f(x)$ at $x = a$ may be visualized in the following manner. Take successive values $x_1, x_2, \ldots$, etc., of x that form a sequence converging to a. Substitute these values of x in $f(x)$. This results in a sequence of values $f(x_1), f(x_2), \ldots$, etc. If this sequence converges to a number $L, f(x)$ has the limit L at $x = a$. A limit exists if L is finite. The operation of taking the limit of $f(x)$ is denoted by $\lim_{x \to a} f(x) = L$.

The function $f(x) = 1 + 1/x$ approaches the limit 1 as $x \to \infty$ (x approaches infinity). However, this result cannot be obtained by substituting ∞ for x in $1 + 1/x$ because $1/\infty$ does not equal zero. $A/B = C$ implies that $A = B \cdot C$. If $1/\infty = 0$, then $1 = (\infty) \cdot (0)$. Since this is untrue, the problem must be resolved by a different reasoning, namely by an application of the definition of the limit. In fact, ∞ is not a number, but rather a direction. Its appearance in a formula is equivalent to the command to list the positive integers in increasing order and go as far as possible, i.e., to take the limit. The value of y can be made to differ from 1 by less than 0.1 by selecting a value for x greater than 10. If $x = 20$, $1 + 1/x = 1.05$, which differs from 1 by only 0.05. Likewise, y can be made to differ from 1 by less than $1/1,000,000$ by selecting a value for x greater than 1,000,000. The difference between the value of y and the number 1 can be made smaller than any prespecified number by taking an x that is sufficiently large.

The function $f(x)$ is continuous at the point $x = a$ if the following con-

ditions are fulfilled: (1) $\lim_{x \to a} f(x)$ exists, (2) $f(a)$ exists, (3) $f(a) = \lim_{x \to a} f(x)$.†
The function is continuous in the interval $a < x < b$ if it is continuous at
every point in the interval. This definition of continuity implies that
the function must be "continuous" in the everyday sense of the word:
one must be able to draw the graph of the function without lifting the
pencil from the paper.[1]

The Derivative. Assume that the function $y = f(x)$ is continuous in
some interval. If the independent variable x changes by a small quantity
Δx, the value of the function will change by the quantity Δy. Hence
$y + \Delta y = f(x + \Delta x)$. The change in the value of the function can be
expressed as

$$\Delta y = f(x + \Delta x) - f(x) \tag{A-3}$$

Dividing both sides of (A-3) by Δx:

$$\frac{\Delta y}{\Delta x} = \frac{f(x + \Delta x) - f(x)}{\Delta x} \tag{A-4}$$

The average rate of change of y per unit change of x for the interval x
to $x + \Delta x$ is given by (A-4). For example, imagine that if one walks
another half-hour, one covers an additional distance of 2 miles. The
independent variable time is changed from x to $x + \frac{1}{2}$ hours; $\Delta y = 2$
miles, $\Delta x = \frac{1}{2}$ hour, and $\Delta y / \Delta x =$ average speed $= 4$ miles per hour.
The derivative of $f(x)$, denoted by $dy/dx, f'(x)$, or $\dot{y}$, is defined as the rate
of change of $f(x)$ as Δx approaches zero:

$$\frac{dy}{dx} = f'(x) = \lim_{\Delta x \to 0} \frac{f(x + \Delta x) - f(x)}{\Delta x} \tag{A-5}$$

The derivative is the rate of change or the speed in terms of the above
example, or, to put it differently, the limit of the average rate of change
(average speed) as Δx (the time interval) approaches zero. If the graph
of $f(x)$ is plotted, the derivative calculated at the point $x = a$ is the slope
of the curve representing $f(x)$ at the point $x = a$. The average rate of
change is the slope of the secant between two points on the curve, and

---

† At the point $x = a$ the value of the function must be finite, and this value must
equal the limit of the function as x approaches a. The function $y = 1$ when x is an
odd integer and $y = 0$ for any other value of x is not continuous when x is an odd
integer. If $f(x)$ and $g(x)$ are two functions which are both continuous at $x = a$,
then $f(x) + g(x), f(x) \cdot g(x)$, and $f(x)/g(x)$ (provided that $g(x) \neq 0$) are also continuous.

[1] Note that a function that has "corners" or "kinks" but no gaps is continuous.
The absolute value of a number x (denoted by $|x|$) is defined as follows:

$$|x| = x \quad \text{if } x \geq 0$$
$$|x| = -x \quad \text{if } x < 0$$

The function $y = |x|$ has a kink at $x = 0$, but is continuous.

the derivative is the slope of the tangent to the curve at a given point. These concepts are illustrated by Fig. A-1.

The derivative of a derivative is a second derivative, denoted by d^2y/dx^2, and is defined as

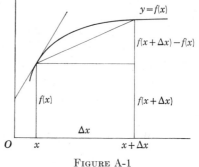

$$\frac{d^2y}{dx^2} = \lim_{\Delta x \to 0} \frac{f'(x + \Delta x) - f'(x)}{\Delta x} \quad \text{(A-6)}$$

The second derivative is the rate of change of the first derivative, i.e., the rate at which the slope of the function is changing. In terms of the previous example it is the acceleration or the rate of change of speed.

FIGURE A-1

Higher-order derivatives are defined similarly.

Techniques of Differentiation. To differentiate a function is to find its derivative. Some of the more important techniques of differentiation are stated below without proof:[1]

1. $f(x) = c$ (constant), $f'(x) = 0$
2. $f(x) = x^n$, $f'(x) = nx^{n-1}$
3. $f(x) = g(x) \cdot h(x)$, $f'(x) = g'(x) \cdot h(x) + g(x) \cdot h'(x)$
4. $f(x) = g(x)/h(x)$, $h(x) \neq 0$, $f'(x) = [g'(x) \cdot h(x) - g(x) \cdot h'(x)]/[h(x)]^2$
5. $f(x) = g[h(x)]$, $f'(x) = g'[h(x)] \cdot h'(x)$ (function of a function rule)
6. $f(x) = \log x$, $f'(x) = 1/x$ (log to base e)
7. $f(x) = e^{ax}$, $f'(x) = ae^{ax}$
8. If $y = f(x)$ is single-valued and continuous, and can be written in inverse form as $x = g(y)$ such that $f'(x)$ is continuous and $\neq 0$, $f'(x) = 1/g'(y)$ or $dy/dx = 1/(dx/dy)$ (inverse-function rule).

Maxima and Minima. A function of one variable $y = f(x)$ has a (relative) maximum at the point $x = a$ if $f(a) \geq f(x)$ for all values of x in a small neighborhood about the point a. The value $f(a)$ is not necessarily larger than values of $f(x)$ outside the small neighborhood about a. Similarly, $f(x)$ has a minimum at $x = b$ if $f(b) \leq f(x)$ for all x in a small neighborhood about b.

Sufficient conditions for maxima and minima can be indicated intuitively as follows. A function that has a maximum (or minimum) is, by definition, neither increasing nor decreasing at its extreme point. But the first derivative is the function's rate of increase. It must therefore equal zero at an extreme point. A function first increases, becomes stationary, and then decreases in the case of a maximum. Thus the

---

[1] Proofs can be found in any standard elementary text on calculus. See R. Courant, *Differential and Integral Calculus* (London: Blackie, 1934), pp. 136–140, 173, 175, or H. B. Fine, *Calculus* (New York: Macmillan, 1937), chaps. III and VII.

second derivative (the rate of change of the first derivative) is negative at a maximum. For similar reasons it is positive at a minimum. These conditions on the first and second derivatives are sufficient for maxima and minima.

A more rigorous proof of necessary and sufficient conditions runs as follows. Assume that $y = f(x)$ is a continuous function with continuous first- and second-order derivatives. The theorem of the mean states[1] that its average rate of change between two points (the slope of its secant) is equal to its derivative (slope of the tangent) evaluated at some point within the interval:

$$\frac{f(x + \Delta x) - f(x)}{\Delta x} = f'(x + \theta \Delta x) \qquad 0 < \theta < 1 \qquad \text{(A-7)}$$

If $f(x)$ is a maximum, $f(x + \Delta x) - f(x) \leqq 0$. Then the fraction on the left-hand side of (A-7) is nonpositive for positive values of Δx and nonnegative for negative values of Δx. Let Δx approach zero from the right (i.e., through positive values). Then the limit of the fraction in (A-7) must itself be nonpositive. Letting Δx approach zero from the left (i.e., through negative values), the limit of the fraction must be nonnegative. But the limit of the fraction in (A-7) as Δx approaches zero is $f'(x)$; this must be neither positive nor negative and hence must equal zero. A necessary condition for a maximum or minimum is that the first derivative equal zero. This condition on the first derivative is the *first-order* condition for a maximum or minimum.

An additional condition must be fulfilled for a maximum or minimum. Expanding $f(x)$ in Taylor series[2] with remainder term about the point x,

$$f(x + \Delta x) = f(x) + \Delta x \, f'(x) + \frac{(\Delta x)^2}{2} f''(x + \theta \, \Delta x) \qquad 0 < \theta < 1 \qquad \text{(A-8)}$$

Since $f'(x) = 0$ when $f(x)$ is a maximum, (A-8) becomes

$$f(x + \Delta x) - f(x) = \frac{(\Delta x)^2}{2} f''(x + \theta \, \Delta x) \qquad \text{(A-9)}$$

This implies that $f''(x + \theta \, \Delta x)$ is nonpositive for all values of Δx within a small neighborhood of x. By the continuity of the second derivative $\lim_{\Delta x \to 0} f''(x + \theta \, \Delta x) = f''(x)$, and this must be nonpositive. Hence, the first derivative must equal zero, and the second derivative must be nonpositive for a maximum.[3] These conditions are necessary, but not sufficient. Their insufficiency is illustrated by the function $y = x^3$. Its

---

[1] Proved in any standard text on calculus. See Courant, *op. cit.*, pp. 102–104, or Fine, *op. cit.*, pp. 104–105.

[2] See Fine, *op. cit.*, pp. 208, 214–215, or any other standard text on calculus.

[3] Courant, *op. cit.*, pp. 159–163.

first and second derivatives vanish at $x = 0$, yet the function has neither a maximum nor a minimum at that point. Sufficient conditions can be stated as follows: a zero first derivative and a negative (positive) second derivative implies that the function attains a maximum (minimum). However, this statement does not provide necessary conditions, since the second derivative may vanish although $f(x)$ attains a maximum or minimum. As an example consider the function $y = x^4$ which possesses zero first and second derivatives at $x = 0$, yet has a minimum at that point.

Necessary and sufficient conditions for a maximum (minimum) are as follows: $f(x)$ attains a maximum (minimum) at $x = a$ if and only if (1) $dy/dx = 0$ at $x = a$, (2) the first $(n - 1)$ (n even) derivatives are all zero and the first nonzero derivative (the nth) is negative (positive) at $x = a$.

In general, the maximum and minimum values of a function are found by determining and solving the equation $f'(x) = 0$, then substituting the values of x for which the first derivative vanishes into $f''(x)$ and evaluating its sign. If it is negative, the corresponding value of $f(x)$ is a maximum; if it is positive, the corresponding value is a minimum. If the second derivative is zero, there are three possibilities: (1) $d^3y/dx^3 \neq 0$, (2) $d^3y/dx^3 = 0$ and $d^4y/dx^4 \neq 0$, or (3) $d^3y/dx^3 = 0$ and $d^4y/dx^4 = 0$. If (1) holds, the function has an inflection point (i.e., the first derivative has an extreme value) rather than a maximum or minimum. If (2) holds, the function has a maximum or minimum according to whether the fourth derivative is negative or positive. If (3) holds, the signs of the fifth and sixth derivatives must be examined and (1) and (2) applied with d^5y/dx^5 replacing d^3y/dx^3 and d^6y/dx^6 replacing d^4y/dx^4.

The examples in Chapters 2 through 8 are based on functions which fall into a class with the property that the second derivative is nonzero for extreme values. Necessary and sufficient conditions for functions in this class involve only the first and second derivatives. The above refinement involving higher-order derivatives is not mentioned in the text, but should be kept in mind. The conditions on the second derivative are the *second-order* conditions.

Average and Marginal Curves. Assume that $R = pq$ and

$$p = \frac{R}{q} = f(q)$$

The functional relationship $p = f(q)$ is frequently referred to as an average curve.[1] The curve the ordinate of which measures the rate of change

---

[1] The relation $p = f(q)$ is an average curve because it relates values of p to the average values (with respect to q) of the variable R. An economic example is provided by the demand curve where q is quantity sold, p is price, and R is total revenue.

of R (the change at the margin) is the marginal curve or the curve marginal to $p = f(q)$. Substituting the value $f(q)$ for p in $R = pq$ and differentiating with respect to q

$$\frac{dR}{dq} = f(q) + qf'(q) \qquad\qquad (A\text{-}10)$$

Let q be restricted to nonnegative values. [The relationship (A-10) implies that the marginal curve will lie below the average curve if the average curve is decreasing and above it if the average curve is increasing, since $f'(q) < 0$ and $q > 0$ imply $f(q) > dR/dq$ for all positive values of q and conversely for $f'(q) > 0$.] Hence the average curve is rising when the marginal curve is above the average, and the average is falling when the marginal is below the average. It also follows that if the average curve has an extreme point (i.e., a point at which $f'(q) = 0$), the marginal curve intersects the average curve at this point.

When $q = 0$, (A-10) becomes

$$\frac{dR}{dq} = f(0) \qquad\qquad (A\text{-}11)$$

The value of p from the average curve is $p = f(0)$. Hence the average curve and the curve marginal to it intersect at the point where they both meet the p axis. The slope of the average curve is $dp/dq = f'(q)$, and the slope of the marginal curve is

$$\frac{d^2R}{dq^2} = f'(q) + f'(q) + qf''(q) = 2f'(q) + qf''(q)$$

If the average curve is a straight line, $f''(q) = 0$, and the slope of the marginal curve is twice the slope of the average curve. On the basis of this information the marginal curve can be constructed diagrammatically with ease if the average curve is given.

A-3. Calculus: Functions of Many Variables

Partial Derivatives. The definitions of a limit and continuity are easily generalized to a function of n independent variables

$$y = f(x_1, x_2, \ldots, x_n)$$

The partial derivative of y with respect to x_i is

$$f_i = \frac{\partial y}{\partial x_i} = \lim_{\Delta x_i \to 0} \frac{f(x_1, x_2, \ldots, x_i + \Delta x_i, \ldots, x_n) - f(x_1, x_2, \ldots, x_n)}{\Delta x_i}$$

which is the rate of change of the function with respect to x_i, all other variables remaining constant. The techniques of differentiation are the same as those for a function of a single variable; all variables other than x_i are treated as constants. For example, if

$$y = 3x_1x_2^2 + x_2 \log x_1$$

then $\quad \dfrac{\partial y}{\partial x_1} = 3x_2^2 + \dfrac{x_2}{x_1} \quad$ and $\quad \dfrac{\partial y}{\partial x_2} = 6x_1x_2 + \log x_1$

Higher-order derivatives are determined by successive partial differentiation; $\partial^2 y/\partial x_i^2$ is the partial derivative of f_i with respect to x_i, also denoted by f_{ii}; $\partial^2 y/\partial x_i\,\partial x_j$ is the partial derivative of f_i with respect to x_j (one of the second cross partial derivatives) and is denoted by f_{ij}. For the previous example

$$\frac{\partial^2 y}{\partial x_2\,\partial x_1} = 6x_2 + \frac{1}{x_1}$$

If the first and second cross partial derivatives are continuous, $f_{ij} = f_{ji}$. The partial derivatives of the implicit function $f(x_1,x_2, \ . \ . \ . \ ,x_n) = 0$ are obtained by assuming that $y = f(x_1,x_2, \ . \ . \ . \ ,x_n)$ and calculating $\partial y/\partial x_1$, $\partial y/\partial x_2$, etc.

The Total Differential. For a function of a single variable

$$\frac{dy}{dx} = f'(x)$$

The symbol dy/dx denotes the derivative and was not interpreted as a fraction composed of the quantities dy and dx. Defining dx as an increment or change in the independent variable, dy can be defined as

$$dy = f'(x)\,dx \qquad\qquad (A\text{-}12)$$

This is the *differential* of $f(x)$. At a given point x^0 the value of the function is $y^0 = f(x^0)$, and (A-12) can be rewritten in terms of deviations from this point as

$$y - y^0 = f'(x^0) \cdot (x - x^0) \qquad\qquad (A\text{-}13)$$

which is the equation of the tangent to $y = f(x)$ at the point (x^0,y^0). Hence, (A-12) is the general form of the equation of the tangent to the function. For small changes of x (A-13) gives the approximate value of the corresponding change of $f(x)$.

The *total differential* of a function of n variables is defined as

$$dy = f_1\,dx_1 + f_2\,dx_2 + \cdots + f_n\,dx_n \qquad\qquad (A\text{-}14)$$

which is the general form of the equation of the tangent plane (or hyperplane) to the surface (or hypersurface) defined by $y = f(x_1,x_2, \ . \ . \ . \ ,x_n)$.

It also provides an approximate value of the change in the function when all variables are permitted to vary, provided that the variation in the independent variables is small. The total derivative of the function with respect to x_i is

$$\frac{dy}{dx_i} = f_1 \frac{dx_1}{dx_i} + \cdots + f_i + \cdots + f_n \frac{dx_n}{dx_i} \qquad \text{(A-15)}$$

or the rate of change of y with respect to x_i when all other variables are permitted to vary and where all x_j are specified functions of x_i.

Given the implicit function $f(x_1, x_2, \ldots, x_n) = 0$, the partial derivative $\partial x_1 / \partial x_2$ is obtained by first finding the total differential

$$f_1 \, dx_1 + f_2 \, dx_2 + \cdots + f_n \, dx_n = 0$$

dividing by dx_i

$$f_1 \frac{dx_1}{dx_i} + f_2 \frac{dx_2}{dx_i} + \cdots + f_j \frac{dx_j}{dx_i} + \cdots + f_i + \cdots + f_n \frac{dx_n}{dx_i} = 0$$

and setting all differentials other than dx_j and dx_i equal to zero. Then

$$f_j \frac{\partial x_j}{\partial x_i} + f_i = 0$$

and

$$\frac{\partial x_j}{\partial x_i} = -\frac{f_i}{f_j} \qquad \text{(A-16)}$$

Equation (A-16) is the *implicit-function rule*.

Assume that $y = f(x_1, x_2)$, $x_1 = g(w_1, w_2)$, and $x_2 = h(w_1, w_2)$. The partial derivatives of y with respect to w_1 and w_2 are determined by the *composite-function rule* derived below. Taking total differentials

$$dy = \frac{\partial y}{\partial x_1} \, dx_1 + \frac{\partial y}{\partial x_2} \, dx_2 \qquad \text{(A-17)}$$

$$dx_1 = \frac{\partial x_1}{\partial w_1} \, dw_1 + \frac{\partial x_1}{\partial w_2} \, dw_2 \qquad \text{(A-18)}$$

$$dx_2 = \frac{\partial x_2}{\partial w_1} \, dw_1 + \frac{\partial x_2}{\partial w_2} \, dw_2 \qquad \text{(A-19)}$$

and substituting (A-18) and (A-19) into (A-17) and collecting terms on dw_1 and dw_2,

$$dy = \left(\frac{\partial y}{\partial x_1} \frac{\partial x_1}{\partial w_1} + \frac{\partial y}{\partial x_2} \frac{\partial x_2}{\partial w_1} \right) dw_1 + \left(\frac{\partial y}{\partial x_1} \frac{\partial x_1}{\partial w_2} + \frac{\partial y}{\partial x_2} \frac{\partial x_2}{\partial w_2} \right) dw_2 \quad \text{(A-20)}$$

The expression (A-20) is itself a total differential in which the first bracketed term equals $\partial y / \partial w_1$ and the second one equals $\partial y / \partial w_2$. Hence

$$\frac{\partial y}{\partial w_1} = \frac{\partial y}{\partial x_1}\frac{\partial x_1}{\partial w_1} + \frac{\partial y}{\partial x_2}\frac{\partial x_2}{\partial w_1}$$
$$\frac{\partial y}{\partial w_2} = \frac{\partial y}{\partial x_1}\frac{\partial x_1}{\partial w_2} + \frac{\partial y}{\partial x_2}\frac{\partial x_2}{\partial w_2}$$

(A-21)

If the independent variables of a function $f(x_1,x_2)$ are themselves functions of some other variables w_1 and w_2, $f(x_1,x_2)$ is differentiated partially with respect to w_1 and w_2 according to (A-21). This is the *composite-function rule*.

Envelopes. Let $f(x,y,k) = 0$ be an implicit function of the variables x and y. The form of this function is assumed to depend on the magnitude of the parameter k. In general, $f(x,y,k) = 0$ describes a curve in the xy plane. A different curve corresponds to each possible value of k. The envelope of this family of curves is itself a curve with the property that it is tangent to each member of the family. The equation of the envelope is obtained by taking the partial derivative of $f(x,y,k)$ with respect to k and eliminating k from the two equations

$$f(x,y,k) = 0$$
$$f_k(x,y,k) = 0$$

This method of obtaining the envelope is generally applicable, provided that $f_{kk} \neq 0$ and $f_x f_{yk} - f_y f_{xk} \neq 0$.†

Maxima and Minima without Constraints. The definitions of maxima and minima are similar to those for a function of a single variable. Necessary and sufficient conditions are difficult to derive. Only sufficient conditions are stated here.[1] It is sufficient for a maximum or minimum that the following conditions be fulfilled: (1) *all* first partial derivatives must equal zero: $f_1 = 0, f_2 = 0, \ldots, f_n = 0$; (2) forming the *Hessian* determinant $\mathbf{A}$ of the second partial derivatives:

$$\mathbf{A} = \begin{vmatrix} f_{11} & f_{12} & \cdots & f_{1n} \\ f_{21} & f_{22} & \cdots & f_{2n} \\ \cdots & \cdots & \cdots & \cdots \\ f_{n1} & f_{n2} & \cdots & f_{nn} \end{vmatrix}$$

and using $\mathbf{A}_i$ to denote the principal minor of $\mathbf{A}$ which is obtained by deleting the last $(n - i)$ rows and $(n - i)$ columns of the array A, the principal minors must alternate in sign for a maximum: $\mathbf{A}_1 < 0, \mathbf{A}_2 > 0,$

† For proof see W. F. Osgood, *Advanced Calculus* (New York: Macmillan, 1925), pp. 186–193; Fine, *op. cit.*, pp. 272–274.

[1] See W. F. Osgood, *op. cit.*, pp. 173–179; R. G. D. Allen, *Mathematical Analysis for Economists* (London: Macmillan, 1938), chap. XIX; P. A. Samuelson, *Foundations of Economic Analysis* (Cambridge, Mass.: Harvard University Press, 1948), appendix A.

$\mathbf{A}_3 < 0, \ldots, \mathbf{A}_n(-1)^n > 0.$† All principal minors must be positive for a minimum.[1] The conditions on the signs of the principal minors are the second-order conditions. Extreme values are determined in a manner analogous to that employed in the single-variable case. The n equations $f_1 = 0$, $f_2 = 0$, $\ldots$, $f_n = 0$ are solved for the n variables $x_1, x_2, \ldots, x_n$. The signs of the principal minors of the Hessian are calculated for each solution. If their signs are as required for a maximum (minimum), the function $f(x_1, x_2, \ldots, x_n)$ attains a maximum (minimum) for that solution.

Constrained Maxima and Minima. Many maximum and minimum problems in economics are such that the independent variables are not permitted to take on all possible values; the variables are "constrained" to satisfy some side relation. The constrained-maximum problem is to maximize the function $f(x_1, x_2, \ldots, x_n)$ subject to the constraint that only those values of $(x_1, x_2, \ldots, x_n)$ that satisfy the equation

$$g(x_1, x_2, \ldots, x_n) = 0$$

are admissible. For example, the function

$$f(x_1, x_2) = (x_1 - 1)^2 + (x_2 - 2)^2$$

has an unconstrained minimum at the point $x_1 = 1$, $x_2 = 2$. However, if this function is subject to the requirement that $x_1 - x_2 - 2 = 0$, its minimum value is achieved at the point $x_1 = \frac{1}{2}$, $x_2 = -\frac{3}{2}$. The function $f(x_1, x_2)$ defines a surface in three-dimensional space. The equation $x_1 - x_2 - 2 = 0$ defines a straight line in the horizontal $x_1 x_2$ plane. The constrained-minimum problem is one of finding the lowest point of the surface defined by $f(x_1, x_2)$ such that this point is above the straight line defined by the constraint. These concepts are illustrated with

---

† In the two-variable case this means that $f_{11} < 0$ and $f_{11}f_{22} - (f_{12})^2 > 0$, which also implies that f_{22} must be negative.

[1] The second derivative must be negative (positive) for a maximum (minimum) in the one-variable case if one disregards the possibility of a zero second derivative. The second total differential (d^2y) must be negative (positive) for a maximum (minimum) in the many-variable case, disregarding again the possibility of a zero value. The second total differential

$$d^2y = \sum_{j=1}^{n} \sum_{i=1}^{n} f_{ij} \, dx_i \, dx_j$$

is a quadratic form in the variables dx_i. It can be shown that a quadratic form is negative definite ($d^2y < 0$ for all values of the dx_is except $dx_i = 0$ for all i) if the principal minors of the Hessian alternate in sign as indicated and is positive definite if they are all positive.

reference to a maximum problem in Fig. A-2. The unconstrained maximum occurs at the point M. The constraint is given by the line AB.

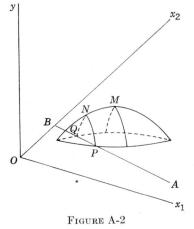

All points on the surface other than those lying above the line AB, namely the points along the curved line PNQ, are irrelevant. The constrained maximum occurs at the point N. The result will generally differ from the unconstrained case, and the constrained maximum will generally be lower than the unconstrained maximum.

There may be more than one constraint, but the number of constraints must be smaller than the number of variables. The following discussion is confined to the case of a single constraint, since cases with more than one constraint are relatively rare in economics.[1]

FIGURE A-2

Method 1. If it is possible to solve the equation $g(x_1, x_2, \ldots, x_n) = 0$ for one of the variables, say $x_1 = h(x_2, \ldots, x_n)$, the solution for x_1 can be substituted in $f(x_1, x_2, \ldots, x_n)$ to give $f[h(x_2, \ldots, x_n), x_2, \ldots, x_n]$ which is a function of $n - 1$ variables. Denote this function by $H(x_2, \ldots, x_n)$. The maximization of $f(x_1, x_2, \ldots, x_n)$ subject to the constraint is equivalent to the unconstrained maximization of $H(x_2, \ldots, x_n)$ with respect to $x_2, \ldots, x_n$. The constrained-maximum problem is thus reduced to an unconstrained one that is handled in customary fashion.

Method 2. The procedure outlined above involves a loss of symmetry depending upon which variable is expressed in terms of the others from the constraint. A more general procedure involves the use of *Lagrange multipliers*. Form the function

$$V = f(x_1, x_2, \ldots, x_n) + \lambda g(x_1, x_2, \ldots, x_n) \qquad \text{(A-22)}$$

The function (A-22) is a function of the $(n + 1)$ variables $x_1, x_2, \ldots, x_n$ and λ, which is the undetermined Lagrange multiplier (different from zero). Maximizing V is equivalent to maximizing $f(x_1, x_2, \ldots, x_n)$, subject to $g(x_1, x_2, \ldots, x_n) = 0$. In addition, $f(x_1, x_2, \ldots, x_n)$ is identically equal to V only for those values of the variables that satisfy the constraint.

[1] For an exception see W. J. Baumol, "Income Effect, Substitution Effect, Ricardo Effect," *Economica*, n.s. vol. 17 (February, 1950), pp. 69–80.

The first-order conditions require that the first partial derivatives of V must vanish for both maxima and minima.   This condition gives $(n + 1)$ equations in $(n + 1)$ variables

$$\frac{\partial V}{\partial x_1} = f_1 + \lambda g_1 = 0$$

$$\cdot \cdot \cdot \cdot \cdot \cdot \cdot \cdot \cdot \cdot \cdot$$

$$\frac{\partial V}{\partial x_n} = f_n + \lambda g_n = 0 \qquad \text{(A-23)}$$

$$\frac{\partial V}{\partial \lambda} = g(x_1, x_2, \ldots, x_n) = 0$$

The last equation ensures that the constraint is satisfied.   The solution of this system of simultaneous equations gives the point or points at which $f(x_1, x_2, \ldots, x_n)$ achieves a maximum (or minimum) subject to $g(x_1, x_2, \ldots, x_n) = 0$.†

Denote the second partial derivatives of V by V_{ij} and form the determinants

$$\begin{vmatrix} V_{11} & V_{12} & g_1 \\ V_{21} & V_{22} & g_2 \\ g_1 & g_2 & 0 \end{vmatrix}, \begin{vmatrix} V_{11} & V_{12} & V_{13} & g_1 \\ V_{21} & V_{22} & V_{23} & g_2 \\ V_{31} & V_{32} & V_{33} & g_3 \\ g_1 & g_2 & g_3 & 0 \end{vmatrix}, \ldots,$$

$$\begin{vmatrix} V_{11} & V_{12} & \cdots & V_{1n} & g_1 \\ V_{21} & V_{22} & \cdots & V_{2n} & g_2 \\ \cdot & \cdot & \cdot & \cdot & \cdot \\ V_{n1} & V_{n2} & \cdots & V_{nn} & g_n \\ g_1 & g_2 & \cdots & g_n & 0 \end{vmatrix}$$

which are obtained by bordering the principal minors of the Hessian determinant of second partial derivatives of V by a row and a column containing the first partial derivatives of the constraint.   The element in the southwest corner of each one of these arrays is zero.   By the second-order conditions all these bordered determinants must be negative for a minimum and must alternate in sign, starting with plus, for a maximum; i.e., the signs of the determinants from left to right must be $+$, $-$, $+$, etc. The above conditions on the signs of the determinants together with (A-23) are sufficient for maxima and minima.[1]

† Note that it makes no difference whether the function V is formed by writing $f - \lambda g$ or $f + \lambda g$.

[1] See Samuelson, op. cit., appendix A; Allen, op. cit., chap. XIX; and for a rigorous treatment of some aspects of this problem, G. Debreu, "Definite and Semi-definite Quadratic Forms," Econometrica, vol. 20 (April, 1952), pp. 295–300.

Jacobians. Consider the system of simultaneous equations

$$f^1(x_1,x_2, \ldots ,x_n) = y_1$$
$$f^2(x_1,x_2, \ldots ,x_n) = y_2$$
$$\cdots \cdots \cdots \cdots \cdots \cdots$$
$$f^n(x_1,x_2, \ldots ,x_n) = y_n$$

(A-24)

The Jacobian of (A-24) is the determinant of the first partial derivatives of the functions f^i and is denoted by

$$J = \frac{\partial(y_1,y_2, \ldots ,y_n)}{\partial(x_1,x_2, \ldots ,x_n)} = \begin{vmatrix} \dfrac{\partial y_1}{\partial x_1} & \dfrac{\partial y_1}{\partial x_2} & \cdots & \dfrac{\partial y_1}{\partial x_n} \\ \cdots & \cdots & \cdots & \cdots \\ \dfrac{\partial y_n}{\partial x_1} & \dfrac{\partial y_n}{\partial x_2} & \cdots & \dfrac{\partial y_n}{\partial x_n} \end{vmatrix}$$

(A-25)

The importance of Jacobians is clear from the following two theorems:

1. If the functions $f^i(x_1,x_2, \ldots ,x_n)$, $(i = 1, 2, \ldots , n)$, are continuous and possess continuous first partial derivatives, it is necessary and sufficient for the system of equations (A-24) to possess a solution $x_i = \phi^i(y_1, y_2, \ldots ,y_n)$, $(i = 1, 2, \ldots , n)$, that the Jacobian be nonvanishing in a neighborhood about a point $(x_1^0,x_2^0, \ldots ,x_n^0)$ for which (A-24) holds.

2. The existence of a function $H(y_1,y_2, \ldots ,y_n) = 0$, i.e., functional dependence among the equations of (A-24), is necessary and sufficient for the Jacobian of (A-24) to vanish identically or to vanish at every point in a neighborhood around $(x_1^0,x_2^0, \ldots ,x_n^0)$.

Proofs are given for the sufficiency parts of the theorems in the two-variable case. The proof of the first theorem utilizes the *lemma* that a continuous function $f(x_1,x_2) = y_1$ with continuous first partial derivatives possesses the solution $x_1 = \phi(x_2,y_1)$ if $f_1 \neq 0$.† Consider the two-variable system consisting of the equations

$$f(x_1,x_2) = y_1 \tag{A-26}$$
$$g(x_1,x_2) = y_2 \tag{A-27}$$

If the Jacobian does not vanish, not all partial derivatives may equal zero. Assume that $f_1 \neq 0$. Then one may write

$$x_1 = \phi(x_2,y_1) \tag{A-28}$$

Substituting in (A-27),

$$F = g[\phi(x_2,y_1),x_2] - y_2 = 0 \tag{A-29}$$

Then

$$\frac{\partial F}{\partial x_2} = g_1\phi_1 + g_2 \tag{A-30}$$

† See W. F. Osgood, *op. cit.*, pp. 133–135.

Substituting (A-28) in (A-26),

$$G = f[\phi(x_2, y_1), x_2] - y_1 = 0$$

Since G is identically equal to zero, its partial derivative with respect to x_2 also equals zero:

$$\frac{\partial G}{\partial x_2} = f_1\phi_1 + f_2 = 0 \tag{A-31}$$

Solving (A-31) for ϕ_1 and substituting its value in (A-30),

$$\frac{\partial F}{\partial x_2} = g_1\left(-\frac{f_2}{f_1}\right) + g_2 = \frac{f_1 g_2 - f_2 g_1}{f_1} \tag{A-32}$$

Since by hypothesis the Jacobian (the numerator) and f_1 do not vanish, $\partial F/\partial x_2 \neq 0$ and (A-29) can be solved for x_2. Therefore

$$x_2 = h(y_1, y_2) \tag{A-33}$$

Substituting (A-33) into (A-28) gives the solution for x_1.

To prove the second theorem, assume that there exists a functional dependence $H(y_1, y_2) = 0$. Taking the total derivative,

$$H_1 \, dy_1 + H_2 \, dy_2 = 0$$

Substituting for dy_1 and dy_2 their values obtained by differentiating (A-26) and (A-27) and collecting terms,

$$(H_1 f_1 + H_2 g_1) \, dx_1 + (H_1 f_2 + H_2 g_2) \, dx_2 = 0$$

Since this must hold for all values of dx_1 and dx_2, the bracketed terms must each equal zero:

$$H_1 f_1 + H_2 g_1 = 0 \qquad H_1 f_2 + H_2 g_2 = 0$$

Moving the second terms to the right-hand side and dividing the first equation by the second,

$$\frac{H_1 f_1}{H_1 f_2} = \frac{-H_2 g_1}{-H_2 g_2}$$

or

$$f_1 g_2 - f_2 g_1 = 0 \tag{A-34}$$

The left-hand side of (A-34) is the Jacobian which equals zero.

As an example, consider the functions

$$x_1{}^2 - 2x_2 - 2 = y_1$$
$$x_1{}^4 - 4x_1{}^2 x_2 + 4x_2{}^2 = y_2$$

The functional dependence between them is given by $(y_1 + 2)^2 - y_2 = 0$. The Jacobian

$$\frac{\partial(y_1, y_2)}{\partial(x_1, x_2)} = \begin{vmatrix} 2x_1 & -2 \\ 4x_1{}^3 - 8x_1x_2 & -4x_1{}^2 + 8x_2 \end{vmatrix}$$
$$= (-8x_1{}^3 + 16x_1x_2) - (-8x_1{}^3 + 16x_1x_2) = 0$$

vanishes identically.

If the functions (A-26) and (A-27) are linear, the first theorem reduces to the familiar proposition that the determinant of the array of coefficients must be nonvanishing. This condition is fulfilled if the number of equations equals the number of variables and if the equations are not functionally dependent. If the Jacobian of a system of linear equations vanishes, the equations are linearly dependent (see Sec. A-1).

A-4. Integrals

The integral of a function $f(x)$ is another function $F(x)$ which has the property that its derivative equals $f(x)$; $F'(x) = f(x)$. An integral is unique except for an arbitrary additive constant c, since a constant vanishes on differentiation. Thus if $F(x)$ is an integral of $f(x)$, so is $F(x) + c$. Integration is the process of finding the integral and is in a sense differentiation in reverse. The integral $F(x) + c$ is known as the indefinite integral and is denoted by

$$\int f(x) \, dx = F(x) + c$$

The techniques for finding the indefinite integrals of various kinds of functions are fairly difficult and are not treated here.

Integration can be used to calculate the area under a curve. The function $f(x)$ is plotted in Fig. A-3. To calculate the area between the x axis and the curve between points a and b, subdivide the distance $(b - a)$ into segments of width Δx_i, and then erect rectangles of height $f(x_i)$ over each segment.

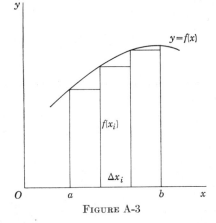

FIGURE A-3

The height of each rectangle is the value of the function evaluated at the left-hand boundary of each segment. The required area A is approximately $\Sigma f(x_i) \, \Delta x_i$.† As the width of the rectangles becomes smaller, the expression $\Sigma f(x_i) \, \Delta x_i$ comes closer to the true

† The sum of these rectangles underestimates the area under the curve. If the height of the rectangles were given by the value of the function corresponding to the right-hand boundary of each segment, the approximation would overestimate the correct area. Either method is permissible for the analysis.

area A.   In fact,

$$A = \lim_{\Delta x_i \to 0} \Sigma f(x_i)\, \Delta x_i$$

provided that this limit exists.[1]   Now change the right-hand-side boundary b of the area under consideration to a variable boundary x. The area from a to a variable right-hand-side boundary x is a function of x and will be denoted by $A(a,x)$.   A somewhat larger area would result if the right-hand-side boundary were somewhat farther to the right, i.e., if this boundary were $x + \Delta x$.   The resulting area will be denoted by $A(a,x + \Delta x)$.   The difference between these two areas is

$$A(a,x + \Delta x) - A(a,x) = A(x,x + \Delta x)$$

The area between the points x and $x + \Delta x$ is also given by the width of the interval Δx multiplied by the value of the function $f(x)$ at some point between x and $x + \Delta x$.   Denote this value of x by x_0:

$$A(a,x + \Delta x) - A(a,x) = f(x_0)\, \Delta x$$

or
$$\frac{A(a,x + \Delta x) - A(a,x)}{\Delta x} = f(x_0)$$

When Δx approaches zero, $x + \Delta x$ approaches x, and hence x_0 approaches x, since x_0 is between x and $x + \Delta x$.   Taking limits

$$\frac{dA}{dx} = \lim_{\Delta x \to 0} \frac{A(a,x + \Delta x) - A(a,x)}{\Delta x} = f(x)$$

This proves that the derivative of the area under a function is the function itself or that the integral of a function is the area under it.   The area $A(a,b)$ is the *definite* integral of $f(x)$ between the points a and b.   If $F(x)$ is an indefinite integral of $f(x)$, the definite integral between a and b is

$$\int_a^b f(x)\, dx = F(b) - F(a)$$

Integration is important for the solution of *differential equations*.   A differential equation is one in which a derivative occurs.   An example is $dy/dx - 3y + 2 = 0$.   To solve this equation means to find a formula $f(x)$ which satisfies the equation when it is substituted into it.   In the case of the above equation one has to find an expression for y in terms of x which has the property that if one differentiates it and subtracts from the derivative three times the expression and adds two, the result is zero. Such a solution is given by $y = e^{3x} + \frac{2}{3}$, as can be checked by substituting this expression in the differential equation above.

[1] The limit exists if the function $f(x)$ is continuous.

A-5. Difference Equations

Consider the sequence of numbers 1, 4, 9, 16, 25, etc., and denote them by $y_1, y_2, \ldots, y_t, \ldots$ The first differences of this sequence are $\Delta y_1 = y_2 - y_1 = 3$, $\Delta y_2 = y_3 - y_2 = 5$, $\Delta y_3 = y_4 - y_3 = 7$, etc. The second differences are the differences between the first differences or $\Delta^2 y_1 = \Delta y_2 - \Delta y_1 = 2$, $\Delta^2 y_2 = \Delta y_3 - \Delta y_2 = 2$, etc. In this particular sequence of numbers the second differences are constant and equal 2. This can be written as

$$\Delta^2 y_t = 2 \tag{A-35}$$

Equation (A-35) can also be written as the difference between two first differences, or

$$\Delta y_{t+1} - \Delta y_t = 2 \tag{A-36}$$

Each of the first differences in (A-36) can be written as the difference between two members of the sequence, or

$$(y_{t+2} - y_{t+1}) - (y_{t+1} - y_t) = y_{t+2} - 2y_{t+1} + y_t = 2 \tag{A-37}$$

Equation (A-37) is a *difference equation*, since it was obtained by taking differences of a sequence of numbers. It relates the $(t + 2)$th member of the sequence to the $(t + 1)$th and the tth members. In general, difference equations relate the tth member of a sequence to some previous members. The general linear difference equation of nth order with constant coefficients is

$$a_0 y_t + a_1 y_{t-1} + a_2 y_{t-2} + \cdots + a_n y_{t-n} + b = 0 \tag{A-38}$$

Equation (A-38) is linear because no y is raised to any power but the first and because it contains no products of ys. It is an nth-order equation because the most distant value of y upon which y_t depends is y_{t-n}. Thus (A-37) is a linear difference equation of second order with constant coefficients. A difference equation is homogeneous if $b = 0$. Both (A-37) and (A-38) are nonhomogeneous.

The Nature of the Solution. The homogeneous first-order equation is

$$y_t = a y_{t-1} \tag{A-39}$$

Given the information that $y_0 = 2$, $y_1 = 2a$ can be determined from (A-37) by substituting the value of y_0 on the right-hand side. Then $y_3 = a(2a) = 2a^2$. In this fashion it is possible to calculate the value of y for any value of t. This procedure is cumbersome and can be avoided by finding a general solution for the difference equation. A general solution is an expression, usually a function of t, which gives the value of y_t immediately upon substitution of the desired value of t. A function of t must be found such that $y_t = f(t)$. Any such function is a solution if it satisfies the difference equation. In the first-order case the solution $f(t)$ must satisfy[1]

$$f(t) = af(t - 1) \qquad\qquad (A\text{-}40)$$

In addition the solution must also be consistent with the *initial conditions*. The initial conditions are a statement about the value of y at one or more specified points in the sequence. The number of initial conditions must be the same as the order of the equation in order to obtain a complete solution. Only one initial condition is necessary in the first-order case. This was given by $y_0 = 2$ in the previous example. The problem is to find the solution or solutions that satisfy the difference equation and then to select the solution that also satisfies the initial conditions.[2] Subsequent discussion is confined to linear difference equations of first and second order with constant coefficients.

Homogeneous First-order Equations. Equation (A-39) can be written as

$$\frac{y_t}{y_{t-1}} = a \qquad \text{for all } t$$

Therefore,

$$y_t = \frac{y_t}{y_{t-1}} \frac{y_{t-1}}{y_{t-2}} \cdot \cdot \cdot \frac{y_2}{y_1} \frac{y_1}{y_0} y_0 = a^t y_0$$

The term a^t is itself a solution since it satisfies (A-39):

$$a^t = a(a^{t-1})$$

If $f(t)$ is a solution, so is $cf(t)$ where c is a constant. Thus assume that the general solution is $y_t = ca^t$. This satisfies the difference equation because

$$ca^t = a(ca^{t-1})$$

The parameter a is given by the difference equation and c is determined on the basis of the initial condition such that the general solution ca^t is consistent with it. In the previous example the initial condition was given by $y_0 = 2$. $y_0 = ca^0 = c = 2$, and the general solution is $y_t = 2a^t$.

Homogeneous Second-order Equations. The homogeneous linear second-order equation is

$$ay_t + by_{t-1} + cy_{t-2} = 0 \qquad\qquad (A\text{-}41)$$

---

[1] A difference equation can also be regarded as defining y as a function of t. To every value of t there corresponds a value of y with the proviso that the independent variable t can take on only integral values, i.e., 0, 1, 2, 3, etc.

[2] In the subsequent discussion, most proofs are omitted, and the ones given are sketchy at best. The reader is referred to W. J. Baumol, *Economic Dynamics* (New York: Macmillan, 1951), chaps. IX–XI, and S. Goldberg, *Introductioh to Difference Equations* (New York: Wiley, 1958), chaps. II–III.

Any function of t is a solution if it satisfies the difference equation. A solution is provided by x^t where x is a number as yet undetermined, as can be verified by substituting x^t into (A-41):

$$ax^t + bx^{t-1} + cx^{t-2} = 0 \tag{A-42}$$

and dividing through by x^{t-2}

$$ax^2 + bx + c = 0 \tag{A-43}$$

Equation (A-43) is a quadratic equation which is solved by the customary formula

$$x = \frac{-b \pm \sqrt{b^2 - 4ac}}{2a} \tag{A-44}$$

This generally gives two values of x: x_1 and x_2. Then $x_1{}^t$ and $x_2{}^t$ are both solutions of (A-42).† It is known that in this case $k_1x_1{}^t + k_2x_2{}^t$ is also a solution. This, in fact, is the general solution of the homogeneous second-order difference equation where k_1 and k_2 are constants determined in accordance with the initial conditions. Two initial conditions are needed in the second-order case. Assume that these are $y_0 = 3$ and $y_1 = 4$. Then

$$\begin{aligned}
k_1x_1{}^0 + k_2x_2{}^0 &= k_1 + k_2 = 3 \\
k_1x_1{}^1 + k_2x_2{}^1 &= k_1x_1 + k_2x_2 = 4
\end{aligned}$$

This system of equations can be solved for k_1 and k_2, since x_1 and x_2 are already known.

In some cases $b^2 - 4ac$ is negative. This introduces a complication because, according to (A-44), one would have to take the square root of a negative number.[1] In such a case the solution is obtained by a different method and involves the trigonometric functions sine and cosine. The solution is merely stated here. Introduce the following notation:

$$v_1 = -\frac{b}{2a}$$

$$v_2 = -\frac{b^2 - 4ac}{2a}$$

$$R = \sqrt{v_1{}^2 + v_2{}^2}$$

† If $b^2 - 4ac = 0$, the two roots of the quadratic equation are not distinct, i.e., $x_1 = x_2 = -b/2a$. Then set $x_1{}^t = (-b/2a)^t$ and $x_2{}^t = t(-b/2a)^t$. See Baumol, *op. cit.*, p. 178.

[1] The square root of a negative number is an imaginary number, denoted by the letter i, e.g., $\sqrt{-16} = 4i$. The quantity x (sum of a real and an imaginary number) is a complex number. See Baumol, *op. cit.*, pp. 181–195.

Find the angle z the sine of which is $v_2/\sqrt{v_1{}^2 + v_2{}^2}$ and the cosine of which is $v_1/\sqrt{v_1{}^2 + v_2{}^2}$.† The solution is

$$y_t = R^t[w_1 \sin{(tz)} + w_2 \cos{(tz)}] \qquad \text{(A-45)}$$

where w_1 and w_2 are constants determined in the usual fashion in accordance with the initial conditions.

Nonhomogeneous Difference Equations. Two steps are required to find the solution of a nonhomogeneous difference equation. The first one is to find the solution $f(t)$ of the corresponding homogeneous equation. The second one is to find the *particular solution* denoted by $g(t)$. The final general solution is $f(t) + g(t)$. Finding the particular solution is illustrated with reference to a second-order equation. The nonhomogeneous equation is

$$ay_t + by_{t-1} + cy_{t-2} + d = 0 \qquad \text{(A-46)}$$

The solution of the homogeneous part of (A-46) is $k_1x_1{}^t + k_2x_2{}^t$. To find a particular solution substitute in (A-46) $y_t = K$ (constant) and solve for K:

$$aK + bK + cK + d = 0$$

and
$$K = \frac{-d}{a + b + c} \qquad \text{(A-47)}$$

provided that $a + b + c \neq 0$. Then the general solution is

$$y = k_1x_1{}^t + k_2x_2{}^t + \frac{-d}{a + b + c}$$

where k_1 and k_2 are now determined in accordance with the initial conditions. If $a + b + c = 0$, assume that the particular solution is $y_t = Kt$, substitute this in (A-46), and solve for K. Then the general solution is $y_t = k_1x_1{}^t + k_2x_2{}^t + Kt$, provided that $(-b - 2c) \neq 0$. If $-b - 2c = 0$, substitute Kt^2 and proceed analogously. In the first-order case either $y_t = K$ or $y_t = Kt$, and in the second-order case either $y_t = K$, or $y_t = Kt$, or $y_t = Kt^2$ leads to the correct particular solution.

SELECTED REFERENCES

Aitken, A. C., *Determinants and Matrices* (New York: Interscience, 1951). A concise reference work that is too difficult for the beginner.

Allen, R. G. D., *Mathematical Analysis for Economists* (London: Macmillan, 1938). A survey of the calculus with many economic illustrations.

Baumol, W. J., *Economic Dynamics* (New York: Macmillan, 1951). Chapters IX–XI contain an introduction to linear difference equations.

† The angle z can be determined by using tables of trigonometric functions.

Birkhoff, G., & S. MacLane, *A Survey of Modern Algebra* (rev. ed.; New York: Macmillan, 1953). A comprehensive text. Not easy, but useful for a thorough understanding of determinants and matrices.

Courant, R., *Differential and Integral Calculus* (London: Blackie, 1934). A classic treatise. Highly recommended as a reference for advanced students.

Fine, H. B., *Calculus* (New York: Macmillan, 1937). An intermediate text.

Goldberg, S., *Introduction to Difference Equations* (New York: Wiley, 1958). A beginning text with many examples drawn from economics.

Goursat, E., *A Course in Mathematical Analysis,* vol. I, trans. by E. R. Hedrick (Boston: Ginn, 1904). A classic treatise. Recommended for intermediate and advanced students.

Milne-Thompson, L. M., *The Calculus of Finite Differences* (London: Macmillan, 1933). Chapters XI–XVII contain a comprehensive treatment of difference equations.

Osgood, W. F., *Advanced Calculus* (3d ed.; New York: Macmillan, 1935). A text more advanced than Fine.

Perlis, S., *Theory of Matrices* (Cambridge, Mass.: Addison-Wesley, 1952). A specialized treatment of determinants and matrices.

Samuelson, Paul A., *Foundations of Economic Analysis* (Cambridge, Mass.: Harvard University Press, 1948). A mathematical approach to economic theory. An appendix contains a survey of some of the mathematical tools employed in the text. The treatment will prove difficult for all but advanced students.

Woods, F. S., *Advanced Calculus* (new ed.; Boston: Ginn, 1934). A text recommended for advanced students.

INDEX

CANISIUS COLLEGE LIBRARY
HB171 .H52 c. 1
Microeconomic theory

3 5084 00086 6239